$39.95

AMERICAN FOREIGN POLICY IN A HOSTILE WORLD
Dangerous Years

AMERICAN FOREIGN POLICY IN A HOSTILE WORLD
Dangerous Years

Simon Serfaty

PRAEGER

PRAEGER SPECIAL STUDIES • PRAEGER SCIENTIFIC

New York • Philadelphia • Eastbourne, UK
Toronto • Hong Kong • Tokyo • Sydney

Library of Congress Cataloging in Publication Data

Serfaty, Simon.
    American foreign policy in a hostile world.

    Includes index.
    1. United States—Foreign relations—1945–
I. Title.
E744.S4698 1984   327.73   84–8277
ISBN 0–03–071996–8

Published in 1984 by Praeger Publishers
CBS Educational and Professional Publishing
a Division of CBS Inc.
521 Fifth Avenue, New York, NY 10175 USA

© 1984 by Praeger Publishers

456789 052 987654321

Printed in the United States of America
on acid-free paper

For
Gail Fitzgerald
and
Alexis Leigh

PREFACE

Four presidents and a lifetime ago, I wrote a book that was intended to provide a short analytical review of American foreign policy since the end of World War II.[1] Such a review, I warned in the preface of that book, had neither heroes nor villains. For, I added, observers of foreign policy are very much like the judge-penitent Albert Camus described in one of his novels: they pass judgments reluctantly because judgments can all too often be passed upon them as well. This is also true of this volume. Success and failure in foreign policy are hardly ever lasting. Events unfold, usually unexpectedly. They make the best policies fail and, on occasion, the worst policies succeed—until, that is, new events and new circumstances reverse the initial appraisals of their results. Accordingly, today's hero is frequently tomorrow's villain, and vice-versa.

Much has happened since *The Elusive Enemy* was first published. The very difficult decade of the 1960s was quickly forgotten in the midst of the even more difficult decade of the 1970s. Out of Vietnam, OPEC, and Watergate there emerged a new world, at home and abroad—a hostile world that lacked both the simplicity and the security that had seemed to prevail in earlier years.

The purpose of this book is therefore twofold. In the first part, appropriately entitled "The Elusive Enemy," I return to my treatment of the years 1945–69 to examine some of the main events and issues that shaped U.S. foreign policies in Europe and Asia during the dangerous years of the cold war. This, in a sense, is a revised, expanded, and reorganized edition of the book I published in 1972. I have not, of course, tried to rewrite it, or even correct it, except in those instances where errors or omissions warranted it. But I have tried to take into account the abundance of material that has come to light over the past decade. In addition, economic and political questions (which had been neglected in the earlier volume) have been introduced within a general structure that is different from the one used more than ten years ago.

The second part of this book covers the evolution of U.S. foreign policy *since* the cold war. It is a sort of sequel to *The Elusive Enemy*. It incorporates ideas and themes that I have developed, in greater or lesser detail, in a number of essays published elsewhere.[2] Focused about evenly on adversary and alliance relationships, this second section presents and analyzes the policies developed by four successive administrations to face or escape the normalcy of coercion and inequality in interstate relations.

All in all, this book has evolved out of the courses I have taught at the Johns Hopkins School of Advanced International Studies in Bologna, Italy, and in Washington, D.C. I am grateful to the students who were involved in these courses. Two of them, however, deserve specific recognition. Peter Fromuth made valuable contributions, especially for the chapters that deal with the early years of U.S.–Soviet relations and the latter years of the Vietnam War. Mark McDonough's thorough research and intelligent insight were also much appreciated for issues related to adversary relations in the 1970s.

Finally, my wife, Gail Fitzgerald, and my son, Alexis Leigh, both contribute to my life in so many ways that my gratitude to them, and my love for them, can only be expressed to both equally on the dedication page.

NOTES

1. Simon Serfaty. *The Elusive Enemy: American Foreign Policy Since World War II* (Boston: Little Brown, 1972).
2. These include: "No More Dissent," *Foreign Policy* (Summer 1973); "America and Europe in the 1970s: Integration or Disintegration?" *Orbis* (Spring 1973); "The Kissinger Legacy: New Looks and Old Obsessions," *World Today* (March 1977); "Brzezinski: Play It Again, Zbig," *Foreign Policy* (Fall 1978); "Une politique étrangère introuvable," *Politique Internationale* (Winter 1979–1980); "The United States and Europe," *Washington Quarterly* (Winter 1980–1981); "Waiting for Reagan," *SAIS Review* (Winter 1980–1981); "Atlantic Fantasies," *Washington Quarterly* (Summer 1982); "Reagan à mi-course: les limites du renouveau," *Politique Internationale* (Winter 1982–1983); and "An Ascending Europe?" *Harvard International Review* (September–October 1983).

CONTENTS

PART ONE

The Elusive Enemy

CHAPTER ONE

Nation
and Empire

Nation or Empire?

There is in the manner in which America discusses and conducts its foreign policy an open invitation to debate it and struggle for the undisputed privilege of directing it. This tendency can first be explained by the way in which American foreign policy is presented to the public, wrapped in a sweeping rhetoric that commits the country to grandiose but often unrealistic objectives. Overly responsive to what needs to be said at home, policymakers lose sight of what can be done abroad, thereby generating national frustrations that ultimately lead to "great debates." International decline and renewal, ideological confusion and consistency, national objectives and purpose then become the recurring themes of a protracted discourse on the United States and its role in the world.

A propensity for public debates is further related to the ambiguity of who makes foreign policy. The president alone holds responsibility for any action at any one time. But his decisions are made against a background that includes many institutional and individual actors who regard themselves qualified to announce policy, denounce it, abandon it, and, most of all, comment on it.[1] With foreign policy therefore drowned in

3

this steady flow of democratic verbosity, congressional compliance periodically gives way to congressional resistance toward policy initiatives taken by the Executive in the name and at the expense of the American people but, allegedly, without the advice and consent of their elected representatives in Congress.

Finally, public debates are also promoted by the vacuum of information provided to, and until recently sought by, the general public. Long in the dark age of international ignorance, the American people have remained receptive to a Manichean and jingoistic description of the world, a description in which national forces of good, justice, and freedom can easily be opposed to foreign forces of evil, injustice, and tyranny. On numerous occasions, this vacuum has facilitated the deceptive practices of U.S. administrations, which have hidden their policies behind a much-inflated rhetoric. As Walter Lippmann once wrote, U.S. presidents "announce, they proclaim, they disclaim, they exhort, they appeal, and they argue. But they do not unbend and tell the story, and say why they did what they did, and what they think about it, and how they feel about it."[2]

That America should repeatedly have been engaged in major controversies over the nature, the objectives, and the instruments of its foreign policy is by itself not very startling. Inasmuch as they questioned America's role in the world—nation or empire?—these controversies began even before the Republic was founded and have been pursued uninterruptedly ever since. Throughout the eighteenth century, the colonists resented the burdens inflicted upon them by wars waged in America for the sake of non-American interests. They argued that the colonies were the tools of the European Great Powers, then the main actors in the world politics. It was shocking, wrote Thomas Paine in 1776, that "America, without the right of asking why, must be brought into all the wars of another, whether the measure be right or wrong, or whether she will or not." The Republic about to be formed would equate its independence from external domination with independence from entanglement in other states' disputes. Noninvolvement in the "contests, broils, and wars of Europe," as Hamilton later put it, was therefore the ultimate objective. "England to Europe, America to itself," concluded Thomas Paine, who described as "common sense" his belief that the true interest of America was to steer clear of European contentions.[3] So convinced of this was Jefferson that he anticipated a day when "we may formally require a meridian of partition through the ocean which separates the two hemispheres, on the hither side of which no European gun shall ever be heard, nor an American on the other."[4]

The search for isolation from the political ills that plagued the European continent was prudent and necessary, based as it was on the intrinsic weakness of the new American state and its need to provide more substance and cohesion to its territorial skeleton. "Young as we are," wrote Jefferson at the turn of the nineteenth century, "and with such a country before us to fill with people and with happiness, we should point in that direction the whole generative force of nature."[5] A seed time was required to absorb the flow of immigrants, reconcile local interests, and explore, exploit, and develop all available resources. America's isolationist impulse thus emerged as a tactical approach to foreign policy—a means toward national goals of internal expansion and external preservation. But in order to be achieved, such goals might occasionally require American intervention in European affairs: in his Farewell Address, George Washington pointedly recommended that the principle of nonentanglement be discarded in "extraordinary emergencies," if this proved to be necessary to keep America's defenses "respectable."

In anticipating the need for U.S. interventionism, Washington was already experiencing the inherent difficulty of determining when to intervene and when not to intervene. Not surprisingly, he favored the latter. Yet, the guidelines defined by the first American president were so general as to depend almost entirely upon the ill-defined circumstances that would shape some unknown situation in the unforeseeable future. When would emergencies be truly extraordinary, and when would America's defensive posture threaten to be no longer respectable? In other words, when should the ordinary policy of isolation give way to an extraordinary policy of intervention, where, and for how long?

Clearly extraordinary was the situation in 1778, when the colonists concluded an alliance with the king of France to gain their independence from England. But was America's national interest threatened in 1812, when, in the midst of the Napoleonic wars then being waged in Europe, the United States declared war on Great Britain—a war that may well have remained over the years the most unpopular war that this country has ever fought, not even excepting the Vietnam conflict.[6] At the time, many deplored an action that threatened to convert national felicity into insecurity and humiliation. They believed that America did not have the resources needed to fulfill its objectives in entering the war against Britain. Already, they derided overbearing commitments to national self-abnegation: "The United States," Madison had proclaimed in 1804, "owes to the world as well as to themselves to let the example of one government at least protest against the corruption which prevails."[7] But these early dissenters also denied that any part of America was endangered by England or by any of its land-locked allies: "Happy in its local relations; removed from the bloody theater of Europe ... with territorial possessions exceeding every real want ... from invasion nothing to fear; from acquisition nothing to hope," America had little to gain from such a conflict.[8] Conversely, it was feared that being on the side of France and against the rest of Europe, the country would be exposed after the war either to retaliation from the other European powers (now free to join hands against the United States) or to the vassalage of the victorious French emperor.

Yet, intervention appeared to be required, because in 1812, as at any other time, it showed America's resolve to prevent, actively when necessary, the conditions in Europe that might lead any nation or group of nations to contemplate a direct attack upon the United States. As Jefferson put it at the time, "We especially ought to pray that the powers of Europe may be so poised and counterpoised among themselves that their own security may require the presence of all their forces at home leaving the other parts of the world in undisturbed tranquility."[9] Thus, intervention and nonintervention complemented each other within the continued balance of power in Europe, and the American position varied according to the shifts of the balance. Having been on the side of British ascendancy on the ocean in 1806, the United States was wishing success to

Napoleon the following year, when, after the *Chesapeake* affair in June 1807, war with Great Britain appeared probable. But in the summer of 1808, with Napoleon invading Spain, Jefferson again turned toward Great Britain, because he now feared that a French victory in Spain might spell America's misfortune even more directly by forcing Spain to concede the Floridas to France. As Alexander Hamilton frankly explained it, the "coolest calculations of interest" prevented America from becoming the instrument of, or allied to, the ambitions of any single European nation. The threat was thought to be self-evident: such a nation, "aggrandized by new acquisitions and her enemies reduced by dismemberments," might then become "the mistress of Europe, and consequently, in a great measure, of America."[10]

As the nineteenth century wore on, however, isolation took the appearance of a divine privilege, the perceived outcome of American national widom and superior virtue. Yet, still unanswered, earlier questions continued to be argued in a protracted debate. What was America's national interest? Was it limited to the Western Hemisphere, or did it extend beyond continental bounds and necessitate the support of any group throughout the world fighting for similar democratic ideas? And if the latter, what form should American support of such groups take?

These questions had all been raised and debated during the Napoleonic wars. But throughout the nineteenth century they gained new intensity as the prudent and sober calculations of the early years of the Republic gave way to a growing confidence in the nation's capacity not only to defend its interests but also to uphold justice for all. In the 1820s for example, public enthusiasm for Greece's resistance against Turkey had to be restrained by John Quincy Adam's portrayal of the United States as "the well wisher to the freedom and independence of all, [but] . . . the champion and vindicator only of her own."[11] In opposing President Monroe's temptation to intervene in Greece, John Quincy Adams, then secretary of state, also questioned America's relationship with Europe and the conservative Holy Alliance, which had been formed following the defeat of France in 1815. Did such an alliance affect the security of the United States, either territorially or spiritually, by undermining the humanistic foundation upon which the new Republic rested?

Speaking, however ambiguously, in favor of intervention, Daniel Webster, then at the beginning of his political career, advocated that as one of the nations of the world, "a part we must take, honorable, or dishonorable, in all that is done in the civilized world." And Webster asked that the American people actively oppose "the doctrines . . . [that] prostrate the liberties of the entire civilized world."[12] Those against intervention, on the other hand, wanted the United States to give priority to domestic matters over foreign issues and to limit its objectives to the prosperity and security of its own citizens. Americans had enough to do at home, they suggested, without adding the problems of other nations whose relevance to America's safety and well-being was, to say the least, dubious. They saw America's resources as too scarce to implement a policy of active opposition to more powerful European nations. "Because the world is full of oppression," wondered Representative Silas Wood of New York, "is this government the Hercules that is to free it from the monsters of tyranny and slavery? And are we bound to emulate the chivalrous achievements of the renowned Knight of La Mancha, by engaging in conflict with every windmill that we may, in the delirium of our frenzy, imagine to be a tyrant?"[13]

Later on, in 1851, public support for Hungary peaked when Louis Kossuth, the Magyar leader, visited the United States. Kossuth was one of the first revolutionary leaders to experience America's combination of verbal recklessness and moderate actions. So, Daniel Webster, by then secretary of state, warmly applauded "Hungarian independence, Hungarian self-government, Hungarian control of Hungarian destinies." However, he carefully stressed that such preference did not imply America's willingness to depart from its proclaimed neutrality. As in the case of Greece earlier, Webster's conception of an American intervention did not imply more than using "the vast moral force" of public opinion. President Filmore added to this his own pledge that America would "pray" for Kossuth and the Hungarians, whatever might become of them.[14] But beyond the rhetoric, most of those involved, in and out of office, agreed with Henry Clay's assertion that "far better it is for ourselves, for Hungary and for the cause of liberty; that adhering to our wise pacific system and avoiding the distant wars of Europe, we should keep our lamp burning brightly on this western shore, as a light to all nations, than to hazard its utter extinction, amid the ruins of fallen republics in Europe."[15]

Isolationism, however, or "American continentalism" as the historian Charles Beard called it, was not a self-denying policy: from the beginning, America's effort to avoid an active role in the world scene was repeatedly challenged not only from within but from without as well. Throughout the nineteenth century, European nations attempted to gain America's participation in the search for international order. But Americans remained adamantly opposed to multilateral intervention, whether by policy, such as the Holy Alliance for which Russia's Czar Alexander offered America full membership, or by mediation, such as when America was asked to help devise a settlement on the future status of the Congo in the Berlin Conference of 1884. At the same time, however, successive administrations in Washington practiced a policy of unilateralism that paid limited attention to the interests of other nations: the naval expeditions against the Barbary Pirates in North Africa (1801–1805), the involvement (mostly diplomatic) in Liberia in the 1820s, the incidents surrounding Commodore Perry's opening of commercial relations with Japan in 1854, the intervention in China where British soldiers were rescued by an American force in 1859, and the shooting in Korea in 1871. In all such cases the United States displayed the flag where and when words were no longer sufficient. Thus, President McKinley's remark, in the aftermath of the war with Spain, that "in a few short months [America] has become a world power" was a misleading assessment of America's earlier abstention as well as a misrepresentation of America's rise as a world power,[16] for such a position had been reached much earlier: in the ten years that preceded the "little glorious war of 1898," as Secretary John Hay called it, the United States had decisively faced Germany over the Samoa scramble in 1889; Italy over the New Orleans lynching bee in 1891; and Great Britain over the Venezuela boundary question in 1896. But in each instance serious trouble was avoided, and none of these crises erupted into war.

The confusion between isolationism and interventionism reached its peak with World War I. America entered the European war when Germany seemed about to achieve hegemony in Europe and acquire the mastery of the Atlantic Ocean. The very month that war was declared by America, Britain lost 880,000 gross tons of shipping, several times more than it could possibly replace. In that same month, mutinies in the French army made France's future in the war questionable. Russia, the third member of Europe's Triple Entente, was but a few months away from its internal collapse. Much of this, however, was not explained by President Wilson at the time, and, in justifying America's intervention, Wilson gave precedence to confused national ideals over principles of national interest. At first, the American president explained his decision to the American people on legal grounds by defending ancient concepts of neutral rights upon the seas. Later, in need of public support, Wilson raised his approach to a still higher moralistic level and transformed the war into a philanthropic crusade—"to serve and save the world at whatever cost for America"—a crusade that would end all wars and make the world safe for democracy.[17] "It would be," as Wilson put it in his Message to Congress on January 18, 1918, "the culminating and final war for human liberty." Speaking in favor of the president's War Message of April 1917, Representative Ferris' words represented a typical public-minded endorsement of the presidential belief: "Ours," he stated, "is a war against crime, against murder, against autocracy, against militarism, against the overthrow of our freedom and liberty, against imperialism; ours is a war for democracy, for justice, for freedom, for liberty, and that the republics of the world may endure and live."[18]

Having oversold the war, the Wilson administration proceeded to oversell the peace. The American people were promised a concert for peace among democratic nations, a "league of honor, a partnership of opinion," which would eliminate the war-like plottings of inner circles.[19] President Wilson further predicted the international abandonment of selfish national purposes for the common and peaceful purposes of enlightened mankind. "The interests of all nations," he declared on September 27, 1918, "are our own also. . . . There is nothing that the United States wants for itself that any other nation has."[20] America was the first nation to substitute goals of self-abnegation for the more traditional ones of self-preservation, Wilson argued throughout 1919. The country had entered the war neither for its redemption, as it had not been directly attacked, nor for its salvation, as it had not been immediately in danger, but only for the salvation of mankind. President Wilson predicted that other nations would follow suit once the way had been shown.

In the aftermath of the war, a comparison was unavoidably made between the causes of intervention (as presented to the American public) and its results. Clearly, great expectations for peacetime had come out of the lofty expectations raised in wartime. These could not be, and were not, satisfied. The compromises secured from President Wilson at the peace conference of Versailles by European statesmen more concerned with security than with moral principle could not easily be understood and accepted by the American people, who rejected Versailles, Wilson, and Europe altogether.

It is not surprising that this first total challenge to nonparticipation in world affairs was followed by a counterreaction of withdrawal. Never since the early years of the nineteenth century had the American people been exposed to the realities of either interventionism or isolationism. Their security unaffected by the necessities of national expediency, with no threatening great power as a neighbor, and developing in a century of relative international order between 1815 and 1914, Americans grew accustomed to equating their ideal expectations with international realities. During that same period, at a time when standing armies in Europe reached several hundred thousand men, the United States Army was almost always below thirty thousand. The lesser relevance of world affairs was also illustrated by the ever-diminishing status of America's secretaries of state. In early American history, being secretary of state was a major step on the way to the presidency: before 1861, six secretaries of state had become presidents. After the Civil War, however, no secretary of state ever became president. Moreover, the ambiguity of the Western cause during World War I played a substantial part in forcing an isolationist revival, as historians soon began to reappraise the outbreak of the war as well as the causes of American participation in it.

World War II could be more easily understood as a just and necessary war as Hitler's rhetoric was being implemented and the German blitzkrieg was gaining momentum. That the security argument was well considered is illustrated by a letter that William C. Bullitt, then U.S. ambassador in Paris, sent to President Roosevelt on May 16, 1940. "The moral for us," Bullitt wrote, "is that unless some nation in Europe stands up to Germany publicly, France and England may face defeat and such defeat would mean the French and British fleets in the hands of the Germans and the Italians. We should then have the Japs in the Pacific and an overwhelming fleet against us in the Atlantic."[21] The perspective of a German victory was repugnant to Roosevelt too. On June 10, 1940, he described the United States' posture as an island of peace in a world of brutal force as a "delusion." "Such an island," Roosevelt argued, "represents to me and to the overwhelming majority of the Americans today a helpless nightmare of a people without freedom—the nightmare of a people ... fed through the bars from day to day by the contemptuous, unpitying masters of other continents."[22] After the passage of the Lend Lease bill in 1941, such concerns with America's security interests in Europe were taken out of the closet in which they had been hidden for the duration of the 1940 presidential campaign. Indeed, to many, Lend Lease seemed to signify the death of isolationism. "We have tossed Washington's Farewell Address into the discard," Senator Vandenberg, then an ardent isolationist, complained in his diary. "We have thrown ourselves squarely into the power politics and the power wars of Europe, Asia, and Africa. We have taken the first step upon a course from which we can never hereafter retreat."[23]

Not just a change of heart but changes of circumstances seemingly made isolationism, in the words of General Marshall, "just wrong generally."[24] No longer could Great Britain or any other great power be counted upon to prevent an expansionist nation from gaining hegemony in Europe. No longer could geography protect America's security as technological developments made obsolete the protection provided by the Atlantic. Conceived as a necessary policy, isolationism became a policy of choice when the weaknesses of the infant Republic appeared overcome and the conditions that made such isolationism possible appeared forgotten. Originally regarded as an "extraordinary" option, intervention became all the more "ordinary" as the American continent drifted closer and closer to Europe and to Asia, and as the conditions that had made protracted periods of isolation possible were irreversibly transformed. In 1945 and thereafter, America was too great a power to remain out of power politics.

The Rise of Globalism

The rise of the United States' role in the world was shaped by President Truman's Message to the Congress in March 1947. Understood as a policy action, the president's message was realistic in its motivation, restricted in its application, and moderate in its requirements. Since the early years of the nineteenth century, Great Britain had prevented Russia from gaining control over the Dardanelles on the assumption that Russian domination would threaten the European balance of power by providing Moscow with a major outlet in the Mediterranean. But early in 1947, no longer able to fulfill this function, Great Britain asked the Truman administration to assume it.[25]

That Russian expansion in the area needed to be contained was sufficiently clear at the time. Greece, particularly, was on the verge of collapse, economically, militarily, and politically. Yet Greece was the strategic key to the Middle East and an important psychological key to the future of a Western Europe also on the point of panic. It seemed vital to American security that Greece be strengthened, and circumstances were such that only the United States could provide the required assistance. This support was not an endorsement of the Greek regime: "The extension of aid by this country," emphasized Truman in his statement, "does not mean that the United States condones everything that the Greek government has done or will do." It was not even to be considered as an endorsement of Great Britain's past policies in Greece. Instead, this was a decision taken for reasons of national security, a decision that could easily be implemented as the problem in either country was largely within American economic and technical capabilities.

Understood as a policy action, then, Truman's Message attempted to satisfy specific objectives for a specific area at a specific time. The president asked for $400 million in aid for both countries—a litttle more than .1% of the money spent during World War II—and no military involvement was sought beyond assisting in the reconstruction. But understood as a "doctrine" through Truman's own description of the implications of his policy, the message appeared to commit the United States to the unlimited and vague containment of an ill-defined ideology. Through these implications, Greece became, as Truman put it, the symbol of a worldwide ideological clash between alternative ways of life, the totalitarian way and the democratic way. "It must be the policy of the United States," concluded the president in his Message, ". . . to help free people maintain their institutions and their national integrity against aggressive movements that seek to impose upon them totalitarian regimes." Such a policy would be "no more than a frank recognition that totalitarian regimes imposed on free people by direct or indirect aggression undermine the foundations of international peace and hence the security of the United States."

Admittedly, the Truman administration hardly made the rhetoric of its doctrine operational. In part, Truman was plainly responding to the Republican majority in Congress, whose bipartisan support of his foreign policy was made dependent on such harsh language. In part, too, this presentation of the communist challenge was expected to arouse the resolve of the American people, whose isolationist spirit was a cause for concern.[26] Yet for the balance of the decade, a pattern of Soviet expansion appeared to argue compellingly on behalf of an American posture that would provide the administration with the capability required to implement its rhetoric. This argument was best codified in the National Security Council Paper Number 68 (NSC-68).

NSC-68 offered a simplified definition of the Soviet threat and an overly programmed response to that threat. Soviet objectives, the paper argued, were threefold: (1) to preserve the internal position of the communist regime and to develop the Soviet Union as a base for that power; (2) to consolidate control over the Soviet satellites; and (3) to weaken any opposing center of power and aspire to world hegemony.[27] With the Soviet leadership said to be able to sustain rapid economic growth

while maintaining large military expenditures, NSC-68 emphasized the inadequacy of the West's ability to meet Soviet-
inspired military challenges and concluded that "more, much
more was needed to be committed in effort and resources by the
United States if the American strategic situation were not to
deteriorate steadily."[28]

Even though the Truman administration had been articu-
lating the general guidelines of NSC-68 throughout the country
since early 1950, the catalyst for its adoption came from the
North Korean attack of June 25, 1950, at which time a corollary
was appended to the Truman doctrine. "The attack upon Korea,"
declared Truman on June 27, "makes it plain beyond doubts
that Communism has passed beyond the use of subversion to
conquer independent nations and will now use armed invasion
and war." Earlier hesitations about Soviet intentions, previous
inhibitions about American power, and former restrictions
about the scope of U.S. interests were thereby dismissed, and the
Truman doctrine now had a specific target against which it
could be enforced. The cold war had begun.

Yet, even before the corollary of June 1950, the Truman
administration had started to build a global network of alliances
that was to frame the extended containment of later years. At
first, the Rio Pact had merely reaffirmed the U.S. commitment
to the defense of the entire Western Hemisphere. Next, the
North Atlantic Treaty (1949) had committed the United States
to the defense of much of Western and Southern Europe. But
this was just the beginning. Soon came ANZUS (1952), which
committed Washington to the defense of Australia and New
Zealand; and the Southeast Asia Treaty (SEATO) and, by
association, the Central Treaty (CENTO, 1954) which filled the
alliance gap in Asia from Iran to the Philippines. Simultaneously, bilateral security arrangements were concluded with
Japan (1951), South Korea (1953), and the Republic of China
(1954); and, last, the Middle East Resolution (1957) pledged
America to the defense of the Arab states against internal
subversion. Thus, in only ten years, the United States had
become a member of four regional defense alliances and an
active participant in a fifth alliance, had signed mutual defense
treaties with 42 different nations, was a member of an
increasingly large number of international organizations, and

maintained diplomatic missions in nearly all existing countries. Lost among all these was an ambiguous commitment to South Vietnam, where the desirability of this wide distribution of American resources was to receive its first true public challenge.

But first, what a Republican administration had made possible, a democratic administration was to make desirable as John F. Kennedy embarked upon the task to make people feel that in the year 1961 "the American giant began to stir again, the great American boiler to fire again."[29] Indeed, there could not be heard a more rousing celebration of globalism than that stated by a youthful president making "the same solemn oath our forebears prescribed nearly a century and three quarters ago." For, speaking on the day of his inauguration, Kennedy could not be any more expansive in describing U.S. commitments around the world: "Let every nation know, whether it wishes us well or ill, that we shall pay any price, bear any burden, meet any hardship, support any friend, oppose any foe to assure the survival and success of liberty." To the foolhardy who might think of any area not covered by the grand sweep of his rhetoric, Kennedy promised, "this much we pledge, and more." And to the fainthearted who might fear the scope and the implications of these commitments Kennedy warned: "In the long history of mankind, only a few generations have been granted the role of defending freedom in its hour of maximum danger." By the end of the fateful decade thus launched by Kennedy, the United States had over 500,000 soldiers stationed in approximately 30 countries, not including the troops fighting in Vietnam and the Atlantic and the Pacific fleets that amounted to 650,000 men, and operated 429 major bases overseas and 2,297 lesser bases that cost approximately $4.8 billion a year.

It was not so much, then, that the United States had suddenly become morally and politically "overcommitted," to use the expression that was particularly fashionable among foreign policy critics in the second half of the 1960s. Overcommitment, if overcommitment there was, had been with America for many years before it became a national issue in and over Vietnam. But its discovery was related to a "new" perception of American interests and American needs, both abroad and at home—a perception that deemphasized the urgency and scope of the external threat to American security while it reemphasized the urgency and scope of the domestic threat to America's own order. That foreign policy requirements were less important than domestic reforms appeared to be particularly plausible because the test case for foreign policy needs occurred in the worst place (Asia had not been a part of the United States postwar foreign policy consensus) and at the worst time (a growing dismemberment of the domestic consensus followed President John F. Kennedy's assassination).

Under such circumstances, no administration could establish a satisfactory relationship between international values, national goals, and the global balance of power. Throughout the 1960s, applauding American involvement because it grew from deep and flowing springs of moral duty became difficult at a time when the old vision of America's moral duty was being discarded not only in large areas of the world but within large sections of America as well. That American actions should continue to be explained by the indivisibility of international peace also proved to be hardly convincing at a time when America witnessed the divisibility of its own domestic peace. Not surprisingly, the Vietnam War, therefore, became the source and symbol of a foreign policy debate that sought a descent from the globalism of earlier years. For through that war the abstract and ideological commitments of yesteryear had become the concrete and practical realities of the present, although no valid case could be made that these realities still related to the inflated moral rhetoric of the past.[30]

Descent from Globalism

During the second half of the 1960s, the uniqueness of the foreign policy debate in the United States was not due to the mere existence of dissent, nor even to the passion and bitterness that the war in Vietnam progressively aroused. Such passion and bitterness had existed on numerous occasions in the past. In April 1847, for example, the Massachusetts legislature had overwhelmingly adopted a resolution against the Mexican War:

"that such a war of conquest, so hateful in its objects, so wanton, unjust, and unconstitutional in its origin and character, must be regarded as a war against freedom, against humanity, against justice, against the Union . . . and against the free states."[31] What was new in the 1960s was the inability of two successive administrations to manage the dissent they faced at home, an inability particularly striking in wartime.

President Johnson's failure to manage such dissent was related to the unusual opposition he encountered. Going beyond party lines and ideological affiliations, the new critics came from the very groups that had faithfully supported American foreign policy since the end of World War II. These had been the great internationalists who had encouraged the growth of American commitments since World War II and had rejected the arguments used by early foreign policy skeptics. For, as the United States system of alliances was spreading, such criticism, however scarce, had nevertheless been heard. Reinhold Niebuhr, for example, had repeatedly warned against a "budding American imperialism" engineered by "eminent proconsuls . . . partly drawn from the army and partly from business."[32] American power in the service of American imperialism, Niebuhr predicted, would create situations that would be difficult to correct. And Walter Lippmann, speaking out before the Korean War had led to the globalization of America's policy of containment of communism, had attacked a foreign policy that required the "recruiting, subsidizing and supporting of a heterogeneous array of satellites, clients, dependents, and puppets." Once completed, Lippmann argued in 1947, such a "coalition of disorganized, disunited, feeble, or disorderly nations, tribes and factions," would present America with "accomplished facts that we did not intend . . . crises for which we are unready . . . [and] an unending series of insoluble dilemmas."[33]

Throughout the 1960s, as such prophecies appeared to be proved right, these arguments were resurrected and enlarged upon by an increasing number of national figures who had previously ignored them. Consequently, foreign policy questions were brought to popular attention in various ways, including the 1968 presidential elections, when peace in Vietnam grew into one of the major and most divisive issues of the campaign.

The growth of dissent continued despite repeated attempts to explain and to justify American policy in Southeast Asia. In turn, these justifications often raised new limits to presidential action. In May 1970, President Nixon's dispatch of troops into Cambodia created enough unrest throughout the country to compel the president to set specific limits in time and space to the military action he had just ordered.

Significantly, it was not only the war in Vietnam that was brought to public debate. To many of the dissenters, the war could not be accepted either as an accident caused by bad luck or as an aberration stemming from the ineptitude of some high-level officials. Instead they described it, and criticized it, as the logical outcome of a policy that had always made such outcomes possible. Thus, within the framework of the 1960s the same unanswered questions were being raised that had been asked in the 1820s. How much intervention did America need for its security? How much intervention could it afford? Where, when, and how should it be undertaken? There was one major difference between these questions and those of a century before, however—namely, that this time the debate was no longer one between interventionists and isolationists. Instead, this debate pitted interventionists among themselves. As one of these critics put it at the time, in "American policy today, the controversy arises not so much from the fact that we are intervening abroad as from the scale and character of our interventions . . . the objection is to excess—a failure of political judgment and discrimination."[34] In sum, dissenters were seeking a limitationist foreign policy, which, however ambiguously, would achieve a reduction of international commitments they considered excessive.

The limitationist argument was further enhanced by the antiwar feelings that the Vietnam War helped substantiate: "not simply against the war in Vietnam but against war itself, not against bombing Vietnam but against the slaughter of bombing anywhere at any time for any reason, not simply against the slaughter of innocents in an unjust conflict but against the slaughter of those who may be far from innocent in a just conflict."[35] In a way the outrage at the war reflected the impact of television, which ended the anonymity of war deaths and at the same time increased the revulsion of a public already puzzled by the causes and objectives of the war itself. It is this aspect of the war that was instrumental in steering the opposition toward moral issues. For in truth the Vietnam war was no more cruel than other wars America had waged. During the Korean War, in less than a year every major city in both Koreas was leveled. By contrast, in Vietnam, the first city that suffered from a comparable treatment was Hue, during the communist Tet offensive of January 1968. In Korea, civilian casualties were estimated unofficially at a minimum of two million—an average of 700,000 casualties a year, much higher than the yearly rate of civilian casualties in Vietnam.

Confusion over the war was also translated into general doubt and reappraisal of America's goals and methods, not only in Vietnam and in the present, but anywhere and throughout the nation's history. No longer did the war in Vietnam alone have obscure beginnings and uncertain causes. So did the cold war and even the Korean War, as self-styled revisionists derided the findings of an outdated "court history" and offered new explanations, usually harsher on America's role and softer on the communist role. New historical schools found conspiracies everywhere: "President Truman's use of the short-lived American atomic monopoly to blackmail the Soviet Union and to force it to withdraw from Eastern Europe"; "the capitalist manipulation of the Marshall Plan, used to put down the genuine revolt of the European masses"; "the Korean War, undertaken so that the military commitment of America to anticommunist regimes in the Far East might be firmly anchored"; "the nuclear folly of John Foster Dulles' massive retaliation, and the conventional folly of McNamara's flexible response"—all these reflected a new state of mind that doubted America's purpose and policies.

In Congress, too, questions were increasingly raised about the respective roles of the Executive and the Legislative in making commitments and waging wars. For many years, Truman's decision to intervene in Korea had remained an admired model for his successors, whose preoccupation with military issues had shaped the parameters of an assertive presidential leadership. It is such obsessive preoccupation that had left progressively little room for a meaningful congressional role on issues of war and peace.[36] After the Korean War, between 1954 and 1964, the Formosa Resolution, the Middle East Resolution, the Cuban Resolution, and the Gulf of Tonkin Resolution had provided the Executive with a congressional blank check which, in practice, covered all areas of the world. This fact of congressional tolerance coincided with the appearance of presidential success in making foreign policy.

But, in the mid-1960s, when the pain of failure emerged in Indochina and the fear of excess in the Caribbean, applause gave way to acrimony, and a presidency now described as exceedingly imperial was said to be in need of reform. "If the president can deal with the Arabs," it was later argued in Congress, "and if he can deal with the Israelis, and if he can deal with the Soviets, then he ought to be able and willing to deal with the U.S. Congress."[37] Repeatedly the Executive had bypassed the Congress through the device of executive agreements—7,300 of them between 1946 and 1977, including SALT I in 1972 and the Paris Peace Agreement on Vietnam in 1973—which had essentially the same legal force as treaties. But now, over the remaining years of the Vietnam War, the 1970 Cooper–Church amendment (which marked the first time that legislative restrictions on the president's capacity as commander-in-chief were voted by one chamber in the midst of a shooting war), the 1972 Case Act (which aimed at controlling the secrecy of executive actions), and the War Powers Act of 1973 (which restricted the commitment by the Executive of U.S. troops to 60 days unless congressional authorization was sought and received) were the initial steps of a determined effort in Congress to engage in the day-to-day management of foreign policy. Indeed, it increasingly seemed that America was pursuing two foreign policies, thereby introducing an image of oscillations and confusion that persisted and sharpened further after the end of the Vietnam War. One policy was defined by the executive branch of the government and still operated within a generally interventionist framework. Thus, even as he was about to launch a retrenchment of American power, President Nixon echoed Truman's earlier fears as he, too, sensed a dangerous "temptation to turn inward—to withdraw from the world, to back away from our commitments."[38] But granted such neo-isolationist mood, it still presented a character markedly different from that of a generation earlier (and possibly that of a decade later, too). In 1950, neo-isolationism had implied a rejection of Europe as the cornerstone of United States national interest, a "the hell with the allies" outlook, and the refusal to negotiate with the communist world. By 1971, neo-isolationism implied precisely the reverse: a rejection of Asia as the cornerstone of United States national interest, a complaint that the allies were not backing up American policies, and the desire for a negotiated settlement of existing disputes with the Soviet Union and China. The apprehension of the Truman years—that the United States might not remain willing to intervene—had been transformed, in the early 1970s, into the apprehension that it had become excessively eager to intervene. (A decade later, entering the 1980s, the dominant concern was once again over a dangerous reluctance to confront present and future threats in the midst of an ever-hostile world, as the Reagan administration promised a new beginning through the resurgence of American power.)

Thus, going into the 1970s, doubts over America's resilience in dealing with other nations (because of its alleged inexperience in such matters) had been replaced by fears that somehow the United States had gone from historical immaturity to historical senility as, according to some critics, it persisted in offering outdated solutions for new problems. For, to these same critics, America's timidity in relying upon power had given way to a so-called arrogance of power, while old myths, instead of being finally corrected, had simply grown older, and hopes of a peaceful and just world had perished in revolutionary warfare.[39]

Accordingly, in the streets and in Congress these critics sought a different foreign policy that would limit America's involvement in world affairs to areas of truly vital national interests, reduce defense expenditures to a minimum, and reassert the primacy of domestic politics over international matters. But with the critics seriously failing to make the limits they advocated any more precise, differences between these two foreign policies remained relatively slight because their respective visions of America's predominant power both entailed a world where changes could occur only in certain ways and where other changes remained altogether forbidden.

Escape from Normalcy

More than a debate over Vietnam, or over America's foreign policy, the debate of the 1960s was also a debate over the American philosophy of international relations—a philosophy unsuited to the circumstances of the time and unrelated to the policies needed to meet such changes. Speaking shortly before he became special adviser to President Nixon on foreign affairs, Henry Kissinger stated: "Vietnam is more than a failure of policy, it is really a very critical failure of the American philosophy of international relations. . . . We have to assess the whole procedure and concepts that got us involved there . . . if we are not going to have another disaster that may have a quite different look but will have the same essential flaws."[40] The direct outcome of a given experiential context—the earlier isolationist impulse turned inside out—globalism, and the type of situation that it permitted, reflected some of the most persistent patterns of America's international life.

Foremost among these patterns was America's traditional belief in a utopian community of nations, where the struggle for power is forever ended and where the state of war ceases to be the most characteristic feature of international relations. Such utopia had grown out of America's own national experience, an experience so luckily disassociated from that of other countries that the United States lived for two hundred years in a state of "perpetually renewed historical virginity."[41] As a result, Americans merely learned about history from a distance and reluctantly, and liked so little of it that a point was soon reached when the only history America accepted and worshipped was that of its own institutions and culture, the lessons of which it attempted to transpose on the world scene.

One of the characteristics that Americans cited most proudly was the minimal role that power had played in the development of their country. Having had little contact with the distortions that a constant struggle over national self-preservation may have on the fiber of international morality, the United States could easily dispute the role of power in the international arena. With the exception of the Civil War (quite an exception at that), Americans recalled that the thirteen colonies had peacefully cooperated and integrated into the wealthiest and strongest country ever. Why, then, could not other countries learn from this experience? Why could they not learn to depend less on force and more on good intentions? Similarly, why not compare the unification of the American colonies to that of Europe? Or the American revolution to the national revolutions of the post–World-War-II period?

But the uniqueness of America's past usually made its projection in the rest of the world simply irrelevant. When President Madison needed to settle American differences with Great Britain on the Canadian border, he sent an expeditionary corps of 6,000 men, at about the same time when Napoleon was sending an army of 600,000 men to settle France's quarrel with Russia. Yet the latter failed while the former succeeded. For better or for worse, all nations could not measure their adversaries according to the Mexicans and Indians who had impeded the American march forward to the Pacific. Similarly, the states involved in America's unification were colonies with no specific tradition, already united in the same experience of rejection, and by and large enclosed within a single linguistical unit. By contrast, Europe consisted of a multitude of nations, jealous of their traditions and their prerogatives, speaking different languages, using different currencies, and facing different problems in different ways. America's national revolution had been essentially a domestic struggle, whereas the revolutions of new African and Asian countries were waged, often violently, against an alien colonial power determined to preserve its domination.

The implications of this narcissistic outlook cannot be overlooked. Plunged into a contemplation of its own national virtues and history, the United States relied on a distorted and simplistic version of present reality. Instant historical analogies (Hitler and Stalin, Munich and Korea, Korea and Vietnam) and a self-serving faith in the altruism of American policies (that is, the hubris of believing that U.S. intentions cancelled out U.S. actions) distorted this reality even further, so that they made both policies and goals irrelevant to specific cases.[42] Now, in the 1960s, the use of American force in Vietnam, too, was said to pave the way for a time when coercion would be eliminated from the system of nations as it had been from the American system of states. "It is a very old dream," mused President Johnson in April 1965, "but we have the power and now the opportunity to make that dream come true."[43] This, of course, was the dream of a world that, in Johnson's words, would be "free of marching invaders and aggressors, free of terror in the night, free of hunger and ignorance and crippling diseases."[44] But until that dream came true, the world needed to be policed, and it was incumbent upon the United States to help fulfill that role, with force if and when necessary.

The assertion of a national interest that entailed conquest and coercion at the expense of other nations was deemed somehow unacceptable to the American people. When America took up arms, it was not only the flag of America that was waved but that of humanity. "I hope we shall never forget," Wilson had once said, "that we created this Nation not to serve ourselves, but to serve mankind."[45] If the United States fought a war it was in the name of a universal interest, as embodied in the Four Freedoms and the Atlantic Charter during World War II. That same rhetoric was applied to the war in Vietnam where victory would be, according to the then Secretary of State Dean Rusk, "a victory for all mankind . . . a world-wide victory for freedom."[46] Vietnam was the last hurdle before ultimate victory, a victory that would be the prelude to the emergence of what former President Johnson wanted to build: the great society of independent nations, each with their own institutions and each settling their disputes by peaceful means.[47] This utopia remained so typically American that it was found even among the most outspoken American critics. Michael Harrington, one of the many self-proclaimed intellectual leaders of the American left, criticized the American establishment for having burdened its people with an excessively good conscience. Yet his program made the more traditional American utopia modest in comparison. For his program was no less than "to finish the creation of the world."[48]

The utopia had not yet been fulfilled, but it was the role of the American people to ensure the millenium, and the laissez-faire principle inherent in the free-enterprise system was, when translated into foreign affairs, a "laissez-nous-faire" principle.[49] America was "the watchman on the walls of world freedom," the self-appointed "guardian at the gate."[50] Former White House adviser Theodore Sorensen said of President Kennedy that he was at his best when his responsibilities did not have to be shared.[51] This was true of American statesmanship as a whole, and Americans never ceased to be amazed when this leadership was being disputed. To dispute American leadership was to dispute its intentions as well. But these intentions were too pure to accomodate any argument. At all times, even America's real and potential enemies could not but be aware of America's altruism, self-control, and self-mastery. "They [the Russians] know, and the world knows," had claimed Dean Acheson at the time of America's nuclear monopoly, "how foreign is the concept of aggressive war to our philosophy and our political system."[52]

Assuredly, America could be trusted because it was the Chosen Nation, "the justest, the most progressive, the most honorable, the most enlightened nation in the world," and as such it had not only the right but also the duty to use whatever means were necessary, including force, to do justice and to assert the right of mankind.[53] Earlier in the twentieth century, Wilsonian diplomacy, which wanted "to teach the South American republics to elect good men," had found "something sacred and holy in . . . warfare" and thus "refused to cry 'peace' as long as there is sin and wrong in the world."[54] In the late 1960s, the time to cry peace had not yet arrived. "When we are gone," asked President Johnson in March 1968, "what other nation in the world is going to stand up and protect the little man's freedom everywhere in the world?"[55] Fifteen months later the same troubled concern was voiced by his successor, who was worried over the prospect of an America that might become a "dropout" in assuming the responsibility for defending peace and freedom in the world.[56]

But neither America's utopia nor its faith in the exceptional nature of its mission would have been possible without a strong infusion of romanticism. For America still thought of itself as the last—if not the first and only—romantic nation in the world. It helped its sister nations, with no objective other than winning their gratitude. It sought no gain. Wilson had said: "There is nothing so self-destructive as selfishness . . . whereas the nation which denies itself material advantage and seeks those things which are of the spirit works . . . for all generations, and works in the permanent and durable stuffs of humanity."[57]

The cynic would soon have pointed out the internal motivation of this inflated rhetoric. As George Kennan once put it, the question in these circumstances "became not: how effective is what I am doing in terms of the impact it makes on our world environment? but rather: how do I look, in the mirror of domestic opinion, as I do it? Do I look shrewd, determined, defiantly patriotic, imbued with the necessary vigilance before the wiles of foreign governments? If so, this is what I do, even though it may prove to be meaningless, or even counter-productive, when applied to the realities of the external situation."[58] Yet, such rhetoric, when repeated as often as it had been through the years, became credible to a trusting public. Indeed, the American public grew so sensitive to it that the rhetoric itself seemed indispensable if public support was to be gained. Indoctrinated as an instrument of foreign policy, the public had thus emerged as its directive force. A policy that merely intended to be packaged into a hard-hitting doctrine might soon be absorbed by the doctrine itself, thereby ensuring the translation of the doctrine into policy.[59]

Nation and Empire

In the late 1960s, America fought abroad and argued with itself to reaffirm its faith in its illusions and its omnipotence, for some, or to face the consequences of the end of both, for others. With most factions at last recognizing the realities and responsibilities of power, the debate centered on the scope, the nature, and the frequency of its use. Indeed, it is likely that during that debate the American people learned more about international relations than they did during the whole prior history of the American Republic.

Twenty years earlier, Dean Acheson had warned against unlimited interventionism:

People will do more damage and create more misrepresentation . . . by saying our interest is merely to stop the spread of
Communism than in any other way. Our real interest is in
those people as people. . . . It is important to take this
attitude not as mere negative reaction to Communism but
as the most positive affirmation of the most affirmative
truth that we hold, which is in the dignity and right of every
nation, of every people, and of every individual to develop in
their own way, making their own mistakes, reaching their
own triumphs but acting under their own responsibility. . . .
On their own, they will make their own decisions . . . and on
occasion they will make their own mistakes. But it will be
their mistakes, and they are not going to have their
mistakes dictated to them by anybody else. . . . American
assistance can be effective when it is the missing component
in a situation which might otherwise be solved. The United
States cannot furnish all these components to solve this
question. It cannot furnish the will and it cannot furnish the
loyalty of a people to its government.[60]

The war in Vietnam confirmed these warnings and eventually showed that the broad margin of error historically
permitted to American diplomacy could no longer be counted
upon. But the war also put an end to an "illusion of perfect
efficacy"[61] which had now become all the more remote as a
foreign policy often seemed especially successful when nothing
happened. Finally, the war in Vietnam also raised questions
about America's omnipotence: there were limits to what America could do, and it was over the determination of these limits
that the debate unfolded.

Unlike previous eras, what was disputed in the 1960s was
not so much intervention as its modalities—its causes and its
effects, its goals and its means. First in Europe and in Latin
America, then nearly everywhere following the war in Korea,
interventionism had become an established principle of American foreign policy. Generally, it was well accepted by the
American public and well tolerated by the noncommunist
international community. In the 1960s, however, the excesses of
military intervention in the Dominican Republic and its increasingly visible failure in Vietnam acted as catalysts to
launch a debate over whether the United States had not gone

beyond the threshold of legitimate goals and available means. Even when the existence of American interests was perceived in such a way as to make the ends appear as acceptable, there remained at issue the relationship between U.S. interests and the methods employed to attain these. Subject to debate was whether the methods chosen had any probability of fulfilling those interests.

Furthermore, a new balance was looked for: a balance between security and purpose, between commitments and means—a balance that was much affected by the world's own diversity and by the multiplicity of the possible responses to the many questions it raises. For beyond the policy dilemmas created by the diversity of the world, another essential question America finally needed to face and answer was whether it could be both a nation and an empire, whether it could build at home a Great Society, or a Just Society, or an Equal Society, as various political slogans of the time had it, and police a just and peaceful world abroad. Or should the United States instead do more of one and less of the other, with much of the self-denial that such a choice entailed?

During the years of the cold war, U.S. foreign policy had found its rationale in the rhetoric articulated by President Truman. But entering the post-cold war era, another presidential Message to Congress was to seek an alternative to "old policies that have failed."[62] Thus, as stated by President Nixon on February 18, 1970, the central thesis of the new doctrine was that America would "participate in the defense and development of allies and friends, but . . . cannot—and will not—conceive *all* the plans, design *all* the programs, execute *all* the decisions and undertake *all* the defense of the free nations of the world. We will help," Nixon concluded, "when it makes a real difference and is considered in our interest."

The Nixon Doctrine ostensibly rested on the conviction that the United States had been carrying too much of the burden of maintaining world peace. Part of this burden would now have to be assumed by America's allies: the withdrawal of American troops from Indochina, as well as renewed debates over the withdrawal of U.S. troops from Europe and elsewhere, reflected the immediate implications of the new doctrine. Thus, although the Nixon Doctrine made it explicitly clear that the United

States would continue to honor all its treaty commitments, it was also serving notice that it would now expect a higher level of self-reliance: America will, President Nixon warned, "look to the nation directly threatened to assume the primary responsibility of providing the manpower for its defense."[63]

For the new American president, military intervention was justified primarily when a domestic insurgency had shaded into external aggression, and only where and when it made a decisive difference and was considered in America's interest. Apart from the unclear and unrealistic problem of defining external aggression, such a conception of military intervention still left unanswered the questions of when and where America would intervene with military force. It described or defined neither America's interests nor interventionist decisiveness. That the United States did not intend to conceive, design, execute, and implement all the plans, programs, and decisions was nothing new. Now, according to Nixon, future commitments would be considered after a careful appraisal of America's capacity "to counter those threats at an acceptable risk and cost."[64] Such a conviction seemed to recreate a more fundamental equation between objectives sought, means available, and the degree to which the latter might help fulfill the former. Yet Nixon's statement merely referred to new commitments— not to old ones. What about those former commitments whose relevance to present American interests was being disputed? "We are not involved in the world," asserted President Nixon, "because we have commitments; we have commitments because we are involved. Our interests must shape our commitments rather than the other way around."[65] But until the limits of America's involvement and the scope of its interests were more precisely defined did not such a principle leave the United States in the position previously defined by President Truman? Unlimited involvement called for unlimited commitments. In Indochina, for instance, it was argued that once the United States had deployed troops in a given area, the American interest was to ensure that they were not driven off the field —hence President Nixon's decision to send U.S. forces into Cambodia: "If we allow American men by the thousands to be killed by an enemy from privileged sanctuaries the credibility of the United States would be destroyed in every area of the world where only the power of the United States deter aggression."[66] With the same reasoning applied elsewhere, involvement in any one country of the world might create involvement (and hence commitment) everywhere else. Thus, if the old commitments were now going to be maintained, how would U.S. interests and involvement be modified? But no less importantly, if the involvement justified the commitment, what specifically justified the involvement?

President Nixon's view, even as he was enforcing a progressive withdrawal of American ground forces from Vietnam, was still that the United States had entered the war for a worthy purpose, namely, to allow the South Vietnamese people "to decide their own future free of outside interference" and to strengthen "long-term hopes for peace in the world."[67] The former objective—to foster self-determination without geographical, political, or economic qualification—coincided with President Truman's ambition "to support free peoples who are resisting subjugation by armed minorities or by outside pressure." There was in Nixon's pledge no promise for a reduction of U.S. involvement abroad. "If," confided Nixon, "I lived in another country that wanted to be sure and retain its rights to self-determination, I would say: 'Thank God that the United States exist at this moment in history.'"[68] Nixon's assertion might entail a global containment of communist encroachments anywhere. "A just peace in Vietnam," the president stated on June 3, 1970, "is essential if there is to be a lasting peace in other parts of the world."

But since the Korean War, the endorsement of global containment had been an integral part of a position according to which the major policy objectives of the United States must be the worldwide containment of totalitarian forces. President Nixon confirmed suspicion of a bias for global primacy in an interview with television news commentator Howard K. Smith on July 1, 1970: "If the United States leaves Vietnam in a way that we are humiliated or defeated . . . this will be immensely discouraging to the 300 million people from Japan, clear around to Thailand in free Asia. And even more important, it will be ominously encouraging to the leaders of communist China and the Soviet Union who are supporting the North Vietnamese. It will encourage them in their expansionist policies in other areas."

In and of itself, such a position did not quite reflect, as Nixon had it, a "major shift in United States foreign policy"[69] and appeared inconsistent with his assertion that the post–World-War-II era in foreign affairs had passed. Or, as stated by Nixon on April 30, 1970: "If, when the chips are down, the United States acts like a pitiful helpless giant, the forces of totalitarianism and anarchy will threaten free nations and free institutions throughout the world."[70] Such a rationale might also read ominously like a colloquial revision of the Truman Doctrine: the United States must act like a formidable giant willing to intervene throughout the world to deter aggression by the forces of totalitarianism. In sum, the "new" American foreign policies of the 1970s still left unanswered the fundamental questions brought forth by the Vietnam War—a reappraisal of America's vital interest: a redefinition of the minimum objectives for the fulfillment of which America might be willing to fight, alone or with its allies; a reevaluation of the military containment of the adversaries, and an examination of substitute policies; and a revision of the alliances that reflected America's continued commitment to such containment. Eventually, the Vietnam War would end, but the protracted debate over America's role in the world—nation and empire—would continue.

NOTES

1. Raymond Aron, "Reflections on American Diplomacy," *Daedalus* (Fall 1962), p. 719.
2. Walter Lippmann, *New York Herald Tribune*, January 29, 1942, reprinted in *The Essential Walter Lippmann*, ed. Clinton Rossiter and James Lare (New York: Vintage Books, 1965), p. 470.
3. Daniel Conway, ed., *The Writings of Thomas Paine*, Vol. 1 (New York: G. P. Putnam's Sons, 1894–96), p. 88.
4. Arnold Wolfers and Lawrence W. Martin, eds., *The Anglo-American Tradition in Foreign Affairs* (New Haven, Conn.: Yale University Press, 1956), p. 162.

5. Ibid., p. 161.
6. Samuel Eliot Morison et al., *Dissent in Three American Wars* (Cambridge, Mass.: Harvard University Press, 1970), p. 3.
7. Quoted in Paul Varg, *Foreign Policies of the Founding Fathers* (Baltimore, Md.: Penguin Books, 1970), p. 160.
8. From an address of the Minority of the House of Representatives to their constituents, 1812, in Dorothy B. Goebel, ed., *American Foreign Policy: A Documentary Survey*, 1776–1960 (New York: Holt, Rinehart and Winston, 1961), p. 52.
9. Wolfers and Martin, *Anglo-American Tradition in Foreign Affairs*, p. 162.
10. Ibid., p. 145.
11. Selig Adler, *The Isolationist Impulse* (New York: Macmillan, 1957), p. 14.
12. From a speech to the House of Representatives, January 19, 1824, in Goebel, *American Foreign Policy*, p. 70.
13. From a speech to the House of Representatives, January 21, 1824, cited in Goebel, *American Foreign Policy*, p. 72.
14. Adler, *Isolationist Impulse*, p. 15.
15. For Clay's statement, see Goebel, *American Foreign Policy*, p. 93.
16. For a development of this theme see Thomas A. Bailey, "America's Emergence as a World Power: The Myth and the Verity," *Pacific Historical Review* (February 1961), pp. 1–16.
17. See Wilson's address to Congress asking for declaration of war, April 2, 1917, and his address on Fourteen Points, in *A Day of Dedication: The Essential Writings and Speeches of Woodrow Wilson*, ed. Albert Fried (New York: Macmillan, 1965), pp. 301–10 and 321.
18. Quoted in Robert E. Osgood, *Ideals and Self-Interest in America's Foreign Relations* (Chicago: University of Chicago Press, 1953), p. 260.
19. Message to Congress, April 2, 1917. Fried, *Day of Dedication*, p. 306.
20. Wilson address on Five Points, September 27, 1918. Fried, *Day of Dedication*, pp. 334–39.
21. Reported in the *New York Times*, April 26, 1970.
22. Quoted in Robert A. Divine, *Roosevelt and World War II* (Baltimore: Penguin, 1969), p. 31. Yet throughout the campaign Roosevelt continued to pledge nonintervention: "To you mothers and fathers, I give one assurance . . . : Your boys are not going to be sent in any foreign war." Ibid., p. 37.
23. Arthur H. Vandenberg, Jr., ed., *The Private Papers of Senator Vandenberg* (Boston, Mass.: Houghton Mifflin, 1952), p. 10.

24. As quoted by Dean Acheson, address before the Civic Federation of Dallas, June 13, 1950, Department of State *Bulletin*, Vol. XXII, p. 1038 (hereafter cited as *Bulletin*).

25. For a thorough account of this period, see Joseph M. Jones, *The Fifteen Weeks: An Inside Account of the Genesis of the Marshall Plan* (New York: Viking Press, 1951).

26. "This country," Truman later remembered, "was being flooded with isolationist propaganda under various guises, and many of us were apprehensive lest the isolationist spirit again become an important political factor." *Memoirs*, Vol. 1, *Year of Decisions* (Garden City, N.Y.: Doubleday, 1955), p. 97.

27. See Glenn Paige, *The Korean Decision* (New York: Free Press, 1968), p. 61; also see Paul Y. Hammond, "NSC-68: Prologue to Rearmament," in *Strategy, Politics, and Defense Budgets*, ed. Warner R. Schilling, Paul Y. Hammond, and Glenn H. Snyder (New York: Columbia University Press, 1962).

28. Hammond, in Schilling et al., *Strategy, Politics, and Defense Budgets*, p. 307.

29. Quoted in Henry Fairlie, *The Kennedy Promise* (New York: Dell Publishing, 1974), p. 60.

30. Robert W. Tucker, *Nation or Empire? The Debate over American Foreign Policy* (Baltimore, Md.: Johns Hopkins University Press, 1968), p. 23.

31. Morison, *Dissent in Three American Wars*, p. 49.

32. See Reinhold Niebuhr, "The Foreign Policy of American Conservatism and Liberalism," in *Christian Realism and Political Problems*, ed. Reinhold Niebuhr (New York: Scribner's, 1953), pp. 58–64.

33. Walter Lippmann, *The Cold War: A Study in U.S. Foreign Policy* (New York: Harper & Row, 1947), pp. 21–23.

34. William Pfaff, "A Case against Interventionism," in *A Dissenter's Guide to Foreign Policy*, ed. Irving Howe (Garden City, N.Y.: Doubleday, 1968), p. 95.

35. Richard Rovere, *Reflections on United States Policy* (London: Bodley Head, 1968), p. 43.

36. Alton Frye, *A Responsible Congress: The Politics of National Security* (New York: McGraw Hill, 1975), p. 187; also, Jacob K. Javits, with Don Kellerman, *Who Makes War: The President versus Congress* (New York: William Morrow, 1973), pp. 250–51.

37. Majority leader Tip O'Neil, U.S. Congress, *Congressional Record*, November 7, 1981, p. 49644.

38. *New York Times*, February 26, 1971.

39. J. William Fulbright, *Old Myths and New Realities* (New York: Vintage Books, 1963), and *The Arrogance of Power* (New York: Vintage Books, 1967).

40. Richard M. Pfeffer, ed., *No More Vietnams? The War and the Future of American Foreign Policy* (New York: Harper & Row, 1968), p. 13.

41. Stanley Hoffmann, *Gulliver's Troubles, or the Setting of American Foreign Policy* (New York: McGraw Hill, 1968), p. 110.

42. Pfeffer, *No More Vietnams?* p. 123.

43. Address at Johns Hopkins University, April 7, 1965. *Bulletin*, Vol. LII, pp. 606–10.

44. Address to the Veterans of Foreign Wars, March 12, 1968, *Bulletin*, Vol. LVIII, p. 439.

45. Quoted in Osgood, *Ideals and Self-Interest in America's Foreign Relations*, p. 177.

46. Quoted in Edmund Stillman and William Pfaff, *Power and Impotence: The Failure of America's Foreign Policy* (New York: Random House, 1966), p. 6.

47. Ibid., p. 10.

48. Michael Harrington, "American Power in the Twentieth Century," in Howe, *A Dissenter's Guide.* pp. 9–10.

49. William A. Williams, *The Tragedy of American Diplomacy* (New York: Delta Books, 1961) p. 21.

50. Phrases used by President Kennedy and President Johnson, respectively; quoted in Richard J. Barnet, *Intervention and Revolution: America's Confrontation with Insurgent Movements around the World* (New York: World Publishing Company, 1968), p. 11.

51. Sorensen, *Kennedy* (New York: Harper & Row, 1965), p. 563.

52. From Acheson's address to the University of California, Berkeley, March 16, 1950, *Bulletin*, Vol. XXII, p. 477. Some of Acheson's most representative statements have been compiled in *The Pattern of Responsibility*, ed. McGeorge Bundy (Boston, Mass.: Houghton Mifflin, 1951).

53. Cited in Williams, *Tragedy of American Diplomacy*, p. 63.

54. The first statement is quoted by Williams, *Tragedy of American Diplomacy*, p. 64. The second statement is quoted by Osgood, *Ideals and Self-Interest in America's Foreign Relations*, p. 176.

55. Address to the Veterans of Foreign Wars. *Bulletin*, Vol. LVIII, p. 439.

56. *New York Times*, June 5, 1969.

57. Quoted in Osgood, *Ideals and Self-Interest in America's Foreign Relations*, p. 177.

58. George F. Kennan, *Memoirs, 1925–1950* (Boston, Mass.: Little, Brown, 1977), p. 53.
59. Tucker, *Nation or Empire*, p. 23.
60. From Acheson's remarks to the National Press Club, January 12, 1950, *Bulletin,* Vol. XXII, p. 114.
61. Charles Burton Marshall, *The Exercise of Sovereignty* (Baltimore, Md.: Johns Hopkins University Press, 1965), pp. 47 ff.
62. "U.S. Foreign policy for the 1970's: A New Strategy for Peace," Report to Congress, February 18, 1970, *Bulletin,* Vol. LXII, p. 276.
63. Ibid., p. 294.
64. Ibid., p. 277.
65. Ibid., p. 276.
66. *New York Times*, March 10, 1971.
67. A New Strategy for Peace," *Bulletin*, Vol. LXII, pp. 298, 297.
68. From columnist C. L. Sulzberger's interview with President Nixon, *New York Times*, March 10, 1971.
69. *New York Times*, November 4, 1969.
70. Ibid., March 10, 1971.

CHAPTER TWO

Conciliation and Showdown

The Strained Alliance

The time of peace is a time of regret. The peacemaker lives yesterday's events so that he will not repeat the mistakes that made the present what it is. The time of peace is a time of hope, too, and the peacemaker concerns himself with yesterday's world so that tomorrow's world is the better one to which he aspires.

Peacemaking, like warmaking, is a perennial activity of man. He wages war in the name of peace; he often makes peace as if he wanted more war. That the peace that everyone wanted as World War II was nearing an end was not given a chance is a particular source of regret when one considers the unanimity with which it was hoped for. In 1945, the victorious allies were all-powerful, at least insofar as their adversaries were concerned. The only substantial enemy they faced was an internal one—confrontation among themselves. "If we were to win the peace after winning the war, we had to have Russian help," Truman remembered thinking in the spring of 1945.[1] "The only hope for the world," Churchill wrote as late as January 1945, "is the agreement of the three great powers."[2] And Stalin was to concur as he warned against the "greatest danger" to world peace: "conflict among ourselves. We must . . . think how to secure unity in the future, and how to guarantee that the three Great Powers (and possibly China and France) will maintain a united front."[3]

It is hardly possible to be sure that these statements were made in good faith. Because of the events that had occurred previously, it was everyone's hope that they were. Because of the events that have occurred since, it is everyone's regret that they were not fulfilled. But calling for future collaboration was not enough, especially in view of the various tensions that had plagued the alliance in wartime. Only if these tensions, often serious, were to be resolved, only if the mutual, and occasionally justified, suspicion that each side of the alliance had displayed for the other could end—only then could the Grand Alliance survive the defeat of its common enemy and ensure the peace that had eluded the victorious powers in 1919. That these tensions were not ended provides a first clue to the confrontation between America and the Soviet Union.

From the summer of 1941 on, and even before America's entry into the war, Stalin's complaint that the Germans were not being prevented from moving forces to the Eastern front with impunity placed a constant strain on the coalition. From Moscow's viewpoint, such a complaint appeared generally warranted as, throughout most of the conflict, the Soviet Union bore the brunt of Germany's war effort in a way that was at first acknowledged by Moscow's allies. "Russians," Roosevelt wrote Churchill in early 1942, "are today killing more Germans and destroying more equipment than you and I put together."[4] Later, reviewing the military operations scheduled for 1943, Winston Churchill criticized the "poor contribution" of the Western allies whom he described as "playing about" with half a dozen German army divisions while the Russians were facing 185 divisions. "Everywhere," wrote Churchill to General Ismay in March 1943, "the British and Americans are overloading their operational plans with so many factors of safety that they are ceasing to be capable of making any form of aggressive war."[5] Not surprisingly, what Churchill called "poor"—and Secretary of War Henry L. Stimson labeled "half-baked" diversionary schemes[6]—was dismissed as "insignificant" by Stalin, whose resentment strengthened his fears and prejudices.

In order to relieve the German pressure in the East, Moscow repeatedly asked for the opening of a second military front. This had been prematurely promised by President Roosevelt after Molotov's first visit to Washington in May 1942, when an ambiguous understanding was reached between the United States and the Soviet Union "with regard to the urgent tasks of creating a second front in Europe in 1942." But for material and strategic reasons that were duly emphasized to the Soviets at the time,[7] the implementation of the understanding was postponed for two full years, during which each Soviet recrimination was systematically followed by a Western profession of good faith.

While undoubtedly meant to draw off from the Russian front sizable portions of the Germany army, Roosevelt's resolve to enter the war in Europe quickly was motivated by domestic concerns. It was, FDR told General George Marshall in late 1941, "very important to morale to give this country a feeling that they are in the war, [and] to give the Germans the reverse effect, to have American troops somewhere in active fighting across the Atlantic."[8] Such a strategy was vigorously endorsed by American military planners who were apprehensive about Stalin's ability to repel another German summer offensive. As General Eisenhower saw it, "We would be guilty of one of the grossest blunders of all history if Germany should be permitted to eliminate an Allied army of 8,000,000 men."[9] But neither "Round-Up," the American plan for a massive cross-Channel invasion in the spring of 1943, nor "Sledgehammer," a complementary emergency landing on the French coast for the summer of 1942, could take place without British participation—and Churchill, perhaps with the memories of the enormous casualties suffered during World War I, vetoed the implementation of either proposal. While such veto enraged American military chiefs, who saw ulterior political motives in the proposed Mediterranean alternative, code-named "Torch," Roosevelt acquiesced in the interest of Anglo-American unity and thus endorsed London's proposal for a North African operation as the next-best thing. Such an operation, however, did not significantly help the Soviet Union. Instead, a momentarily reassured Germany was reported to have shifted twenty-seven of its army divisions to the Eastern front, away from an Atlantic coast which appeared no longer threatened.[10]

The inability and/or unwillingness of the Western allies to play a more immediate role in the defeat of the German forces enhanced Stalin's suspicion that, under Churchill's influence, the strategy of the Western nations consisted in letting the Soviets and the Germans fight one another until the physical exhaustion of both states.[11] At that point, the Soviet leader reasoned, it would be relatively easy for the West to dictate its conditions of peace both to the Nazis and to the communists.

Earlier, such a suspicion had already been entertained during the 1938 Munich conference. Prior to, and during, that ill-fated meeting between France, Great Britain, and Germany over the fate of Czechoslovakia, the Soviet government attempted to cement a united front against Hitler. How genuine such Soviet efforts were remains uncertain. Obviously, it was to Moscow's interest to harden Czechoslovakia's resistance, as this unfortunate state represented one further step in Germany's eastward advances. But neither Czechoslovakia, nor France, nor Great Britain were anxious to make Soviet intervention possible—assuming that it was, in the aftermath of purges that had reached some 30,000 officers, and in the light of considerable problems of logistics that would have hampered significantly any Soviet military action in Czechoslovakia. Did the Western democracies, Moscow now feared, plan to settle Europe not only without the Soviet Union but against it? The question is worth raising only inasmuch as it reflects Soviet suspicions, both at the time and later, during and after World War II. Clearly, as Stalin saw it, the Western powers preferred to see Germany fight eastward rather than westward, if it fought at all. Moreover, Moscow's vision of a capitalist "conspiracy" was enlarged, again in Stalin's estimation, by the events in the Far East, where Japan was engaged in a full-scale conflict with China—one further step in Japan's westward advances. Thus Moscow could implicate Washington in the Anglo-French "conspiracy" whenever the American and the Japanese governments undertook conciliatory negotiations. In August 1939 fear of isolation drove Moscow into the Nazi camp as the Western powers could not decide upon the value of a military agreement with Moscow. At Yalta, Stalin, in an expansive mood, confided to Churchill: "If the British and French had sent a mission to Moscow in 1939 containing men who really wanted an agreement with Russia the Soviet government would not have signed the pact with Ribbentrop."[12]

Soviet fears of Western treachery were paralleled by fears of the Western allies that Moscow might seek a separate peace, which, eventually, would place it in a position to dictate its own terms at the end of the conflict. The Peace of Tilsit (when Czar Alexander signed a separate peace with Napoleon), the Peace of Brest Litovsk in 1917 (when Lenin signed a separate peace with Germany), and the Pact of Non-Aggression of 1939 emphatically suggested that no Russian government, czarist or communist, would preclude the idea of a separate peace with another foreign government if Russia's national interest justified a search for an immediate end to the hostilities.

From December 1942, when the German Army was encircled at Stalingrad, to the German summer offensive at Kirsk in early July 1943, Stalin's numerous peace probes provided ample substantiation for such fears. Unlike Roosevelt, Stalin subordinated military to political strategy.[13] Following his success at Stalingrad in March 1943, he still faced a long road to total victory. As long as the opening of the second front was delayed, Soviet losses were certain to be considerable. Accordingly, the activities of the Red Army diminished to a minimum, and, conspicuously enough, Stalin dissociated himself from the call for unconditional surrender issued by Roosevelt and Churchill after their meeting in Casablanca in 1943. There could be no guarantee, it was reasoned in Moscow, that the Americans would agree to Soviet territorial terms. The Germans, however, might, and as Soviet official pronouncements continued to encourage a compromise, Stalin sought unsuccessfully to trade a military settlement with Berlin in return for a restoration of the Soviet Union's 1941 borders.

Aware of the allies' doubts over each other's staying power, Hitler sought ways whereby charges and countercharges within the opposite coalition would proliferate. Late in the war, therefore, the German High Command shifted the main pressure from one front to another, hoping thereby to give more credibility to the possibility of an impending double cross. "If," Hitler argued in December 1944, "we can deliver a few more heavy blows, then at any moment this artificially-bolstered common front may collapse with a gigantic clap of thunder."[14]

The German chancellor met with little success in raising Western suspicions when he threw his last major offensive in the Ardennes while the Soviet troops were rolling on in the East, now favored by a depleted German front. But when contacts between Germany and the Western nations were attempted in Bern, Switzerland, without the presence of Soviet representatives, Stalin's suspicions apparently reached a new high. Informed of these meetings by his own sources, the Soviet generalissimo attributed Western discretion on such matters to the "strange and unaccountable" absence of German resistance on the Western front. "At this moment," Stalin complained bitterly, "the Germans have stopped fighting against English and Americans while they continue the war against Russia—an ally of England and America."[15] That the war on the Western front had not stopped, as Stalin claimed, did not end his alleged indignation. As to the substance of the disagreement, the whole incident was blown out of proportion and proved awkward to President Roosevelt, who had steadfastly believed that Stalin had full confidence in him personally.

In part at least, this incident accounted for Roosevelt's growing change of attitude shortly before his death. The American president was all the more distressed because the Western allies had actually notified the Russians that their interest in pursuing the German overtures did not go beyond a willingness to present German emissaries (who never came to Bern) with a draft copy of Germany's capitulation. Seen from Washington, Soviet recriminations implicitly reflected a dogmatic and irreversible Soviet opposition: hence Stalin's tendency to inflate any minor incident into a major confrontation. Seen from Moscow, this alleged attempt at separate negotiations illustrated Western bad faith. Seen from Berlin, the incident appeared to confirm Hitler's earlier assumption. Thus, in a last desperate measure following the sudden death of Roosevelt and reminiscent of Prussia's mode of terminating the Seven Years' War, Himmler, the German Gestapo Chief, formally offered to surrender his forces on the Western front while resistance would be continued on the Eastern front, "at least for a time."[16] Once again both Washington and London rejected any part of this offer even though, from Paris, Charles de Gaulle found the offer and the analysis that came with it moderately appealing.[17] A week after Churchill had informed Stalin of Himmler's offer and the Western rejection, the Soviets held secret talks of their own to negotiate a surrender of Berlin. While the talks quickly broke down, the allies were, of course, never informed.[18] As the war was coming to an end, Stalin had become so conditioned to the possibility of a separate peace that the Red Army was constructing defensive facilities in Austria and warning that "the greatest treason in world history is under way."[19] Later, Stalin's official acknowledgement of Germany's final and unconditional surrender was delayed as he still assumed that the fighting against the Russian troops might go on for some time.[20]

From Roosevelt to Truman

The alliance between the Soviet Union and the Western democracies was a convenient arrangement, concluded to face an immediate threat and despite the many differences and mistrust that existed between the new partners. But a wartime rhetoric that extolled the virtues of the Russian people and its leadership had helped build expectations in the United States that the alliance would survive the defeat of the common enemy: "one hell of a people", claimed the March, 1943 issue of *Life* magazine, "who look like Americans, dress like Americans, and think like Americans."[21] This claim was echoed a few months later in General Malinovski's celebration of the common virtues of the two people: "Russians are like Americans. You love life as we love life. You like to sing and dance and be happy. And we do to. You like music. You like colors. You fight well. You can be gay and you can be sad. And so can we Russians. Ah yes . . . the Russians and the Americans are so much alike."[22]

Not only the Russian people but also their ideology and their leadership were endowed with new and unsuspected qualities. Thus, Joseph E. Davies' *Mission to Moscow,* an American best-seller in 1942 and later a popular motion picture, now suggested that "all believers in Christ and Christ's teachings are theoretical communists to the degree that they are for the brotherhood of men."[23] As for Stalin, wrote the former U.S. Ambassador to Moscow, "a child would like to sit in his lap and a dog would sidle up to him."[24] And for those presumably not ready yet to entrust their children and pets to the Generalissimo, there was still room for comfort in the light of Stalin's reported "great deal of charm and magnetic personality," as written in *Fortune* in January 1945.[25]

Such extraordinary romanticization of the Soviet Union was nourished by Stalin's own efforts to rally internal support for the war by downplaying ideology and invoking patriotic feelings through a conspicuous tolerance of the Russian Orthodox Church, the abolition of the Comintern, and the resurrection of pre-revolutionary heroes, among other well-orchestrated gestures.[26] These helped cultivate a persistent American inability—one that had been experienced many times before and would be experienced many times again—to assess realistically Soviet objectives, capabilities, and purpose. Now, during the war years, the mood was one of optimism, and foremost among the optimists was President Franklin D. Roosevelt. "The only way to have a friend is to be one," he stated wishfully in his final inaugural address of January 10, 1945, in an obvious reference to the Soviet Union. Friendship between the two nations, Roosevelt believed, would be cemented by America's patience and tolerance until Moscow's confidence in the West was sufficiently built up. But by then time was running out on Roosevelt's efforts to build a basis for lasting postwar cooperation with Stalin. Since the Russian victory at Stalingrad, the president had appeared resigned to an eventual Soviet dominance in Eastern Europe because, he argued, a broad understanding between the United States and the Soviet Union required a mutual accomodation of each other's security needs.[27] Yet, such an entente could not be achieved without wide domestic support whose prerequisite in the United States was self-determination in Eastern Europe—that is, exactly what was needed to be sacrificed if the unity of the Grand Alliance was to have any chance of being preserved in the aftermath of the war.

Never sure of the solution to this dilemma, Roosevelt at first entertained some fanciful notions about Stalin's forebearance and understanding. Stalin, Roosevelt was reported to have argued in August 1943, "doesn't want anything but security for his country, and I think that if I give him everything I possibly can and ask nothing in return, noblesse oblige, he won't try to annex anything and will work with me for a world of democracy and peace."[28] Later in the year, after the Teheran Conference, Roosevelt wistfully hoped that planned referendums for Eastern Europe would conveniently result in governments "friendly" to Moscow anyway, thus enabling him to satisfy Stalin's call for friendly border states while maintaining the ideal of self-determination.[29] Still later, Roosevelt hoped to persuade Stalin that the defeat of Germany represented a better guarantee for Soviet security than territorial gains in Eastern Europe.

Thus, Roosevelt traveled two separate and contradictory ways. Abroad, he appeared to accept in advance a Soviet sphere of influence in Eastern Europe. At home, he promised the American people an end to the "system of unilateral action and exclusive alliances and spheres of influence and balances of power and all the other expedients which have been tried for centuries and have failed."[30] Believing in the promises Roosevelt made to them, the American people were not prepared for those accommodations to Stalin that the American president made at Yalta. And, among them, Truman may well have been one of those who were least prepared.

As Daniel Yergin has explained well, there were in those years two schools of thought that competed to influence U.S. policy toward the Soviet Union.[31] The "Riga school," named for the Latvian capital where U.S. State Department analysts were stationed before the establishment of diplomatic relations with the Soviet Union, postulated that Soviet foreign policy was the necessary and inevitable product of totalitarianism at home. To the Russian fear of physical insecurity was added an ideological fear of political insecurity, which made the Soviet leadership irreversibly bent upon worldwide and unlimited expansion. Accordingly cooperation with the Soviet state was said to be not only impossible but also counterproductive. Viewed as a sign of weakness, efforts at cooperation would invite increasingly exorbitant demands rather than lead to compromises. The Nazi–Soviet Pact, the Russian note on the partition of Poland, the winter war in Finland, the annexation of Bessarabia, the Baltics, and the Balkans, all were said to confirm this view.

Primarily based at the State Department and, after 1933, at the U.S. Embassy in Moscow, the Riga group went into eclipse after the German invasion of the Soviet Union in June 1941. For Roosevelt, the exigencies of meeting a common enemy demanded a more serviceable and more flexible doctrine, one that would permit the incorporation of the Soviet Union in a Great Power consortium—also including China and Great Britain—whose task it would be to maintain sufficient armed forces to impose peace in their respective regions. Accordingly, Roosevelt rejected the ideological explanation of Soviet foreign policy in favor of one that emphasized the conventional motives of an authoritarian, imperialist power. It was not only possible but necessary to negotiate and compromise with such a state, because the alternative would be a postwar world comprised of hostile blocs that would ultimately drift toward another world war.

Because its emphasis was placed on high-level personal contacts, the "Yalta school" never developed any lasting institutional base. Instead, it was limited to Roosevelt and a few trusted advisers around him. That it dominated the making of U.S. foreign policy toward the Soviet Union as long as Roosevelt remained president comes as no surprise. From the very moment of Moscow's entry into the war, the State Department had advised against extending unlimited aid to Stalin. Bureaucratic snarls that slowed down American aid annoyed Roosevelt, who felt that the Russians were getting the runaround in the United States. Accordingly, he appointed a special assistant to direct the supply effort and sent another one to Moscow to look into the pessimistic appraisals that were made by State Department military experts about Moscow's staying power.[32] As the years passed by, Roosevelt increasingly abstained from consulting the State Department in his major foreign policy initiatives. But following Roosevelt's death on April 12, 1945, the positions of the Riga school appeared to suit better the views of the new president. As a much-quoted example, Truman, then a Senator, had suggested after Germany's invasion of the Soviet Union: "If we see that Germany is winning the war we ought to help Russia, and if Russia is winning we ought to help Germany, and in that way let them kill as many as possible."[33] Although largely dictated by domestic considerations, such a statement reflected Truman's profound mistrust toward the Soviet regime. At any rate, it did not do much to further Stalin's confidence in the new American leadership.

Truman's attitude may have become all the more firm as the success of the first atomic test provided him with a new sense of military strength. It was Churchill's evaluation that a fortified Truman now became a "changed man" and, in a most emphatic manner, "told the Russians just when they got on and off and generally bossed the whole meeting."[34] Yet the impatience that Truman was to display toward Moscow had manifested itself long before the Potsdam conference and the New Mexico test of July. The new president had decided as early as April 17, five days after he had assumed the presidency, to "lay it on the line with Molotov."[35] And three days later, to Averell Harriman, who had just reminded him that any negotiation requires reciprocal concessions from both sides, Truman replied that "he understood that and would not expect 100 per cent of what he proposed. But [he] felt that [the United States] should be able to get 85 per cent."[36]

Truman's attitude was inspired by the Munich syndrome of the time, a syndrome that described any search for accomodation as appeasement and any appeasement as the prelude to a new world war. A self-styled interpreter of history, Truman believed that most of the problems a president faced had their roots in the past, and many of their solutions therefore had to be shaped by its lessons. "I had trained myself," Truman confided, "to look back into history for precedents, because instinctively I sought perspective in the span of history for the decisions I had to make. That is why I read and re-read history."[37] The Munich syndrome became particularly significant when the Kremlin, too, began to act and react as if it believed in the lessons of Munich. Said Zhdanov, one of the most influential men in Moscow in the 1940s: "Just as in the past the Munich policy untied the hands of the Nazi aggressors, so today concessions to the new course of the United States and the imperialist camp may encourage its inspirers to be even more insolent and aggressive."[38]

Both sides had learned their lessons seemingly too well. Understandably, the guidelines that security policies attempt to follow are anchored in the past. But the past is not always fully understandable either to the observer or to the policymaker. Thus, one of the "lessons" taught in Munich was that, in August 1938, a show of force would have deterred Hitler. But a show of force did take place earlier that year in May, when military measures were adopted by Czechoslovakia to compel a diplomatic retreat by Hitler. Yet, the very success of Czechoslovakia's policy made the adversary more determined, as Hitler, now angered by his "humiliation," cancelled a previous directive that had repudiated military action against Czechoslovakia. At the same time, Prague's show of force weakened British–French support for Czechoslovakia, whose diplomacy was not to the taste of its Western allies. Coercive diplomacy and appeasement came hand in hand: Hitler's appeasement in the spring had become coercion in the fall, while Czechoslovakia's coercion in the spring led to the West's frightened appeasement in the fall. The case against the Anglo–French policy of appeasement was made persuasive by the subsequent discovery that Germany was not ready for war in September 1938 and that Hitler's ambitions were unlimited. If met with Western coercion, Hitler's attempted takeover of Czechoslovakia might have turned into another withdrawal, at least until he was better prepared. But such favorable components of the situation were not known at the time.

Another significant aspect of the Munich syndrome was Washington's refusal to associate itself with the search for a settlement. In his appeal to Hitler on September 27, 1938, Roosevelt had proposed a major international conference, which, however, the United States would not attend. "With no political involvements in Europe," Roosevelt informed Hitler, the United States would assume "no obligations in the conduct of the present negotiations."[39] In that indirect way, it was reasoned, Roosevelt bore part of the responsibility for the Munich debacle. In sum, through the Munich syndrome, America eventually relived in the late 1940s the Munich Conference by doing not only what it thought it should have done in the late 1930s (enter into a formal agreement with European democracies), but also what it thought European democracies should have done themselves (use force to deter aggression in its early stages).

Truman alone, however, would not bring about a reversal of American policy from one of conciliation to one of showdown. To be sure, the scolding given Molotov on April 24, the confrontation with Tito in early May, and Truman's apparent endorsement of Harriman's plan to use economic leverage against Moscow[40] seemed to reflect a rising reliance on confrontational politics,* which Roosevelt had shunned up to his death.[41] Within the U.S. government, this drift did not go unnoticed. "FDR's appeasement of Russia is over," approvingly wrote Senator Vandenberg in his diary following Truman's heated meeting with Molotov.[42] And Secretary Forrestal urged Truman that "if the Russians were to be rigid in their attitude we had better have a showdown with them now rather than later."[43] But such drift was ended quickly after the Soviet and American delegations had treated one another with equal acrimony at the U.N. San Francisco Conference. To patch things up, Truman sent Harry Hopkins, Roosevelt's confidant, to Moscow for a meeting with Stalin, in the course of which the question of

---

*As early as November 1941, Congress had balked at Roosevelt's request that the Lend-Lease program be extended to the Soviet Union. Under the bill, the president was authorized as he saw fit to lend, lease, sell, and barter arms, ammunitions, food, and any defense information to the participating nations. By the end of the war, American deliveries to the government of the Soviet Union added up to more than eleven billion dollars' worth of the widest variety of requirements—including tire plants, chemical factories, petroleum refineries, food, machinery, metal, diverse vehicles, and even $1,647,000 worth of buttons. Such aid represented approximately one-fourth of the total Lend-Lease aid from the United States to the allies. But during the last year of the war, congressional opposition to the extension of Lend-Lease to the Soviet Union increased. As a result, the Fourth Russian Supply Protocol was delayed from July 1944 until April 1945. In fact, the deciding vote was cast by then-Vice President Truman who, as president of the senate, broke the tie on a Republican-sponsored amendment that called for the prohibition of Lend-Lease deliveries for postwar relief and reconstruction—a direct reference to Soviet requests for additional equipment and machinery.

Poland appeared to be resolved to Stalin's satisfaction. Although there would be only token representation of the London Poles, although all the delegates would have to be screened by Stalin, and although there was no mention either of elections or of British participation, Truman, surprisingly but significantly, expressed complete satisfaction with the results of the agreement reached between Hopkins and Stalin.[44] At a subsequent press conference, Truman carefully deflected questions about the fate of 16 Polish delegates arrested while en route to Moscow for discussions about the formation of a government in Warsaw. "I want to make no statement," Truman explained, "that will in any way embarrass the Russian government."[45] This was a long way from showdown.

Similarly, at Potsdam, there was little evidence of Truman's alleged intransigence. Certainly, as conference chairman, Truman could be pugnacious and impatient. When Anglo–Russian bickering and Churchill's digressions elongated the proceedings, Truman often interrupted with the warning that "if they did not get to the main issues [he] was going to pack up and go home."[46] But there is little evidence of the sort of refusal of compromise that characterizes intransigence. In fact, it is with Truman's explicit support that Secretary of State James Byrnes offered several successful compromises which—however short-lived they soon proved to be—gave Potsdam the appearance of having provided the Grand Alliance with a new lease on life. These included a reparations settlement which, though somewhat unfavorable to the Soviets, came together with a U.S. acquiescence of a "provisional" but plainly irreversible settlement of Poland's western borders.[47] Regarding the political future of the other East European countries, American policy at Potsdam did not truly differ from the precedents set at Yalta, that is, a call for elections in the "near future" and without 3-Power supervisions.[48] And for those who had missed the point, Byrnes frequently reminded the conferees that the United States did "not wish to become involved in the elections of any country."[49]

Foreign policy hardly ever lends itself to the dramatic reversals that a revisionist history of the cold war later uncovered. Instead, by 1945 international relations were less involved with men than with circumstances. The agreements signed at Yalta and Potsdam reflected strategic conditions as they had been understood to exist then. Occasionally, several varying interpretations of these agreements were possible, and, in such cases, the interpretation most closely connected to the strategic landscape of the moment prevailed. Later on, of course, as these temporary circumstances faded away, criticism, now related to a different "reality," became fashionable. For example, General Patrick Hurley, former United States ambassador to Peking, said in June 1951: "America was in a position at Yalta to speak the only language the Communists understand, the language of power."[50] But could it really? Substantially delayed by the last great German counteroffensive in the Ardennes, Western forces did not reach the Rhine until March 2, 1945 (after the Yalta Conference) though the Soviets had reached the Oder River, near Frankfurt, by February 7 (during Yalta). With a Soviet army in possession of almost all prewar Poland, approximately 40 miles from Berlin and within 80 miles of Vienna, the question faced by the Western Allies was less one of determining what they would allow the Russians to do than one of determining what the West could persuade them not to do. As Dean Acheson put it: "The Russians had in their power not only to take what was conceded to them, but much more besides." Yalta, therefore, merely gave them the basis for a legal claim to something considerably less than they might have taken without a legal claim.[51] And to this relative and limited extent, in the words of the then Secretary of State Edward Stettinius, the Soviet Union made more concessions to the United States and Great Britain than were made to the Soviet Union.[52]

Furthermore, whatever concessions were made at Yalta to the Russians, they were ultimately based on Washington's explicit need to secure Soviet assistance in the war against Japan.* While the Yalta Conference was being held, the

---

*The most significant and questionable concession made to the Soviets at Yalta was probably the restoration to Russia of a share in the Chinese Eastern and Southern Manchurian Railroads. This, together with the lease of Port Arthur as a naval base, could well have led to a Soviet domination of the Yellow Sea and of Manchuria, unless China emerged after the war as a strong and unified state—a prospect already unlikely at the time.

Combined (United States and British) Chiefs of Staff still foresaw that the end of the war against Japan would take eighteen months beyond the end of the war against Germany.[53] Japan, it was estimated at the time, had stationed approximately 700,000 troops in Manchuria and 1,235,000 troops in China, all of whom MacArthur would later describe as "as fine ground troops as I have ever known."[54] Later it would be learned that the Japanese armies in Manchuria and Korea had been greatly depleted, both in quality and in quantity, as Tokyo wanted to counter American assaults elsewhere. But this information was not available to the policymakers in early 1945. And because the impending campaign was based on the assumption that American ground forces should not engage the Japanese army on the Asian continent, Soviet help was judged to be indispensable.

The decision to spare American ground forces from further confrontation with Japanese ground forces was itself understandable within the perspective of the slaughters that had just occurred on the two islands of Iwo Jima and Okinawa. When Iwo Jima was finally secured, in March 1945, the American marines had lost 4,891 men and the wounded amounted to 15,594. Out of a Japanese garrison of 22,000 men, 212, all wounded, were taken as prisoners. All others had died in battle, in line with the Japanese military code of honor. The following month at Okinawa, 11,939 marines died and 35,905 were wounded, while, on the other side, 7,400 Japanese soldiers were taken prisoner and 131,000 died.[55] Partly on the basis of these events, the anticipated losses for an invasion of the Japanese islands were placed at a minimum of 500,000 killed on the American side, with many more on the Japanese side, and still on the premise that the invasion, scheduled to start on November 1, 1945, could bypass the Asian mainland thanks to the Russian intervention.

In February 1945, shortly after the Yalta Conference, General MacArthur still argued that the invasion of Japan proper should not be undertaken unless the Russian army was previously committed to action in Manchuria.[56] His estimate was confirmed by all the Joint Chiefs of Staff. MacArthur himself felt that at least 60 Russian army divisions were needed for the invasion to be successful. The Joint Chiefs of Staff additionally planned to clear a Pacific supply route through the

Soviet Union, and such plans were not cancelled until April 24, the very day of Truman's stormy meeting with Molotov.[57] What could be disputed is whether such concessions as those made by Roosevelt at Yalta were needed to secure Russia's agreement to enter the war against Japan. Indeed, such aid had already been pledged by Stalin, even prior to the Yalta Conference. In other words, the political payment was made to Stalin for something he had every intention of doing anyway, perhaps even without any compensation at all.[58] But even then, the American president's action at Yalta could still reflect a desire to let no loophole or frustration prevent implementing what was regarded as indispensable to American capabilities and objectives.

Several months after Yalta and on the eve of his journey to Potsdam, Roosevelt's successor continued to regard Russia's entry into the war against Japan as the "compelling reason" for holding a conference. Coming before the atomic test of July 16, the intelligence report submitted to Truman on July 8, possibly the last received before the strikes were ordered, warned that "the basic policy of the present government [in Tokyo] is to fight as long and as desperately as possible in the hope of avoiding complete defeat and of acquiring a better bargaining position in a negotiated peace."[59] Even after the atomic test proved successful, no one was able to ascertain precisely the actual capability of these new weapons, so that most of the existing military plans for Japan's invasion were maintained just in case such weapons were ineffective. Indeed, a cable from the Tokyo government to its ambassador in Moscow, dispatched by the Japanese and intercepted by Washington on July 21, corroborated the earlier intelligence projection as it confirmed once again Japan's unwillingness to "accept unconditional surrender in any situation."[60]

Yet, during the last months of the war in the Pacific, a tripolar confrontation slowly evolved, with Japan playing less and less active a role, caught between the United States and the Soviet Union. Such a confrontation was particularly significant with regard to the use of atomic bombs at Hiroshima and Nagasaki. Truman said afterwards that he had never had any doubt that they should be used, and, with very few exceptions that included then-General Eisenhower, everyone within the political, military, and scientific communities concurred with him. Indeed, the Committee on the Atomic Bomb recommended that the bomb be used against the enemy as soon as possible. They further urged the president that it should be dropped without specific warning and against a target that would clearly show its devastating power. Their debates always centered on how and when to use the bomb, never on whether to use it. Yet the consensus within the administration was also that the Japanese had already been militarily defeated. More than half of Japan's main cities had been burnt to the ground—Tokyo, Osaka, Nagoya, Kobe, Yokohama—and with them the major industrial areas that had supported Japan's war effort. Short of planes, skilled pilots, gasoline, and parts, the Japanese air force was almost inactive, and American bombers could now come and go as they pleased and without escort. Moreover, Japan was seeking mediation from Stalin, who informed Truman at Potsdam. In sum, it was the opinion of the Joint Chiefs of Staff that the unconditional surrender of Japan was likely to occur without the atomic bomb and prior to the invasion. Should they be wrong in their estimate, the invastion itself was not scheduled to start before November 1, and the rate of casualties would probably remain low during the summer months that would precede it as the Japanese leaders wanted to preserve their scarce remaining forces for the defense of the homeland.[61]

That two atomic bombs were nevertheless dropped when they were thus reflects America's concern not only with the military requirements of the war against Japan—as these could be perceived in July–August 1945—but also with the political requirements imposed by the imminence of a Soviet intervention in the Far East. Such intervention had been contractually sought at Yalta, when Roosevelt had found it imperative to secure it. Now, atomic weapons looked like the most effective way of concluding the war in the Pacific with the shortest delays, thus not allowing Soviet claims for active participation in the future occupation of Japan. By making its own impression, the bomb would also contain the Soviet armies, who might otherwise go further into Manchuria even after Japan had been defeated. "I would not allow the Russians any part in the control of Japan," later confided Truman in his *memoirs,* "I decided to take no chances in a joint setup with the Russians. . . . We were not going to be disturbed by Russian tactics in the Pacific."[62] And Secretary Stimson confirmed it: "The thing to do was to get this surrender through as quickly as we can before Russia could get down in reach of the Japanese homeland . . . [and] before the Russians could put in any substantial claim to occupy it and help rule it."[63] Stalin had pledged to enter the war within three months following the end of the conflict in Europe: the deadline was August 8. The Soviet army was then to begin to fulfill whatever political and military objectives Moscow might have had in the Far East. Occurring as they did on August 6 and 9, the bombings of Hiroshima and Nagasaki, which led to Japan's surrender on August 14—six days after the beginning of the Soviet offensive in Manchuria—represented both the last military acts of World War II and the first political acts of the emerging confrontation between the United States and the Soviet Union.

The Rise of the Soviet Threat

At no time during the interwar period and since the Second World War has any given U.S. administration been able to achieve a firm and lasting consensus on the nature and scope of the Soviet threat. Accordingly, American policy has been condemned to oscillate and stagger in its repeated attempts to identify the focus of the Soviet challenge and implement the actions best suited to contain it.

Already in the immediate aftermath of the Soviet Revolution, Walter Lippmann, then at the beginning of his long and celebrated career, noticed the contradictions of an approach that persisted in presenting the Soviet Union as "both a cadaver and a world-wide menace."[64] Analyzing the coverage of the Soviet revolution, Lippmann observed that the *New York Times* had reported the collapse of the Soviet government no less than 91 times during the first two years of the Soviet Republic, while the capital city of Petrograd was said to have been recaptured six times, on the verge of capture three more times, burned to the

ground twice, in a state of absolute panic twice, in revolt against
the Bolsheviks six times, and in a state of starvation constantly.
How, Lippmann asked at the time, was it possible to refer to the
overwhelming advances of Polish troops deep in Russia and
simultaneously fear the imminent Russian invasion of Europe?
Twenty-five years later, World War II was barely over when the
same contradictions were emerging, pointing to the disastrous
state of affairs in the Soviet Union ("Is it true that they eat
human bodies there in Russia?" asked Congressman Rankin
from former Ambassador to Moscow Bullitt)[65] and the imminence of a Soviet takeover of Europe.

Every so often, therefore, reports about the nature of Soviet
intentions and the size of Soviet military capabilities have been
issued either to urge the United States to regain the initiative
and return to the offensive in a protracted conflict with Moscow,
or else to deplore U.S. excesses in the light of the moderation of
the Soviet Union. In the 1960s, such a pattern could be seen once
again as historians of the cold war were going the full swing of
the pendulum. Earlier critics had attacked U.S. policies for
supposedly turning over the fruits of World War II victory to the
Russians. Now, the self-styled revisionists of the Vietnam era
described American postwar policies as the unnecessary containment of a destroyed and largely impotent Soviet Union,
whose only postwar claims were legitimate: compensation for
the enormous destruction caused by Germany and security from
a potential revival of German militarism. These later revisionists overlooked several aspects of the relationship that evolved
between the United States and the Soviet Union after World
War II. First, they ignored the ideological outlook of the Soviet
regime and the political psychology of its rulers. While not "the"
cause of the confrontation with the East, these factors could not
be put aside as if they did not exist. Second, the revisionists
overlooked Western perception of Soviet intentions: they overlooked Western fears. To dismiss them as unjustified because of
alleged Soviet weakness, or as not genuine but part of a
jingoistic mentality aimed at frustrating a rising movement for
social justice, is not sufficient. To the extent that these fears
were indeed felt at the time, American policies could still be
regarded as a policy of response after all. Third, the cold war
revisionists gave too little credit to U.S. restraints, at least until

the outbreak of the Korean War. To be sure, as will be seen, the Truman administration did not attempt to share its nuclear monopoly, and it did make some tactical mistakes that might have justified in part Soviet fears of Western intentions. But the United States did not attempt to exploit directly its nuclear advantage. Nor did it attempt, until after June 1950, to build up its atomic and/or conventional forces in a way that would have made an American military attack on the Soviet Union possible. Finally, and tying these together, the revisionist history of the cold war plainly ignored the security interests that the policies of the Truman administration sought to achieve. The assumption can be made now that these interests were not threatened then in view of Moscow's reduced capabilities and limited objectives. Whether or not such an assumption is valid, it is not surprising that a convincing case could not be made at the time. In retrospect, the tragedy is that the only policy either side could legitimately have regarded as one that did not present any serious threat was a policy that placed that country's security at the mercy of the other. In sum, the revisionists paid too much attention to American ideology, Soviet fears, Soviet restraint, and Soviet security, and not enough to Soviet ideology, American fears, American restraint, and American security.

The impact of research on early, "traditional" cold war scholarship should, however, not be underestimated. The willingness of the revisionist historians to seek new answers—however excessive these may have been at times—to old questions helped correct an interpretation of cold war history that had been often too benign in its assessment of the role played by the Truman administration in the unfolding conflict with the Soviet Union. For instance, an examination of Herbert Feis' *Japan Subdued* (1961) and *The Atomic Bomb and World War II* (1966) reveals significant differences and adjustments, on the basis of which one of the leading members of the first generation of cold war historians came to acknowledge, however reluctantly, a partial causality between an American attempt to influence and direct postwar relations with the Soviet Union and the use of the atomic bomb against Japan.[66] Thus, in *Japan Subdued*, Feis had written: "It *may* be also—*but this in conjecture*—that Churchill and Truman and some of their colleagues conceived that besides bringing the war to a quick end, dropping the bomb at Hiroshima would improve the chances of arranging a just peace. For would not the same dramatic proof of Western power that shocked Japan into surrender impress the Russians also?" But five years later, Feis amended his analysis: "It is *likely* that Churchill and probably also Truman conceived that bringing the war to a quick end would improve the chances of arranging a just peace. Stimson and Byrnes *certainly had that thought in mind.*" What had been confined to mere "conjecture" had now become "likely," "probable," and even "certain," without, however, degenerating into the discovery of a U.S. policy of "atomic blackmail" against the Soviet Union.[67]

Nobody wanted or sought the cold war. The United States and the Soviet Union had been foreseen for a long time as the two main actors on the international scene. In the 1830s, Tocqueville had described the two nations as "marked out by the will of heaven to sway the destinies of half the globe."[68] By that time, they were already two of the greatest land empires in the world, and over the following decades both became inhabited by a larger population than were the great powers of the late nineteenth century—Great Britain, France, and Germany. At however different a pace, America and Russia were both on their way toward unparalleled industrialization. In 1919, only a mythical belief in isolationist principles in the United States and a domestic upheaval in Russia delayed their ascendancy. By 1945, the collapse of the traditional sources of power in Europe combined with continued or renewed growth in the United States and Russia made them superpowers by position if not by choice. Their confrontation, too, was one of position, if not of choice, as the island power of the West sought to prevent the land power of the East from filling the various power vacuums then existing within the international system. Such divisive factors as the Soviet Union's communist ideology and America's short-lived monopoly of atomic weapons enlarged the conflict further, shaping some of its unique features, even though, admittedly, these factors did not actually cause it.

The confrontation that grew out of World War II was, then, one of the many struggles fought in history to maintain or to restore the balance of power in Europe. And as in the previous struggles, the American people were involved, whether they wanted to be or not. In several respects, however, the conflict between the United States and the Soviet Union was quite different from previous general European wars. First, there was a new distribution of power that deprived of any significant meaning the former power multipolarity. The new bipolarity preempted any national claim of independence by the old nation states, especially those of Europe whose decline was accentuated by the rising expectations of their colonial possessions.[69] Within this bipolar framework ideological antagonism intensified superpower rivalry. Other European wars, too, had implied a measure of ideological opposition, but never before had the lines been so clearly drawn according to ideological criteria. In repeated instances, communist ideology could be adapted to the requirements of anticolonial revolutions so that the advent of postwar nationalism in the third world also became part of the cold war.

Following a phase of uncertainties between 1945 and 1950, the challenge of such a revolutionary ideology was greatly and unfortunately overemphasized during the 20 years that followed the outbreak of the Korean War. Often communism merely displayed great opportunism in taking advantage of domestic weaknesses and eventually worsening these weaknesses, rather than causing them. Yet, to the extent that each side eventually allowed itself to believe in the ideological rhetoric of the other, each side could conceivably be understood as seeking to establish its rule all over the world, even though military means were physically and psychologically unavailable to both sides. In 1945, the homeland of communism, evidently tired by a war it had been instrumental in winning, could not seriously think of militarily exporting its avowed gospel. Nor were the Western democracies capable of a serious effort at rolling communism back across an already devastated European battle-ground. Hence, a second peculiarity of this confrontation: both Moscow and Washington implicitly resolved that they would avoid employing force against each other. Paradoxically, the decision largely rested on a balance of illusions as, even while each nation was inflating the other's military capabilities far beyond what they actually were, both nations proceeded with an accelerated demobilization of their respective forces. Thus, the Truman administration lost no time in "bringing the boys back home." By June 30, 1949, U.S. military personnel had been reduced from approximately 12 million four years earlier to 1,450,000. Most of the remaining troops were insufficiently trained and generally not ready for combat, as was to be shown during the first months of the Korean war. In the meantime, the Soviet military forces had also been considerably reduced, from a wartime high of 11.4 million to a possible low of 2.9 million. The Soviet demobilization nearly matched America's, given the huge land borders that these forces had to protect plus the internal needs that the army might be called upon to assume within the Soviet Union. In addition, American forces were one part only of Western forces that included, among others, the 750,000 men made available by Great Britain.[70]

Nevertheless, both nations took relatively great risks. They progressively spread their confrontation throughout the world, threatening one another with all the paraphernalia of indirect aggression and subversion that they could devise. In this game of action and reaction, probing and containment, each party helped the pendulum move from one side to the other. Ultimately, the two sides had to face the consequences of their diplomatic bluffs being called. During the Hungarian crisis of October 1956, the Eisenhower administration tacitly conceded that it had neither the resources nor the inclination to move into the Soviet sphere of interest in Eastern Europe. During the Cuban missile crisis of October 1962, it was shown that Soviet infiltration in Latin America, the American sphere, had limitations that were not to be overstepped. Once the two superpowers understood the limits of the action they might take against one another, areas of accommodation began to appear, first before the escalation of the Vietnam war, and next after it had ended.

Side by side with such an evolution grew the seeds of a better understanding of each nation's respective goals. Earlier, everywhere and about everything, ideological as well as political, yet by and large demilitarized, the cold war developed within a framework of total opposition and inability to communicate. Given the almost complete opposition that characterized the past experiences and characters of the two protagonists, there was a basic incomprehension of the other side's historical past. So, the Soviet Union, always aware of its national weakness and territorial insecurity in the face of the ever-possible invasion from the West, faced a self-assured America, certain of its national strength and geographic security. Similarly, an often humiliated Russia, whose military success had usually been the culmination of a series of defeats and which had traditionally looked to the world outside for much-needed help in completing its modernization, coped with a self-righteous America, supposedly never defeated in war, proud of its greatness and eager to propagate it abroad.

But each nation also misunderstood the other's future, as neither side could understand why the other side was not living up to its expectations. The Soviet Union assumed that, following the conclusion of the war, a bitter and frustrated America would soon lapse into isolation, in order to face the enormous problems of reconversion, recession, and unemployment. At Yalta, Roosevelt himself had stated that the withdrawal of American forces from the Continent would be completed less than two years after the end of the war. Why then, asked the Russians, was Truman now speaking as if he foresaw an unlimited involvement of his country in the affairs of Europe? Why this departure from what the Soviets understood to be the traditional policy of the United States? Why these friendly overtures toward the Western zone of Germany and why such concern with the remilitarization of the Western European states, as if they were indeed to undertake the "liberalization" of the Eastern European states from Soviet control? Why such American amity and generosity toward Japan, a traditional threat to Russia? As asked by an American observer of Soviet foreign policy, "Was the construction put upon American policy in the summer of 1947 much more extravagant than the belief held in the West between 1945 and 1949 that the USSR was about to unloose her armed hordes across Europe to the English Channel?"[71] Apparently, both Washington and Moscow lacked the empathy that was needed if they were to understand one another and in neither did any substantial expertise exist about the other—only, at best, varying degrees of ignorance. Disillusionment with misrepresented expectations thus maximized each country's suspicions.

America, too, faced its own illusions. A weakened Russia was expected to give in to the requests of an America made irresistible by atomic weapons. In the spring of 1945, Truman was being advised that "the bomb might well put us in a position to dictate our own terms at the end of the war."[72] Secretary of State James Byrne hoped with others that America's atomic monopoly might force Russia to agree to an American plan for a lasting world peace. Such weapons might be, in Truman's words, the "greatest thing in history."[73] Furthermore, Russian losses in the previous war went far beyond what America could visualize as acceptable. Between 15 and 20 million Soviet citizens had been killed and another 25 million had been deprived of shelter though the destruction, complete or partial, of 15 large cities and innumerable towns and villages. Russia's economic situation was little short of disastrous. In the aftermath of such suffering and destruction, how, Americans asked, could the Russian people long accept the yoke of communist dictatorship? Already the Kremlin was reported as having lost the allegiance of several million representatives of minority groups. How much longer, then, would it be possible to keep the demobilized Russian soldiers harassed and deprived of their fundamental liberties? Had not the time come for the long-awaited collapse of the Soviet regime? And what about the "orgy of good feeling" that seemed to have spread over Russia, whose "almost delirious friendship" toward the American people was reported by George Kennan from the Moscow embassy?[74] But instead of fulfilling Washington's expectations, Moscow pursued its take-over of what it regarded as the legitimate fruits of the war in Eastern Europe. Suspicion bred still more suspicion.

To examine the outbreak of the cold war is to travel through the sinuous paths of conditional history. What would have happened if the allies had been in a position to satisfy faster the Soviet request for a second front? What would have happened if the Soviets had been led by a man other than Stalin, a man according to Khrushchev's later analysis, "everywhere and in everything . . . saw 'enemies,' 'two-facers' and 'spies'."[75] As hardly anyone could ever determine what Stalin was up to, it became everyone's prudent behavior to assume that he was up to the worst. What would have happened if Roosevelt had not died, or if Henry Wallace had not been replaced in 1944 as Roosevelt's running mate, or if Churchill had been reelected? But, above all, what would have happened if the United States had accepted a Soviet sphere of influence in Eastern Europe?

Such a principle had been recognized in an agreement concluded between Churchill and Stalin in October 1944.[76] According to this agreement, Stalin was to be left free to organize his own favored elements in Rumania and Bulgaria, while Hungary and Yugoslavia were equally shared and Greece left to the control of Great Britain. By and large, Stalin lived up to the agreement, which he regarded as a natural extension of traditional European history. In Bulgaria, a part of "his" sphere, the coalition government was ended quickly in August 1945 when the parties of the opposition—the Agrarian and the Social Democratic parties—were captured by communist nominees following the forced resignation of their leaders.[77] In Rumania, too, Moscow forced the abdication of King Michael in favor of a so-called National Democratic Front government. In Hungary, on the other hand, relatively free elections were held in the fall of 1945, and the communist take-over did not take place until 1947 with the imprisonment of the Hungarian leaders, Bela Kovacs and Imre Nagy. The rise of a communist regime in Yugoslavia was essentially the work of domestic forces following the destruction of the old political structure. But when Tito tried to export his revolution to Greece, he encountered the opposition of Stalin, anxious in 1945 to respect Britain's free hand and in 1947 not to engage U.S. forces now openly committed to the defense of Greece.

Much more critical were the questions raised with regard to Poland: what would be the boundaries of postwar Poland, and who would rule it? At Yalta, it had been decided that a "democratic" Poland would receive compensation in the West for its substantial territorial losses in the East. At Potsdam, Poland's eastern frontiers were tentatively agreed upon, but neither the question of its western frontiers nor that of its domestic institutions was settled. By that time, and in a way that combined symbolic, political, and strategic considerations, Poland had already become too complex an issue to permit concessions by either side. In addition, of course, spheres of influence were intrinsically unacceptable to the American philosophy of international relations. World War II might not be a war to end all wars, but at least it would bring forth an alternative to power politics and the related evils of secret or open alliances, balances of power, and spheres of influence where the weaker state had its fate decided upon by the stronger state. All these were to be replaced, in Roosevelt's words, by a "universal organization in which all peace-loving nations will finally have a chance to join."[78] This goal had been the essential objective of Cordell Hull's wartime tenure as secretary of state, the high tide of which had been reached, in his own estimation, with the Moscow declaration on general security of November 1, 1943. At that time, the United States, the Soviet Union, Great Britain, and China had pledged to establish at the earliest practical date a general international organization, based on the sovereign equality of all peace-loving states and open to membership by all such states for the maintenance of international peace and security.

But America's objections to de facto Soviet gains in Eastern Europe dealt a further blow to any remaining hope of continued collaboration. Soviet suspicions of American high-spirited ideals were all the more aroused as they saw the United States practice with a good conscience the very principle against which they preached. The place was, of course, Latin America, "our little region over here which never has bothered anybody," as Secretary Stimson once put it.[79] For the United States, just like Russia, was behaving according to tradition. Collective security for the one already endowed with continental security, regional security for the other, who is little concerned with global security when the potential aggressor is at its door—this was the old pattern of the idealist employing realist means while facing the realist who was using an idealist cover.

The End of Security

Indeed, a tragic world evolved out of the military victories of a triumphant alliance. In August 1945, the dawn of the cold war also meant the dawn of the nuclear era, as the United States now enjoyed atomic capabilities that its major adversary on the international scene lacked. Instinctively, the Truman administration based America's national security on such new weapons. "America's security," wrote President Truman in his *Memoirs*, "and the security of the free world depend to a large degree on our leadership in the field of nuclear energy."[80] Loose in the wrong hands, nuclear weapons would spell disaster both for the United States and for the rest of the world, and it increasingly appeared to America that, in the words of Secretary James Forrestal, "it could exercise a trusteeship over the atomic bomb on behalf of the United Nations and agree that we would limit its manufacture for use on such missions as the United Nations should designate."[81]

The adoption of a policy of nuclear hegemony did not go unchallenged. Throughout the latter half of 1945 and 1946, the higher echelons of the Truman administration were involved in a major debate over national versus international control of the atom. To many, including Secretary of War Henry Stimson, the atomic bomb had revolutionized international relations in a manner that made reliance on traditional notions of national security dangerous, if not obsolete. Different approaches to the search for security needed to be tried, including the eventual demilitarization and denationalization of the new technology. Relations with the Soviet Union, Stimson argued in September 1945, "may be perhaps irretrievably embittered by the way in which we approach the solution of the bomb with Russia. For if we fail to approach them now and merely continue to negotiate with them, having this weapon rather ostentatiously on our hip, their suspicions and their distrust of our purpose and motives will increase."[82] Consequently, Stimson, about to retire from public service, urged that direct arrangements with Russia be worked out by the United States (and Britain) to control the production and use of the bomb. Stimson further recommended that work on the improvement or manufacture of the bomb be ended, provided the Russians agreed to do likewise. He finally suggested that existing U.S. bombs be impounded, with the proviso that they would never be used without the joint approval of the three governments.[83]

Stimson's proposal was hardly based on an inflated vision of Soviet willingness to cooperate. At Potsdam, he had often expressed his concern over Moscow's policies, and following his return, the aging secretary could not shake the spectre of Soviet oppression that he had vividly experienced throughout the conference.[84] Nonetheless, Stimson believed that the Kremlin had to be tested once more. Truly, problems and differences between the two countries were considerable; but they were, in Stimson's view, exacerbated by the atomic bomb. If "ostentatiously" displayed, the bomb would be a dangerous incitement to confrontation.

In opposition to Stimson (whose proposal remained short of sharing the atomic bomb with Russia), there was a growing temptation to base a long-awaited Pax Americana on such U.S. atomic monopoly. The bomb, Secretary of State James Byrnes emphasized, had placed America "in a position to dictate [its] terms" to the rest of the world.[85] At Yalta and at Potsdam, Stalin had spoken the language of power. The language of power would now be spoken to him, and Byrnes strongly advocated that the United States preserve and strengthen its atomic capabilities. "We must use our best efforts," he argued, "to develop better bombs and more of them."[86]

Seen in retrospect, both Stimson and Byrnes showed a comparable concern over a future they deemed to be predictable. To Stimson, a gradual and verifiable program of mutual exchange of scientific information and collaboration in the development of atomic power might convince Moscow of America's good will and preserve a semblance of harmony between the two superpowers. To Byrnes, the bomb might make the Soviets docile and subservient as they would, however reluctantly, respect America's atomic power. But Stimson and Byrnes wanted to act quickly, because both based their expectations on the assumption that America's atomic monopoly would not last long—no more than "from seven to ten years"—so that if any initiative were to be launched in either direction—conciliation or showdown—it needed to be launched at once.[87]

At first glance, the proposal made at the United Nations on June 14, 1946 by the United States—a proposal subsequently known as the Baruch Plan—indicated that Truman was following, at least in part, the Stimson recommendation of presenting the bomb as part of an international heritage. The plan provided for an international agency that would own and control all nuclear energy facilities and the necessary materials. After such international control had been asserted, the United States would be committed to stop its production of nuclear weapons, destroy existing stockpiles, and make available to all information concerning nuclear technology.[88]

However, from a Soviet viewpoint, the Baruch Plan neglected a number of legitimate Soviet concerns. First, while this system of international ownership and regulatory controls was being created and tested in transitional stages, the United States was to be allowed to continue to manufacture and stockpile atomic weapons if it so chose. By postponing the American sacrifice until the Soviet sacrifice should have been made, the proposal therefore assumed that Moscow was prepared to grant Washington the confidence that Washington was unprepared to grant Moscow. The Soviets had reason to ask what would then prevent Washington from reneging on its commitment once Moscow had been made incapable of achieving atomic parity. Moscow's refusal to take the first step matched Washington's own refusal to do the same. To Molotov, who warned on November 7, 1945: "We will have atomic energy and many others things too,"[89] Truman replied seven months later: "We should not under any circumstances throw away our gun until we are sure the rest of the world can't arm against us."[90] Both statesmen proved true to their word.

Second, even if the United States did not renege on its pledge to stop its production, destroy its stocks, and submit to the same inspection as other members of the accord, a state of inequality would still remain an intrinsic part of the intended arrangement. For, under the Baruch Plan, the United States would inevitiably preserve a know-how far more sophisticated (despite any further exchange of information) than that of a Soviet Union pledged, like other states, to abandon nuclear arms research and testing. In denying the Russians a try at atomic parity, the Baruch Plan was unacceptable to the Soviets. Third, beyond Moscow's perception of America's good faith were problems raised by the projected international agency. Given the voting distribution at the United Nations, the abandonment of the veto power that the Baruch Plan required would leave the Kremlin in a semipermanent minority. In the words of one of the Soviet leaders, Moscow would then be dominated by "a majority on whose benevolent attitude . . . the Soviet people cannot count."[91] Conversely, being itself in a semipermanent majority, the United States would be in a position to control the development of both the military and the industrial uses of nuclear energy within the Soviet Union. As any violation of the agreement was expected to be met with "immediate, swift and sure punishment," the Soviet Union would be at the mercy of measures taken by a majority largely directed from Washington. As seen by Dean Acheson, such a provision "could be interpreted in Moscow only as an attempt to turn the United Nations into an alliance to support a United States threat of war against the USSR unless it ceased its efforts."[92]

It was not, of course, America's stand alone that caused and fed the atomic arms race already in the making. However imperfect it might have been in some areas, the Baruch Plan entailed important and generous concessions and real risks for the United States, not the least being the abandonment of one of its major instruments for balancing the superior military manpower of the Soviet Union. Further concessions would have encountered strong and insurmountable opposition from the Congress. American policymakers could rightly assume that the Baruch offer was a first step in a lengthy process, a step that needed to be matched with Soviet concessions rather than with Soviet demands for additional American concessions. Instead, Moscow's counterproposals at first consisted of calling for the destruction of atomic stockpiles, whether in a finished or semi-finished condition, and prior to the elaboration of adequate and verifiable measures of control. This proposal would have implied a unilateral destruction of the American advantage, and the Soviet plan too grossly attempted to postpone the Soviet sacrifice until the execution of the American sacrifice.

In October 1946, the U.S. rejection of marginal Soviet concessions on international inspection and the elimination of the veto rule on day-to-day inspection ended this initial try at nuclear arms control. No part of the American proposal, it was now indicated, was open to discussion: it would be accepted or abandoned in toto. Its abandonment confirmed Stimson's and Byrnes' earlier prediction: a nuclear arms competition of unparalleled magnitude between the two superpowers. "As long as an international agreement for the control of atomic energy could not be reached," concluded President Truman, "our country had to be ahead of any possible competitor."[93] But as long as one country remained ahead, the other would attempt to catch it. The evidence is now strong: by that time, Stalin had given first priority to the development of a nuclear weapon.[94]

NOTES

1. Harry S. Truman, *Memoirs*, Vol. 1, *Year of Decisions* (Garden City, N.Y.: Doubleday, 1955), p. 246.
2. Quoted in John L. Snell, *Illusion and Necessity: The Diplomacy of the Global War* (Boston, Mass.; Houghton Mifflin, 1963), p. 121.
3. As quoted by Winston Churchill, *Triumph and Tragedy* (Boston, Mass.: Houghton Mifflin, 1953), p. 355.
4. Winston Churchill, *The Hinge of Fate* (Boston, Mass.: Houghton Mifflin, 1950), p. 274.
5. Ibid., p. 935.
6. See John Lewis Gaddis, *The United States and the Origins of the Cold War, 1941–1947* (New York: Columbia University Press, 1972), p. 70.
7. Anthony Eden, *The Reckoning: The Memoirs of Anthony Eden, Earl of Avon* (London: Cassell, 1965), p. 330.
8. Quoted in Gaddis, *United States and Origins of Cold War*, p. 66.
9. Ibid., p. 67.
10. Churchill, *Hinge of Fate*, pp. 745 ff.
11. See Milovan Djilas, *Conversations with Stalin* (New York: Harvest Books, 1962), pp. 73–74.
12. Churchill, *Triumph and Tragedy*, p. 364.
13. See Vojtech Mastny, *Russia's Road to the Cold War* (New York: Columbia University Press, 1979), pp. 73–80.
14. Quoted in Chester Wilmot, *The Struggle for Europe* (New York: Harper & Brothers, 1952), p. 578.
15. Quoted in Adam B. Ulam, *Expansion and Coexistence: The History of Soviet Foreign Policy* (New York: Praeger, 1968), p. 381.
16. Truman, *Memoirs*, Vol. 1, p. 91.
17. Charles de Gaulle, *Mémoires d'espoir* (Paris: Librairie Plon, 1959), p. 206. See also Truman, *Mémoirs*, Vol. 1, pp. 88 ff.
18. Mastny, *Russia's Road to Cold War*, p. 272–73.
19. Ibid., p. 270.
20. See *Final Entries, 1945. The Diaries of Joseph Goebbels*, ed. Hugh Trevor-Roper (New York: G.P. Putnam's Sons, 1978), passim.

21. Cited in William N. Neuman, *After Victory: Churchill, Roosevelt, Stalin and the Making of Peace* (New York: Harper & Row, 1969), p. 90.
22. Quoted in Leslie A. Rose, *After Yalta: America and the Origins of the Cold War* (New York: Charles Scribner's Sons, 1973), p. 6.
23. Joseph E. Davies, *Mission to Moscow* (New York: Simon and Schuster, 1941), p. XVI.
24. Ibid., p. 357.
25. *Fortune*, January 1945, No. 31, pp. 146–47.
26. Gaddis, *United States and Origins of Cold War*, p. 33.
27. Ibid., pp. 138–39; Mastny, *Russia's Road to Cold War*, pp. 248–53; Lloyd J. Gardner, *Architects of Illusion. Men and Ideas in American Foreign Policy*, 1941–1949 (Chicago: Quadrangle Books, 1970), p. 52.
28. Quoted in Gaddis, *United States and Origins of Cold War*, p. 64.
29. See ibid., pp. 36–37; Rose, *After Yalta*, p. 20; and Robert A. Divine, *Roosevelt and World War II* (Baltimore, Md.: Johns Hopkins University Press, 1969), pp. 92–93.
30. Gaddis, *United States and Origins of Cold War,* p. 52.
31. Daniel Yergin, *Shattered Peace. The Origins of the Cold War and the National Security State* (Boston, Mass.: Houghton Mifflin, 1977), pp. 32–55.
32. Roosevelt's envoy to Moscow, Harry Hopkins, left Stalin convinced that Russia would not surrender in 1941. "There is unbounded determination to win," he cabled Roosevelt. Cited in Robert Sherwood, *Roosevelt and Hopkins: An Intimate History* (New York: Harper & Row, 1950), pp. 339, 342–43. See also Divine, *Roosevelt and World War II,* pp. 80–83.
33. Quoted in D. F. Fleming, *The Cold War and Its Origins* (Garden City, N.Y.: Doubleday, 1961), p. 135.
34. Quoted in Herbert Feis, *The Atomic Bomb and the End of World War II* (Princeton, N.J.: Princeton University Press, 1966), p. 87. However, Feis does not believe that Churchill's perception of Truman's mood is justified by the minutes of the Potsdam Conference.
35. Truman, *Memoirs,* Vol. 1, p. 50.
36. Ibid., p. 71.
37. Harry S. Truman, *Memoirs. Volume 2, Years of Trial and Hope, 1946–1952* (Garden City, N.Y.: Doubleday, 1956), p. 1.
38. Quoted in Walter LaFeber, *America, Russia and the Cold War* (New York: John Wiley, 1967), p. 62.
39. Robert A. Divine, *Roosevelt and World War II*, p. 22.

40. James B. Reston, *Prelude to Victory* (New York: Pocket Books, 1942), p. 46. Quoted in Rose, *After Yalta*, p. 39. See George C. Herring, *Aid to Russia, 1941–1946. Strategy, Diplomacy, the Origins of the Cold War* (New York: Columbia University Press, 1976).
41. Gaddis, *United States and Origins of Cold War*, pp. 183–84; Rose, *After Yalta*, p. 48.
42. Arthur H. Vandenberg, Jr., ed., *The Private Papers of Senator Vandenberg* (Boston, Mass.: Houghton Mifflin, 1952), p. 175.
43. Truman, *Memoirs*, Vol. 1, pp. 77–78.
44. Rose, *After Yalta*, pp. 42–45; Mastny, *Russia's Road to Cold War*, p. 286.
45. Rose, *After Yalta*, p. 45.
46. Truman, *Memoirs*, Vol. 1, p. 360.
47. Adam A. Ulam, *The Rivals* (New York: Viking Press, 1971), p. 75.
48. Gaddis, *United States and Origins of Cold War*, pp. 163–64.
49. James F. Byrnes, *Speaking Frankly* (New York: Harper & Brothers, 1947), p. 73.
50. See General Hurley's testimony to the Senate Committees on Armed Services and Foreign Relations. U.S. Senate, *Hearings* on the Military Situation in the Far East, 82nd Congress, 1st Session (1951), pp. 2827–62.
51. Ibid., pp. 2948–3053.
52. Edward Stettinius, *Roosevelt and the Russians: the Yalta Conference* (Garden City, N.Y.: Doubleday, 1949), p. 6.
53. Quoted in Martin Herz, *Beginnings of the Cold War* (New York: McGraw Hill, 1969), p. 5.
54. U.S. Senate, *Military Situation in the Far East*, p. 58.
55. United States Strategic Bombing Survey, *The Campaigns of the Pacific War* (Washington, D.C.: Government Printing Office, 1946), pp. 323, 331.
56. Walter Millis, ed., *The Forrestal Diaries* (New York: Viking Press, 1951), p. 31.
57. Gar Alperovitz, *Atomic Diplomacy: Hiroshima and Potsdam* (New York: Vintage Books, 1967), p. 31. This meeting worried both Stimson and Marshall, who feared that the Russians might subsequently delay their entry into the Pacific war until, observed Marshall, America "had done all the dirty work." Feis, *Atomic Bomb*, p. 36.
58. George Kennan, *Russia and the West under Lenin and Stalin* (Boston, Mass.: Little, Brown, 1960), p. 354.

59. Quoted in Rose, *After Yalta*, p. 60.
60. Ibid., p. 59.
61. Barton J. Bernstein, ed., *The Truman Administration: A Documentary History* (New York: Harper & Row, 1966), p. 8.
62. Truman, *Memoirs*, Vol. 1, p. 412.
63. From the Stimson Diary, August 10, 1945. Quoted in Alperovitz, *Atomic Diplomacy*, p. 190.
64. Walter Lippmann and Charles Mertz, "A Test of the News," *The New Republic*, August 4, 1920, and August 11, 1920. Quoted in James Aronson, *The Press and the Cold War* (New York: Bobbs-Merrill, 1970), pp. 26–27.
65. Aronson, *Press and Cold War*, p. 32.
66. See Gar Alperovitz's review of Herbert Feis' work, in *Cold War Essays* (Garden City, N.Y.: Doubleday, 1970), pp. 51–73.
67. Herbert Feis, *Japan Subdued* (Princeton, N.J.: Princeton University Press, 1961), p. 12; *Atomic Bomb and End of World War II*, pp. 194–95; and *Japan Subdued*, p. 14.
68. Alexis de Tocqueville, *Democracy in America*, Vol. 1 (New York: Vintage Books, 1954), p. 452.
69. George Liska, *Imperial America: The International Politics of Primacy* (Baltimore, Md.: Johns Hopkins University Press, 1967), p. 5.
70. See Adam Ulam, *Expansion and Coexistence*, pp. 403–4; and Thomas Wolfe, *Soviet Power in Europe, 1945-1970* (Baltimore, Md.: Johns Hopkins University Press, 1971), pp. 10–11.
71. Ulam, *Expansion and Coexistence*, p. 448.
72. Truman, *Memoirs*, Vol. 1, p. 87.
73. Ibid., p. 421.
74. Kennan, *Memoirs*, Vol. 1, p. 241.
75. Khruschev's posthumous attack on Stalin was delivered at a closed session of the Twentieth Party Congress in February 1956. It appears in *A Documentary History of Communism*, Vol. 2, ed. Robert V. Daniels (New York: Random House, 1962), pp. 224–31.
76. See Churchill's own account of his agreement with Stalin in *Triumph and Tragedy*, pp. 226 ff.
77. See Hugh Seton-Watson, *The East European Revolution*, 3rd ed. (New York: Praeger, 1956), pp. 167–230.
78. Quoted in Louis Halle, *The Cold War as History* (New York: Harper & Row, 1967), p. 53.
79. Quoted in Gabriel Kolko, *The Politics of War: The World and United States Foreign Policy, 1943–1945* (New York: Random House, 1968), p. 471.
80. Truman, *Memoirs*, Vol. 2, p. 294.

81. Walter Millis, *Forrestal Diaries*, pp. 94–96.
82. Henry L. Stimson and McGeorge Bundy, *On Active Service in Peace and War* (New York: Harper & Row, 1948), p. 642.
83. On September 21, 1945, at the last cabinet meeting attended by Stimson, the proposal of the Secretary of War was supported by Acting Secretary of State Dean Acheson, Undersecretary of War Robert Patterson, and Secretary of Commerce Henry Wallace. Opposed to it were notably Secretary of the Treasury Fren Vinson, Attorney General Thomas Clark, and Secretary of the Navy James Forrestal. See Truman, *Memoirs*, Vol. 1, pp. 525–27. According to Dean Acheson, "the discussion was unworthy of the subject. No one had a chance to prepare for its complexities." *Present at the Creation. My Years in the State Department* (New York: W. W. Norton, 1969), p. 123.
84. Richard G. Hewlett and Oscar E. Anderson, Jr., *The New World: 1939–1946* (University Park, Pa.: Pennsylvania State University Press, 1962), p. 416.
85. Truman, *Memoirs*, Vol. 1, p. 87.
86. James Byrnes, *Speaking Frankly*, p. 275.
87. Ibid., p. 261.
88. Hewlett and Anderson, *New World*, pp. 531–619.
89. Quoted in ibid., p. 461.
90. Quoted in Walter Lafeber, *America, Russia, and Cold War*, p. 35.
91. Inis L. Claude, Jr., *Swords into Plowshares: The Problems and Progress of International Organization* (New York: Random House), p. 317.
92. Dean Acheson, *Present at Creation*, p. 155.
93. Truman, *Memoirs*, Vol. 2, p. 306.
94. Dean Acheson, *Present at Creation*, p. 125.

CHAPTER THREE

Expansion
and Containment

The Collapse of Europe

"What is Europe now?" asked Winston Churchill in mid-1947. "It is a rubble heap, a charnel house, a breeding ground of pestilence and hate."[1] indeed, it was. Five years of war had left the entire European continent in shambles, a collection of hopeless nations in the most complete state of hunger, poverty, desperation, and chaos. In the midst of the relative affluence of later days, it became all too easy to forget the general atmosphere of past atrocities, actual collapse and future disturbances. Apparently, Great Britain could better resist the onslaught of the German armies than the endless and devastating winters that followed the war. As to Britain's former enemy—a nation that only a few years earlier was building a new empire expected to last a thousand years—it now lay prostrate, divided into four occupied and ravaged areas. Everywhere, the diet of bread and potatoes for the European urban dweller without access to farm products, the lack of clothing and the scarcity of shoes, the desperate search for coal, the innumerable black markets—all these appeared far too remote one generation later.[2]

Continental Europe alone, exclusive of England, required 12 million tons of food in 1946 to avoid large-scale starvation.

Food production had fallen by 25% from its prewar levels, with 17 million more people than before the war. In the 1930s, most European countries had already been unable to feed their people out of their own resources. In Britain, only one-third of the total food needs had been home-grown; it had amounted to less than one-half in Belgium, and four-fifths in France. But after 1945, the ability of each nation to produce foodstuff was further reduced, not only by war damages but also by a dramatic succession of "acts of God." In the summer of 1945, drought struck in France. In 1946, an exceptionally harsh winter ruined the wheat crops in England, France, and Germany. The winter was followed by severe floods in the spring, and more disruption was caused in the summer by excessively dry weather.

Industrial output had also collapsed. It reached only one-third of the prewar (1938) volume in Belgium, slightly over 50% in Italy, less than 80% in France. By 1947, Europe's industrial production was 15% below prewar levels. Inadequately fed and sheltered, without much incentive to work as increases in prices and taxes steadily reduced their purchasing power (in France, for instance, wholesale prices rose 80% in 1946), Europeans showed little enthusiasm in the reconstruction effort. In sum, beyond the human losses, beyond the destruction of cities, factories, mines, railroads, the war had dislocated the very fabric of Europe's economies.[3]

Not only was Europe unable to regain on its own the limited standard of living it had enjoyed before the war, it was not even in a position to prevent further deterioration. Everything had to be imported—food, raw material, industrial equipment, agricultural machinery—but these imports needed to be paid for, and Europe had no substantial foreign exchange reserves left. During the period between the end of the war and the beginning of the Marshall Plan, the United States supplied Western and Southern Europe with roughly $11.3 billion to help these countries face interim difficulties.[4]

The collapse of Europe, however, was not merely economic or financial. It was also military, political, and social. The military establishments of all continental nations had not only been weakened but discredited as well. Defeated was the French army, supposedly the strongest and most dependable force on the continent in the 1930s. In June 1940, outfought, outmaneuvered, and outequipped, it had surrendered to Germany after a few weeks of serious fighting. Gone, too, was the German army and its short-lived aura of invincibility, as well as the Italian army whose moment of national glory did not long survive the Ethiopian campaigns of 1936. With manpower made plentiful by chronic unemployment, military forces might possibly be reconstituted. But there was no collective will to fight, and neutralist pressures were exerted by populations thoroughly exhausted by war and understandably reluctant to join new conflicts for which, once again, Europe would provide the battleground.

Political establishments had also been discredited, before and during the war, and a widespread crisis of political confidence afflicted each nation. The old accounts of the 1930s were being settled under cover of an assumed postwar justice. Collaborators were found everywhere, and everywhere they were eliminated, physically or politically. In France alone, 2,000 death sentences were passed, together with 40,000 detentions and even more condemnations for national indignity.[5] Many of these affected individuals who, at one level or another, had held positions that now needed to be filled by new men and women who were not always available and not always competent. Thus, in most European countries a leadership vacuum existed, and there could not be found a lasting majority able to revive the will of the nation and to reorganize its productive resources.

Such a political crisis was especially convenient for local communist parties. Forced to go underground in the aftermath of the Russo–German Pact of 1939, European communists had joined underground movements of resistance when the Soviet Union entered the war against Germany. Their reorganization helped them to become rapidly the main force of these movements, a status symbolically enhanced because German forces everywhere persecuted them. These parties were now rewarded by the electorate—19% of the total vote in Italy (June 1946) and 28% in France (November 1946). In France, in Italy, and in Belgium, the communists were members of governments of national unity. But such unity was conceivable only as long as the facade of East–West cooperation was maintained. In these countries, therefore, small cold wars grew together with the cold war proper, and none of these governments long survived America's Truman Doctrine. With the presidential Message to Congress delivered on March 11, 1947, the communists ceased to be part of the government on March 12 in Belgium, on May 4 in France, and on May 31 in Italy. The threat to Europe's security was now seen as coming from within as well as from without.

When the German armies swept across Europe in 1940, all European states were transformed, willingly or unwillingly, into dependencies of the Nazi Empire. In every one of these states, thousands of people had turned against their own countrymen and fought alongside the enemy. The very notion of the nation state had been dismembered, thereby compounding the ineffectiveness with which postwar problems of reconstruction were tackled. Consequently, in 1945, throughout Europe—with the possible exceptions of England and such neutral countries as Switzerland and Sweden—nationalism appeared suspect. Source of all evil, the nation state was transcended, at least for a while, by movements in favor of European unification. It was not surprising that in the three major countries on the continent some of the leading political figures came from borderlands. Robert Schuman in France and Alcide de Gasperi in Italy had formerly held dual nationality; Konrad Adenauer in Germany had promoted separatist movements in the aftermath of World War I. Everywhere, public and private figures called for the creation of a United States of Europe. But born out of destruction and misery, these calls failed to survive subsequent reconstruction and recovery.

The postwar years enlarged the vacuum that the war had created in Europe. Economically deprived, politically unstable, and militarily impotent, the old European states faced the world outside with uncertainty and weariness. In traditionally predominant nations, such as France and Great Britain, policy-makers wondered what direction they should give to their policies. What was the status of their countries now? Were they still great powers in their own right? Could they find salvation in neutrality or should they seek their security through an alliance with one of the superpowers? In France, under de Gaulle's leadership, old diplomatic patterns reappeared even before the conclusion of the war. Signed on December 10, 1944, the Franco–Russian alliance pledged automatic cooperation in preventing a resurgence of Germany's power that might lead to a new German aggression. Diplomatically, Moscow greeted the new treaty as a sign of France's reentry among the great powers: "On the continent Germany will remain placed between Russia and France," declared the Soviet ambassador to France. "That is why the Franco–Soviet pact allows us to think that Frenchmen and Russians with all their allies, will be able to assure to Europe a stable and durable peace."[6] To accomodate de Gaulle, American policy planners, too, recommended satisfying French wishes and treating this embattled nation according to its potential power and influence rather than its present strength.[7]

Although the Anglo–American relationship was being widely labeled as "special," numerous tensions reflected the different perspectives of the two countries involved—one reluctant to acknowledge its fall from world power, the other not always clear over the implications of its rise to world predominance. Between 1945 and 1948, the most notable differences between Washington and London included the negotiations of the Anglo–American Loan Agreement of 1945–46, the development of a British nuclear program, and the negotiations over Palestine. In all of these instances, Prime Minister Clement Attlee pointedly warned that Great Britain had "to hold up [its] position vis-à-vis the Americans. We couldn't allow ourselves to be wholly in their hands, and their position wasn't always awfully clear anyway."[8] There was, Attlee added on another occasion, "always the possibility of their withdrawing and becoming isolationist once again."[9] After the monetary debacle of 1947–48, public opinion pollsters in Britain reported an increasingly favorable attitude toward the Soviet Union and an alarming increase in anti-Americanism. As the conservative weekly *The Economist* put it at the time, "American opinion should be warned that over here in Great Britain one has the feeling of being driven into a corner by a complex of American actions and inconsistencies which in combination are quite intolerable."[10]

But both in France and in Great Britain attempts to reassert national prestige and independence often offended public wishes for new solutions. Such efforts also conflicted with the compelling necessity of relying upon outside aid for economic recovery and military defense. For Europe, the choice was one of means, and policies were, as always, being dictated by circumstances. That most states decided to go along with the United States is hardly surprising, not only because of the real sense of commonalities that tied the two sides of the Atlantic together, but also because the United States alone was able and willing to provide Europe with the assistance it needed. Nevertheless, such decisions were not always approved by a general public that remained suspicious of U.S. objectives and intentions and regarded the growing schism between Moscow and Washington as a choice between the lesser of two evils. To Washington, European doubts, whenever perceived, appeared horrendous. They were often dismissed as an obvious communist plot.

The Politics of Confrontation

Yet, it is all too easy to seek an explanation of the resulting discord between the United States and the European left in the fundamental irreconciliability of the general views they held. To be sure, each side was the natural adversary of the other. In addition, however, the United States quickly became the pawn in a game for power that was often managed by local conservative forces—especially in France and in Italy, where these forces were competing with the political parties of the left to form a viable and lasting majority. To assume therefore that American pressures alone imposed a polarization of political forces in these countries—first, forcing the dismissal of the French communists and the Italian communists from their respective coalition governments and, next, achieving their isolation as foreign national pariahs—is to ignore the extent to which U.S. officials were manipulated in these early years by noncommunist forces in Europe.[11]

These defined the choice they faced as an either/or proposition. "There are only two real forces in France today, the Communists and I," de Gaulle told U.S. Ambassador to France Jefferson Caffery in May 1945.[12] "I am almost alone in the world of our responsible friends to desire" the expulsion of the Italian communist party from the government, complained Prime Minister Alcide de Gasperi two years later, as he pledged to carry out such expulsion nevertheless, "at any cost, running all the risks that I know."[13] To remove whatever hesitation there might still exist among the policymakers in Washington, the communist opposition was said to be firmly and unquestionably under Soviet control. "If the communists win," de Gaulle warned in November 1945, "France will become a Soviet Republic."[14] Italy, Ambassador in Washington Alberto Tarchiani noted, is "directly linked to Russia through Yugoslavia. . . . It would serve to flank Greece and Turkey, to extend communist influence north to Germany and Austria, west to France and Spain . . . and facilitate communist penetration into North Africa."[15] To balance the Soviet support of the communist parties, American aid was urgently requested. "If I get any breaks at all," de Gaulle pointed out, "especially in the international field, I will win," in which case, of course, "France will stay independent." Without such aid, de Gaulle also warned, he would have "to work with the Soviets . . . even if in the long run they gobble us up," as they had already gobbled up the French communist party.[16] Speaking through Tarchiani, de Gasperi, too, sought U.S. assistance in comparable terms. "If the Italian populace had any thought they were choosing between the United States and the Soviet Union in their support of the communist party, there would be no doubt of their decision."[17]

This was blackmail diplomacy, and none of these arguments should have gone unchallenged. Neither in France (undoubtedly) nor in Italy (probably) was the communist party close to achieving power, either under the cloak of legality or by force. In both countries, the first postwar election made of the more moderate socialists the dominant parties of the left. De Gaulle's and de Gasperi's either/or analysis simplified the political landscape of France and Italy to the point of irrelevance. This is not to say that these communist parties did not expect to come to power in the future. Relegitimated by their role in the underground war against Germany, both the French and the Italian communists had regained their national images, with tangible electoral results. By promoting postwar groupings and fronts that included the socialists and accepted a strategy of political alliances with bourgeois parties, the communists expected further electoral gains, especially as their superior organization made it relatively easy for them to dominate these coalitions.[18] Force, therefore, was not needed, even if, as Ambassador Caffery indicated, its availability "should not be doubted."[19]

That such a strategy of nonviolent takeover was followed by the European communist parties with the explicit advice and consent of Moscow should not be questioned. By 1943, the earlier prewar differences between the Italian communists and the leadership of the Comintern had been smoothed over. On April 1, 1944, Togliatti's public *svolta di Salerno* (that is, his declared willingness to enter the government before the King's withdrawal) followed closely Stalin's recognition of the government of Italy on March 13: understandably, the Soviet Union preferred to maintain a political presence in the conduct of Italian affairs. Similarly, the French communists, too, were now willing to participate in a government headed by de Gaulle. As Stalin is reported to have said, revolution was no longer necessary everywhere.[20] Peace through compromises between the United States and the Soviet Union on the one hand, between the communist and the bourgeois parties on the other, would permit an eventual communist rise to power. Caution was a matter of necessity: "With the Americans in France," French communist leader Maurice Thorez later reflected, "the revolution would have been annihilated."[21] In short, the way to Soviet hegemony went through Togliatti's *partito nuovo* and Thorez's *voie démocratique*.

Presented with a choice that was unequivocally dramatized by conservative interlocutors in France and in Italy, the United States went into battle with a determination that increased quickly as the expectations that there might be East–West cooperation in Europe soon faded away. Not surprisingly, U.S. aid proved to be a major weapon in the resulting battle. Léon Blum and de Gasperi, who both went to Washington to secure such aid, emphatically stressed, upon their return, that they never faced any condition of any kind, military, political, or diplomatic, or any suggestion or even by insinuation.[22] And, indeed, investigating the record divulges little evidence that points to explicit and direct pressures exerted by the American government on the French and Italian governments to exclude the communist parties from their respective majorities. What can be uncovered are numerous innuendos and indirect promises that gained ever more urgency with the unfolding of international events that surrounded the enunciation of the Truman Doctrine. These, however, were for the most part sought by the French and Italian prime ministers themselves. The communist scare was the key to faster deliveries or larger amounts of U.S. aid. Caffery and U.S. Ambassador to Rome James Dunn significantly complained of the excessive passivity of the Truman administration in the face of the political situations in France and in Italy; they would have liked more decisive actions to be taken at once to contain communist gains that resulted from the overall dissatisfaction of the public with the pace of recovery.[23] In other words, although it clearly met with Washington's approval, the decision to expel the communists from the French and Italian governments was made in Paris and in Rome. It is only after the decision had been made and implemented that U.S. policies became overtly and covertly supportive of the new majorities and explicitly opposed to a return that the communists themselves expected to be imminent.

After May 1947, U.S. intervention in the internal affairs of European allies was more evident and, in some cases, remarkably successful.[24] Indeed, no foreign state, including the Soviet Union, was more involved in the legislative elections held in Italy in April 1948 than the United States. The electoral contest was transformed by all sides into a referendum over the nature and the scope of the ties between the United States and Italy, and the Truman administration, time and again, interfered to explain, justify, defend, and define its policies.*

---

*Togliatti and his allies also helped to make the American connection the main issue of the 1948 elections. Indeed, rereading from the record of the campaign, one is left with a sense of disbelief over the inventions, the distortions, and the deletions—the rumor, for example, started by the communist newspaper *Unità* according to which 150 famous Italian paintings (including masterpieces by Raphael, Tintoretto, and Titian) were to be given to the United States in return for American aid; or Togliatti's attacks against de Gasperi as the "Austro-American Chancelor." It is during this campaign therefore that Togliatti committed himself and his party to a foreign policy that remained essentially unchanged until at least 1956. Throughout that period and beyond, the grand and ferocious party battles against the Marshall Plan at every step of the way, against the Atlantic Alliance, against every effort at European unity show, in form and substance, how poorly American objectives and interests would have been served had the PCI gained the role it was revendicating at the time.

A favorable predisposition toward the United States was a factor of considerable importance in facilitating American influence in Italy. With substantial numbers of emigrants of Italian origin, most of them still heavily involved with the relatives they had left behind, the United States was directly and intimately involved in the daily lives of many Italians, especially in the South. More than anywhere else in Western Europe, these family ties helped in turn to develop a romantic image of America, an image of facility, opportunities, and affluence, which the free spending and informal living of American soldiers stationed in Italy helped to promote further. In the midst of the extreme poverty that prevailed in the aftermath of the war, many Italians found the prospect of emigration, especially emigration to the United States, particularly appealing. Thus, polls taken between 1946 and 1948 revealed an extraordinarily high number of Italian adults (between 25 and 29%) anxious to leave Italy permanently, while another 16 to 23% would have liked to move away temporarily. Among these, nearly half (between 45 and 49%) would have chosen to go to the United States.[25] With emigration laws tightened up and the flow of Italian emigrants thereby reduced—with surprisingly little bad will generated in the process—the next-best thing to going to America was, in a sense, to welcome it to Italy. This was all the more true as the U.S. presence meant substantial economic assistance, which, as the Truman administration repeatedly emphasized, would be discontinued should the left gain control of the country. In sum, to Italians, America as a country, and the Americans as a people, were something more than a geographic place and the human groups in it. They represented instead an abstraction that embodied the pursuit of a dream whose fulfillment was said to be impossible in Italy proper. Accordingly, nowhere else in Europe (save, for obvious reasons, West Germany) could U.S. influence be exerted as effectively and as openly as in Italy.[26]

Although the economic dependence of war-devastated France was no less flagrant than that of Italy, the impact of U.S. policies was far less determining there than in Italy. For one thing, contrary to Italy, there existed in France a prejudice of relative hostility toward the United States. In a most general sense, the anti-Americanism of France was but the specific expression of French xenophobia. If there was in Italy a long tradition of accomodation to the pressures of an external great power, there was in France a tradition of confrontation with those states that might threaten France's own status as a great power. Simply put, even in 1945 the French preferred themselves and their way of life to others. With Great Britain on the decline and Germany soundly defeated, the potential foci of French nationalism were confined to two—the United States and the Soviet Union—neither of which was perceived as a true competitor from the standpoint of French grandeur: "two technocracies," François Mauriac wrote in early 1950, "which view themselves as antagonists but are dragging humanity toward the same dehumanization."[27] Thus, in 1945, the French considered the Soviet Union far ahead of the United States in matters of social welfare, legislation, and public education; they found the United States leading in science and sports. Later, they rated the Americans first only in the areas of practicality and progressiveness, while the Soviets were first in the dubious areas of cruelty and backwardness. In 1948, the French thought of themselves as much more intelligent, much more generous, more courageous, and much less domineering than either the American or the Russian people. Emigration was an option contemplated by only a few, even if and when conditions at home worsened: from 16 to 18% between August 1946 and March 1947. Of these, only 3% would have chosen to go to the United States, as most still preferred the alternative (unavailable in the case of Italy) of transplanting their way of life into the Empire.[28]

Thus, the French tolerated their progressively close ties with the United States with many reservations and much ambivalence. Theirs was not only a nationalism of bitterness born out of the humiliations of their recent past. Theirs was also a nationalism of prudence and suspicion, soon confirmed by allegedly misguided U.S. policies, which threatened French security (over Germany and the Soviet Union) while making inroads into French national sovereignty (through the Marshall Plan and in the Empire). In sum, France was too weak to avoid an alliance with the United States, but it was also politically too fragile to make such an alliance an exclusive one. "An alliance with the West?" asked Foreign Minister Georges Bidault, "Of course. . . . But an alliance with the East also. . . . France will never permit itself to be limited to the Western part of the world."[29]

The French perception of the threat evolved continously, and so did, therefore, the Franco-American clash over what a proper security policy should be. To the United States, one policy was imposing itself: greater military cooperation within the Western community of democratic nations, including West Germany, as already announced by Secretary of State James Byrnes in early 1947. The French agreed that such cooperation should be sought. At first, however, they wanted this cooperation to be achieved against Germany but with Soviet assistance: the Franco–Russian alliance of December 1944, the Anglo–French alliance of 1947, and even the Atlantic alliance of 1949 were said to satisfy the French objectives in a complementary way. Yet, the public fear of Germany subsided exceptionally quickly, and during the years between 1948 and 1950 (but prior to the Korean war) the fear of an East–West confrontation began to take precedence over that of a renewed German military adventure. The threat perception now became dual. Among the French communists, the United States replaced Germany as the number one enemy. Elsewhere, the Soviet Union began to replace Germany, even though U.S. dependability in facing it continued to be seen by many in France as part of the security problem. Only after the outbreak of the war in Korea did the French cease to assume that participation in an East–West conflict, should there be one, could be avoided. They agreed therefore with the Truman administration that some form of German participation should be secured, even though they continued, more than ever, to seek ways whereby guarantees against U.S. unpredictability might be devised.

Western Europe's internal debate was a real one. What could Western Europeans do? Where could they go? If the military threat raised by Moscow was realistically assessed by Washington, the states of Western Europe were too weak to join in any protective alliance. If the perception of that threat was not realistic, the Western European states were too divided at home to join in any political or ideological challenge to the

communist doctrine. Western Europe was deterred from endorsing American policies by the fear of offending Stalin, whose
reaction it could ill afford to face. But it was also deterred from
rejecting those policies by the fear of offending Truman, whose
assistance it could ill afford to lose.

The delicacy of Europe's attempted balance between
Washington and Moscow was particularly apparent in the
Atlantic Alliance, which was entered into by states (Great
Britain and France) that had signed prior treaties with the
Soviet Union.[30] These treaties had pledged the contracting
parties not to conclude any alliance or take part in any coalition
directed against either party. To satisfy the requirements of an
alliance with America without risking an immediate invalida-
tion of the alliance with the Soviet Union, Western Europeans
wanted to reduce the anti-Soviet direction of the Atlantic
Alliance by discarding the high phraseology of the Truman
Doctrine. Yet, they also attempted to impale the U.S. administration on the specifics of the American commitment to Europe,
even though the European denial of an immediate Soviet threat
largely diminished America's interest in the alliance.[31]

Whether or not these concerns were justified at the time is
less important, for our immediate purposes, than the state of
mind they reflected—and would continue to reflect throughout
the subsequent years of cooperation *and* discord between the
Atlantic allies. For such a state of mind was shared by many in
Western Europe who were as hostile to Moscow's ideology as
they were to Washington's. Born out of a European nationalism
of frustration, bitterness, and humiliation, this was a state of
mind that acknowledged American strength, wealth, and good
intentions, to be sure—but nevertheless looked upon these as all
the more potentially dangerous as they serviced a distorted
vision of what the European countries regarded as the realities
of the world.[32] But with economic aid and military protection
truly indispensable, Europeans eagerly seized the opportunity of
the Marshall Plan and promoted the Atlantic Alliance as an
alliance of nations that might provide national problems with
international solutions. Later, when U.S. aid became less vital
and the effectiveness of U.S. protection less compelling, such
divisions, fears, and criticism reappeared to disrupt the relations between America and the states of Western Europe.

The Birth of the Western Coalition

Following the end of World War II, the United States thought of Europe as "an organism with a soft shell,"[33] and the primary concern of the United States was to reorganize the countries that faced the Soviet lines. "Europe," said President Truman, "is still the key to world peace."[34] Accordingly, U.S. foreign policy was initially a Europe-first, if not a Europe-only, foreign policy.

U.S. policies also aimed at displacing Soviet influence in Eastern Europe, expecting that in time the Soviets would inevitably withdraw. But such a withdrawal would occur only if the Western nations held firm in the face of Soviet pressure. Washington applied the lessons it had learned from two previous world conflicts: cooperation between the two sides of the Atlantic needed to be formally recorded, and a multinational alliance—as opposed to a number of bilateral alliances—was the best way to ensure such cooperation. Said Dean Acheson in March 1949: "If the free nations do not stand together, they will fall one by one. . . . We and the free nations of Europe are determined that history shall not repeat itself in that melancholy particular."[35]

The strategic dependence of American security on that of Europe was not substantially and persuasively disputed at the time. In retrospect, it might be argued that this dependence was exaggerated. But then, as now, there could hardly be any doubt that the fall of Western Europe would make America if not insecure, at least much less secure. At the most, a Soviet domination of Western Europe would shift the global distribution of power against the United States and ultimately create a direct threat to America's physical security. At the least, a Soviet domination of Western Europe would create an indirect threat to America's security by forcing the creation of an American fortress that would strain the nation's resources, which would have been already depleted by the loss of European resources, and slowly erode its democratic institutions.

America's nascent policy of containment was attributed to George Kennan, whose controversial "X article" (a lengthy cable that he sent from the American embassy in Moscow to the then

Secretary of the Navy James Forrestal) provided the Truman administration with the conceptual framework eagerly sought at the time.[36] Kennan's analysis suggested that the main thread of Soviet communism was unlimited domestic authority. Having seized power while they were still a small minority, the communists had wanted to secure their rule against both internal and external enemies. "Until such time as that security might be achieved, they placed far down on their scale of operational priorities the comforts and happiness of the peoples entrusted to their care."

With time, Kennan continued, this Soviet absolutist conduct could not be successfully completed. On the contrary, it produced a violent counterreaction as the ruthlessness of the party steadily increased opposition to a level even higher than in 1917. In the aftermath of World War II, therefore, the Soviet leaders found themselves taken in by their own ideological logic. Because capitalism no longer existed inside Russia, opposition to their rule was attributed to foreign agitators and the retention of their dictatorial power justified by the menace of capitalism abroad.

Because of its quest for security, the main objective of the Soviet regime in foreign affairs was to fill every vacuum by exerting a "cautious, persistent pressure toward the disruption and weakening of all rival influence and rival power." This pressure, Kennan argued, could be contained by America through the "long-term, patient but firm and vigilant" application of "counter-forces, at a series of constantly shifting geographic and political points, corresponding to the shifts and maneuvers of Soviet policy." (Later, Kennan limited containment to the three areas of the world other than the United States and the Soviet Union where "the sinews of modern military strength could be produced in quantity"—the Rhine valley with its adjacent industrial areas, England, and Japan.)[37]

If successfully managed, containment would also imply rollback, as American actions were expected to influence the internal developments of a state that had "within it the seeds of its own decay." Faced with America's external pressure, burdened with insoluble domestic problems, and subjected to the additional strains of its dominion in Eastern Europe, Soviet Russia, predicted Kennan, "might be changed overnight from one of the strongest to one of the weakest and most pitiable of national societies. Thus, the future of Soviet power may not be by any means as secure as Russian capacity for self-delusion would make it appear to the men in the Kremlin."

Kennan's analysis too easily exposed the worldwide character of Soviet expansionist aims, without explaining how Soviet expansion would take place and how it should be contained. That Kennan himself later criticized his own analysis as ambiguous, careless, and indiscriminate is a meager solace. That he disapproved of the Truman Doctrine, which was, after all, in line with his expose, merely points to the problem of communication between those who plan or devise policies and those who implement them. For now, armed with the rhetoric of the doctrine (to which, Kennan feared, Moscow might respond with no less than a declaration of war)[38] and the rationale of containment, America resolved to revive, stabilize, and strengthen Western Europe to deny Stalin any expansionist temptation.

Whether or not military aggression was ever seriously contemplated by Stalin is questionable.* Most Kremlinologists subsequently found behind the Soviet dictator's irrational quirks considerable calculation and caution in foreign policy.[39] Nevertheless, by March 1948, following the coup in Czechoslovakia, all Eastern European countries had become Soviet satellites, and Iran, Greece, and Turkey continued to be under strong communist pressure. One could well argue that the Soviets were attempting to fulfill traditional national interests and that, by staying carefully away from the American sphere, they were in no way challenging American power. It would then

---

*In April 1948, George Kennan tried to explain his view of containment in a letter, which he never mailed, to Walter Lippmann, whose columns had spearheaded a controversy over containment in the late summer and fall of the previous year. "The Russians don't want," Kennan wrote, "to invade anyone. It is not their tradition. . . . They . . . prefer to do the job politically. . . . That does not mean without violence. But it means that the violence is nominally domestic, not international violence. . . . The policy of containment related to the effort to encourage other peoples to resist this type of violence and to defend the internal integrity of their countries." *Memoirs*, p. 361.

follow that a settlement between the two superstates was still possible with a mutual recognition of each other's interests. Former Vice-President Henry Wallace was advocating this position when he ran for the presidency on a third-party ticket in 1948. But, however plausible now, is it surprising that such an interpretation was not seriously considered by policymakers (and the American electorate) then? How was it possible to distinguish between direct and indirect aggression when the leaders of the French and Italian communist parties were announcing that they would welcome Soviet troops in Paris and in Rome—troops already stationed in occupied Germany and elsewhere in Eastern Europe?[40] In the 1940s, then, the U.S. guarantee against direct and indirect aggression would take the form the countries of Europe had sought in vain in 1919: a formal alliance linking America's security to that of Europe. The initiative, however, rested not with the Truman administration but with Europe to request the alliance, and with the U.S. senate to approve it.

Europe's initiative was taken through the Brussels Pact, which was signed by France, Great Britain, Belgium, Luxembourg, and the Netherlands in March 1948. Unlike the Anglo–French treaty of Dunkerque, concluded the previous year, the Brussels Pact had no explicit anti-German focus. It provided automatic assistance in the event of an unspecified aggression in Europe against any one of the participants and also envisaged the creation of a permanent consultative council. That the pact was concluded so rapidly was in part a reaction to the February coup in Czechoslovakia. In the United States, approval of the pact came at once. On the day of its signing, following requests by the French and British Foreign Ministers, President Truman officially pledged that American willingness to help Europe would match Europe's willingness to help itself with collective (regional) action.

To make this promise possible, Truman sought prior support from the senate, which quickly responded with the Vandenberg Resolution. The resolution stated the senate's approval of American participation in "such regional and other collective arrangements as are based on continuous and effective self help and mutual aid, and as affect [United States] national security." By relying on Article 51 of the United Nations Charter, which permitted regional defense, the resolution enabled the United States to operate within the United Nations, but outside the veto constraints of the Security Council. Most importantly, the Vandenberg Resolution showed that, for the first time in its history, the United States was now willing to enter into an alliance outside the Western Hemisphere in peacetime.

The resolution was approved by the Senate with only four dissenting votes. Less than four weeks later, negotiations officially began between the United States, Canada, and the members of the Brussels Pact. During the next few months, five new participants (Italy, Iceland, Norway, Denmark, and Portugal) joined the talks. When signed, on April 4, 1949, the North Atlantic Treaty contemplated optimum defense efforts from the 12 participating countries and considerable aid and supplies from the United States. After the Korean War, further institutional arrangements for military, diplomatic, and financial cooperation progressively transformed the Atlantic Alliance into a regional organization as well as a guarantee pact.[41] Ultimately, this organization involved a Permanent Council, to coordinate the activities of the alliance; a Military Committee, responsible to the Council and consisting of the Chiefs of Staff of the member states (with the exception of Iceland, which had no army); several regional planning groups, foremost among them the European Command, under the Supreme Allied Commander, Europe (SACEUR); a Secretary General, appointed by the Council for an undefined period; and an international staff of several hundred. Three more states were subsequently admitted to the alliance—Greece and Turkey in 1951, and West Germany in 1955. For political reasons, and despite its strategic importance, Spain was excluded from the alliance, as well as Yugoslavia, whose participation was briefly considered by the Western states.

The North Atlantic Treaty, like most treaties, was a general declaration of intentions. The pledge of mutual support was open to substantial escape clauses, and little in its text justified Senator Robert A. Taft's fear that it had placed America "at the mercy of the foreign policies of eleven nations."[42] The treaty was strictly defensive. It was applicable only in case of armed attack. Should an armed attack occur, each nation was to take, individually or collectively, "such action as it deemed necessary." This commitment did not mean, as Dean Acheson told the Senate Foreign Relations Committee, that "the United States would be automatically at war if one of the nations covered by the pact is subjected to armed attack."[43] The seriousness of the attack, and its relevance to America's vital interests, would be considered first. Thus, the report of the Senate Committee stated: "What we may do to carry out that commitment . . . will depend upon our own independent decision in each particular instance." Contrary to what was subsequently argued, in no part of the treaty was the United States obligated to react to an attack on a European city in the same way as it would react to an attack on an American city.[44] Finally, each government was expected to operate within strict constitutional restrictions, a requirement carefully inserted in Article 11 of the treaty.

Should indirect aggression threaten the territorial integrity, political independence, and security of any member, only consultation was pledged. But, should a revolution be aided and abetted from without, such foreign assistance might be considered an armed attack. NATO intervention in a civil war within a Western European state was, therefore, conceivable. In later years, the status of Algeria (specifically mentioned by name in the treaty) became a source of controversy among the Atlantic allies. But the French government refused to consider the hostilities in Algeria as an external war. Instead, it argued that the Algerian situation was a domestic matter, and, as the French refused to appeal for aid or consultation, the alliance remained officially unconcerned with it.

The treaty of April 1949 was also limited in space and in time. It extended to a finite geographic area that included the territories of the member states but excluded their colonial possessions. Nothing in the language of the treaty compelled the allies to render aid to the French in Indochina, to the British in Malaya, or to the United States in Korea. If there were doubt as to whether or not an armed attack had occurred within the "North Atlantic area" (an attack upon a ship or an aircraft, for example) each member state was left free to determine on its own the nature and the significance of the attack. The treaty could be modified after 10 years, and each nation reserved the right to withdraw after 20 years, on a one-year notice. Europe's efforts to secure a 50-year commitment were opposed by America's objection to forecasting international developments in such a distant future.[45]

In 1949, it was essentially believed in Washington that a statement of American intentions was sufficient to deter aggression in Europe. Despite the occasional tenseness of the situation, there was no sustained fear of a military attack on Western Europe. With the information he had gathered from the U.S. government and from the heads of European governments, John Foster Dulles, who was a senator from the state of New York at the time when the North Atlantic Treaty was being debated, had concluded: "The Soviet Union does not now contemplate large-scale military aggression in Europe."[46] Vis-à-vis the Russians, the treaty would set up a new Monroe doctrine that warned them to stay out of Western Europe.[47] European governments hoped that the treaty would be the bolt of lightning that transformed apathy and despair into hope and confidence in facing the staggering problems of reconstruction and defense with American assistance. They did not believe the imminence of a Soviet attack in and against Western Europe, and many expected that Europe would not have to become involved in any conflict waged between the two superpowers outside of Europe. To everyone, the treaty was a vivid reminder of America's Europe-first policy. If peace and security could be achieved in the North Atlantic area, it was reasoned, they could easily be achieved in other areas as well.

Already, however, this partnership was a troubled one, and within the alliance itself each nation looked at its partners with suspicion and uncertainty. America could not easily forget France's early military and political collapse in June 1940. It saw in France a weakness that needed to be overcome if a unified Western coalition was ever to exist. Conversely, the French were suspicious of what they regarded as collusion between Washington and London. The French government was anxious to assume in the eyes of the American government the leadership of continental Europe. Yet, it thought that somehow America was "more generous" and "more friendly" toward the British government.[48] The Italians, too, entered the alliance with mixed emotions. Riots broke out throughout the country, and fist fights occurred in parliament. The issue became a domestic one as the majority coalition identified the Italian communist opposition with the "threat" raised by the Soviet Union. Great Britain was still trying to reconcile its relationship to Europe, its obligations to the Commonwealth, and its special relationship with the United States. It ultimately antagonized them all.

The Atlantic Alliance was all things to all people. The French presented it as a follow-up on the Franco-Russian alliance of December 1944; they still looked upon Germany as the major menace to their security. The British regarded the alliance as the restoration of the old power game in Europe where, thanks to their influence in Washington, they would still continue to hold the balance. To the Italian government, the alliance provided the best available means of seeking an early revision of its peace treaties with the United States, Great Britain, and France, while securing more support against Yugoslavia for Italy's claims over the port of Trieste.

Paradoxically enough, the war in Korea helped to bridge these differences by providing the new allies with a recognizable danger and urgency. In June 1950, Western Europe, which had remained relatively passive while Soviet expansion in Eastern Europe had become a fait accompli, now grew more responsive to America's call for general and accelerated rearmament. "From now on," emphasized Dean Acheson, "it is action which counts and not further resolutions or further plans or further meetings."[49] The war in Korea provided the alliance with a new unity. It was, as McGeorge Bundy has suggested, a good opportunity "to adopt openly a policy urgently recommended in private for some months previous."[50] But the unity achieved was at most military; political and strategic differences between allies were not resolved. They were merely postponed.

The unanimity reached periodically at every interallied meeting was based on a general agreement about its basic aims. Countless special groups, liaison teams, and standing committees regularly agreed, first, to build up defense forces, second, to devise a common defense strategy, and, third, to preserve the sound and stable economy necessary to support such a defense effort. Such agreement, however, was not always extended to the way in which these objectives could be satisfied or even, in some instances, reconciled. For example, could the alliance build up adequate strength and at the same time preserve a sound and stable economy? With a per capita income of approximately one-third that of America, Europe faced obvious difficulties in diverting its scarce resources toward rearmament. Everywhere, there were demands for lower taxes, better food, more houses, and more consumer goods, even if few guns, planes, and tanks were manufactured. But Europe's minimal contribution in turn irritated America, particularly as the costs and burdens of Western defense continued to rise while military targets agreed upon by the allies were not met. For in America, too, the claim was being made that military expenditures covered too large a share of national wealth, thus endangering economic stability.

Regardless of the cost, the efficacy of conventional rearmament was also disputed by European allies. Could the Western alliance ever gather conventional forces strong enough to face Russia's? In 1949, the military power of the Soviet Union was assumed to exceed the combined military power of Russia and Germany in 1939. Yet, during the war, 200 German divisions, well armed and well led, had been unable to defend the Third Reich. How, then, could 40 to 60 army divisions now defend the whole continent against a Russian invasion? Conventional defense might be effective if, and only if, 100 to 150 American divisions were deployed in Europe even before the beginning of the hostilities.

This was Western Europe's response to America's call for strengthening the conventional forces of the alliance. Washington, however, did not favor a large American ground presence in Europe. "Are we going to be expected to send substantial numbers of troops over there as a more or less permanent contribution?" Senator Bourke Hickenlooper asked Secretary Acheson during the NATO hearings. "The answer to that question," Acheson replied, "is a clear and absolute 'no'."[51] An American air force (supplemented with American nuclear capability), a British navy, and a European ground force would be sufficient to deter the Soviets. But, assuming that this division of military labor was acceptable to the European allies—and it was not—what would be the place of West Germany within this force? The Atlantic Alliance could not dedicate itself to the defense of a Europe that included Germany without having the Germans themselves participate in the common effort. Yet how could one secure Germany's military participation without some German rearmament? One answer was to have German soldiers but no German army, or even a German army that would be strong enough to defeat the Soviet army and yet weak enough to be defeated by the French or British army. Obviously, this was not possible.

To the Europeans, still feeling the ravages of the last war, Germany could not easily be dismissed as a threat of the past. At least part of the protection they sought was related to a potential revival of Germany's military capability. To Washington, however, the threat that needed to be deterred came from the Soviet Union. The more urgently Washington perceived that threat, the less attention it paid to other problems. As part of a regional grouping or as a single entity, Germany had to be rearmed if the defense of Europe was to be organized in any effective way at all. So, despite repeated pledges to the contrary, the Truman administration officially asked, in September 1950, that Germany contribute 10 of the 60 army divisions that were expected from the Western European allies.

As has often been true since 1945, France took the lead in expressing Europe's opposition to the United States request. In October 1950, the French response was to use European unity as the framework within which Germany might altogether disappear as a nation. The previous year, unable to convince its Western allies that the industrial resources of Germany's Ruhr complex should be internationalized, the French government had successfully sponsored the formation of the Coal and Steel Community as a supranational organization wherein France, Germany, Italy, Belgium, the Netherlands, and Luxembourg would pool their coal and steel resources. With the United States now requesting Germany's rearmament, the new French offer, the so-called Pleven Plan, was to set up a European Defense Community (EDC), under the executive command of a European Political Community. The purpose of this plan was not so much to create a united Europe as to avoid the restoration of Germany's military capability. "Europe" was the instrument chosen for the absorption of a country which, it had now been demonstrated, could neither be dismembered nor neutralized, neither disarmed nor pastoralized. But even such a framework was acceptable to France only if Great Britain's participation was secured, on top of further U.S. guarantees. These guarantees would ensure that the European experiment was still conducted within an Atlantic framework. France would not take the risk of locking itself up in a "small, dark box" where it might ultimately be unable to match German dynamism and where, therefore, no counterpoise to Germany's eventual domination of the new entity could be found.

Ultimately, the collapse of the EDC was ensured by Great Britain's opposition to joining it in 1951–52, even though its death certificate was finally signed by the French Assembly when it refused to ratify the proposed treaty in late August 1954. The whole history of Great Britain explained such a distaste for the integration of the British army into a supranational European army. Yet it was only during the months that followed the French proposal that the combined threat of Russian imperialism and German militarism might conceivably have generated a Europe-wide consensus for the EDC; by 1953, it was too late. With the war in Korea ended, with Stalin dead, and with renewed hopes that East–West detente was on its way, the call for European unity through such a dramatic initiative as the EDC had lost its urgency and raison d'être. Nevertheless, it remained one of the gravest crises faced by the Atlantic allies in the 1950s. American threats of an "agonizing reappraisal" were matched by the reemergence of various European groups asking for neutrality for Europe.

After the demise of the EDC, Great Britain made its commitment to the Continent and pledged to keep a few contingents of British forces there as long as its European allies wanted them. For Great Britain, this step alone was revolutionary: never before in modern times had British forces been specifically committed to service on the Continent, except in wartime. This commitment paved the way for the Paris Pact (October 1954), which recognized the full sovereignty of West Germany. The Brussels Treaty Organization of 1948 was enlarged into a Western European Union (WEU), which was joined by West Germany and Italy. Through WEU, West Germany was to contribute 12 army divisions to the defense of Europe, more than the number President Truman had asked for in the first place. But several safeguards were included: West Germany unilaterally renounced the right to manufacture atomic, biological, and chemical weapons, as well as guided missiles, large naval vessels, and bombers. At the same time, the American and British pledges to maintain their continental forces were restated, thus providing a sense of security in Europe that proved to be sufficient to permit the admission of West Germany to NATO in May 1955.

The Management of Europe's Economic Recovery

Sharp friction over economic policy between the United States and other economic powers occurred frequently throughout the interwar years.[52] By the end of the war, Secretary of State Cordell Hull believed that a liberal world of free trade and multilateral payments arrangements was a necessary, perhaps even sufficient, foundation for any peaceful postwar order. Fascism, totalitarianism, war, and depression were all supposedly linked to the excesses of economic rivalries that had characterized the prewar period, with its increasing reliance on competitive devaluations, quotas, ever-higher tariff walls, and world-wide fragmentation into exclusive economic blocs. It is a "fact," Hull argued, "that war did not break out between the United States and any country with which we had been able to negotiate a trade agreement. . . . The political line-up followed the economic line-up."[53]

In July 1944, the international economic order sought at the Bretton Woods Conference resulted primarily from a dialogue between the United States and Great Britain. As formulated by John Maynard Keynes, the British plan called for the creation of an International Clearing Union, with $26 billion worth of liquidity expressed in a new international unit of account (the so-called "bancor").[54] Essentially a credit system that would preserve maximum freedom for nations to pursue their own domestic economic policies, the Keynes plan was designed to protect the interests of a debt-plagued imperial state beset with the added problem of sterling overhang and led by a political party committed above all to full employment.

In opposition, the American plan, as put forth by Harry Dexter White, favored the creation of a significantly smaller Stabilization Fund, with only $5 billion in conditional credit facilities.[55] Relying primarily on the internal adjustment of payment imbalances, the White plan reflected the position of a country that held two-thirds of the world's gold reserves. It was not less clearly designed to protect the interests of a creditor nation dominated by a conservative economic philosophy with regard to the international economic responsibilities of debtor nations, and it assumed that, following a short period of adjustment, the world would rapidly move toward political and economic equilibrium—an assumption that was soon to be shattered.

Although the agreement reached at Bretton Woods was presented as a compromise between the Keynes and White plans, it closely resembled the latter conception. To be sure, the newly created International Monetary Fund (IMF) did include a "scarce currency clause" that was applicable to persistent creditor nations, thereby implying, as Keynes had wanted it, that surplus countries would be subjected to the same discipline as debtor countries. But the clause was never invoked, and the Fund squarely placed primary responsibility for the adjustment process on the deficit nations. Voting power in the IMF was based upon a nation's total quotas and borrowing rights from the Fund, thus ensuring a dominant U.S. influence that reflected the anticipated economic, political, and military influence of the United States in the postwar world.

Such dominant influence was quickly confirmed between 1945 and 1947, as circumstances revealed that the structures devised at Bretton Woods were unable to provide for Western interests in economic recovery and political stability. Neither the IMF's $8.8 billion in liquidity credit tranches that were designed to meet temporary balance of payments problems, nor the World Bank's $10 billion fund available for the reconstruction of Europe, were sufficient to satisfy the needs of the participating nations and sustain the rigors of the open world of free trade and payments multilateralism that had been envisioned by Cordell Hull. Thus, in early 1946, a U.S. loan to

Great Britain amounting to $3.75 billion had been made conditional on the renewed convertibility of the pound sterling. But in July 1947, when the time came for Britain to fulfill a commitment that it had made reluctantly, the British Treasury lost more reserves in one week's time that it had throughout the entire previous year. Such disastrous experimentation with a premature return to convertibility and, beyond Britain, the contemptation of a Europe frozen in the throes of grossly inadequate dollar reserves convinced the Truman administration that a new economic approach was needed if Western Europe was to avoid further political and economic collapse.

The dollar gap was, indeed, startling. In 1947, the European balance of payments deficit with the rest of the world had risen to $7.6 billion, and by 1948 Western Europe had only $6.7 billion in reserves to pay for its even larger deficits. Conversely, the U.S. trade surplus amounted to $10.1 billion in 1947, and U.S. reserves grew to $25.8 billion in 1948.[56] With traditional economic relations with Eastern Europe disrupted by the politics of U.S.–Soviet confrontation and with the former imperial routes already hampered by the emerging process of decolonization, most of Western Europe's vital supplies and outlets could only be found in the dollar area. Yet far from offering remedies to such existing difficulties, the IMF's conservative lending policy served to aggravate the worsening economic and political crises. As Richard Gardner has pointed out, "The Fund was not going to grant assistance to members unless it was assured that the aid would be used for short-term stabilization purposes and not for purposes of reconstruction. Since few members could give such assurances in the first half of 1947 the Fund engaged in virtually no exchange operations."[57]

Heralded as America's decisive assumption of world responsibilities, the Marshall Plan aimed at the reconstruction of a world economy so as to permit the creation of political and social conditions in which democratic institutions could exist.[58] But it was also designed to facilitate the postwar multilateralism envisaged by U.S. negotiators at Bretton Woods: European integration was linked to the eventual creation of a liberal free trade order based on a better balanced relationship between the two sides of the Atlantic. Yet, even while Europe was receiving the needed dollar reserves to pay for dollar area imports, it opened the umbrella of economic protectionism to ensure a recovery that would be conducive to such a balance. Thus, in July 1950, the European Payments Union (EPU) was formed to allow for multilateral international payments, within Western Europe but not in regard to the dollar area. During a period of acute dollar shortage, the Truman administration therefore accepted to subordinate trade to politics as it tolerated short-term economic discrimination against U.S. exports in the name of the long-term security gains that would result from strengthened Western European economies.[59] With the European Recovery Program (ERP) moving the United States to the status of a central banker to the world, and with the EPU reflecting Washington's acceptance of a discriminatory European bloc, Hull's universal vision was set aside, however temporarily, in favor of policies more compatible with European needs.

With U.S. encouragement, Britain and most other West European countries devalued their currencies by about 30% against the dollar in September 1949. As a result, the Truman administration expected to see the recipients of Marshall aid increase their exports to the dollar area in such a way as to facilitate the restoration of Western Europe's balance of payments equilibrium, even if this were to be achieved at the expense of U.S. trade surpluses. Since the American priority was to improve the position of Europe and Japan, there was much satisfaction in the fact that some of these countries were restoring their depleted reserves. When such dollar accruals were used to purchase gold from the United States, this, too, was welcomed.[60] Indeed, throughout the 1950s, repeated U.S. balance of payments deficits provided needed international liquidity to finance growth in world trade and European recovery as the United States asserted its hegemonial role in the system not so much as a result of deliberate ambition as the unintended consequence of a war that had left the economy of every state but the United States in eclipse.[61]

That Western European central banks accepted willingly such increasing amounts of deficit-financed dollars as reserves should come as no surprise. Unlike gold, the dollar as the world's key reserve currency was an interest-bearing asset. Furthermore, the dominance of the dollar derived from the widespread opinion that the U.S. economy was a formidable bastion of unparalleled strength and potential—with relative price stability, high technology dominance, and unrivaled productivity in key industrial and agricultural sectors. In addition, U.S. payments deficits helped to prevent competitive exchange depreciations or domestic deflations even as wartime exchange controls and trade restrictions were being quickly lifted. In sum, for most of the 1950s, U.S. deficits—which averaged about $1.5 billion a year—were hardly a source of tensions in transatlantic relations, as they would prove to be in later years. Quite the reverse, they actually served to prevent monetary instability or policy disputes.[62]

When the European Recovery Program was curtailed in 1952, it was in part offset by an increase in U.S. military expenditures in Europe, which averaged about $1.5 billion a year between 1954 and 1959.[63] Thus, with the United States financing the defense of Europe and with Europe financing the U.S. payments deficits, there emerged a transatlantic bargain that appeared to work well and to the general benefit of all. Whatever division there might have been over economic issues was quickly obscured by the primacy given to security issues. With an eye on the escalating cold war, the Truman administration warmly heralded the formation in 1952 of the European Coal and Steel Community as a testimony to the rapprochement between France and Germany and another step toward the eventual goal of the political union of Europe. The success of these policies seemed impressive. The ad hoc arrangements of the ERP and EPU soon helped national governments in Western Europe regain economic and political self-confidence.[64] Already by the year 1950, all ERP countries had returned to prewar productivity levels, and economic recovery soon gave way to growth. Industrial production increased by more than 60% between 1952 and 1960.[65] Throughout the decade during which the Atlantic bargain worked best, rates of investment and productivity growth were significantly higher in Europe than in the United States, owing in part to lower defense spending.[66] The revival of Europe's economic strength and the expansion of its economic power relative to the United States were seen as the vindication of the U.S. commitment to European security. By the pivotal year of 1958, the results were sufficient to permit a return in Europe to full convertibility (i.e., an end to EPU) and a start toward a still more ambitious effort aimed at economic integration within the framework of the newly ratified Rome Treaty.

Expansion and Containment

It is common to observe the wide divergence between the world as it is and the world as it is perceived. A further source of distortion is added when one seeks to perceive, and understand, the world as it was. Any historical record ought to be read in relation to the conditions prevailing when the events in question occurred. Unfortunately, the record is too often read in retrospective relation to subsequent developments.

America's containment policy in Western Europe succeeded, inasmuch as nothing happened: Soviet aggression, assuming that it was ever planned, never occurred. Yet the success of American policy also spelled its undoing. Achieved with America's assistance, the recovery of Western Europe placed the Soviet Union in a new defense posture. Admittedly, Stalin's main recourse in the military field lay in balancing American atomic and air power with Soviet land power. With no strategic weapons capable of reaching the continental United States, the Soviet military posture lent itself to deterrence only if the Soviet capacity to overrun Europe to the Atlantic was made to be credible.[67] Should the Soviets be unable to preserve the credibility of their conventional superiority, they could conceivably be served with a nuclear ultimatum from Washington, whose policy, as they might have perceived it, was to expel Moscow from Eastern Europe. Washington described its policy as the containment of Soviet expansion. But to Moscow this policy reflected America's decision to expand beyond its traditional sphere of influence. Should such expansion go unchecked, it would ultimately roll back Moscow's own line of containment. In a striking instance of the reversal of cause and effect, America's very success in the containment of the Soviet Union in Western Europe went far toward creating the necessity for containment.

The success of containment also made its adoption in other areas tempting—particularly in Asia, as will be seen. The American recipe for global containment of communism thus came to include the three major ingredients used in Europe: at the economic level, foreign assistance; at the political level, regional unification: at the military level, formal alliances.

However successful, the Marshall Plan nevertheless failed to fulfill several of its objectives. From a national viewpoint, the plan helped bring about economic recovery, but it did not succeed in ending the electoral strength of the communist parties in France and Italy. Inadequate information was in part responsible for this failure: a survey of French opinion conducted early in the program revealed that 70% of those Frenchmen who had heard of the Marshall Plan felt that it was bad for them.[68] In 1953, 22.7% of the electorate voted for the Communist party in Italy, as opposed to 19% in 1946. In the summer of the same year, 26% of the French electorate voted communist, as opposed to 28% five years earlier.

Nor did the Marshall Plan succeed in moving Western Europe toward unity. The Organization for European Economic Cooperation (OEEC), set up to determine the long-term economic needs of the area and to ensure the most effective satisfaction of these needs, was never accepted by most of its 18 members as a major vehicle for European unification. Its secretariat remained ineffective and without real power, despite initial efforts by the French government to have Marshall aid handled by a supranational organization. Furthermore, the OEEC could not easily be conceived as both an inducement for prompt economic recovery and a vehicle for political unification. It was doubtful that the economic recovery of Western European states could help achieve their political unification. On the whole, a united Europe remained, in Europe, an intellectual idea with little mass support. It only gathered political momentum in time of crisis. Thus, the more successful the Marshall Plan, the less likely it was to generate European unity.

Western Europe's receptiveness to foreign aid was unique. Western European states already possessed an integrated economic infrastructure, lived in a market economy, and had an impressive array of managerial and technological skills and a long-established entrepreneurial tradition. Europe did not lack the many intangible factors that, in other areas, made economic growth so laborious. What was needed for Europe's economic recovery could be defined and provided within a limited period of time. In other words, there was in Europe a short-term problem that had but a distant relation to the long-term dilemmas that foreign aid attempted to resolve elsewhere.

America's endorsement of the idea of a united Europe was understandable, considering America's own background. Yet it seemed that American policy quickly lost the sensitivity to European aspirations that it had displayed in earlier years. American based its thinking too much on the cold war, and not enough on those problems that Europe had encountered traditionally. America's entry into an entangling alliance was, indeed, a major revolution in its foreign policy—a revolution that accounted for some of the initial errors. But a European army, where France and Germany, Belgium and Italy would have shared the same uniform only five years after the agonies and the atrocities of World War II, was also a major revolution in Europe's foreign policies—a revolution that accounted for the soul searching and the quest for ever more guarantees. Neither side displayed much empathy for the other's hesitation.

Finally, too much was made of the assumption that a major Soviet military attack was imminent. As Washington believed that Europe's rearmament had prevented such an attack from taking place, it was tempted to establish NATO-like alliances everywhere else, without first examining the differences that another place, another enemy, and another time might introduce in America's interests and commitments. These differences were to become the focus of the foreign policy debates of the 1960s.

NOTES

1. Quoted in George Ball, *The Discipline of Power* (Boston, Mass.: Little, Brown, 1968), p. 29.
2. See Richard Mayne, *The Recovery of Europe, 1945–1973* (New York: Anchor Books, 1973).
3. As presented in Secretary Marshall's speech at Harvard Uni-

versity, on June 5, 1947. See *Department of State Bulletin*, Vol. XVI, pp. 1159–60 (hereafter cited as *Bulletin*).

4. Harry B. Price, *The Marshall Plan and Its Meaning* (Ithaca, N.Y.: New York University Press, 1955), p. 31.

5. Jacques Fauvet, *La IVème république* (Paris: Presses Fayard, 1960), pp. 32–33.

6. Quoted in A. W. DePorte, *De Gaulle's Foreign Policy, 1944–1946* (Cambridge, Mass.: Harvard University Press, 1968), p. 80.

7. Herbert Feis, *Roosevelt, Churchill and Stalin: The War They Waged and the Peace They Sought* (Princeton, N.J.: Princeton University Press, 1957), p. 477.

8. Francis Williams, *Twilight of Empire: Memoirs of Prime Minister Clement Attlee* (New York: A.S. Barnes, 1962), p. 118.

9. Ibid., p. 119.

10. Quoted in Donald C. Watt, *Personalities and Policies: Studies in the Formulation of British Foreign Policy in the Twentieth Century* (Notre Dame, Ind.: Notre Dame University Press, 1965), p. 70.

11. See Simon Serfaty, "An International Anomaly: The United States and the Communist Parties in France and in Italy, 1945–1947," *Studies in Comparative Communism*, Spring/Summer 1975, pp. 123–47.

12. Quoted in Steven P. Sapp, "The United States, France and the Cold War: Jefferson Caffery and American–French Relations, 1944–1949," unpublished Ph.D. dissertation, Kent State University, 1978, p. 99.

13. Quoted in Sari Gilbert, "From Armistice to Alliance: Goals and Methods in Italian Foreign Policy, 1943 to 1949," unpublished Ph.D. dissertation, Johns Hopkins University, 1969, p. 142.

14. Quoted in Sapp, *United States, France, and Cold War*, p. 99.

15. See *Foreign Relations of the United States*, 1947, Vol. III, pp. 904–8.

16. Quoted in Sapp, *United States, France, and Cold War*, pp. 90 and 70, respectively.

17. Memorandum of meeting between Ambassador Tarchiani and H. Freeman Matthews, Director, European Affairs, Department of State, May 8, 1947.

18. See Mario Einaudi, Jean Marie Domenach, and Aldo Garosci, *Communism in Western Europe* (Ithaca, N.Y.: Cornell University Press, 1951).

19. As cabled to Secretary Byrnes on June 18, 1946. Cited in Sapp, *United States, France, and Cold War*, p. 115.

20. Milovan Djilas, *Conversations with Stalin* (London: Pelican Books, 1969), p. 113.
21. Quoted in Georgette Elgey, *La république des illusions,* Vol. 1, 1945–1951 (Paris: Fayard, 1965), p. 23.
22. For Blum, see Elgey, *République des illusions,* p. 140, and Alexander Werth, *France, 1940–1955* (London: Robert Hale, 1957), pp. 315–16. De Gasperi's statement was reported in *The New York Times,* January 9, 1947.
23. As argued by Ambassador Dunn, for example, in early May 1947. See *Foreign Relations of the United States,* 1947, Vol. 3, pp. 890–91.
24. See Ernest Rossi, "The United States and the 1948 Elections," unpublished Ph.D. dissertation, University of Pittsburgh, 1964.
25. Mary M. Benyamin, "Fluctuations in the Prestige of the United States in France. A Description of French Attitudes toward the United States and its Policies, 1945–1955," unpublished Ph. D. dissertation, Columbia University, 1959.
26. See Simon Serfaty, "The United States and the PCI: The Year of Decision, 1947," in *The Italian Communist Party: Yesterday, Today and Tomorrow,* ed. Simon Serfaty and Lawrence Gray (Westport, Conn.: Greenwood Press, 1980), pp. 59–74.
27. Quoted in Edgar S. Furniss, Jr., *France, Troubled Ally. De Gaulle's Heritage and Prospects* (New York: Harper & Brothers, 1960), p. 87.
28. Benyamin, *Prestige of United States in France,* pp. 34, 51, and 64–65.
29. In *L'Année politique, 1944–1945* (Paris: Editions du grand siècle, 1946), p. 66.
30. The Anglo–Russian alliance of 1942 and the Franco–Russian alliance of 1944 were terminated in May 1955, following West Germany's entry into the Atlantic Alliance.
31. See Robert E. Osgood, *NATO, the Entangling Alliance* (Chicago: Chicago University Press, 1962).
32. Foremost among these realities was, of course, the atomic bomb, and European leaders remained pointedly sensitive to any such reference by an American leader. Thus, on November 30, 1950, as the Chinese were launching their offensive in Korea, President Truman indicated in a press conference that he would "take whatever steps are necessary to meet the military situation." In response to a specific question, he further indicated: "There has always been active consideration of [the] use" of the atomic bomb. This quickly prompted a lecture from Prime Minister Attlee,

following consultation with French Foreign Minister Georges Bidault. See Truman, *Memoirs*, Vol. 2, *Years of Trial and Hope, 1946–1953* (Garden City, N.Y.: Doubleday, 1956), p. 395. In fact, the Joint Chiefs of Staff had already recommended against its use in North Korea.

33. From Acheson's statement to the Senate Committee on Foreign Relations, August 8, 1949. Cited in McGeorge Bundy, ed., *The Pattern of Responsibility* (Boston, Mass.: Houghton Mifflin, 1951), p. 71.
34. Truman, *Memoirs*, Vol. 2, p. 380.
35. From a radio address, March 18, 1949. *Bulletin*, Vol. XX, p. 384.
36. X (George Kennan), "Sources of Soviet Conduct," *Foreign Affairs*, July 1947, pp. 556–82.
37. Kennan, *Memoirs* (Boston, Mass.: Little, Brown, 1967), p. 358.
38. Ibid., pp. 365–67. See also Joseph H. Jones, *The Fifteen Weeks* (New York: Viking Press, 1955), pp. 385–87.
39. Adam Ulam, *Expansion and Coexistence* (New York: Praeger, 1968), p. 439. See also Marshall D. Shulman, *Stalin's Foreign Policy Reappraised* (Cambridge, Mass.: Harvard University Press, 1963).
40. In October 1948, for example, in response to the question: "What would you do if the Red Army occupied Paris?" Maurice Thorez, then the head of the French communist party, replied with a declaration of all-out support for the Russian army even if it should enter French territory. Shulman, *Stalin's Foreign Policy*, p. 58.
41. Osgood, *NATO*, p. 23.
42. Lawrence S. Kaplan, ed., *NATO and the Policy of Containment* (Lexington, Mass.: D.C. Heath, 1962), p. 21.
43. From Acheson's radio address, March 18, 1949. *Bulletin*, Vol. XX, p. 387.
44. State Department, *American Foreign Policy, 1950–1955: Basic Documents,* Vol.1 (General Foreign Policy Series 117), p. 836.
45. Ibid., p. 843.
46. Osgood, *NATO*, p. 50.
47. As Acheson stated in the Senate hearings on the Atlantic Alliance. See some extracts in Bundy, *Pattern of Responsibility*, p. 65.
48. Alexander Werth, *France, 1940–1955* (London: Readers Union, 1957), p. 315.
49. From Acheson's news conference, December 22, 1950. *Bulletin*, Vol. XXIV, p. 3.

50. Bundy, *Pattern of Responsibility*, p. 77.
51. Senate Committee on Foreign Relations, U.S. Senate, *Hearings on the North Atlantic Treaty*, 81st Congress, 1st Session (1949), p. 47.
52. See David P. Calleo and Benjamin M. Rowland, *America and the World Political Economy: Atlantic Dreams and National Realities* (Bloomington, Ind.: Indiana University Press, 1973), pp. 61–65.
53. Quoted in Richard N. Gardner, *Sterling Dollar Diplomacy: The Origins and the Prospects of Our International Economic Order* (New York: McGraw-Hill, 1969), p. 9.
54. Ibid., pp. 77–80.
55. Ibid., pp. 71–77.
56. Joan Edelman Spero, *The Politics of International Economic Relations* (New York: St. Martin's Press, 1977), p. 34.
57. Gardner, *Sterling Dollar Diplomacy*, p. 297.
58. Mayne, *Recovery of Europe*, p. 119.
59. Calleo and Rowland, *America and World Political Economy*, p. 43.
60. Robert Solomon, *The International Monetary System, 1945–1976* (New York: Harper & Row, 1977), p. 19.
61. Harold van B. Cleveland, *The Atlantic Idea and Its European Rivals* (New York: McGraw-Hill, 1966), p. 72.
62. Benjamin J. Cohen, *Organizing the World's Money: The Political Economy of International Monetary Relations* (New York: Basic Books, 1977), p. 98.
63. Solomon, *International Monetary System*, p. 21.
64. Lawrence B. Krause, *European Economic Integration and the United States* (Washington, D.C.: The Brookings Institution, 1968), pp. 25–28.
65. Solomon, *International Monetary System*, p. 21.
66. Angus Maddison, *Economic Growth in the West: Comparative Experience in Europe and North America* (New York: Norton, 1964), pp. 60–63.
67. Thomas W. Wolfe, *Soviet Power and Europe, 1945–1970* (Baltimore, Md.: Johns Hopkins University Press, 1970), pp. 34–35.
68. Price, *Marshall Plan and Its Meaning*, p. 397.

CHAPTER FOUR

Limited War and Expanded Commitments

The Fall of China

In contrast with Europe, the nature and scope of America's interests in Asia remained under review throughout the immediate postwar period. Thus, on November 1, 1945, Secretary of War Robert Patterson requested from Secretary of State James Byrnes guidance on what involvement the United States would accept and what consequences it would tolerate in order to preserve "minimum interests" in the Far East, particularly in Manchuria, Inner Mongolia, North China, and Korea. An answer to this question, the secretary of war insisted, was urgent if military plans were to be made against unacceptable aggression in that region.[1] The department's ambiguous answer reflected doubts as to what such interests were. Only in a negative sense could an agreement be reached between all concerned: American ground forces should not be used for combat on the mainland of Asia.

Dean Acheson, then secretary of state, attempted to define U.S. minimal interests in January 1950, in a speech that was to become famous after the outbreak of the Korean War. "It must be clear that no person can guarantee these areas against military attacks," Acheson said of a defensive perimeter that did not include Korea, Taiwan, and Southeast Asia. Military aggression, the origin of which Acheson was unable to foresee ("one hesitates to say where such an attack could come from"), would have to be met not by the United States alone, but by the "peoples attacked . . . and . . . the commitments of the entire civilized world under the charter of the United Nations." Thus, the Asian peoples were expected to be "on their own." "We can help," continued Acheson, "only where we are wanted and only where the conditions of help are really sensible and possible."[2] But within a few months, the Truman administration drastically revised and enlarged its vision of what was sensible and possible, thereby permitting what had previously been ruled out: two ground wars, one in Korea, the other in Indochina.[*]

The extension of America's policy of containment from Europe to Asia grew from America's refusal to intervene in the Chinese civil war. After Japan's surrender in August 1945, China was, in the words of President Truman, a "geographic expression" led by a fragile government that had been fighting for its survival since 1927.[3] From within, the nationalist government of Chiang Kai-shek faced a communist opposition that controlled one-sixth of the country proper (exclusive of Manchuria) and one-fourth of the overall population (116 million people). In the field the communists had over 1 million troops, generally well trained, well led, and moderately well equipped with captured Japanese weapons.[4]

Government forces, on the other hand, comprised approximately 3 million men. They held an overwhelming superiority in basic weapons, a near monopoly of heavy equipment and transport, and total control of the air.[5] Throughout 1946, government forces achieved major advances in areas formerly controlled by the communists; but in so doing, they overextended themselves, as they had neither the military strength

---

[*]Later critics of Dean Acheson all too often forgot that similar assessments of U.S. interests in the Far East had been made by others, too. Thus, "the line of defense" that was described by General MacArthur in 1949 ran through the chain of islands fringing the coast of Asia precisely in the same manner as Acheson's, the only difference being that the secretary listed the islands from North to South, while the General listed them from South to North (Joseph Goulden, *Korea: The Untold Story of the War* [New York, 1982], p. 31).

nor the political skills needed to garrison and administer these holdings.

Mao's troops seized the initiative in 1947. They exerted superior pressure at points of greatest government overextension, destroyed isolated bodies of troops, and cut communications. They also seized much-needed weapons.[6] By 1949, it was estimated that 75% of all the material provided by the United States to the nationalist government, both during and after the war against Japan, had been captured by the communist forces.[7] As communist victories multiplied, nationalist resistance disintegrated. The latter had entered 1948 with an estimated 3-to-1 advantage that remained generally constant through mid-September. Yet by February 1, 1949, the communist forces outnumbered the total nationalist strength, and had even achieved an estimated 3-to-2 superiority in combat effectiveness.[8]

President Truman's decision against intervention in the Chinese civil war reflected limitations on existing U.S. military capabilities. Within one month after the defeat of Japan, American troops were discharged at the rate of 15,200 a day. By June 1946, when the fighting in Manchuria began to spread throughout the country, U.S. forces available in the entire Pacific area amounted to 830,000 men. And by February 1948, a date generally regarded as the last feasible opportunity for an effective large-scale American intervention, total force levels in the Far East amounted to no more than 140,000 men.[9] This was insufficient.

American intervention in China also faced a problem of political effectiveness. Admittedly, military forces alone—even if available—could not eliminate Chinese communism. The civil war had been a political puzzle long before it became a military question.[10] Yet the United States had no control over the political means needed to solve these political problems. Referring to his own unsuccessful efforts, General Marshall bitterly emphasized that American "advice [was] always listened to very politely but not infrequently ignored when deemed unpalatable."[11] In time, the Chiang government grew incapable of adapting its policies to the requirements of the situation. The head of the U.S. military mission, Major General David Barr, called it "the world's worst leadership."[12] The American ambassador, Leighton Stuart, found it, by August 1948, "no longer capable of changing and reforming or discarding inefficient associates in favor of competent ones. . . . [The nationalist government] ignores competent military advice and fails to take advantage of military opportunities offered, due . . . to the fact that the Generalissimo selects men on the basis of personal reliability rather than military competence."[13]

The United States had neither the capability nor the will to fight against Mao for Chiang. Two options remained theoretically available: either to mediate a reconciliation between the two embattled factions, or to create a political third force around the moderate elements that might be found throughout China.

The first option was explored in 1946 during the so-called Marshall Mission. As spelled out by the president, General Marshall's task was to persuade the Chinese government to call a national conference of representatives of the major political elements to bring about the unification of China, and, concurrently, to affect a cessation of hostilities.[14] In so doing, Truman hoped to help Chiang preserve as much authority as possible within what were judged to be the capabilities of the United States.[15] During the first half of the year, Marshall's mediation met with relative success. An unconditional and immediate cease-fire was organized, pending the convocation of a national assembly, scheduled for the following May. Late in February, an agreement was reached that called for a unified Chinese army of 60 divisions, with 50 nationalist divisions and 10 communist divisions. But both sides then chose not to implement the parts of these agreements least favorable to them, and Marshall's efforts became increasingly hopeless. American inability to intervene militarily limited the pressure that Marshall could exert on the communist forces. But American inability to generate an alternative to Chiang-Kai-shek also inhibited the pressure that could be exerted on the nationalist forces. Late in the year, the evidence of Marshall's failure was made inescapable when the Chinese national assembly was convened without communist approval or participation. In any case, there as elsewhere, a coalition government presupposed the ability to join together, in a practical and lasting way, groups and factions that had been killing each other for decades. It was, as Henry Kissinger put it within the context of Vietnam, "an absurdity . . .

a gimmick or an excuse, not a solution that works best when it is least needed."[16]

Apart from the communists, however, there was no readily available alternative to Chiang. "He is the one who holds this vast country together," reluctantly admitted Ambassador Leighton Stuart in his previously quoted report. Standing between Mao and Chiang, a third force would have required America's full support—politically, economically, and, most of all, militarily—until it had gained sufficient internal legitimacy to stand on its own against both extremes. But the Truman administration had neither the inclination nor the resources needed to provide such open-ended assistance in a struggle that many in Truman's official entourage perceived as already lost. Any political solution could only be a roundabout route to a military intervention of the United States into the Chinese civil war. In subsequent years, this would also be true of Vietnam.

Thus, the decision against military intervention decisively set the limits of American policy in China. Chiang could not win the civil war unless he launched a series of economic, political, and social reforms opposed by the very forces that kept him in power through the years. Without direct intervention, America could not promote a third force that might undertake such reforms, since, devoid of much initial support within China, a third force would have been largely an American creation requiring American protection. Finally, without direct armed intervention, America could not prevent the Chinese communists from defeating Chiang, as his troops had neither the morale, the leadership, nor the stamina to resist their opponents. In short, to quote Dean Acheson, "Nothing that this country did or could have done within the reasonable limits of its capabilities could have changed that result; nothing that was left undone by this country had contributed to it. It was the product of internal Chinese forces, which this country tried to influence but could not."[17]

Nanking, the nationalist capital, fell to the communists on April 24, 1949. On October 15, the new capital, Canton, also fell. By December 8, 1949, the nationalist capital was moved onto the island of Taiwan. Nevertheless, even after such communist triumphs, the Truman administration attempted to pursue its policy of nonintervention. American policymakers still reasoned that China might be used as a counterpoise to Russia in the Far East, as it was felt—correctly, it later turned out—that border disputes and other historical antagonism would ultimately eradicate ideological ties. Any other policy, warned Acheson, "would deflect from the Russians to ourselves the . . . anger, and the wrath and the hatred of the Chinese people."[18] Thus, the U.S. administration rejected any intervention in the pending conflict over Taiwan, the last stronghold of Chiang's armies. On December 23, 1949, the State Department sent "a secret" memorandum to all its diplomats abroad to prepare for the expected fall of Taiwan. On January 5, 1950, following leaks to the press and pressure from the Republican opposition, President Truman issued a formal, written statement that, first, the United States would not give military aid or advice to Chiang; second, it would refrain from any action that might lead to involvement in the Chinese civil conflict; and, third, confirmed China's territorial sovereignty over Taiwan, as stated in wartime conferences.

But this hands-off policy was drastically altered following North Korea's invasion of South Korea. "I have ordered the Seventh Fleet to prevent any attack on Formosa," announced President Truman on June 25, 1950. "The determination of the future status of Formosa must await the restoration of security in the Pacific, a peace settlement with Japan or consideration by the United Nations." For the first time, then, American forces were directly involved in the Chinese civil war, because the communist victory in China would remain incomplete as long as Chiang held Formosa.

A Sour Little War

Decided at the 1943 Cairo Conference, the postwar partition of Korea was expected to be a five-year arrangement based on military convenience and even courtesy from the Russians. The demarcation line was convenient because it determined which nation, America or Russia, would accept Japan's surrender in a given locality.[19] The dividing agreement was also an act of Russian courtesy because the 38th parallel was chosen despite

America's military inability to reach it, so that the United States might preserve the symbolic satisfaction of accepting the Japanese surrender in Korea's ancient capital city of Seoul. "If we had been guided solely by how far north we could get our troops [in Korea] if there was oppposition," President Truman has testified, "the line would have had to be drawn considerably further south on the peninsula."[20]

Soon, however, it became apparent that the two super-powers could not implement their trusteeship policy and ensure the reunification of Korea into a free and independent nation. In September 1947, therefore, the Truman administration brought the matter to the General Assembly of the United Nations with the hope of breaking the deadlock and achieving the reunification of the Korean peninsula. Actually, coming when the United Nations was being frequently bypassed by American actions elsewhere, such reliance on the international organization conceivably reflected Washington's desire to reduce its commitment in the area. This interpretation was confirmed in October 1947, when the Joint Chiefs of Staff, of whom General Eisenhower was the unofficial chairman, asked that the 45,000 American troops stationed in Korea be evacuated. The Joint Chiefs reasoned that in the context of a general war, Korea was indefensible and of "little strategic value" to the United States.[21] With America about to withdraw from Korea—despite CIA estimates that found it "improbable that any South Korean government can maintain independence after U.S. withdrawal"[22]—the General Assembly of the United Nations recommended that free elections be held throughout the country under its supervision. The North Korean authorities, however, refused to grant the United Nation's Control Commission access to North Korea, and the election was limited to South Korea. The General Assembly voted to recognize the newly elected government of Syngman Rhee as the "only lawful government" in Korea. Within a few months the Soviets countered by setting up, north of the 38th parallel, the Democratic People's Republic of Korea. By the end of 1948, with or without the approval of the United Nations, there were two Republics of Korea. With different social outlooks and political organizations, neither zone appeared to have a capacity for economic self-sufficiency: the southern, primarily agricultural, zone, even though it included the majority of Korea's largest cities, had historically

supplied rice for the entire country, while the northern zone—
larger but more sparsely populated—had most of Korea's
industrial plants.

During the first half of 1949, both the Soviet Union and the
United States hurriedly completed the military evacuation of
their respective zones of occupation—the Soviet Union in
January, the United States in June. But within one year of the
American withdrawal, on June 25, 1950, an invading force of
approximately 90,000 North Korean troops crossed the 38th
parallel. Within 24 hours, the Rhee government's request for
military assistance had been satisfied by Truman's authorization to use American air and naval forces to support South
Korean troops. Within five days, the use of American ground
units had also been approved by the Truman administration.
Thus began a "police action" that was to last three years and
cost America 142,000 casualties, including approximately
34,000 dead. As to Korea, this "sour little war" cost South Korea
over 800,000 casualties and North Korea more than 500,000,
while the People's Republic of China suffered approximately
1,000,000 casualties.

"It seemed close to certain," according to Dean Acheson,
"that the [North Korean attack] had been mounted, supplied,
and instigated by the Soviet Union."[23] The U.S. military action
in Korea was conceived from the start as a prolongation in Asia
of the containment effort undertaken in Europe. It was not
South Korea proper that needed to be defended, a South Korea
that even in the midst of the war was not regarded as "vital" to
American security.[24] The Truman administration assumed that
the North Korean action against South Korea and the impending Chinese action against Taiwan were both part of a
world-wide communist military offensive directed by and from
Moscow. Accordingly, American strategy was reappraised at
three different levels: in Europe, the rearmament of the North
Atlantic countries was accelerated; in Korea, American troops
hastily returned; in the Taiwan Straits, the Seventh Fleet was
sent in with the avowed purpose of neutralizing the area.

However convincing it may have seemed at the time,
American policy was based on a misunderstanding of the
policies and objectives of China, whose involvement in planning
North Korea's aggression was probably marginal.[25] First, Mao's

influence in North Korea was limited. Most North Korean leaders had been trained in Moscow, where they continued to pledge their allegiance. The new Chinese government did not have any diplomatic representation in North Korea until August 1950. Already, it had publicly endorsed a blueprint for the future, a blueprint that called for localized "wars of liberation" as opposed to the overt force employed by the North Koreans. Furthermore, China's interest demanded that it complete its unity through the recovery of the Tibet territories and, more particularly, through the absorption of Formosa, whose invasion was widely predicted for the summer of 1950. Implicitly, the forthcoming loss of Formosa had been accepted by the Truman administration: why, then, would the government in Peking risk losing Washington's repeated pledge of neutrality in the Chinese civil war? If China's objective was to replace Stalin's revolutionary influence in Asia, backing the North Korean action was ill-chosen, given North Korea's ideological preference for Moscow. But if China's objective was the more traditional one of creating a buffer zone between itself and Japan, which was on the verge of signing a peace treaty with the United States, then, too, the means were ill-chosen, since they allowed for the possibility (regardless of what Dean Acheson and others might have previously said) of American troops returning to an area that they had just evacuated, and at a time when China was about to recover an integral part of its territory.

Similarly, China's involvement in planning the Korean War with the Soviet Union is doubtful. It implies such a close harmony between the two communist countries as to convince China to face American forces on behalf of its Soviet ally, should the Truman administration choose to intervene. But such harmony, too, is highly questionable. In 1949, Mao's victory on China's mainland did little to endear him to Stalin.[26] In 1927, Stalin had tacitly endorsed Chiang's repression of his communist opposition, and throughout the 1930s, the Soviet leader continued to support the anti-Maoist faction within the Chinese communist party. During the war against Japan, most of the Soviet assistance went directly to the Chiang government, which Moscow recognized until 1949. After his victory, Mao still had to fight Stalin's ambitions in Manchuria and the Sinkiang area, and during the lengthy negotiations of a Sino–Soviet Pact the Chinese leader sharply criticized Moscow's refusal to honor its 1924 pledge that Outer Mongolia be returned to China.

China's decision to enter the Korean War was implemented reluctantly. Repeatedly, Peking warned Washington of the specific circumstances that would make Chinese intervention unavoidable; an invasion of its neighbour by US. forces.[27] Evidence subsequently uncovered also shows how cautiously the Chinese intervention unfolded during the weeks that followed the crossing of the 38th parallel by U.N. forces in early October 1950. Nor were the Chinese prepared for a war that was waged at first with many of the old weapons that had been salvaged from the war against Chiang Kai-shek—until, that is, the later arrival of Soviet-made weapons.[28] In short, the Chinese entered the war because of the direct threat to their security, which, as they perceived it, would be created by the arrival of a major and hostile military force along the Yalu river. "Everybody," later suggested Senator McMahon to General MacArthur, "that had to do with [China's intervention in Korea] turned out to be wrong." To which the general replied: "Practically, although . . . everybody realized that that risk was involved."[29]

By contrast, Soviet interests in sponsoring the Korean War were considerable and varied. First of all, South Korea might have represented, in Stalin's eyes, a rare opportunity to assert his presence in Asia, influence the impending peace treaty with Japan, and alter favorably the distribution of ideological power between himself and Mao. With Korea seemingly placed outside the American defensive perimeter, the risks of American intervention there could be regarded as minimal, especially in view of the absence of any domestic interest in the area: unlike Poland, for example, no influential Korean ethnic group lived in the United States. Furthermore, Americans had known misgivings about Syngman Rhee and his government. Early in 1950, the United States Department of State publicly protested Rhee's disregard of basic constitutional rights, and Truman described the South Korean president as a man who had "little patience with those who differ with him. . . . I did not care," the American president indicated, "for the methods used by Rhee's police to break up political meetings and control political enemies."[30] Indeed, America's distrust of Rhee was reminiscent of its distrust of Chiang. In the elections of May 30, 1950, anti-Rhee factions within South Korea had won more than half of the National Assembly, and the South Korean president had been forced to form a coalition government that promised to be precarious, bitterly contested, and possibly short-lived. If Washington had been unwilling to intervene in China to defend Chiang Kai-shek, why would it intervene in Korea to defend Syngman Rhee, a "zealous, irrational and illogical fanatic," as a presidential envoy was to describe him at the close of the war?[31] In Stalin's view, the small risk of Washington's intervention was worth taking when compared with the considerable gains that would result from a North Korean victory (which the military unpreparedness of South Korea made all the more likely), should the United States choose not to intervene. First, the victory might block the impending alliance between Japan and the United States by serving notice to Japan, and to the other countries of the area as well, that no arrangement in Asia or elsewhere could be worked out without the prior agreement, if not participation, of the Soviet Union. Moreover, a Moscow-sponsored invasion of South Korea would restore Moscow's prestige as the true revolutionary center in Asia, as well as in Europe, at a time when this position was being challenged in both areas. A North Korean victory would therefore be as much a communist victory over the capitalist camp as it would be a Soviet victory within its own camp.

Substantial gains were possible for the Soviet Union even if the Truman administration, despite its previous announcements, opted for military intervention. Such intervention would weaken America's hand in Europe as it would divert American resources away from the European continent to Asia. Consequently, Soviet situations of strength could rapidly be created not only in Western Europe but also in Eastern Europe, particularly in Yugoslavia and Bulgaria. Assuming the worst, a military defeat of North Korea would still be of some profit to Stalin: in addition to asserting Moscow's revolutionary elan, it would place the Soviets in the position of peacemakers defending the weak hybrid state against the powerful industrial superstate. This peacemaking function was actually assumed by the Soviets from the start of the hostilities, more or less eagerly, depending on the fluctuations registered on the battlefield.

More than 30 years after the event, it is difficult to give any credence to the hypothesis that the North Koreans might have acted without prior approval from Moscow. It remains even more difficult, of course, to imagine, as some have, that the North Korean action was precipitated by a conspiracy organized, with the support of the South Koreans, by a small American clique led by General MacArthur and John Foster Dulles.[32] For one thing, the idea of a conspiracy itself overlooks the many conflicts that divided the two men. Thus, upon his return from Tokyo where he had been visiting MacArthur at the very moment when the North Koreans were about to cross the 38th parallel, Dulles lost no time in recommending to Truman that MacArthur be "hauled back to the United States immediately."[33] But, more substantively, it is hardly possible not to make much out of the North Korean attack as a causal fact in starting the Korean War. According to some radical critics of U.S. foreign policy, the North Korean forces were merely engaged in a "limited campaign" that was "directed . . . toward Seoul alone,"—in other words, a campaign aimed at a "relatively small part of a nation."[34] Indeed, it is difficult to conceive as limited a military campaign that aims at the capital of the adversary—and it is no less difficult to accept an analysis that presents the South Korean army as being so overwhelmingly superior to the "small counteroffensive" launched in desperation by the North Koreans that it allegedly engaged in a strategy of "deliberate withdrawal" intended to justify a pre-planned U.S. intervention. After one week of fighting, the losses of the South Korean army amounted to 44,000 men, killed, captured, or missing—that is, one-half of its initial force of 98,000.[35] The fact of North Korean aggression was then, and has remained since, unquestionable.

What can be questioned more convincingly is the role and the objectives of the Soviets in the actual launching of the war.

Up to that time, in the words of George Kennan, the Soviet policy in Asia had been generally a "fluid resilient policy of maximum power with minimum responsibility."[36] But now, a Soviet-sponsored military attack against South Korea presented considerable risks. To be sure, past American pronouncements pointed to a likely U.S. abstention from any direct involvement. Yet, if past experience could be relied on, the only thing predictable about American behavior appeared to be its unpredictability. The Truman administration had sent an ultimatum to Moscow over the Republic of Azerbaidjan, but it had not intervened on behalf of Czechoslovakia; similarly, an administration that had refused to fight in China might decide to fight in Korea. In that case, to stop the confrontation of two armies would be more difficult than to end frontier maneuvers as in the Turkish affair, or to lift a blockade, as in Berlin.

If Moscow's objective was to gain control of South Korea, other means short of the overt use of military force were still available at the time. From without, North Korea's ambitions might be fulfilled through guerilla and psychological warfare, political pressure, and intimidation. From within, the Rhee government had been weakened by the elections held the previous May, and an enlarged coalition government might have proved more amenable to the negotiation of an eventual reunification with North Korea. In addition, since January 1950 the Soviet boycott of the Security Council of the United Nations had virtually left the U.N. in American hands. With its representative scheduled to assume the presidency of the Council as of August 1, Moscow had an obvious interest in awaiting further developments within South Korea and holding back the North Korean attack in the meantime.

This leads to two tentative interpretations, neither of which can be truly confirmed because the necessary documents are not accessible. One possibility is that, having received a green light from Stalin, the North Koreans chose to attack at a time of their own choosing. If so, the North Korean timing might have been precipitated either by the political rivalry which, since the fusion of the communist parties of South and North Korea, had opposed Kim Sung and the influential South Korean communist leader, Pak Hon Yong,[37] or because Kim, aware of the Chinese plans for an invasion of Taiwan and already pressured by Pak for a quick thrust into South Korea, may have wished to strike first. A U.S. administration willing to stand by while the Chinese communist forces were invading Formosa might have been reluctant to abstain again in and over Korea.

Another plausible explanation regarding the timing of the war places direct responsibility on Stalin. Thus it might be argued that Stalin's policy in Korea focused not so much on the United States as on China. At a time when he was engaged in major purges of communist parties everywhere, the Soviet leader was troubled by Mao's ascendancy. Without a U.S.

reaction, a successful North Korean attack on South Korea before Mao's attack against Taiwan would place China in a Soviet nutcracker; but even with a U.S. reaction, the return of U.S. forces to Korea might at least frustrate China's intentions in Taiwan, and at best involve China in a war against America, which would ruin any rapprochement between these two countries, thereby leaving China fully dependent on Moscow.

The Truman administration, however, did not pause to ponder the extent of Sino–Soviet involvement and collusion. Instead, it took these for granted in a swift and instinctive reaction, which reflected the prevailing anti-Munich mood of the postwar era: aggression met by appeasement inevitably bred more aggression until ultimately it would generalize into a world war. President Truman described his mood when, in the plane taking him back to Washington on June 25, he recalled other occasions when his generation had seen the strong attack the weak: "I recalled some earlier instances: Manchuria, Ethiopia, Austria. I remembered how each time that the democracies failed to act it had encouraged the aggressors to keep going ahead. Communism was acting in Korea just as Hitler, Mussolini and the Japanese had acted ten, fifteen and twenty years earlier. I felt certain that if South Korea was allowed to fall Communist leaders would be emboldened to override nations closer to our own shores. . . . If this was allowed to go unchallenged it would mean a third world war, just as similar incidents had brought on the second world war."[38]

The North Korean attack was widely interpreted as a Soviet test of America's capability and determination to meet force with force. In the easy language of historical analogies, Stalin was now investigating how much of Chamberlain there was in Truman. Of course, it might have been argued that a test over Korea did not necessarily involve more than Korea itself or, at most, Northeast Asia. Other "tests" had been held in other places—how many such tests would it take, and where, to assert the credibility of America's will to resist? But an American administration now anticipating an all-out confrontation thought increasingly in global terms. Korea proper might not be essential to American security—a proposition readily granted by officials in Washington before, during, and after the war—

but its fall was nevertheless unacceptable, inasmuch as it weakened those organizations and alliances to which American security was clearly related.

The collapse of the League of Nations was attributed (erroneously) to the unwillingness of the member states to face military aggression in Manchuria and Ethiopia in the 1930s. It was felt that North Korean aggression now tested the very foundations and principles of the new international organization. On June 26, 1945, President Truman had appraised the past and prophesied the future when he stated: "If we had this Charter a few years ago and above all the will to use it—millions now dead would be alive. If we should falter in the future in our will to use it, millions now living will surely die."[39] In Korea, then, collective security was being challenged, and there could be no United Nations (and no international peace and order) without collective security. Thanks to the United Nations, American intervention was also, conveniently, provided with the additional respectability of a multinational endorsement that the absence of the Soviet delegate from the Security Council made possible. Ultimately, 41 member states, in addition to the United States, offered some material assistance, and 15 of these contributed armed forces—even though the American share of U.N. forces in Korea still amounted to 50% of the land forces, 86 percent of the Navy, and 93 percent of the air forces.[40] The war itself was fought under the flag of the United Nations, even though in the field the United States preserved full command. Said General MacArthur: "The controls over me were exactly the same as though the forces under me were all American."[41]

The strengthening of America's alliances, too, was of paramount importance. It was anticipated that Korean-type aggression might occur elsewhere in the world at any moment, particularly in Europe where the threat of "disguised aggression through a satellite" was alluded to by Dean Acheson. "In the absence of defense forces in being," he warned in February 1951, "satellites might be used for such disguised aggression in the hope that they could get away with it."[42] Throughout the fighting in Korea, the maintenance of adequate forces in Europe remained one of the major concerns of a Truman administration worried by the possibility that the Soviets might take advantage of Washington's involvement away from the main theater of confrontation.[43]

Another potential American ally was Japan. A few weeks before the outbreak of hostilities in Korea, President Truman had announced that a peace treaty with Japan had the highest priority, and that it would be signed on the basis of Japanese independence and the long-term presence of American military bases throughout Japan. The announcement had been received in the communist world with a series of actions that showed an intense determination to oppose it as best they could.[44] A North Korean victory would reduce America's credibility in Asia and, as noted by John Foster Dulles, would place Japan "between the upper and lower jaws of the Russian bear."[45]

Korea was thus regarded as the first military encounter of a global war that was still avoidable, provided that such communist aggressions were defeated. "Our best hope of peace," said Dean Acheson, "lies in our ability to make absolutely plain to aggressors that aggression cannot succeed."[46] To place the conflict in a global perspective helped to limit it, even though such global interpretation was based on a fallacious analysis of the causes of the war—an erroneous analysis from which the right decisions were made but the wrong conclusions drawn.

Limiting the War

The United States intervened in Korea because the Truman administration believed, rightly or wrongly, that in Korea the Soviets were "probing" for weaknesses in America's commitments; that they were "testing" America's will to fight; and that they were taking advantage of "opportunities" that America itself had opened. Such intervention remained limited because the Truman administration also assumed that one of Moscow's main objectives was to divert American resources away from other more strategic points, so that when the real attack took place American capabilities would be too depleted to withstand it. President Truman remained determined to keep America's commitment, and consequently its objectives, as limited as possible: "We would not become so deeply committed in Korea that we could not take care of such other situations as might develop."[47] Only for a short period were American objectives escalated beyond a restoration of the status quo ante bellum. This occurred when, following MacArthur's crossing of the 38th parallel, the U.N. Resolution of October 7 advised U.N. forces to seek the reunification of the whole Korean peninsula. It would be "sheer madness," said Dean Acheson, for China to intervene.[48] As events came to prove, it was, instead, sheer madness to expect that they would not intervene, when they had made it clear that they would. By March 1951, as a result of China's intervention, the status quo ante bellum had become once again the stated American objective in Korea.

In short, the war in Korea remained limited less out of choice than out of necessity. In limiting the conflict, Washington had two objectives: to keep the Russians out of the war, while saving scarce military resources for possible military confrontations elsewhere. The U.S. concern over Soviet reaction was candidly acknowledged by General Marshall, then secretary of defense, during the MacArthur Hearings: "If . . . there was no danger whatsoever of a Soviet intervention, I would say that certainly the bombing [in China] would start almost immediately."[49] The reasoning was obvious. A Soviet intervention would cause an escalation that might transform the Korean "police action" into World War III. As the police action had been undertaken precisely to prevent a world conflict, Korea had to remain limited as much as possible—a proposition readily endorsed by the other side.

The major limitation that both sides agreed to respect was their refusal to employ the most potent weapons at their disposal. The U.S. decision not to use atomic weapons was first dictated by tactical considerations. No target in Korea would have justified their use.[50] Furthermore, the scarcity of these weapons and means of delivery made it imperative at the time that they be used with the utmost care. As late as July 10, 1951, the Strategic Air Command had only 87 B36 bombers ready for action, and the production rate was only two or three a month.[51]

A very limited atomic stockpile needed to be guarded and preserved for more decisive encounters.* The United States probably could have delivered a major assault on China's or Russia's urban-industrial centers, but such a blow would not have been decisive. The Soviet Union was already capable of a small retaliatory strike against the United States or, more probably, against the hostage cities of Europe. As an ultimate although unlikely gesture, Moscow might have "loaned" some of its very few atomic bombs to China for a retaliatory raid on South Korea, Japan, and Okinawa. As for the Chinese, they were eager to dispel the notion that such weapons might deter them from undertaking actions they deemed vital to their national security. "Atomic bombs," admitted General Nieh Jung-chen, a Chinese Deputy Chief of Staff, "may kill a few million people." But, he went on, "China lives on the farms. What can atom bombs do there?"[52]

The United States also had the capability, which it did not use, of launching conventional air attacks on China. Such attacks could have closed the Manchurian air bases, disrupted the supply lines, and seriously damaged the Chinese economy by destroying industrial centers or blockading the coast. This was so carefully avoided that even the bombing of bridges over the Yalu river was ordered to be confined to their Korean half only. In North Korea, too, major targets such as some hydroelectric

---

*The question of nuclear weapons is one shrouded in utmost secrecy. In 1950, nowhere in any document in the president's office, in the Atomic Energy Commission, in any governmental agency, could anyone find the exact number of bombs available or scheduled for production. Nevertheless, the evolution of America's arsenal during the Truman presidency can be followed through Truman's own remarks. Such evolution appears to be as follows: in 1946, the number of bombs was "disappointing" and those available had not been assembled yet (*Memoirs*, Vol. II, p. 296). In 1947, it was still "inadequate" both quantitatively and qualitatively, and progress was "dangerously slow" (p. 299). By early 1949, America was beginning to have a stockpile, but it was still regarded as "inadequate in number and not keeping up with technological progress" (p. 304). In July 1949, the president strongly urged that "production of atomic weapons should be stepped up," and by January 1953, two months after the first successful explosion of an H-bomb, Truman could boast that he had left his successor with "a stockpile of atomic bombs, together with the means for delivering these bombs to the target" (p. 314).

plants were not touched for two full years after the outbreak of the war. Deep concern with Soviet reaction further prevented the bombing of targets close to Soviet territory. On the ground, no American unit was allowed within approximately 15 miles of the border of northeast Korea with Siberia.[53] But, in return, communist forces did not attempt, in however limited a way, to attack excellent and crucial targets in South Korea (such as Inchon or Pusan), or American airfields in Japan and in Okinawa. American naval vessels were also spared from air attacks.

Finally, both sides avoided using military manpower that the other might find offensive. No Russian volunteer was ever reported in the war, even though Moscow had numerous forces not too far away, in the vicinity of Vladivostok, Dairen-Port Arthur, and Harbin. Chiang Kai-shek's forces were not used either. On June 29, 1950, his offer of 330,000 troops was turned down, as America's Joint Chiefs of Staff felt that the troops would be as "helpless as Syngman Rhee's army against the North Korean attacks."[54] Besides, they were needed for the defense of Taiwan. Later on, larger offers of help by Chiang were still ignored to avoid any escalation of the conflict.

These self-imposed restraints led to a momentous debate when General MacArthur, following his repeated public demands after the Chinese intervention that most of these limitation be lifted, was fired by the President for insubordination.[55] In the narrow sense, MacArthur's insubordination stemmed from a conflict over strategy. Administration spokesmen viewed warfare as a means to an end and found a substitute to victory in the diplomatic search for an accommodation of mutual disagreements, even while the fighting was going on. In Truman's words, "warfare, no matter what weapons it employs, is a means to an end, and if that end can be achieved by negotiated settlements of conditional surrender, there is no need for war."[56] Such a limited view of warfare as a continuation of politics by other means—the so-called "die-for-tie" approach— was rejected by MacArthur and by every single American commander involved in the war, with the exception of Generals Ridgway and Taylor. Instead, MacArthur appeared to view war as the end of politics, on the assumption that by using force both sides implicitly admitted the impossibility of reaching any peaceful settlement. "Once war is imposed upon us," MacArthur dramatically told a joint meeting of Congress on April 19, 1951, "there is no other alternative than to apply every available means to bring it to a swift end. War's very object is victory—not prolonged indecision. In war, indeed, there can be no substitute for victory."[57] MacArthur felt that China's intervention had created a new war that required the "release [of] the power that we now possess so that it can be utilized."[58] "China," MacArthur further complained, "is using the maximum of her force against us . . . and we are not using the maximum of ours against her."[59] No more American ground forces would be needed if 500,000 of Chiang Kai-shek's troops were "unleashed" against China while major Chinese targets were attacked from the air (possibly with atomic weapons) and the Chinese coast was blockaded. MacArthur's forecast of the "decisive and victorious end" that would reward his strategy was skeptically received by his critics. As was often the case, Dean Acheson best summarized the administration's position: "We are being asked to undertake a large risk of general war with China, risk of war with the Soviet Union, and a demonstrable weakening of our collective security system—all of this in return for what? In return for measures whose effectiveness in bringing the conflict to an early conclusion are judged doubtful by our responsible military authorities."[60]

MacArthur denied that such an American offensive would cause a Soviet entry into the war. The Soviets, he argued, did not have the capabilities needed to undertake a major military campaign in Asia.[61] Nor was any part of Stalin's strategy, as MacArthur saw it, related to events in Korea: "[nothing] that happens in Korea, or Asia," declared the general, "would affect his basic decision. . . . He will make his decisions on a higher basis."[62] MacArthur did not believe either that his strategy implied an American participation in a ground war in China, which he staunchly opposed as a "master folly," or the thinking of a man "not in his proper sense."[63] Such an outcome would be avoided because China's inherent weakness made it vulnerable to sustained American air attacks, combined with ground engagements in Korea plus Chiang's diversionary attacks either in China proper or on the periphery.

But the Truman administration, still under the shock of past underestimation of Chinese communist capabilities and intentions, refused to risk a major war with China in Asia while the major enemy was Russia in Europe, and when America's capability of facing either one in either place was open to question.[64] For the United States to go to war with China over Korea would be to fight the wrong war in the wrong place at the wrong time and against the wrong enemy.[65] The Truman administration further argued that such a war would have to be fought essentially alone, a likelihood that was actually welcomed by the MacArthur forces: "If the other nations of the world," said MacArthur, "haven't got enough sense to see where appeasement leads after the appeasement which led to the second war in Europe . . . why then we had better protect ourselves and go it alone."[66]

In a broader perspective, the confrontation between the president and the general was a classic dispute between civilian and military authorities. In his *Memoirs*, Truman emphasized: "If there is one basic element in our constitution, it is civilian control of the military. Policies are to be made by the elected political officials, not by generals or admirals."[67] So, when announcing MacArthur's dismissal, Truman made clear that "it is fundamental that military commanders must be governed by the policies and directives issued to them in the manner provided by our laws and constitution."[68] What he sought was the unconditional approval by the men in the field of the policy goals set by Washington, once these goals had been set. MacArthur at first argued that his policy was in line with the directives sent him by the Joint Chiefs of Staff, whose views, he said, were "practically identical" to his own.[69] Thus, MacArthur could emphatically recognize, as he did, Truman's basic assumption of civilian control over the global strategy. These directives, however, had been issued in the first week of January 1951, when United Nations troops might be forced out of Korea if the Chinese chose to do it—a possibility that "seemed at the time to be verging on a probability."[70] But MacArthur next contended that the administration had no coherent policy at all in Korea, hence no concrete guidelines for him to follow. Indeed, MacArthur argued, he had followed the only policy that the administration had formulated, namely the Truman Doctrine. Reporting on an earlier visit with MacArthur, Averell Harriman had confirmed to President Truman that the celebrated general considered his doctrine "great" and felt only that it should be carried out "more vigorously."[71] "Who is overwhelmingly the main enemy?" asked Senator McMahon. And MacArthur replied, à la Truman, "Communism. . . . All over the world including the interior of many of the fine democratic countries of the world."[72]

Essentially, the Truman–MacArthur controversy mirrored the policy vacuum that existed when the decision to intervene in Korea was taken. Still in the aftermath of the communist victory in China and faced with increasing charges of having lost China and being soft on communism, the Truman administration had failed to articulate a coherent policy for the Far East. At best America's Asian policy was in a state of flux and uncertainty. Decisive policy formulation and implementation was reached only slowly during the war years, and it resulted in measures to which we must now turn.

Expanding Containment

Immediately following World War II, American foreign policy objectives were relatively moderate: to restore political stability in the areas in which hostilities against Germany had taken place. In most cases, Washington was acutely aware that no lasting stability could be achieved without Soviet cooperation, and it was prepared to seek that cooperation through accommodation and coercion.

By 1947, however, the growth of Soviet power and the emergence of a Soviet bloc seemingly waging a war of subversive attrition against the democratic nations led to a shift of priorities. The Truman Doctrine was the earliest indication of that shift, as the program of reconstruction and stabilization that it advocated for Greece and Turkey became part of a general denunciation of totalitarian forces, with Moscow as the obvious target. But, simultaneously conceived, the Marshall

Plan reflected the hesitancy with which that shift was taking place, because Washington still included, however dubiously, the Soviets in this common venture of political and economic restoration.

From then onward other programs of economic reconstruction and political stabilization became increasingly the instruments of a policy of military coalition under American guidance as the only way to contain Soviet expansion. East and West, North and South, there was now but one world, one peace, and one enemy. "We have no intention to sacrifice the East in order to gain time for the West," claimed the Republican platform of 1952. What made such a statement palatable to a large section of the American people was precisely the rhetoric of the Democrats.

Even before Korea, a Democratic secretary of state, Dean Acheson, had defined the policy of meeting strength with strength that a Republican secretary of state, John Foster Dulles, would soon apply faithfully. "The only way to deal with the Soviet Union," Acheson said in February 1950, "is to create situations of strength. . . . Every time one of these situations [of weakness] exists . . . it is . . . an irresistible invitation for the Soviet government to fish in those troubled waters. . . . You can't argue with a river—it is going to flow. You can dam it up, you can put it to useful purposes, you can deflect it, but you can't argue with it."[73]

In 1951, the Truman administration dismissed MacArthur but almost simultaneously adopted parts of his policy, a policy that was further enlarged and implemented by Truman's successor. "The first line of defense for Europe," MacArthur argued, was "right where we are fighting over there in Korea."[74] Hurriedly, then, the policy vacuum of 1950 was filled so that the first lines of defense could be manned. During the last 18 months of the Truman administration and the first two years of the Eisenhower administration, the wall of security alliances that had been devised for Europe was rapidly extended to Asia: on August 30, 1951, to the Philippines; two days later to Australia and New Zealand: on September 8, 1951, to Japan; on October 1, 1953, to South Korea; on September 9, 1954, to Australia, France, Great Britain, New Zealand, Philippines, Pakistan, and Thailand within the Southeast Asia Treaty

Organization; and on December 2, 1954, to Taiwan. In all these places an armed attack on any country was formally described as dangerous to America's own peace and security, and the United States was committed to act to meet the common dangers in accordance with its constitutional process. This understanding was somewhat more general than the NATO principle. But these treaties were thought to be only a first step toward the global implementation of a Pacific Pact regarded as the "desirable ultimate objective of United States policy in the Pacific."[75]

The wisdom of this extension of the containment policy to Asia did not go undisputed. That such a policy could be applied to Europe against the Soviet Union had been regarded by some as doubtful. That it could be applied in Asia primarily to prevent Chinese expansion was regarded by many as absurd. It was then argued, and it continued to be so argued during the war in Vietnam, that in Europe military containment was undertaken to provide a shield behind which European nations could recover, whereas in Asia such containment would help nations not yet formed, where disruption mainly took the form of civil conflicts. The threat that had to be met in Asia was an internal threat, based upon conditions that were genuinely revolutionary, with or without external assistance. Asia needed the political containment of a political threat, not the military containment of a military threat. Furthermore, such an expansion of containment to Asia would commit America to protecting highly volatile regimes whose survivability would become dependent upon American assistance, creating imperial relationships that might ultimately overextend America's military burdens. In other words, such an involvement in Asia would consist of supporting local governments and not peoples, taking charge of problems that were essentially domestic and that these governments could no longer face themselves, not only because of the external pressure to which they were subjected but also because of their own inability to create a more stable domestic consensus upon which they could satisfactorily rely for support. These differences were ignored as the Eisenhower-Dulles foreign policy administration was to make morality an integral part of America's ascending power and historic purpose. Eventually, they would be tested in and over Indochina, despite

President Eisenhower's warning in 1954 that he could not "visualize a ground troop operation in Indochina that would be supported by the people of the United States."[76]

Into the Cold War

Dean Acheson's successor, John Foster Dulles, had been a lawyer for a long time before he became Secretary of State, shortly before his 65th birthday. In his new position, he often reasoned, spoke, and acted like a lawyer. The court he faced was the court of History, where he prosecuted the Soviet Union for crimes against God, liberty, and peace. The legal code he used was that of a God-made moral law which determined right and wrong and ensured the ultimate victory of those conforming to its canons. For a while, because of the war, moral law had been put aside in favor of military expediency. But with the war ended, principle and morality should have been reasserted in the world as a guide to international behavior. America's mission, Dulles thought, was to ensure such a belated restoration. "What we need to do," he pleaded, "is to recapture . . . the kind of crusading spirit of the early days when we were darn sure that what we had was a lot better than what anybody else had. . . . The missionaries, the doctors, the educators, and the merchants carried the knowledge of the great American experiment to all four corners of the globe."[77]

A preacher in the world of politics, the new secretary of state found in the international community a protracted conflict between the forces of good and evil, in the literal sense. More specifically, the forces of evil were those of the international communist conspiracy, a conspiracy against God that needed to be defeated in His name. "When your Secretary and I are discussing matters," once said an Indian diplomat of Dulles, "God always gets between us." "Surely," Dulles had predicted in 1942, "the catastrophies that inevitably overtake those who operate on anti-Christian principles powerfully argue that it is those principles which are true."[78]

Nevertheless, John Foster Dulles was also a politician before he became a preacher, and his legalistic, moralistic, and ideological references were set within a framework that was nonlegalistic, nonmoralistic, and nonideological. During the interwar period, Dulles had criticized the "devil" theory of causation as an ultimate escape from responsibility. He had found at the time little difference between states: "All nations," he wrote then, "are inherently selfish and we are no different from any other."[79] Side by side with a Manichean vision of international politics therefore existed a Machiavellian vision that recognized the primacy of power and national interest; and Dulles, who in the 1950s came to be known for his pactomania, had discarded international agreements that did not respond to the necessities of power and national interest. Shortly before being named secretary of state he observed: "Treaties of alliance and mutual aid mean little except as they spell out what the people concerned would do anyway."[80] Earlier, he had commented, even more abruptly: "In the absence of any central authority to pass judgments one cannot consider treaties, as such, to be sacred, nor can we identify treaty observance in the abstract with law and order. If we do not realize that treaties as such are neither 'law' nor 'sacred' we will fall into the common error of thinking that treaties provide a mechanism whereby international peace can be assured."[81]

Within this Machiavellian framework, Dulles made a simpler distinction between "static" and "dynamic" nations—a distinction that was strictly nonethical. Static nations were regarded as the main obstacle to peace, and Dulles made the need for change the dominant theme of his career. "The concepts and words that matter, in all we say," he once confided, "are simply peace and change. We live in an age of deep change. You can't stop it. What you can do is to bend every effort to direct it—to see that it is evolutionary rather than revolutionary."[82] Only change, Dulles felt, would prevent the institutionalization of injustice: "Change is the law of life and new conditions are constantly arising which call for remedy lest there be injustice."[83] By canceling injustice, change would help promote peace: "A frequent cause of war has been the effort of satisfied peoples to identify peace as a perpetutation of the status quo. Change is the law of life. . . . World order cannot be measured merely by the elimination of violence. There must also be processes of peaceful change whereby justice manifests itself."[84]

But change that involved a compromise with forces unwilling to recognize the basic principles of moral law was strictly ruled out. "If we rely on freedom," reasoned Dulles, "then it follows that we must abstain from diplomatic moves which would seem to endorse captivity. That would in effect be a conspiracy against freedom."[85] At this juncture, Dulles displaced the source of international conflicts from the international system and the related problems of ensuring change toward malignant states with which coexistence was impossible unless they abandoned their nonmoral principles. "This [moral] law," concluded Dulles, "has been trampled by the Soviet rulers and, for that violation, they can and should be made to pay."[86]

The identification of the Soviet Union as "the" malignant state was relatively slow to take shape, and it paralleled the reorientation of Dulles' thinking about the sources of Soviet policy. As late as 1947, he still characterized Russian expansion outside its frontiers as a traditional search for security; but by the time he became secretary of state, Dulles had concluded that the Soviet rulers were enslaved by the doctrine of international communism, and that Soviet policy was nothing but a means to communist ideology. The immediate inference from Dulles' conclusion was that although problems between states could be worked out, they could not be worked out between two opposite ideologies, one of which started from "an atheistic Godless premise." Between Russia and America there was no real dispute at all—the dispute was with an ideology that had captured the minds and bodies of hundreds of millions of people, including the Soviet people. Said Dulles: "If only the government of Russia was interested in looking out for the welfare of Russia, the people of Russia, we would have a state of non-tension right away."[87]

Such a single-minded perception of international communism as the enemy, with the Soviet Union as its agent, closed the secretary's mind to the possibility of any accommodation unless the Soviets and their allies were to abandon altogether the communist way and endorse the American way. Within this Manichean framework, any decrease in Soviet hostility appeared to result from the pressure that America had brought to bear on Moscow, and it provided further evidence that such pressure needed to be maintained and even increased. For example, in April 1953, shortly after Stalin's death, early Soviet pronouncements in favor of detente between the two superpowers were dismissed by Dulles as "rotten apples." "It's obvious," he said, "that what they are doing is because of outside pressures, and I don't know anything better we can do than to keep up these pressures right now."[88] By July 1953, following the settlement of the Korean War, Dulles wanted to increase these pressures further: "this is the kind of time when we ought to be doubling our bets, not reducing them. . . . This is the time to crowd the enemy—and maybe finish him, once and for all."[89] Any Soviet accommodation would now be interpreted as evidence of the correctness of America's decision to stand firm until final victory. Soviet agreement to a summit meeting (in 1955),* or Soviet reductions of their armed forces (in 1956), would be attributed to economic shortages or problems of leadership. Such force-level reductions might also be interpreted as another Soviet treachery: to a newspaperman who had asked Dulles whether it was not a "fair conclusion" that he would have preferred "to have the Soviet Union keep these men in their armed forces," the secretary of state replied: "Well, it's a fair conclusion that I would rather have them standing around doing guard duty than making atomic bombs."[90] Similarly, should Peking appear to accept a proposed Indian compromise for a settlement in Korea, as it was rumored in early 1953, Dulles would react with "sorrow" to the prospect of a "premature"

---

*The initial suggestion for the summit meeting came from Winston Churchill in May 1953. In the aftermath of Stalin's death, Churchill called for an early meeting of the "smallest number of powers and persons possible." America's participation was made dependent upon prior evidence from Russia that the conference would be worthwhile. This condition was met with the Austrian treaty in May 1955 and, the following month, final arrangements for the July meeting were settled. The Summit Conference itself was not very successful. On the one hand, the Soviets were now eager to disprove the claims that their concessions had been made out of weakness. The Americans, on the other hand, were eager to exploit the weakness that had been perceived in Moscow's first "retreat" (in Austria) since the end of World War II. (See Coral Bell, *Negotiations from Strength* [New York, 1963], pp. 100–36.)

settlement: "I don't think we can get much out of a Korean settlement until we have shown—before all Asia—our clear superiority by giving the Chinese one hell of a licking."[91]

While the treachery of the Soviet regime made negotiations dangerous—"there'd be a catch in it"[92]—the superiority of the American system (and American power) over an inept Soviet system made negotiations superfluous. "The fact is," noted Dulles in early 1955, "that they have failed, and they have got to devise new policies. . . . The free nations have banded together, shown their strength, shown their unity. . . . The result is, they have got to review their whole creed, from A to Z."[93] And the secretary of state added three months later: "My analysis of the whole world situation is that the Soviets are overextended . . . [and that] their system . . . is on the point of collapsing."[94]

Ironically, the Manichean side of Dulles' policies was dictated by his Machiavellian perception of the international situation and of America's role within it. Viewing the Soviet menace as a long-range challenge to the United States and other western democracies, Dulles found it necessary to ensure America's continued involvement in the struggle by raising the tone of American inflexibility toward an implacable though fading enemy. But in so doing, Dulles made the nation and himself the captives of the resulting public mood that grew out of such deceptive practices and exaggerated rhetoric.

The outcome of these tactics was made ironical by the evolution of international circumstances as well. Was Dulles' vision of an international communist conspiracy still valid after Stalin's death? In 1953, the new Soviet government abandoned its territorial demands in Turkey, thus unfreezing the hostility that had prevailed since 1945; it extended a hand of friendship to Iran and restored diplomatic relations with Israel, relations that had been broken by Stalin, following the discovery of the so-called doctors' plot in December 1952; it began a rapprochement with Greece, and nonalignment for the first time began to be spoken of with favor; the war in Korea was ended. In 1954-55, other Soviet moves included its withdrawal from Austria; a public apology to Tito for past Soviet errors and a public recognition that all socialist states should be left free to follow their own socialism; the evacuation of Port Arthur and the return to Finland of the naval base of Porkalla; offers for the reunification of Germany (in an extension of Stalin's offer of May 1952 for a unified, rearmed, and neutral Germany within its Potsdam frontiers); attempts to normalize relations with Japan; and certain concessions on disarmament.* Finally, in February 1956, at the Twentieth Party Congress, Khrushchev harshly denounced Stalin and Stalinism and spelled out the new Soviet foreign policy of strengthening its relations with other communist states, improving relations with the Western states, and supporting nonalignment. Clearly, an American policy that had been at best conceived to satisfy a national mood of inflexibility and an international situation of confrontation built a momentum that made it unresponsive to international changes and incapable of modifying the mood that that policy had brought with it. In May 1950, one month prior to the Korean War, Dulles had criticized America's habit of behaving "as though God had appointed us to be the Committee of Admissions to the Free World and as though the qualifications for membership were to be found by our looking into a mirror."[95] In a position of power, however, he quickly found a need to reassert America's chairmanship of that committee and to bar from the committee any nation that did not fulfill the requirements set by America's own image.

---

*Among these steps Soviet policies over Austria and Germany were probably the most dramatic expressions of Moscow's new flexibility. Concluded on May 15, 1955, the Austrian State Treaty permitted the withdrawal of Soviet occupation forces from the Soviet-occupied portion of Austria in return for permanent Austrian neutrality. By driving a 500-mile neutral wedge between West Germany and Italy, the Soviets were effectively splitting the zone of Atlantic defense. With regard to Germany, Soviet proposals in early 1954 and 1955 consisted essentially in calling for an all-European collective security system that would tentatively exclude the United States. Such a security system would be linked to a settlement of the German question, possibly on the basis of general elections that would follow the formation of a coalition government between the Bonn government and the East German communist regime. Offers of this type, because they were not properly tested, or because they were tested too late, may have been lost opportunities for reaching a basic agreement that could have altered the subsequent course of the cold war.

Liberation, Brinkmanship, and Massive Retaliation

The precepts of foreign policy that John Foster Dulles devised and defined during his six years as secretary of state were consistent with both Dulles' and America's theological principles and political temperament. These precepts were also shaped by the political atmosphere of the time. The new Republican administration took office after twenty years of exile in the aftermath of a three-year campaign that had vilified the secretary of state, the policies he had pursued, and the institutions that had tried to implement those policies. Indeed, the bitterness this campaign had aroused was such that in 1961, upon learning of Dean Acheson's appointment as an adviser on NATO, some Republicans expressed amazement that he was still in America.[96]

These attacks had begun to gain momentum in February 1950, when the junior senator from Wisconsin, Joseph R. McCarthy, suggested that a group in the State Department promoted at every moment the communist cause. His charges were endorsed by numerous legislators, and hardly anyone in official Washington escaped the folly of the era. Senator William E. Jenner, a Republican from Indiana, attacked General Marshall, then secretary of defense, as a "living lie . . . an errand boy, a front man, a stooge, or a co-conspirator for the [Truman] administration's crazy assortment of collectivist cut-throat, crackpots and communist fellow-traveling appeasers."[97] Between 1950 and 1953, in the "night of the long knives," as Dean Acheson has called it, charges and countercharges, resignations and dismissals, the growing intolerance of the opposition and the unstated fear of being perceived as not being loyal enough, caused incalculable damage to the governance of the nation and the formulation of its foreign policy. To prove his personal loyalty, the secretary of state had to spend much of his time explaining that he was not a communist and that there were not "a lot" of communists known to him within the State Department. To prove its collective virtue, the State Department had to sacrifice many qualified and irreplaceable career officers who had been attacked by McCarthy. Thus, between February and August 1953, the personnel strength of the State Department dropped by more than half, from approximately 42,000 to 20,000, including 5,000 terminations under the president's security program—despite the fact that during the entire McCarthy era not a single case of disloyalty was ever proved.[98]

In 1953, John Foster Dulles faced the problem of gaining the confidence and the support of the nation for the foreign policy of the Eisenhower administration. To this end, he chose to emphasize the newness of its approach to world affairs. In his Inaugural Address, the president pointedly underlined the general spirit in which American foreign policy would now be conducted—a spirit that "once again" would "know and observe the difference between . . . a thoughtfully calculated goal and spasmodic reaction to the stimulus of emergencies." Shortly thereafter, in his first State of the Union Message, the new president proudly announced that in less than a fortnight he had "begun the definition of a new positive foreign policy."[99] In other words, under a new Republican administration, the United States would have a new foreign policy employing new means toward the fulfillment of new objectives issued from a rejuvenated faith in traditional principles.

The first of these policies was the policy of liberation. In 1952, the Republican platform had pledged that under a Republican administration the policy of containment would be discarded as "an example of non-moral diplomacy." Instead, it was claimed, the 800 million people who had been abandoned by Acheson's policies were to be liberated by rolling the communist empire ever further east. In May 1952, a campaigning Dulles asked the United States "to make it publicly known that it wants and expects liberation to occur."[100] That such a commitment would have immediate political gains was evident enough. As the major areas of liberation lay in Eastern Europe, the endorsement of the principle alone carried over countless Americans of East European extraction. Beyond that Dulles assumed that the espousal of high moral principles was a tremendously potent force that ought not to appear as the monopoly of the communist world.

However, the policy was nothing more or less than a principle itself and was never made operational. During his confirmation at the Senate Foreign Relations Committee, Dulles denied that such a policy might be conducive to war: "A policy which only aims at containing Russia where it now is, is in itself, an unsound policy." But, Dulles continued, liberation "can be done and must be done in ways which will not provoke a general war . . . in ways which will be . . . a peaceful process . . . by moral pressures, by the weight of propaganda."[101] The new sound that America would use to dismantle the Soviet empire would be the sound of freedom, upon which "America had stood as a Christian nation and for which the Church of Christ [stood]."[102] In practice, to adopt the image used by one of Dulles' biographers, liberation would be no more warlike than Joshua's march around the walls of Jericho.[103]

Never had the illusion of American omnipotence received a better tribute than through the assertion that a mere declaration of principles would suffice to bring down the communist empire. Under American leadership, political task forces were to be formed. These forces would then develop freedom programs for each one of the captive nations. Such programs would rely not on military power, not even on economic power, but on the intangibles of power, moral judgment, and world opinion. Yet, could these be sufficient if they were not substantiated by military force if and when needed? And would America be willing to provide such force as might be needed?

An early answer to these questions was provided during an uprising in East Germany in June 1953. Angered by an increase in work norms (which was the equivalent of a cut in wages), East Germans staged mass demonstrations, first in East Berlin, then in most other German cities and in part of the countryside. These were dispersed only after as many as three Soviet divisions were called in by the government of communist leader Walter Ulbricht. These riots appeared to confirm Dulles' belief in the internal erosion of the Soviet empire by the indomitable call for freedom. Yet they also showed that such calls against Soviet troops could not be answered by psychological warfare experts only. In June 1953, there was no reaction from Washington because there could be none. The requirements of power were such that American intervention in Eastern Europe could not be seriously considered unless the United States was willing to wage war with the Soviet Union, which it was not. In practice, liberation meant either war or futility. In 1953, as later in 1956, liberation was implemented via a note of protest and an offer of free food.

Following the East German uprising, the evidence is strong that Dulles became aware of the limits of his own Eastern European pronouncements.[104] But, a prisoner of his own rhetoric, the American secretary of state could not discard his earlier commitments; and he continued to voice his support for a liberated Eastern Europe. A necessarily demilitarized objective within an unavoidable arena of power politics, liberation thus found its logical end when it was tested again in Hungary in late October 1956.

It will never be clear how much American policy led the Hungarians into believing that they would receive American military assistance if they rose against Soviet domination.[105] Most probably, the Hungarian revolution was the product of domestic forces, and its tragic outcome resulted partly from the miscalculations of a Hungarian leadership that misjudged the permissible pace and scope of destalinization. Nevertheless, American pledges of support and exhortations to fight were hardly conducive to more prudence from the Nagy government. But in Hungary, as earlier in East Germany—and later in Czechoslovakia and Poland—there was no American assistance because there could be none. The Atlantic Alliance was in complete disarray in the midst of Washington's bitter opposition to the Anglo–French intervention in Suez. America was in the midst of a presidential campaign, and Dulles' paramount objective was to keep both crises under control, at least until after the elections. In early September, reviewing the then explosive situation in the Middle East, Dulles candidly acknowledged that his main concern was to gain time: "Every day that goes by without some outbreak," said Dulles, "is a gain, and I just keep trying to buy that day. I don't know anything to do but to keep improvising.[106] By October 1956, Dulles himself had begun his bout with cancer, and he followed much of the Hungarian revolution from his hospital bed. Said Robert Murphy, then a high official in the State Department, Dulles

"like everybody else in the department, was terribly distressed."
Yet, no one, "had whatever imagination it took to discover
another solution. We were just boxed."[107] "The . . . trouble,"
others added, "is that we don't have a policy in this crisis, and
you can't try to use a speech as a substitute."[108]

Dulles' second major pronouncement concerned "brinkmanship." In the secretary's words. "You have to take chances
for peace, just as you must take chances in war. The ability to
get to the verge without getting into the war is the necessary
art. If you cannot master it, you inevitably get into war. If you
try to run away from it, if you are scared to go to the brink, you
are lost."[109]

Dulles' pronouncement coincided well with his personal
philosophy. A pessimist in his general understanding of international relations, the secretary of state was fond of observing that
wars had occurred on the average three times every five years
since 1480. The introductory sentence of one of his major pieces
of writing stated: "War is probable . . . not inevitable . . . not
imminent."[110] The probability of war was particularly high in
an international environment disrupted by the forces of atheistic communism. A relaxation of tension was therefore not
necessarily a good thing. "We dare not relax because the
moment of relaxation is the moment of peril."[111] It was the
moment of peril because, in Dulles' view, it would be succeeded
by a renewed threat of war against which the nation always had
to be prepared. In *War, Peace and Change* he had written: "The
creation of a vast armament in itself calls for a condition
between war and peace. Mass emotion on a substantial scale is a
prerequisite. The willingness to sacrifice must be engendered. A
sense of peril from abroad must be cultivated."[112] From Dulles'
viewpoint, maintaining international tension was the only way
through which essentially satisfied and nonmilitaristic nations
could be induced to reverse their natural predilection for
consumer goods over defense expenditures aimed at keeping
America ahead of the power competition. Without some evident
menace from the Soviet bloc, America's will to maintain its
unity and strength might weaken, so Dulles continued to couple
his announcements of an imminence of Soviet collapse with an
exaggerated estimate of their military capabilities.[113]

In practice, brinkmanship consisted of making one's views and politics so ambiguously open to the most extreme assumptions that the enemy would be deterred from taking any action at all. In May 1953, America went to the brink of "a bigger war" when it hinted in New Delhi about its plan to carry the Korean War across the Yalu River into Manchuria.[114] In April 1954, the same strategy was used to aid the French in Dien Bien Phu and to raise more fears in the communist camp over what U.S. reaction might be, should the forthcoming negotiations in Geneva fail to bring a satisfactory truce in Indochina.[115] In January 1955, and again in the fall of 1958, Dulles attempted to deter Peking from attacking the off-shore islands of Quemoy and Matsu by brandishing the possibility of committing American forces to their defense.[116] To this effect, the White House secured passage by the senate of the so-called Formosa Resolution, whereby the president was empowered "to include the securing and protecting of such related positions and territories of that area now in friendly hands and the taking of such other measures as he judges to be required or appropriate in ensuring the defense of Formosa and the Pescadores."

In all of these instances, American diplomacy waved the big stick even if it did not mean to use it. There were rumors of an impending use of nuclear weapons against China in 1953; conventional, even perhaps nuclear, forces were gathered for use in Indochina in 1954; a personal commitment of the American president to Chiang was allegedly made in 1955; units of the Seventh Fleet convoyed nationalist ships supplying Quemoy and Matsu in 1958.[117] In all these instances, too, war was either avoided or ended, and "satisfactory" outcomes were achieved: in Korea, where a truce was signed in July 1953, after two full years of negotiations; in Indochina, where Vietnam was divided on the 17th parallel, one degree south of the French initial request and three degrees north of Ho Chin Minh's first demand; and in the Taiwan Straits, where the communist Chinese were kept at bay. Thus one might possibly argue, as Robert Goold Adams does in his biography of Dulles, that "it was no bad thing for the people in the Kremlin to have that nasty ultimate doubt at the backs of their minds, that some idiot in Washington might not after all loose off an atomic bomb, if Russia went too far."[118] But in pursuing this juggling act of brinkmanship, Dulles also had to conceal the full truth from America's allies, who became the most consistent critics of America's and Dulles' apparent intransigence.

The military policy of the Eisenhower administration was shaped around the so-called doctrine of massive retaliation. Dulles reasoned that nations on the Soviet and Chinese periphery only required indigenous military forces able to hold off external attack long enough to expose aggression and prevent a fait accompli. But once aggression had been exposed, America could use its strategic forces "to retaliate, instantly, by means and at places of [its] own choosing." This capability in turn was expected to restrain Soviet adventurism.[119] In other words, America would rely on its growing strategic power to deter communist aggression, but the forward positions would be sustained by the forward countries themselves. America's participation in local and limited defense operations would be confined essentially to air and sea power, to which might be added small but highly mobile and efficient grounds units.

Such a strategy relied heavily on Dulles' favorite objective: to keep a potential enemy guessing about the action that the United States might take in a given circumstance. But in explaining his strategy, Dulles suffered from the image he had built for himself when endorsing such other policies as "liberation" or "brinkmanship." Massive retaliation gave the impression that America looked upon the possibility of war, even nuclear war, with equanimity. Yet, plainly the Eisenhower administration did not condone the overwhelming use of nuclear weapons in any situation against any adversary at any time. Massive retaliation, Dulles wrote in early 1954, "does not mean turning every local war into a world war. It does not mean that if there is a communist attack somewhere in Asia, atom or hydrogen bombs will necessarily be dropped on the great industries of China or Russia."[120] Massive retaliation only stressed the extreme strategic option open to America in its selection of retaliatory tools, an option that would be neither "necessarily" selected nor "necessarily" ruled out. Retaliation would still be launched on a selective basis. But the important thing, as Dulles saw it, was that the would-be aggressor would now know in advance that he was exposing far more than only those forces that he chose to use for his aggression. Thus aware that he would lose something more than he could win, the aggressor would be deterred.[121]

In effect, massive retaliation attempted to answer a wish for a total solution that suited well the historical mood of the American people, particularly during Asian crises in Korea, Indochina, and Taiwan.[122] It was also a possible answer to the Republican approach to the economics of national strategy. As a result of the Korean War, defense expenditures had grown from $14.3 billion and 5% of the gross national product in 1950, to $49.3 billion and 13.5% of the gross national product in 1953. Anxious to reduce such excessive defense budgets, the Republican administration reasoned that greater reliance upon nuclear weapons would reduce the burden of developing more conventional armaments and maintaining ever larger ground forces in innumerable bases abroad.

In a limited sense, massive retaliation was a negative weapon that did little more than pursue the search for an effective policy of containment without tears by paralyzing the other side with fear. Yet, understood as if it meant what it said, massive retaliation stirred many misgivings and fears among the allies. They wanted to know the meaning of such words as "instantly," "means" and "ours" in Dulles' warning of a retaliation launched "instantly with means of our choosing." More specifically, they wanted to know what would actually happen if the threat failed, that is, if the Soviets refused to be intimidated by it. Was a middle way left between inaction and nuclear holocaust? Which weapons would be used in reprisal, where, and when? Would nuclear weapons have been used in order to meet the communist threat in Greece and in Turkey? Whose basic decision would it be to use such weapons? What would be the level of intra-allied cooperation in implementing a decision that might sanction the annihilation of those nations in 'the defense of which massive retaliation was being exerted in the first place?

The Irony of Power

Throughout the 1950s, numerous other efforts were made to stimulate the perception of a "New Look" in U.S. foreign policy. Yet, for all of these efforts, little was drastically new in

American policy. In truth, the foreign policy of the Eisenhower administration began in June 1950 under the Truman administration. "A free society," Dean Acheson, too, had observed in 1951, "can call upon profound resources among the people in behalf of a righteous cause,"[123] and he had unequivocally pledged: "We can see no moral compromise with the contrary thesis of international communism."[124] Brinkmanship had also been used several times by the Truman administration,[125] and even the threat of massive retaliation could be regarded as a new name for an old policy: in case of open aggression by enemy armies, nations always attempted "to strike back where it hurts, by means of [their] own choosing." But that choice had also been traditionally limited by circumstances—as it had been in Korea. In his inimitable style, Eisenhower himself discarded the notion that massive retaliation was a revolutionary strategy. "To call it revolutionary," the president stated in one of his news conferences, "or to act like it is something that just suddenly dropped down on us like a cloud from heaven is just not true."[126] As to such other pronouncements as the "unleashing" of Chiang's forces, these, too, hinted at an option that had been considered during the previous Democratic administration when Chiang's harassment of China's mainland had been approved no less actively than it would be during the Republican administration. Having publicly unleashed Chiang Kai-shek (as the newspapers put it, although the Eisenhower administration never used the phrase), the administration secretly exacted a pledge from Chiang not to engage in any offensive action without prior American consent.

In short, Dulles' policies were essentially old policies presented within a theological package that was consistent with America's philosophy of international relations. Although Dulles hardly initiated any lasting policy, his rhetoric caused serious doubts among America's allies about U.S. objectives and policies. Within one week of his inauguration, America had warned Western Europe with "a little rethinking of [its] . . . policy in relation to Western Europe." But with time, Western Europe's policies also undertook "a little rethinking." Dulles' interventions on behalf of Chancellor Konrad Adenauer and against Prime Ministers Anthony Eden and Pierre Mendès-France raised furor in Germany, Great Britain, and France, respectively. After the Suez crisis, the threat of being left alone played no small part in convincing France to accelerate the development of its own nuclear force.

To be sure, the Dulles policies prevented any further communist expansion without any direct U.S. participation in a war. Yet, many of the problems awaiting America in the 1960s had their most serious roots in the missed opportunities in the 1950s: the overall rejection of Moscow's peace initiative of 1953–55, the persistent refusal to deal with China after Korea, the stubborn rejection of nonalignment as "an immoral and shortsighted conception," the refusal to hold free elections in Vietnam, the ambivalent Middle East policy over Suez and Lebanon, and the clumsy handling of European allies, to cite but a few.

One year after the Hungarian revolution, Dulles warned against an American illusion of omnipotence: "We are not omnipotent. . . . Our power and policy are but a significant factor in the world . . . in combination with other factors we are able to influence importantly the course of events. But we cannot deal in absolutes."[127] Yet, in January 1961, the illusion was at its peak, and the problems associated with it were lacking easy solutions.

NOTES

1. Tang Tsou, *America's Failure in China, 1941–1950* (Chicago: Phoenix Books, 1963), p. 361.
2. From Acheson's remarks to the National Press Club, January 12, 1950. Department of State *Bulletin*, Vol. XXII, p. 118 (hereafter cited as *Bulletin*).
3. Truman, *Memoirs*, Vol. 2, *Years of Trial and Hope, 1946–1952* (Garden City, N.Y.: Doubleday, 1956), p. 61.
4. See Acheson's statements before the Senate Subcommittees on Armed Services and Foreign Relations. U.S. Senate, *Hearings on the Military Situation in the Far East*, 82nd Congress, 1st Session (June 4, 1951), pp. 1838–57.
5. *The China White Paper*, August 1949 (Stanford: Stanford University Press, 1967), p. 311. Originally issued as *United States Relations with China*, Department of State Publication, 1949.
6. Ibid., p. 315.

7. As a Chinese communist official declared in November 1946: "It's all right for the United States to arm the Kuomintang because as fast as they get it we take it away from them." Quoted in John Melby, *Mandate of Heaven: Record of a Civil War, China 1945–1949* (Toronto: Toronto University Press, 1968), p. 36.

8. U.S. Senate, *Military Situation in Far East*, pp. 1838–57.

9. Truman, *Memoirs*, Vol. 1, *Year of Decisions* (Garden City, N.Y.: Doubleday, 1955), pp. 507–9. Tang Tsou, *America's Failure in China*, pp. 365–66.

10. On September 13, 1943, for example, in addressing the Kuomintang Central Executive Committee, Chiang said: "We should clearly recognize that the Chinese communist problem is a purely political problem and should be solved by political means." *China White Paper*, p. 530.

11. Quoted in Acheson in U.S. Senate, *Military Situation in Far East*, 1838–57.

12. Ibid.

13. From Ambassador Stuart's report to Secretary Marshall, August 10, 1948. *China White Paper*, pp. 885–86.

14. Truman, *Memoirs*, Vol. 2, pp. 67–68.

15. Tang Tsou, *America's Failure in China*, pp. 356–57.

16. Henry Kissinger, *White House Years* (Boston Mass.: Little, Brown, 1981), p. 1032.

17. *China White Paper*, p. xvi.

18. From Acheson's remarks to the National Press Club, January 12, 1950. *Bulletin,* Vol. XXII, p. 115.

19. Truman, *Memoirs*, Vol. 1, pp. 521–22.

20. Ibid., p. 445. Russian forces reached Korea on August 12, while Americans forces only landed in Korea by September 8.

21. John W. Spanier, *The Truman–MacArthur Controversy and the Korean War* (Cambridge, Mass.: Harvard University Press, 1959, Norton Library Edition, 1965), p. 16.

22. Joseph C. Goulden, *Korea, The Untold Story of the War* (New York: New York Times Books, 1982), p. 25.

23. Acheson, *Present at the Creation* (New York: W. W. Norton, 1969), p. 405.

24. See, for example, Marshall's testimony of May 7, 1951. U.S. Senate, *Military Situation in the Far East*, p. 373.

25. On China's motivation in entering the Korean War, see Allen S. Whiting, *China Crosses the Yalu* (New York: Macmillan, 1960).

26. On the earlier phase of the Sino–Soviet split, see Conrad Brandt, *Stalin's Failure in China, 1926–1927* (Cambridge, Mass.: Harvard University Press, 1958).

27. Tang Tsou, *America's Failure in China,* p. 572. See also David Rees, *Korea: The Limited War* (Baltimore, Md: Penguin Books, 1970), p.107.
28. According, for example, to Allen S. Whiting, *China Crosses Yalu,* p. 124.
29. U.S. Senate, *Military Situation in the Far East,* p. 75.
30. Truman, *Memoirs,* Vol. 2, p. 329.
31. Quoted in Goulden, *Korea,* p. vii.
32. Joyce and Gabriel Kolko, *The Limits of Power: The World and United States Foreign Policy, 1945–1954* (New York: Harper & Row, 1972), pp. 578–85.
33. Quoted in Goulden, *Korea,* p. 75.
34. Kolko, *Limits of Power,* pp. 578 and 582.
35. Goulden, *Korea,* p. 83.
36. George F. Kennan, *Memoirs, 1925–1950* (Boston: Little, Brown, 1967), p. 238.
37. Robert R. Simmons, *The Strained Alliance. Peking, P'yongyang, Moscow and the Politics of the Korean Civil War* (New York: Free Press, 1975), pp. 104 ff.
38. Truman, *Memoirs,* Vol. 2, p. 333.
39. Ibid., Vol. 1, p. 289.
40. Rees, *Korea,* pp. 32–33.
41. U.S. Senate, *Military Situation in the Far East,* p. 10.
42. From his statement to the Senate Committees on Armed Services and Foreign Relations, February 16, 1951. Cited in *The Pattern of Responsibility,* ed. McGeorge Bundy (Boston: Houghton Mifflin, 1951) p. 93.
43. For an early analysis of the U.S. reaction to the outbreak of the Korean War, see Alexander C. George, "American Policy Making and the North Korean Aggression," *World Politics,* January 1955, pp. 209–32.
44. See Whiting, *China Crosses Yalu,* pp. 37–38.
45. Quoted in Tang Tsou, *America's Failure in China,* pp. 557–58.
46. From Acheson's address to the General Assembly of the United Nations, September 20, 1950. *Bulletin,* Vol. XXIII, p. 524.
47. Truman, *Memoirs,* Vol. 2, p. 341.
48. In a television interview on September 10, 1950. *Bulletin,* Vol. XXIII, p. 463.
49. U.S. Senate, *Military Situation in the Far East,* p. 397.
50. See Bernard Brodie's comments on this "odd idea" in *Strategy in the Missile Age* (Princeton, N.J.: Princeton University Press, 1959), p. 319.
51. Spanier, *Truman–McArthur Controversy,* p. 28.

52. Quoted in Tang Tsou, *America's Failure in China*, p. 576. See also Rees, *Korea*, pp. 106–7.
53. As indicated by Secretary of Defense Marshall. U.S. Senate, *Military Situation in the Far East*, p. 359. See also Truman, *Memoirs*, Vol. 2, pp. 380–82.
54. Truman, *Memoirs*, Vol. 1, pp. 342–43.
55. In addition to Spanier, *Truman–McArthur Controversy*, see Arthur M. Schlesinger Jr. and Richard Rovere, *The General and the President* (New York: Farrar, Straus and Giroux, 1951).
56. Truman, *Memoirs*, Vol. 1, p. 210.
57. MacArthur's speech may be found in U.S. Senate, *Military Situation in the Far East*, pp. 2553–58.
58. Ibid., p. 207.
59. Ibid., p. 68.
60. Ibid., p. 1720.
61. Ibid., pp. 6, 130.
62. Ibid., p. 9.
63. Ibid., pp. 103 and 29, respectively.
64. Ibid., p. 490.
65. Ibid., p. 732 (from General Bradley's testimony).
66. Ibid., p. 42.
67. Truman, *Memoirs*, Vol. 2, p. 444.
68. Ibid., Vol. 2, p. 449.
69. U.S. Senate, *Military Situation in the Far East*, p. 13.
70. Ibid., p. 370 (from Marshall's testimony). For MacArthur's comments see his own *Reminiscences* (New York: McGraw-Hill, 1964), p. 377.
71. As reported by Truman, *Memoirs*, Vol. 2, p. 353.
72. U.S. Senate, *Military Situation in the Far East*, p. 100.
73. From remarks made on two occasions in February 1950. Cited in Bundy, *Pattern of Responsibility*, p. 30.
74. U.S. Senate, *Military Situation in the Far East*, p. 263.
75. State Department, *American Foreign Policy, 1950–1955: Basic Documents*, Vol. 1 (General Foreign Policy Series 117), p. 911.
76. Quoted in Norman Podhoretz, *Why We Were in Vietnam* (New York: Simon & Schuster, 1982), p. 37.
77. Quoted in John Beale, *John Foster Dulles: 1889–1959* (New York: Harper & Row, 1959), p. 310. See also Hans J. Morgenthau, "John Foster Dulles," in *An Uncertain Tradition: American Secretaries of State in the Twentieth Century*, ed. Norman A. Graebner (New York: McGraw-Hill, 1961), p. 305.
78. Quoted in Ole Holsti et al., *Enemies in Politics* (Chicago: Rand McNally, 1967), p. 40.

79. Quoted in Michael A. Guhin, "Dulles' Thoughts on International Politics: Myth and Reality," *Orbis* (Fall 1969), pp. 865–90.
80. Dulles, "Security in the Pacific," *Foreign Affairs* (January 1952), p. 183.
81. Dulles, *War, Peace and Change* (London: Macmillan, 1939), p. 47.
82. Quoted by Emmet John Hughes, *The Ordeal of Power: A Political Memoir of the Eisenhower Years* (London: McMillan, 1963), pp. 208–9.
83. Address of October 15, 1956. *The New York Times,* October 15, 1956.
84. Dulles, *War, Peace and Change,* pp. 266–67.
85. Speech made in New York, January 25, 1954. *Bulletin,* Vol. XXX, p. 110.
86. David Heller and Deane Heller, *John Foster Dulles: Soldier of Peace* (New York: Holt, Rinehart & Winston, 1960), p. 41.
87. In a broadcast made in Great Britain, October 23, 1958. *Bulletin,* Vol. XXXIX, p. 734.
88. Hughes, *Ordeal of Power,* p. 109.
89. Ibid., p. 137.
90. News Conference, May 15, 1956. *Bulletin,* Vol. XXIV, p. 885.
91. Quoted in Hughes, *Ordeal of Power,* pp. 104–5.
92. Reported by Robert Goold-Adams, *John Foster Dulles: A Reappraisal* (New York: Appleton-Century-Crofts, 1962), p. 293.
93. Senate Committee on Foreign Relations, *Hearings* (February 24, 1956), p. 19. Quoted in Holsti, *Enemies in Politics,* p. 65.
94. Quoted in ibid., pp. 66–67.
95. Guhin, *Dulles' Thoughts,* p. 888.
96. Goold-Adams, *John Foster Dulles,* p. 305.
97. Quoted in Acheson, *Present at Creation,* p. 365.
98. Louis L. Gerson, *The American Secretaries of State and their Diplomacy: John Foster Dulles* (New York: Cooper Square Publishers, 1967), p. 111.
99. Richard P. Stebbins, ed., *The U.S. in World Affairs, 1953* (New York: Harper & Row, 1955), pp. 18–22.
100. See Dulles' article in *Life,* May 19, 1952.
101. Stebbins, *U.S. in World Affairs,* pp. 16–17.
102. Quoted in Coral Bell, *Negotiations from Strength: A Study in the Politics of Power* (Cambridge, Mass.: Harvard University Press, 1964), p. 89.
103. Beale, *John Foster Dulles,* p. 313.
104. Roscoe Drummond and Gaston Coblentz, *Duel at the Brink: John Foster Dulles' Command of American Power* (Garden City, N.Y.: Doubleday, 1960), p. 88.

105. See, for example, Paul Kecskemeti, *The Unexpected Revolution* (Stanford: Stanford University Press, 1961), and Raymond L. Garthoff, *Soviet Military Policy: A Historical Analysis* (New York: Praeger, 1966), pp. 155–72.
106. Hughes, *Ordeal of Power*, p. 178.
107. Robert Murphy, *Diplomat among Warriors* (London: Collins, 1964), p. 526.
108. Hughes, *Ordeal of Power*, p. 217.
109. James Shepley, "How Dulles Averted War," *Life* (January 16, 1956).
110. Dulles, *War, Peace and Change*, p. 317.
111. Quoted in Beale, *John Foster Dulles*, p. 317.
112. Dulles, *War, Peace and Change*, p. 90.
113. Andrew Berding, *Dulles on Diplomacy* (Princeton, N.J.: Van Nostrand, 1965), p. 23.
114. Goold-Adams, *John Foster Dulles*, pp. 74, 102.
115. See Chapter 6.
116. Tang Tsou, *The Embroilment over Quemoy: Mao, Chiang and Dulles* (Salt Lake City, Utah: University of Utah, Institute of International Studies, International Study Paper No. 2, 1959).
117. Goold-Adams, *John Foster Dulles*, passim; Beale, *John Foster Dulles*, p. 207.
118. Goold-Adams, *John Foster Dulles*, p. 200.
119. See Dulles' address, "The Evolution of Foreign Policy," *Bulletin*, Vol. XXX, pp. 107–10.
120. Dulles, "Policy for Security and Peace," *Foreign Affairs* (April 1954), p. 359.
121. See William W. Kaufmann, *Military Policy and National Security* (Princeton, N.J.: Princeton University Press, 1956), pp. 12–38.
122. Brodie, *Strategy in the Missile Age*, pp. 223 ff.
123. From Acheson's statement to the Senate on the relief of General MacArthur, *Military Situation in Far East*, p. 1720.
124. Address at the University of California, Berkeley, March 16, 1950. *Bulletin*, XXXIII, p. 474.
125. See James L. Payne, *The American Threat: The Fear of War as an Instrument of Foreign Policy* (Chicago: Markham Publishing, 1970), pp. 22 ff.
126. Quoted in Goold-Adams, *John Foster Dulles*, p. 122.
127. Dulles, "Challenge and Response in United States Policy," *Foreign Affairs* (October, 1957), pp. 25–26.

CHAPTER FIVE

Enduring Balance and Troubled Alliance

Discord and Collaboration

A traditional view of the Atlantic Alliance is to present it as a harmonious relationship that resulted from the willingness and ability of the powerful, rich, vibrant, and altruistic New World to come to the aid of its European family with which it shared an ethos called "Western civilization." According to this view, the genius of the early generation of Atlantic leaders was to understand the common interests that bind the states of Europe and the United States together, and to develop structures within which occasional differences would be easily overcome. However valid it may be, such a reading of the past remains incomplete. In fact, over the years the history of the Atlantic Alliance has been a history of collaboration and consultation, to be sure, but it has also been a history of discord and unilateral decisions.[1]

In a general sense, such discord resulted from Europe's inability to accept the idea, let alone the fact, of United States leadership. Predictably, from President Truman (as we have seen) to President Reagan (as shall be seen), each U.S. administration has faced an Atlantic crisis of its own: over the rearmament of Germany and the management of the Soviet threat; Suez and the preservation of European interests in the Third World; NATO and the credibility of the Western deterrent; the stability of the dollar and its impact on the European economies; OPEC and the issue of energy supply; economic sanctions against the East and rearmament in the West. Repeatedly, the states of Western Europe feared collision during periods of brinkmanship and collusion during periods of detente; they saw the evidence of U.S. unpredictability during periods of interventionism and assertiveness, as well as during periods of abstentionism and decline. All the issues that have divided the Atlantic allies—political, economic/monetary, and strategic; within the West, with regard to the East and to the South—have erupted with such regularity as to give them all an air of *déjà vu* that dampens one's interest while arousing a measure of impatience if not irritation. Yet in the 1950s and going into the 1960s, the leadership provided by the United States benefited from several assets that helped surmount early crises and made of the Atlantic Alliance America's most successful postwar foreign policy.

Such assets first included the availability and preponderance of American power. At times, of course, there was serious concern in Europe over the form, place, and timing of its use. There was also some resentment over the ascendancy of an extra-European state to a status once reserved for European states only. But with its immediate historical memories shaped by the fear of political extremism, the consequences of appeasement, and the indispensibility of U.S. power for the preservation of an enduring balance in Europe, the noncommunist leadership on the continent sought American assistance to find physical security and achieve economic recovery within a stable political environment. The successful Soviet atomic tests of 1949 and 1953 notwithstanding, few in Europe expected to see the superiority of American power ever challenged by a Russian state traditionally seen as intellectually backward and institutionally inefficient. In this context, the Korean War was a turning point, as it showed both the Soviet predilection for military aggression *and* the U.S. will and capability for containment in an international system that was admittedly dominated by the East–West conflict. At first focused on the international threat raised by communist parties closely tied to Moscow and on the fear of an eventual military resurgence of Germany, Europe's preoccupations with security issues now turned sharply to the Soviet Union.

Related to this surplus of American power was Europe's image of the United States: an assertive country, domineering and sure of itself, eminently successful. To be sure, a rampant anti-Americanism could also be seen everywhere in Europe's facile characterizations and arrogant intellectual rejections of its senior partner.* Yet, this was anti-Americanism-but: in the years that followed the war, those Europeans who could afford it often came to the United States as if they were going to the moon—an overwhelming country of skyscrapers where bathrooms came in pairs, as did cars and television sets, where affluence prevailed for all, democracy won, and success was around the corner. Whatever their rhetoric, a large majority of Europeans still looked upon the United States as a model that was setting a whole range of standards that deserved emulation and aroused envy.

In contrast with this vision of an omnipotent America was the evidence of a weak, divided, and unstable Europe. While initial efforts to build a united Europe seemed to meet with some impressive results in the late 1940s (especially with the institution of the European Steel and Coal Community), the 1950s remained a decade of actual or projected setbacks: the rejection of the European Defense Community in 1954 and the expected collapse of the Rome treaty whose demise the Gaullists, about to return to power in France, were promising from the very moment it was translated into the European Economic Community in 1958. In Italy, after the 1953 election, the Christian Democrats were already beginning their long descent

---

*"It was impossible to live in England or visit any European country," remembered Norman Podhoretz from his first visit there in the early 1950s, "without being forced into a constant awareness of oneself as an American. . . . For protest as we all might, the whole world insisted on regarding us quite simply and unarguably as Americans. . . . The sheer vulgarity of the anti-Americanism one came upon everywhere in Europe pushed many of us into the unaccustomed role of patriotic defenders. . . . No, not all artists were condemned to starvation in America; yes, Americans did care for other things besides money; . . . yes, Alger Hiss had been a communist; yes, civil liberties still existed in America despite McCarthy; no, the country was not going fascist" (*Making It* [New York, 1967], pp. 84–87).

from power, and the first "opening to the left" was soon to be tested in the aftermath of the 1956 Soviet invasion of Hungary. France, then the sick man of Europe, was less governable than ever following the election in 1956 of a deadlocked National Assembly, which, together with the war in Algeria, ensured a swift but painful end to the Fourth Republic two years later. And in 1956, the Suez crisis vividly exposed the impotence of two of the former great powers of Europe when reduced to themselves. Everywhere, the empires were coming home, with only tiny Portugal doggedly able to postpone the inevitable.

Europe's dependencies on the United States were varied, and the Europeans behaved essentially as security consumers. Repeatedly, they stressed their military impotence by pointing to their economic limitations, their political frailty, Soviet conventional capabilities, U.S. strategic superiority, or the horrors of nuclear war. Even isolated national efforts to produce security by waging a colonial war or by developing an autonomous nuclear deterrent were launched and pursued in such a way as to integrate the war within the framework of the East–West conflict or permit the coupling of such a deterrent with the American deterrent.

Accordingly, although persistently questioned, the credibility of the U.S. commitment never declined to the point of incredibility, either from the standpoint of the allies or from that of the Soviet Union. In numerous instances, it provided successive administrations in Washington with much leverage in other (monetary, economic, and political) areas as issues were linked to force the allies into an acceptance or rejection of U.S. leadership *in toto.* Such explicit linkage of general politico–economic issues to military issues could already be seen during the years that preceded the formation of the Atlantic Alliance, when a high and effective measure of dollar diplomacy was used by the Truman administration to ensure Europe's endorsement of its policies on the continent. It could also be seen later in the 1950s, when the U.S. request for a rearmament of Germany was tied to the continuation of U.S. economic assistance and trade privileges; and in the 1960s, in a reverse fashion, when the negotiations of the Kennedy Round (1963–67) were very much affected by Washington's interests in areas other than trade, while the maintenance of U.S. troops in West Germany was linked, during the second half of that decade, to the continued willingness of the government in Bonn to accumulate dollars and accept offset payments.

Throughout, an intrinsic feature of the U.S. leadership package in Europe remained its economic and monetary dimension. Thus, the Atlantic Alliance originated as a subsidiary to the key economic concerns that were the focus of the evolving Atlantic relations after World War II. As we have seen, following an early underestimation of the destruction of the European economies by the war, the policymakers in Washington concluded that recovery could be achieved only to the extent that the United States was willing, as recommended by Assistant Secretary of State for Economic Affairs Will Clayton, "to run the show."[2] A consequence of international circumstances as well as a matter of choice, the postwar monetary system soon became a hegemonial system that left the United States with apparently unlimited freedom of monetary action in return for making available the liquidity needed by the European states for an instant economic recovery. Once recovery had been launched, a long phase of European growth began and was stimulated by the semiprotectionist clauses of the Rome Treaty in 1957. The European Economic Community (EEC) permitted substantial trade expansion from within the Community, primarily to the benefit of German industry and French agriculture, but also to the general gain of all member states. But by exposing European companies to the advantage of an economy of scale within an expanded market, the EEC also improved Europe's competitiveness vis-à-vis other industrial states, now hampered by the higher external tariffs surrounding the EEC.[*]

---

[*]Initially, the EEC's common tariff was averaged arithmetically, without consideration of the value of goods imported in each case. Thus, the low-tariff countries (the Benelux, regarded as one single unit, and West Germany) counted for as much as two high-tariff countries (France and Italy), even though they represented about two-thirds of the Community's imports. In addition, such calculations did not take into account some earlier tariff reductions in Germany and in Italy and, in a number of instances, pushed up the arithmetic average no matter how calculated. This conveniently placed the EEC in a stronger position to bargain with any state seeking to negotiate mutual tariff reductions, as would be seen subsequently.

That the consequences for the United States of such measures would have been tolerated at a time when the dollar was beginning to show distinct signs of wear and tear was due to three considerations. First and foremost, in this cold-war era it was reasoned that the political and strategic gains that would result from a unification of Europe would outweigh any loss or disadvantage that might accrue to the U.S. economy. Second, these losses were in any case likely to be minimal, it was then argued, because of the marginal importance of foreign trade to the U.S. economy (about 7% of the Gross National Product in 1960, as compared to approximately 40% for the countries then in the Common Market), because of the overwhelming U.S. competitiveness in a number of vital trade sectors, and because of the ability of U.S. capital to bypass tariff restrictions through massive direct investments into the Community. Consequently, third, whatever small trade diversion there might be, it was thought, would be compensated for, from the standpoint of U.S. economic interests, by the large amount of trade creation that would follow the emergence of Europe as one thriving trade unit.

Accordingly, the resulting American strategy of the 1960s assumed that a fresh infusion of economic interdependence would strengthen the political and strategic bonds that were required to contain Soviet expansion in Europe and elsewhere. Increasing U.S. trade surpluses would balance the capital outflows generated by military expenditures and rapidly growing direct investments in Europe and thus alleviate an ever larger balance of payments deficit, already seen by President Kennedy as a threat second only to the threat of nuclear war.[3] Linkages between the costs and rewards of U.S. Atlantic leadership were made all too obvious: committed to a trading partnership with the United States, an integrated Western Europe would further shift the global balance of power to the side of freedom. European unity continued to be seen as the logical extension of the postwar Atlantic bargain, and the temporary consequences of high external tariffs (which the Dillon Round of negotiations tried to dismantle even before they were actually applied) were discounted as secondary to the benefits that would accrue to the West if the nations of Europe, including Great Britain, were to form a political unit based on the American model of federalism and supranational institutions.

For most Europeans, however, a continuing relationship based on American primacy and European dependence was tolerated by default only, and with considerable reservations. In France and in Great Britain—and increasingly in West Germany as well—what was feared from the U.S. leadership was a volatile mixture that included a presumed virginity in world affairs, an obsession with military superiority, a cultural influence seen as a threat to Europe's intellectual heritage, and a series of ulterior motives that were specifically directed against Europe's colonial possessions. "If we only pushed on and developed Africa," contended Britain's Foreign Secretary Ernest Bevin in 1948, "we could have the U.S. dependent on us, and eating out of our hands in four or five years."[4] And in the meantime Churchill deplored: "Poor England. They have become so big and we so small."[5]

That such reluctance (most forcefully and most persistently articulated in France) was nevertheless overcome resulted from Europe's obvious lack of alternatives: only in the United States could the policymakers in Europe find the necessary economic aid, the sizeable markets, and the protection required by growing tensions within the international system. In the end, such a necessity undoubtedly served Europe, and the United States, well. Relying as it did on a policy that mixed military instruments, economic tools, and cultural appeal for the masses, the United States contained the communist and procommunist forces in several countries where those forces were seen as a real threat to the continuity or resumption of democratic processes, helped build an anti-Soviet alliance that effectively denied the expansion of the Eastern bloc into Western Europe, facilitated the recovery of West Germany within an integrating Western Europe while postponing if not resolving the dangerous issue of German reunification, and satisfied U.S. economic interests through the availability of large outlets for excess capacity and excess capital. Similarly, from the standpoint of Europe, the Atlantic policy of the United States facilitated a quick recovery through the availability of U.S. monetary assistance, the opening of U.S. markets, and the preservation of low prices for raw materials coming from developing countries where a measure of U.S. influence promptly replaced European imperial control; but it also helped stabilize the political relationships of forces within Western Europe by making sustained economic growth the presumed solvent of social conflicts, eliminated or contained the threats of Germany's military revival and Soviet military expansion, and provided a ready-made rationale for the initial efforts at European integration.

Nevertheless, even during those years when the bargain worked best, European states continued to have doubts over the long-term credibility of U.S. leadership. As Chancellor Konrad Adenauer warned in 1956 before the Suez crisis, "Vital necessities for European states are not always . . . vital necessities for the United States, and vice-versa; there may result differences in political conceptions that may lead to independent political actions."[6] With American policymakers unwilling to recognize that there was a price to be paid for the very success of its contribution in making the recovery of Europe possible, such differences began to gain momentum and visibility in the 1960s.

Change and Security in Europe

Following the events of late 1956, Soviet foreign policy appeared to abandon the caution it had shown during Stalin's later years and the conciliatory tone it had adopted during Khrushchev's early years. Instead, rocket-rattling became one of Moscow's favored ploys, and it could be heard ominously over the landings in Lebanon and at the height of a crisis over the islands of Quemoy and Matsu. Yet, it is over Berlin that the theatricalities of the Soviet leader seemed to be most threatening. Having revealed indirectly that a serious cleavage existed between him and his Chinese allies and having lost ground in the Middle East, Khrushchev now returned to Europe to force a Western recognition of the East German government. Unless the reunification and demilitarization of Berlin was agreed upon within six months, he warned in November 1958, the Soviet half of the city would be turned over to East Germany and a treaty signed with its government (which in turn could have been counted upon to terminate quickly Western rights in Berlin). In practice, this six-month ultimatum was to last four years. During that period, East–West tensions reached the danger level, especially in the summer of 1961, when following President Kennedy's bitter meeting with his Soviet counterpart in Vienna, a world-wide alert of U.S. forces was ordered, and the sudden building of a wall in Berlin symbolized the reality and the dangers of East–West hostility.

In retrospect, it seems that Moscow was engaged at the time in a complex juggling act.[7] On the one hand, the Soviets wanted to reassert a policy of coexistence that would reduce the risks of nuclear war with the United States and increase diplomatic opportunities in a Western alliance in disarray since Suez. But simultaneously, their growing rift with Peking enhanced the Soviet inhibitions against a cooperation with the West that might have accelerated an open break with China. These two contradictory courses converged in Germany by way of the question of nuclear weapons.

Perhaps as a short-lived reward for the tactful support extended by the PRC the previous year, sometime in 1957 the Soviets had agreed to provide Peking with atomic know-how and a sample atomic bomb.[8] But Khrushchev feared that such an offer, if implemented, might be paralleled in the West by a similar U.S. offer to West Germany. Clearly, the availability of nuclear weapons to two historical adversaries would impair Soviet security all the more dangerously as Soviet nuclear capabilities remained themselves limited. For although unknown to the West at the time (the U.S. fear of a "missile gap" peaked during the presidential campaign of 1960), Khrushchev's boast of a rapidly expanding Soviet nuclear arsenal from 1957 to 1961 was but a bold exercise in stategic bluffing.[9] Accordingly, Moscow's promise to China was promptly withdrawn in 1959, and in 1961 Khrushchev asked for atom-free zones in Europe and the Far East.[10] By that time, however, it was already doubtful that the Soviet Union could control China's nuclear program and thus satisfy its part of a deal that would have attempted to exchange the continuous denuclearization of China for that of Germany. By that time too, responsible

U.S. officials had begun to recognize that no missile gap existed after all, and that the United States enjoyed substantial and significant strategic superiority.[11]

Detente between the two superpowers was sought in the aftermath of the Cuban missile crisis in October 1962, when the world leaped to the brink of disaster. Militarily, the primary Soviet object in deploying some 40 medium-range and intermediate-range ballistic missile launchers in Cuba was probably to bridge the strategic gap between Moscow and Washington. Short of ICBM's, the Soviet leadership was moving most of its existing short-range (1,100 to 2,200 mile) missiles closer to continental United States. Politically, the Soviet effort, if successful, would have represented an important victory over Peking, which was then in open confrontation with Moscow over the allegiance of worldwide communist parties and the sponsorship of wars of national liberation. Such a Soviet success was especially needed in view of the failure of Khrushchev's Berlin offensive. In fact, Soviet nuclear bases in Cuba might have been, as the Soviet premier saw it, the decisive factor in enforcing his 1958 ultimatum over Berlin. Finally, this short-cut to strategic equality would have been conveniently achieved at little expenditure for a Soviet economy hampered by lagging growth and pressured by increasing demands for more consumption goods.

Under circumstances of overwhelming U.S. strategic and theater dominance, the Soviet maneuver was intolerable to American security. That American bases were located at the periphery of the Soviet Union as well did not justify that the United States accept a similar situation in a spirit of fairness. In effect, the Cuban missile crisis provided a clear example of massive retaliation in action as President Kennedy warned Moscow of what would happen should these missiles be launched from Cuba: "It shall be the policy of this nation to regard any missile launched from Cuba against any nation in the Western Hemisphere as an attack by the Soviet Union on the United States, requiring a full retaliatory response upon the Soviet Union."[12]

It is not necessary here to go into the details of the 13-day crisis of October 1962.[13] With the Soviet missiles evacuated from Cuba, a mood of sober reflection appeared to provide

Soviet–American detente with some momentum. "Prudence, peace, and the world's security have won," stated the Soviet premier in December 1962.[14] President Kennedy found the analysis sufficiently plausible to launch a series of arrangements that included the signing of the test ban treaty, the establishment of a "hot line" that would facilitate direct communications between Moscow and Washington in times of crisis, and adherence to a United Nations resolution banning nuclear weapons from outer space. To Kennedy, it seemed that the problem of European security had now been solved. "The whole debate about an atomic force in Europe," he told Paul Henry Spaak of Belgium in 1963, "is really useless, because Berlin is secure and Europe as a whole is well protected. What really matters at this point is the rest of the world."[15] Relaxation of tensions between the two superpowers reflected an apparent acceptance of each other's preponderance within their respective spheres of influence, and though this influence would still be probed in Africa, the Middle East, or Southeast Asia, the lines now seemed to be well drawn in Europe. In September 1968, the Soviet invasion of Czechoslovakia all but confirmed again the Western acquiescence of the Soviet sphere in Eastern Europe, as hardly any serious call for American intervention was issued in the United States or abroad. Even President Johnson's belated guarantee of Yugoslavia's and Rumania's territorial integrity was sufficiently ambiguous to make its eventual fulfillment doubtful.[16] Instead, within a few months of the Soviet invasion, President Richard M. Nixon spoke in his 1969 Inaugural Address of the era of conciliation that had succeeded a now-defunct era of confrontation.[17]

Throughout the decade, however, America continued to reason that granted such a stalemate between the United States and the Soviet Union, and even assuming the Kremlin's willingness to discuss the rules that would cover this stalemate, it was more urgent than ever to preserve the cohesion of the Atlantic Alliance for the negotiations that were about to begin. The Kennedy and Johnson administrations held lingering doubts that detente was no more than Moscow's application of the old technique of dividing to conquer better. Obviously, discord within the Western Alliance would create opportunities that Soviet diplomacy might effectively exploit: to this extent, de Gaulle, who rapidly became the symbol of whatever opposition to U.S. policies there was from within the alliance, was Moscow's Trojan Horse.

Yet de Gaulle's opposition to U.S. leadership went far beyond a Washington–Paris rift alone. In 1949 and thereafter, earlier U.S.–European discord had stemmed from the problems of best defining and implementing Atlantic security: What was to be done, how, and why?[18] But now, in the aftermath of the Cuban missile crisis, American–European divisions were part of a conflict that took security at least partly for granted and centered on the means of best defining, promoting, and stabilizing negotiations between the West and the East: Who was going to do it, how, and why? Begun as a debate over ends and means (what was the function of the alliance and how was it going to be fulfilled?) the Atlantic debate spearheaded by de Gaulle had become one of identity (who was going to fulfill such a function and how?). As the 1960s unfolded, the Atlantic Alliance found itself endangered, in Stanely Hoffmann's words, "by the pursuit of the same objective by allies each of which [was] trying to control events [more] than by the pursuit of different objectives by allies that avoid[ed] challenging one another," as had been the case in the past.[19]

Such a debate reflected a growing devolution of power between the two sides of the Atlantic. By 1962, the European Economic Community was producing almost as much steel as the United States; it was the world's second-largest producer of automobiles, first in world imports, second in world exports. The economies of the whole European area grew over twice as fast as the economy of the United States. Not only economically revived, but also colonially disengaged, politically stabilized, and with no serious security apprehension, some in Europe questioned the continued desirability of the alliance. Was it in Europe's interest, they asked, to remain entangled in a relationship that was no longer related specifically to Europe's needs, now that most international crises appeared to take place outside Europe on grounds often alien to Europe's vital interests?

Inasmuch as it indicated Western Europe's recovery, Europe's new assertiveness showed that America's primary objective on the continent had already been fulfilled. Yet Europe's recovery continued to be unstable, since it was emerging within the context of a tacit acceptance of the existing status quo and without the formal resolution of security issues that had plagued the European continent since the end of World War II. These issues were complicated by several factors. As an alliance of status quo countries, the Atlantic Alliance was ill equipped to face demands for change. Understandably, the preservation of Europe's status quo was of least immediate risk to Washington. A new European security system would open a Pandora's box that might provide more or less security depending on which elements of that system were weakened. For example, to reduce the military presence of both superpowers in Europe and thus permit the emergence of an all-European security system would favor the superpower geographically closer to the European continent, namely, the Soviet Union.[20] In addition, the fate of Germany would have to be debated soon. To be sure, to keep Germany divided would satisfy both Europes, East and West. Yet the paradox of reuniting East and West Europe at the expense of a truncated Germany would make the new system dependent on West Germany's continued willingness to substitute the fact of security (guaranteed by the United States) for the promise of reunification (denied by the Soviet Union).

However convenient, especially in view of other problems the United States was facing in Indochina and at home, Europe's status quo could not remain permanent. Over the years, it helped Europe to take security largely for granted; but, paradoxically, taking security for granted was also bound to help raise demands for changes that might harm that security. Such dilemmas were to gain increasing momentum in the following decade.

From Massive Retaliation
to Flexible Response

One of the questions raised in the 1960s was whether or not the Atlantic Alliance could satisfy the renewed search for national independence and national identity in Europe. Another question, however, raised doubts about the credibility of the alliance. The end of the American nuclear monopoly, plus a number of technological revolutions in nuclear weaponry and means of delivery, had opened new perspectives to the search for national security. It was possible to rely on nuclear weapons as an instrument of policy as long as American nuclear superiority was unchallenged. But when such superiority disappeared and the threat or retaliation was balanced with a Soviet counter-threat of comparable reprisal, both Europe and America asked whether any nation could and should risk destruction for the sake of another nation. And, assuming that America was willing to risk its cities for the defense of Western European cities, was such a commitment credible to partners and potential enemies alike?

The question did not permit an easy answer. In June 1963, during his German tour, President Kennedy forcefully stated: "The United States will risk its cities to defend yours because we need your freedom to defend ours."[21] Yet, four years earlier, Christian Herter, then an undersecretary of state, had emphasized: "I can't conceive of the President of the United States involving us in an all-out nuclear war unless the facts showed clearly that we are in danger of devastation ourselves, or that actual moves have been made toward devastating ourselves."[22] The logical conclusion, one of incertitude, was drawn by de Gaulle as he stated, early in 1963: "No one in the world, particularly no one in America, can say if, or where, or when, or how, or to what extent, American nuclear weapons would be used to defend Europe."[23]

In a general vein, the survival of alliances in the nuclear age depended on a fundamental reform of their structures. But such reforms apparently went in contradictory directions. For one, national commitments, if they were to be credible, needed to be made within a much more closely integrated framework. Such integration did not have to be structural, and the engagement of a given nation could simply take forms that, in certain situations, preempted its options. This attitude was known, to use Thomas Schelling's phrase, as being "rationally irrational." An irrational policy might be credible to the other side if cloaked in a rational mantle — for example, by making automatic, through one device or another, nuclear retaliation against an aggressor. At the same time, alliances needed to be disintegrated precisely because of the irrationality of the commitment. In practice, the Munich syndrome was ended when the alternative to appeasement moved dangerously close to mutual annihilation: peace was divisible because destruction might otherwise be indivisible. A nation was not going to commit itself to annihilation — not merely to the possible loss of human lives or territory as in the past — so that another nation might live. In short, the allies would meet force with force, but only up to a point.

Implicit in such a dilemma was the distinction between deterrence (that is, war avoidance) and defense (that is, damage limitation). Some argued that raising the terms of deterrence would make it more effective. According to this reasoning, massive retaliation had eliminated the risk of limited wars: in the later stages of the Vietnam War, many even appeared to think of John Foster Dulles' strategy with regret. But the risks inherent in a strategy that unfolded under the choking shadow of nuclear war were not negligible. Those in the United States and in Europe who argued for a tougher deterrence posture were asking for the irrational to be rationalized into a policy. They wanted to paralyze the other side with fear. Part of the rationale behind the French nuclear force was that contradictory deterrence positions within the alliance (massive retaliation for Paris, flexible response for Washington) would introduce additional doubts in the enemy's calculations. It was assumed, of course, that a rationally irrational policy would be met with rationality. But what if irrationality prevailed on the other side as well? What if deterrence failed? Could defense still be addressed in common and resolved jointly, or would it become instead every country for itself? Whatever seemingly rational answer might be offered on one side of the Atlantic was likely to remain seemingly irrational on the other.

This general debate over whether or not American strategic forces would or should be used for the defense of Europe was enhanced further when the Kennedy administration adopted the so-called strategy of flexible response, which was widely regarded in Europe as a U.S. effort to avoid the use of those weapons to which American territory was most vulnerable.[24]

Flexible response rested on two essential premises. The first was that deterrence might not always work, and that more attention needed to be given to defense. Related to this premise was the belief that a nuclear war was manageable provided that the tools required for such management had been carefully examined and cautiously gathered prior to the outbreak of the war. The second premise was, therefore, that a nuclear war could be kept limited, depending, among other factors, on the targets selected by the two main protagonists. By concentrating on military targets ("counterforce capability"), America would reduce the other side's potential for destruction. At the same time, it would provide the other side with incentives to confine its own strike to military targets as well, thereby limiting damages. A counter-city capability could still be kept in reserve as part of a deterrent force operating during the war itself.[25]

To make the strategy meaningful, it was necessary to develop a strategic capability with a high level of survivability, penetrability, and control against and after a Soviet preemptive first strike. "I should think," argued Assistant Secretary of Defense Paul Nitze in December 1961, "the most important persuader is to be found in Western nuclear capabilities, their survivability against anything his [Khrushchev's] force can do, their penetration capabilities against defenses, their responsiveness to responsible control, and their accuracy, number and power."[26] The deterrent value of this second strike capability would be to maintain a highly reliable ability to inflict an unacceptable degree of damage upon any aggressor at any time during the course of a strategic nuclear exchange, even after absorbing a surprise first strike.[27] Of course, for a second strike to distinguish between civilian and military targets, the aggressor, too, would have to control its own first strike: "In talking about nuclear war," McNamara recognized, "the Soviet leaders always say that they would strike at the entire complex of our military power including government and production centers, meaning our cities. If they were to do so, we would . . . . have no alternative but to retaliate in kind." But the new doctrine at least gave Moscow the "strongest imaginable incentive to refrain from striking [American] cities."[28]

Yet the most effective way of limiting a nuclear war was obviously to avoid it altogether. Accordingly, McNamara attempted to raise the nuclear threshold and to widen the area of conventional warfare by emphasizing the role that conventional forces played in the implementation of America's overall strategy. The American secretary of defense assumed that a wider range of practical alternatives was required to face the new challenges that the Kremlin seemed to be planning. "Unless the Free World has sufficient forces organized and equipped to deal with these challenges at what appears to be the highest appropriate levels of conflict," stated McNamara in February 1962, "we could be put into difficult situations by the communists. In such situations we could lose by default; or we could lose by limiting our response to what appears to be the highest appropriate level—but a level at which we may be inferior; or we could resort to thermonuclear war—the level at which we are superior—but at a cost which could be out of proportion to the issues and dangers involved."[29]

In short, America needed to be able to respond promptly to limited aggressions, possibly in more than one place at a time, in order both "to deter them and to prevent then from spreading into larger conflicts."[30] The inadequacy of conventional capabilities within NATO and beyond therefore became troubling for the Kennedy–Johnson administration. Under a formula devised by former Secretary of State Dean Acheson, the European allies were asked to provide the larger part of 30 active and 30 reserve divisions for Central Europe, instead of the 16 active divisions and scattering of reserves that NATO had available at the time.[31]

McNamara's predilection for noncivilian targets and conventional weapons attempted to institutionalize the earlier NATO theory of a pause between each step on the escalation ladder. Escalation from conventional to nuclear war, and from nuclear exchange to nuclear holocaust, would thus remain gradual, and the chances of avoiding it would be accordingly increased. For, whereas massive retaliation had left very little choice following that pause, flexible response left every possibility open: the use of nuclear weapons was postponed but not eliminated, civilian targets were devalued but not excluded. In sum, McNamara would have liked to keep a war in Europe nonnuclear, or at least to limit any nuclear engagement away from the continental United Stated. Still, such aims were made explicitly secondary to the aim of not losing, as the Kennedy administration emphasized that it would not accept a loss of allied territory or defeat. "In the event of a major aggression that could not be repulsed by conventional weapons," Kennedy explained, America would "take whatever action with whatever weapons . . . appropriate."[32]

Earlier, massive retaliation had been a policy of minimum deterrence calling for minimum involvement in world affairs, inasmuch as the situations where retaliation would be acceptable were by definition strictly limited. Now, flexible response was a policy of extended deterrence, because making retaliation as minimal as possible permitted maximum involvement in world affairs. Such a strategy made U.S. global involvement in world affairs both possible and credible. Military forces, theorized Secretary McNamara, must be able "to respond, with discrimination and speed, to any problem, at any spot on the globe at any moment's notice."[33] Yet, ironically enough, the new strategy was interpreted widely in Europe as a first step toward an eventual American withdrawal.

That the allies would have been generally concerned with the McNamara doctrine should come as no surprise. Obviously, what seemed "controlled" on the American side of the Atlantic did not look the same from the European vantage point. Conventional or nuclear, a war waged in Europe would be "limited" only from a non-European viewpoint. But would any strategy ever gain Europe's favor? If the Soviet Union's nuclear capabilities were neglected and nothing was said of the possibility and consequences of a nuclear war, Europeans accepted the military status quo as satisfactory and were accordingly tempted to decrease their defense expenditures. If, on the other hand, Soviet capabilities were "realistically" estimated and the risks of nuclear war acknowledged, Europeans might well choose to develop their own nuclear forces to ensure a security for which, they thought, America would not fight. If Soviet conventional capabilities were conceded to be large, Europeans argued that their own conventional weapons could hardly shift the balance. If these capabilities were thought to be small, Europeans argued that any additional effort was redundant.

In the 1950s, Europe had found massive retaliation dangerous, because it threatened to escalate any armed confrontation in Europe into a total nuclear war. In the 1960s, Europe found flexible response dangerous as well, because it might encourage Soviet aggression in Western Europe through the implied reduction in the scope of America's retaliation, hence increasing its acceptability. Europeans, who charged both Moscow and Washington with the intention of confining a war over Europe to Europe, would have liked to see such a war confined to American and Soviet territories. In an age of massive retaliation, American territory was the first target of the Soviet missiles. With a flexible response, this was no longer true. The European allies implicitly complained that the McNamara strategy was making the United States more secure at the expense of Europe. Yet the inescapable fact was indeed that Europe remained more insecure than America by definition— the obvious implication of Europe's geographical location. Situated between both superpowers, Europe held the same position as Poland had held in the past, located between two of the great powers of the time (Russia and Prussia). Europe represented both a stake of the conflict and its battleground, and ultimately a war between the two superpowers might remain "limited" to Europe while their own territory would be totally spared. "Who can say," asked de Gaulle at his apocalyptic best, "that if the occasion arises . . . [the Soviet Union and the United States], while each deciding not to launch its missiles at the main enemy so that it should itself be spared, will not crush the others? It is possible to imagine that in some awful day Western Europe should be wiped out from Moscow and Central Europe from Washington."[34] No one could say, to be sure. Yet Western Europe's reluctance to be wiped out by Moscow, possibly for the sake of Washington, could only be matched by Washington's own reluctance to be wiped out from Moscow, possibly for the sake of Western Europe.

The Problem of Nuclear Control

By the mid-1960s, the Atlantic Alliance had become a troubled partnership.[35] Central to such troubles was the question of nuclear control. Already by 1965, few if any scientific secrets concerning earlier bomb designs were left. A dozen nonnuclear countries were easily capable of producing enough plutonium 239 for at least one bomb a year.[36] As nuclear technology continued to spread, the list of potential nuclear powers would grow as well. Delivery systems remained a major technological constraint, but the types of systems required changed from place to place, depending on hypothetical adversaries. Ultimately, a power might even attempt to acquire nuclear weapons without any clear means of delivery, and simply resort to various forms of nuclear terrorism. To be sure, the cost of such weapons remained a major obstacle to nuclear proliferation, especially as frequent technological changes required the endless pursuit of expensive research and development programs on top of the manufacturing costs proper. Altogether, it was estimated in the mid-1960s that a modest nuclear force with its own means of delivery could not be devised by states with a gross national product of less than $10 billion. But this limit still left quite a few candidates. In short, it was feared that the world might have survived the winter of the cold war merely to enter the new uncertainties of a world in which nuclear power had proliferated.[37]

Why any one state might choose to base its defense on nuclear weapons varied from one state or region to another. A first theory held that a small nuclear force might deter aggression if it could inflict on enemy targets greater damage than acceptable. Aggression would then be deterred even if it could not possibly be defeated in the field, of even if the homeland of the aggressor could not be totally devastated. Nuclear weapons were a magic equalizer that would automatically preserve a balance of terror between all states.[38] As all states did not have the same "value" within the international system, all national nuclear forces did not need to have the same destructive capabilities, and one small nuclear force might therefore "equal" a much larger one in deterrent effect.

A second theory held that a small nuclear force could be used to trigger the forces of the superstate within a given alliance.[39] The stability of deterrence would be increased because national nuclear forces would threaten a potential aggressor with a collective retaliation set in motion by a chain reaction of national considerations. Underlying such a theory was the assumption that the terms of a policy of deterrence were as high as the terms of its highest bidder, even if the main share of the deterrent itself was in the possession of the lowest bidder. It was not so much the actual credibility of the dominant power's commitment that was being strengthened, but its perceived credibility. Furthermore, a national nuclear force, independently targeted, could neutralize objectives that, although vital to the smaller state, might not have been hit in the first volley of the superstate's retaliation.

Third, it was argued that a small power might seek nuclear weapons in order to face regional problems that the superstates, either because of their nuclear stalemate or because of a lack of national interest, might be incapable or unwilling to solve. Such a theory therefore had the nonnuclear state seek nuclear weapons not against either superstate, but in order to secure a regional advantage vis-à-vis states that were deprived of any such forces. "To possess atomic weapons," emphasized de Gaulle, "is for a country to be in a position to reduce relentlessly a nation which does not possess any."[40] And, in another instance, the then French president reminded his listeners that, in the nuclear age, "the life of any [nonnuclear] nation is . . . absolutely at the mercy of whomever possesses [nuclear] weapons."[41]

In the 1960s, American policy remained staunchly opposed to any such reasoning and, beyond its opposition to France, was more generally aimed at preventing or postponing the entry of other states into the nuclear club. "I am haunted," President Kennedy confided to one of his aides in March 1963, "by the feeling that by 1970, unless we are successful, there may be ten nuclear powers instead of four, and by 1975, fifteen or twenty. . . . I regard this as the greatest possible danger."[42] The fact is that attempts to explain the national acquisition of nuclear weapons appeared to raise more questions than it answered. A credible deterrent could hardly be based on an incredible act.[43] Would the potential aggressor ever take at face value a retaliatory threat that equated a crippling strike with a deadly strike, or a threat that would be based on the suicidal option of igniting nuclear escalation? If such a force were to be devised on the assumption that it would not have to face a major adversary alone, could it be realistically assumed that the other superpower would indeed become automatically a part of the nuclear chain reaction? To devise a limited and yet effective second strike capability would involve baffling qualitative problems. Whereas nuclear weapons might be a quantitative equalizer, a huge technological gap still made the invulverability and the penetrability of such a second strike difficult to achieve.

Undoubtedly, America's opposition to nuclear dispersion was a sound policy. A small nuclear force could not deter alone, nor oppose alone, a major nuclear power. But, regrettably enough, U.S. opposition to the French *force de frappe* grew in intensity as the force grew in size. For a long time, de Gaulle appeared to assume that he merely needed to build the foundation of France's nuclear force, following which the United States would provide him with the required assistance. In 1959, the French president was still speaking of his force as "whether we manufacture it or buy it."[44] But U.S. objections to an autonomous French force were enhanced by the defense policy of the Kennedy administration. McNamara's strategy implied the indivisibility of a general nuclear war target system: how could the French value-centered strategy be reconciled to the American force-centered strategy? Washington argued that the French force would be essentially useless, since American power was admittedly sufficient. Paris, however, was less interested in the sufficiency of the American arsenal (which was not questioned) than in the conditions and the circumstances of its availability. The Kennedy administration also remained concerned over the trigger effect that the French force might have. Exactly how the trigger would work was never satisfactorily explained—either by those who feared it or by those who wished it—yet somehow a small nuclear power could, out of desperation, act in such a way as to trigger the two superpowers into a nuclear conflict that they would have otherwise wanted to avoid. Such a risk might even necessitate a reappraisal of America's commitment to Europe. A further source of potential harm was related to the Soviet reaction. As it happened, Moscow never expressed much concern over France's nuclear force. Understood as a source of dissension within the Atlantic Alliance, it was even somewhat welcomed. But what would be the reaction of the Soviets if the Germans were to follow the French example? And by reviving national tendencies, were not the French promoting such a possibility?

By and large, from the viewpoint of Washington, America's opposition to France's nuclear force was amply justified on the grounds that such a force was unduly expensive, strategically dangerous, lacking in credibility, and militarily useless. Coming before France's, Great Britain's effort to build and operate its own deterrent had been a losing struggle against the periodic obsolescence of nuclear weapons, against the ever larger cost of such weapons, and against the insurmountable problems of maintaining elementary requirements of deterrent credibility, survivability, and penetrability. Yet, once the French commitment to a nuclear force had become irreversible, continued opposition could only serve to exacerbate the differences between the two countries, and a better American strategy might have been to try to manage it (as was done with Great Britain), not defeat it. The arguments used by Washington lacked, to say the least, empathy. To suggest that the acquisition of nuclear weapons was a waste of financial resources while insisting that comparable resources be spent by the allies to strengthen further their conventional forces was not much of an argument from the viewpoint of Europe. The American policy, one must suspect, was somehow affected by a strong dose of mistrust for Paris and vice versa. This mistrust had been a significant aspect of American policy toward Europe, and French policy toward America, for a long time after World War II. Washington's policy was also affected by its misunderstanding of the French political scene: the Kennedy–Johnson administrations dealt with the Fifth Republic as if it merely reflected the personal wishes of de Gaulle. Yet it was clear to many that the French president followed a policy essentially in line with French tradition in such matters. The nuclear policy of France was launched by the Fourth Republic. It reached adolescence under de Gaulle and began to mature under his immediate successor.

Unwilling to accept national nuclear forces, the Kennedy administration nevertheless devised a number of schemes that might at least provide the Europeans with the illusion, if not the fact, of sharing the control and management of an integrated strategic nuclear force. The best-known outcome of this search was the MLF, a projected multilateral force with a range of 2,000 miles or more.[45] The ships and missiles were to be operated by crews of several nationalities and the decisions were to be reached unanimously by the "major" participants—namely, those nations whose financial contribution would amount to no less than 10% of the overall cost.

The directions that the MLF was expected to take were those of Paris and Bonn. As seen in Washington, the MLF would negate Germany's eventual search for nuclear weapons by giving it access to the control of some part of the Western deterrent. At the same time, the MLF was expected to isolate France in Europe by forcing Germany into an unwanted choice between Washington and Paris. The Soviets could offer reunification to Germany; Paris could offer its sponsorship of German overtures in Eastern Europe; Washington now thought that it, too, had something to offer: a share in the control of nuclear weapons. In fact, Bonn's approval of the MLF went far toward preempting the Franco–German Treaty of Friendship that de Gaulle and Chancellor Adenauer signed in late January 1963. But in return it further embittered the French, who continued to regard the American offer as being essentially anti-French.[46]

Awkward in its objectives, the MLF was also inadequate in its procedures. The unanimity rule gave each participating member a de facto right of veto. But, though a veto from Washington would have left Europe powerless because the MLF represented all of Europe's nuclear capabilities, a veto from the Europeans would have left Washington just as free to take any unilateral action it deemed necessary as the MLF capabilities represented an insignificant amount of the overall American strategic forces. Occasionally, some American officials, including Secretary of State Dean Rusk and Undersecretary George Ball, hinted that ultimately Washington might relinquish its veto, but neither the timing nor the modalities of this eventuality were ever discussed in detail. And it was President Kennedy's own evaluation, as reported by Arthur Schlesinger, that "so long as the United States retained its veto (and he [Kennedy] never mentioned renunciation as a possibility . . .) the MLF was something of a fake. . . . He could not see why Europeans would be interested in making enormous contributions toward a force over which they had no real control."[47] No wonder, then, that Europeans generally ignored the American offer, and that the idea of MLF died during the Johnson administration. West Germany expressed real interest, despite Moscow's and Paris' explicit warnings against German participation in such a nuclear partnership. Greece and Turkey, too, accepted the American scheme in principle, as did Italy. But even these acceptances were often conditional, and the feasibility of these nations manning ships multilaterally was never tested.

However imperfect it might have been, the MLF at least sought a solution to the question of nuclear control within NATO. The problems it encountered were problems that any related search for consultation raised, namely, problems of membership, status, and substance.

When speaking of consultation, it was first necessary to determine who was entitled to participate in the consultation. The MLF appeared to imply that the best criterion was one of financial responsibility. Such a criterion made possible a large number of participants, so long as MLF costs would have remained relatively limited. In his September memorandum in 1958, de Gaulle had suggested, on the other hand, that consultation be confined to a directoire of three members only, who also happened to be the three permanent Western members of the United Nations Security Council as well as the only three nuclear powers within the alliance.[48] But neither the American nor the French criteria were truly operational, because it was as meaningless to pretend to endow the smaller states in Europe with a voice equal to that of the United States as it was to pretend that the other European countries (including West Germany and Italy) would tolerate an exclusive ménage à trois between Washington, London, and Paris.

Could all those participating in the consultation be treated as equal regardless of the issue under discussion? One French suggestion referred to a géométrie variable according to which the status of each participant would depend on the interest it had in a given issue. North Africa, the Caribbean Basin, and East Africa, to cite but three areas of the world, were regions where France, the United States, and Great Britain had determining interests, respectively. Yet such a division of diplomatic labor entailed a recognition of spheres of influence within the noncommunist world, as a matter of fact if not a matter of principle. Furthermore, how would the "geometry" of such consultation be devised for other vital areas, in the Middle East for instance, where the distribution of interests was not so evident? And would the distribution of alliance interests around the world imply the extension of the alliance to the whole world?

All these schemes for strengthening the alliance attempted to adjust intra-alliance relationships to a transformed political and strategic milieu. But any scheme for making consultation more effective was already undermined by the growing divergence of national interests between the United States and Europe, and, within Europe, between European states. In an alliance of independent and sovereign states, consultation could not lead to consensus as it might do in domestic politics, because there is no way for the alliance to induce the minority to adopt the decisions of the majority. Should a nation state become dissatisfied with the way an alliance works, it can always withdraw from it when it concludes that the advantages gained from such a withdrawal will outweigh the disadvantages. In an alliance of independent and sovereign states, consultation indeed presupposes a specific consensus so that, on each specific issue, the consultation may be reduced to the procedure of implementing that consensus.[49]

But cooperation could also be promoted through an eventual integration of America and Europe. This was essentially the idea behind President John F. Kennedy's Grand Design, as expressed in his so-called Declaration of Interdependence of July 4, 1962. "As the American effort for interdependence now approaches a successful close, a great new effort for interdependence is transforming the world around us. And the spirit of that new effort is the same spirit which gave birth to the American constitution. . . . [But] the first order of business is for our European friends to go forward in forming the more perfect union which will someday make this partnership possible."[50] A formal Atlantic community would depend upon the prior formation of a formal European community.

The Management
of Europe's Economic Growth

In 1957, the Treaty of Rome establishing the European Economic Community (EEC) had fit in nicely with U.S. plans to strengthen the Atlantic community politically. The Eisenhower administration assumed that such an economic customs union would lead in time to a political union based on the American preferred model of federalism and supranational institutions. Shaping this assumption was a tenacious belief in the continuing harmony of interests between the United States and Western Europe. The EEC, it was therefore reasoned, would come to represent an outward-looking Europe capable of acting in concert with the United States all the more effectively as it was freed at last of its past penchant for self-destruction. As it was argued at the time, "Union was needed to imprison Europe's evil genie, nationalism, in a solid cage. An objective of this high political importance outweighed any incidental damage to commercial interests."[51]

In any case, such damage was deemed to be at most marginal. A united and dynamic European economy would represent a better and larger trading partner. New opportunities for direct foreign investments would help secure further economic benefits, especially as the eventual access of Great Britain into the EEC would guarantee America's privileged status. In short, Europe was a logical component of the "Atlantic idea" of a decade earlier.

On the other side of the Atlantic, however, the "European idea" gathered much momentum out of the impressive economic successes that the Common Market quickly achieved. Having benefited from the trade discrimination against products from the dollar area that U.S. policies had made possible earlier, the EEC states chose to erect, in lieu of the EPU, a Common External Tariff that was charged against imports coming from non-EEC countries. Thus, international trade liberalization was to be founded on external trade protectionism.[52]

Simultaneously, a further contentious focus of transatlantic relations was emerging with the replacement of the former postwar "dollar gap" with a novel and more ominous post-recovery "dollar glut." Throughout the 1950s, the excess of U.S. gold holdings over foreign dollar holdings had steadily fallen from $18.1 to £0.5 billion. By 1960, as the U.S. balance of payments deficit ballooned to $3.7 billion, foreign dollar holdings came to exceed U.S. gold reserves for the first time, and the end of that year saw the first serious speculative attack against the U.S. dollar.[53]

With the British pound facing an even worse crisis of confidence the following year, the spirit of the White plan at last embraced the spirit of the Keynes plan, and both Great Britain and the United States now urged additional funding facilities for the IMF. The European states, however, were willing to contribute additional funds only to the extent that their influence was enhanced, and the regained strength of Western Europe in international monetary affairs was thus reflected in the December 1961 creation of the General Arrangements to Borrow (GAB), a fund that was significantly placed outside IMF jurisdiction, where U.S. control remained predominant. Created by the Group of Ten (Belgium, France, Germany, Italy, the Netherlands, Sweden, Canada, and Japan, as well as Great Britain and the United States), the GAB could provide additional funding of up to $6 billion to the IMF whenever the Group of Ten collectively determined the need for an extension of credit facilities.

With the transformation of the OEEC into the Organization for Economic Cooperation and Development (OECD) also reflective of the changing nature of the economic dialogue between the United States and its Western allies, two issues now came to be debated between the two sides of the Atlantic. First, to what extent was the United States exporting inflation to other countries through its continuing and rising overall balance of payments deficits and its relatively expansionary monetary policy? And, second, to what extent was the growing inflow of U.S. capital to Europe the result of inadequately developed European capital markets?[54]

Not that the Kennedy administration was itself oblivious to the fact and consequences of such a deterioration in the U.S. balance of payments. To reduce the foreign exchange costs of a number of government programs, foreign aid and overseas military expenditures were tied to procurements in the United States. To this end, military "offset" sales agreements were negotiated with the European allies, especially West Germany, which received about 30% of these shipments between 1960 and 1970.[55] Now emerging as the new "special partner," Germany also pledged to continue to maintain large dollar holdings as reserves to help offset the cost to the United States of stationing large numbers of American troops on German soil. To help reassure America's nervous European creditors, so-called "Roosa bonds" denominated U.S. liabilities in the foreign currencies of the purchasers. The Interest Equalization Tax in 1963 sought to stem short-term capital outflows from the United States to Europe by adding 1% to the cost of foreign borrowing in American money markets. Raising short-term interest rates while keeping long-term rates low (the "Operation Twist") was meant to balance domestic economic needs (namely, to avoid a recession) with balance of payments constraints. Yet all of these measures notwithstanding, these constraints were not allowed to interfere with domestic economic expansion or, for that matter, with those foreign policies deemed vital to U.S. security.

The selective use of capital controls represented only part of Kennedy's rising concern over balance of payments deficits. This concern received further expression in the American effort to improve U.S. trade competitiveness with Western Europe, even though the U.S. basic balance deficits of the early 1960s were primarily the product of capital outflows largely unrelated to the shifting patterns of U.S.–EEC trade.[56] And even though the United States maintained a sizeable surplus in its balance of trade every year during the decade that followed the creation of the EEC, the return to a balance of payments equilibrium was still sought through further increase in trade surpluses as the result of a U.S. determination to permit the capital outflows necessitated by an ambitious foreign policy.

There was, however, little reason to believe that the EEC states remained willing to share in the operational costs of such a policy. Yet Kennedy's Grand Design unfolded around the idea that a waning Atlantic political unity might be revived by a fresh infusion of Atlantic economic interdependence. Accordingly, the American president told the U.S. Congress that "an integrated Western Europe, joined in trading partnership with the United States, will further shift the world balance of power to the side of freedom."[57]

However grandiose a vision, Kennedy's Grand Design could hardly ever be made operational. First, it called for a very specific Europe: an integrated, supranational Europe born out of the same spirit that had given birth to the union of the American thirteen colonies. But there was no indication that such a Europe was wanted by the Europeans themselves. The

American view seemed to be that if there was as yet no unified Europe, it was because of France's opposition; and that indeed Europe had been on the verge of political integration when this was defeated by de Gaulle's singlehanded veto of Great Britain's entry into the Common Market in mid-January 1963. Yet the evidence showed that at no time during the Fourth Republic had there been in France a majority in favor of European integration conceived along supranational lines. Instead, throughout the 1950s, French support for European integration, apart from a minority of "maximalists" dedicated to integration, had been the outcome of external pressures understood as security threats, and "Europe" itself was conceived as the best available means of coping with these pressures.[58] The European Coal and Steel Community had resulted from the inability of the French to promote the International Ruhr Authority; the European Defense Community had been France's answer to calls for a rearmament of Germany; and the European Economic Community had been very much influenced by the fear of isolation that followed the Suez crisis and Khrushchev's ultimatum to Paris and London. Besides, to believe that the entry of Great Britain into the Common Market would strengthen the forces of supranationality ignored Britain's well-established opposition to the very idea of supranationality, as displayed in previous years by its position on various schemes of unification.

Assuming a united, supranational Europe, including Great Britain, that would be speaking with one voice only, would such a Europe make the Atlantic partnership possible? And, above all, would it make it workable? All that a united Europe would mean really was that several nationalisms had been replaced by a larger European nationalism that might raise a far more formidable obstacle to Washington's wishes. The problems inherent in reconciling interests between Washington and Europe, whenever Europe spoke with one voice, were well shown during the protracted discussions on the reduction of tariffs—the so-called Kennedy Round.[59]

Thus, reluctantly, the United States was beginning to take a closer look at the implications of European integration. Where some continued to see the EEC as a vast market with unlimited potential for trade and investment, others now saw it as a threat to the further expansion of important U.S. export sectors. As such, the 1962 Trade Expansion Act (TEA) was expected to deal with such a threat, as it granted the American president authority to negotiate across-the-board tariff reductions of up to 50% and permitted the removal of duties altogether for those products where the combined exports of the United States and the EEC countries amounted to 80% of total world exports. The TEA and the opening of the Kennedy Round thus marked the point at which the harmony between general and trade liberalization and European integration began to break down.[60]

Once again, the position of de Gaulle's France was critical in shaping the positions of the EEC in these negotiations. Already, de Gaulle had shown his resistance to the Grand Design by vetoing Britain's entry into the Common Market in January 1963, citing the inadvisability of allowing an American "Trojan horse" inside a still fragile European community. Now, in matters of trade, de Gaulle's conception of Europe demanded that nothing be allowed to interfere with the Rome Treaty, especially in the area of agriculture where France was particularly dependent on the effectiveness of the EEC's Common Agricultural Policy (CAP).[61] That the CAP would have been left out of the Kennedy Round following intense inter-European and Atlantic bargaining was indeed an important concession, which reflected a U.S. willingness to pay a high price for at least the appearance of Atlantic unity. In addition, the Johnson administration failed to sway the Europeans to accept significant increases in Japanese exports to the EEC countries. At a time of rising unemployment, this, too, was an important U.S. concession in response to the unwillingness of the European allies to permit America to solve its balance of payments problems at Europe's expense—namely, by increasing the U.S. balance of trade surplus with the EEC while reducing its trade deficit with Japan by rerouting Japanese exports toward Europe. More generally, however, the Kennedy Round exposed the limits of a united transatlantic economy and acknowledged the changed environment of international economic affairs: U.S. concessions reflected Western Europe's improved economic standing in the world relative to America. Formally, the Kennedy Round was expected to be a monument to the Bretton Woods system: yet, within six months of its conclusion, foreign exchange markets would be closed in what was to become the most serious financial crisis of the postwar period up to that time. Thus, by the end of the decade, the twin pillars upon which America's leadership has been built—its deterrent and its currency—were being simultaneously shattered.

Troubled Partnership

The Atlantic debates of the 1960s showed that the days of undisputed American leadership were by and large over. Thus at least one basic objective of American policies toward Europe—recovery from economic devastion—had been essentially fulfilled. But the search for a true Atlantic partnership was now made all the more elusive as a recovered Europe appeared to display a renewed taste for independence and assertiveness.

Even if not altogether illusory, the Atlantic partnership that was sought throughout the decade hardly ever came to grips with the two fundamental questions of timing and content: when would the partnership be set up, and what would be shared between the partners? To the question of when, the answer was that Europe first needed to become a power comparable to America in resources and in political organization. This prospect was obviously a very long-term one, particularly if it related, among other factors, to nuclear resources. Furthermore, this question could only be answered by the United States, as it remained up to the senior partner to decide when the junior partner would be allowed to join the organization. It would also be up to the senior partner to decide what kind of junior partner was acceptable. The Kennedy administration simply reasoned that a Europe with a will to share its resources would make sharing effective. But as to what America would share, the answer was, to say the least, dubious. Now and then there were vague hints about giving the European partner hypothetical authority to fire nuclear missiles without preliminary authorization from Washington, but these were always when-and-if hints. According to George Ball, "If Europe were sufficiently far advanced toward political unity, we could hopefully look forward to an effective and integrated Atlantic defense founded on a true nuclear partnership. But this is not the case today nor is it likely to be for some time."[62]

Clearly the fact of sharing could not be postponed to a future admittedly regarded as unlikely for some time. Just as in the 1950s the Europeans sought a partnership based on a need to share American resources, Washington now wanted a partnership based on a growing need to see the Europeans share American burdens. For only then were the terms of the partnership made explicit: a contribution by Europe to the American balance of payments problem, a share of at least the cost of the war in Vietnam, an increased contribution to the cause of foreign aid—this participation would make Europe a true partner.

Thus in the 1960s American policies were generally deficient less in their intent than in their form. The Atlantic Alliance could not yet be replaced, as de Gaulle wanted it, by a classical alliance in which each member was theoretically free to use its autonomous military forces as it saw fit but within a collective framework that implied somewhat automatic support from its allies. The technological revolution of the previous 25 years, the fantastic scale of destruction implicit in any armed conflict, had made a return to a classical balance-of-power game undesirable. Not that a big power was now unable to protect a smaller power. It could do so, provided that the smaller power accepted its strategic subordination to the bigger power and never attempted to force its hand—in other words, provided that the smaller power was willing to relinquish part of its national authority on such essential matters as defense.

But could a nation reasonably accept such a responsibility? The answer was affirmative only as long as there was no need to meet it. Vietnam, for example, was in the process of showing, among many other things, how difficult it was for America to fight a nonnuclear war for someone else. Could one conceive of fighting a nuclear war for someone else? Could Washington ever decide that the salvation of Europe lay in the latter's nuclear destruction, and should it ever decide so itself? Or should such a decision, and its subsequent justification, remain eminently national both in the way it was reached and implemented?

These were questions that could not be answered formally. Those who argued—then as later—for the obsolescence of alliances were also arguing for the obsolescence of warfare. Surely if it was true that alliances were now obsolete because of the nature of war, then it was equally true that the unacceptable level of destruction that nuclear warfare entailed made war itself obsolete—no longer the continuation of politics by other means but now indeed the termination of politics by total means. But yet, was not war deterred precisely because of such alliances? Would not the end of alliances imply the end of the relative security that had prevailed in Europe over the previous 25 years?

In practice, of course, neither war nor alliances were ended. Only circumstances had changed, and because of these changes the Atlantic Alliance now needed some repairs. That these repairs still remained ambiguous reflected the ambiguity of international changes. Only when the direction of these changes could be more firmly determined and their effect more adequately measured would it be possible for United States policymakers to attempt to adjust America's commitments in Europe.

NOTES

1. Some of these arguments have been developed by the author at greater length in such publications as *Fading Partnership: America and Europe after 30 Years* (New York: Praeger, 1979); *The United States, Europe and The Third World: Allies and Adversaries* (Washington, D.C.: Center for Strategic and International Studies, 1979); and "The United States and Europe," *Washington Quarterly* (Winter 1981), pp. 70–86.
2. As reported by Dean Acheson, Clayton's memorandum (May 27, 1947) began by stating: "It is now obvious that we have grossly underestimated the destruction to the European economy by the war." The memorandum concluded: "We must avoid getting into another UNRRA. The United States must run this show." Dean Acheson, *Present at the Creation: My Years at the State Department* (New York: W. W. Norton, 1969), p. 231.
3. As reported in Arthur M. Schlesinger, Jr., *A Thousand Days:*

John F. Kennedy in the White House (Boston, Mass.: Houghton Mifflin, 1965), pp. 654–55.

4. Quoted in R. B. Manderson-Jones, *The Special Relationship: Anglo–American Relations and Western European Unity, 1947–1956* (New York: Crane, Russak, 1972), p. 23.

5. See Alfred Grosser, *Les Occidentaux: Les Etats-Unis et l'Europe depuis la guerre* (Paris: Fayard, 1978).

6. Quoted in Gerald Freund, *Germany between Two Worlds* (New York: Harper & Row, 1961), p. 115.

7. Adam Ulam, *Expansion and Coexistence* (New York: Praeger, 1968), p. 613. See also Coral Bell, *Negotiations from Strength: A Study in the Politics of Power* (Cambridge, Mass.: Harvard University Press, 1964), pp. 197 ff.

8. William E. Griffith, *The Sino–Soviet Rift* (Cambridge, Mass.: Harvard University Press, 1964), p. 351. Also, Ulam, *Expansion and Coexistence*, p. 611.

9. Thomas W. Wolfe, *Soviet Power and Europe* (Baltimore, Md.: Johns Hopkins University Press, 1970), p. 85. See also Arnold L. Horelick and Myron Rush, *Strategic Power and Soviet Foreign Policy* (Chicago: Chicago University Press, 1966).

10. Ulam, *Expansion and Coexistence*, p. 656.

11. Wolfe, *Soviet Power and Europe*, p. 86.

12. *New York Times*, October 23, 1962.

13. See Robert F. Kennedy, *Thirteen Days: A Memoir of the Cuban Missile Crisis* (New York: W. W. Norton, 1969).

14. Ulam, *Expansion and Coexistence*, p. 677.

15. Arthur Schlesinger, Jr., *A Thousand Days*, p. 872.

16. See, for example, Robert L. Pfaltzgraff, Jr., "The Czechoslovak Crisis and the Future of the Atlantic Alliance," *Orbis* (Spring 1969), pp. 210–22.

17. More on Nixon's policy toward the Atlantic Alliance in Chapter 8.

18. Pierre Hassner, *Les deux Europes et les deux grands* (Paris: Centre d'Etude des Relations Internationales, Institut des Sciences Politiques, 1966).

19. Stanley Hoffmann, *Gulliver's Troubles* (New York: McGraw-Hill, 1968), p. 410.

20. See, for example, George Kennan, *Russia, the Atom and the West* (London: Oxford University Press, 1958). For a reply to Kennan, see Dean Acheson, "The Illusion of Disengagement," *Foreign Affairs* (April 1958), pp. 371–83.

21. *New York Times*, June 26, 1963.

22. Hearings on his nomination as secretary of State, Senate Foreign Relations Committee, April 21, 1959, p. 10.

23. News conference of May 15, 1962.

24. The main rationale for the new strategy was first delivered publicly by Secretary McNamara at Ann Arbor, Michigan, June 16, 1962. *Bulletin*, Vol. XLVII, pp. 64–69.

25. Address before the Fellows of the American Bar Foundation, Chicago, February 17, 1962.

26. Remarks to the Institute for Strategic Studies, London, December 11, 1961. Quoted in William W. Kaufmann, *The McNamara Strategy* (New York: Harper & Row, 1964), p. 109.

27. Robert McNamara, address to editors of United Press International, San Francisco, September 18, 1967, *New York Times*, September 19, 1967.

28. In McNamara's address at Ann Arbor, Michigan, *Bulletin*, Vol. XLVII, pp. 64–69.

29. Address before the Fellows of the American Bar Foundation, *Chicago*, February 17, 1962.

30. Robert McNamara, quoted in William W. Kaufmann, *Military Policy and National Security* (Princeton, N.J.: Princeton University Press, 1956), p. 59.

31. Ibid., p. 105.

32. Quoted in Seyom Brown, *The Faces of Power* (New York: Columbia University Press, 1968), p. 176.

33. Quoted in Seymour T. Deitchman, *Limited War and American Defense Policy*, 2nd ed. (Cambridge, Mass.: Massachusetts Institute of Technology, 1969), p. 5.

34. De Gaulle's press conference of November 10, 1962, *New York Times*, November 11, 1962.

35. Henry Kissinger, *The Troubled Partnership* (New York: McGraw-Hill, 1965).

36. Richard Rosecrance, *Problems of Nuclear Proliferation*, Security Studies Project, University of California at Los Angeles, 1966, p. 12.

37. A. Buchan, *A World of Nuclear Powers?* (Englewood Cliffs, N.J.: Prentice Hall, 1966), p. 9.

38. See Pierre Gallois, *The Balance of Terror* (Boston, Mass.: Houghton Mifflin, 1961).

39. See André Beaufre, *Deterrence and Strategy* (New York: Praeger, 1965).

40. New Conference of July 23, 1964, French Embassy, *Speeches and Press Conferences*, No. 208, p. 7.

41. Speech of September 30, 1963. André Passeron, *De Gaulle parle, 1962–1966* (Paris: Fayard, 1966) p. 220.
42. As reported by Arthur Schlesinger, Jr., *A Thousand Days*, p. 897.
43. A detailed discussion of these and other related issues can be found in Michael M. Harrison, *The Reluctant Ally. France and Atlantic Security* (Baltimore Md.: Johns Hopkins University Press, 1981).
44. Simon Serfaty, *France, de Gaulle and Europe* (Baltimore, Md.: Johns Hopkins University Press, 1968), p. 144.
45. See Kissinger, *The Troubled Partnership*, pp. 129–62. The case for the MLF is concisely presented by Robert E. Osgood, *The Case for the MLF: A Critical Evaluation* (Washington, D.C.: The Washington Center of Foreign Policy Research, 1964).
46. Serfaty, *France, de Gaulle and Europe*, p. 128.
47. Arthur Schlesinger, Jr., *A Thousand Days*, p. 872.
48. De Gaulle, *Memoires d'Espoir: Le renouveau, 1958-1962*, Vol. 1 (Paris: Librairie Plon, 1970), pp. 214 ff.
49. Kissinger, *Troubled Partnership*, pp. 223–34.
50. John F. Kennedy, "The Goal of an Atlantic Partnership," July 4, 1962. *Bulletin*, Vol. XLVII, pp. 131–33.
51. Harold van B. Cleveland, *The Atlantic Idea and its European Rivals* (New York: McGraw-Hill, 1966), p. 105.
52. Fred C. Bergsten, *The Dilemmas of the Dollar: The Economics and Politics of United States International Monetary Policy* (New York: New York University Press, 1975), pp. 80–81.
53. Joan Edelman Spero, *The Politics of International Economic Relations* (New York: St. Martin's Press, 1977), p. 38.
54. Robert Solomon, *The International Monetary System, 1945–1976* (New York: Harper & Row, 1977), p. 53.
55. David Calleo and Benjamin M. Rowland, *America and the World Political Economy: Atlantic Dreams and National Realities* (Bloomington, Ind.: Indiana University Press, 1973), p. 291.
56. David Calleo, *The Atlantic Fantasy: The U.S., NATO, and Europe* (Baltimore, Md.: Johns Hopkins University Press, 1970), p. 87.
57. Quoted in Ernst Preeg, *Traders and Diplomats* (Washington, D.C.: The Brookings Institution, 1970), pp. 285–86.
58. Simon Serfaty, *France, de Gaulle and Europe*, pp. 51 ff.
59. For a thorough and highly readable treatment of the Kennedy round and related issues see Gerald Meier, *Problems of Trade Policy* (New York: Oxford University Press, 1973).
60. Cleveland, *Atlantic Idea and Its European Rivals*, p. 105.

61. See Gian Paolo Casadio, *Trans-Atlantic Trade: USA-EEC Confrontation in GATT Negotiations* (Lexington, Mass.: Lexington Books, 1973). p. 26.

62. George Ball, "U.S. Policy Toward NATO," in *NATO in Quest of Cohesion*, ed. Karl Cerny and C. W. Briefs (New York: Praeger, 1965), p. 18.

CHAPTER SIX

The Elusive Enemy

The Heritage in Indochina

From 1940 on, America's enemy in Indochina was a changing and elusive one. During the months that preceded and followed Pearl Harbor, the enemy was Japan, as Indochina provided the setting for the first application of an American change of attitude toward Japan—from a policy of "restraint and patience" to one of "firmness."[1] Later, toward the end of the Pacific war, the main enemy became colonialism, as President Roosevelt supported Indochina's movement toward independence from France. And later still, with the outbreak of the cold war, the enemy became international communism.

Like Korea, Indochina did not engage vital American interests. Indeed, its intrinsic value was little: it was hardly ever a region of major military or industrial importance. True, Indochina represented a valuable source of rice, corn, coal, rubber, and minerals, particularly before it entered three decades of uninterrupted warfare. But even then, Indochina remained somewhat marginal to American interests; and no decisive developments in the international situation would have been determined under normal circumstances by what happened in that area of the world.[2] Yet, between 1940—Japan's invasion of Indochina—and 1970—the U.S. invasion of Cambodia—circumstances never appeared to be normal, and U.S. policies toward the Indochinese peninsula reflected America's concern with Japan and China as Asian powers, with France and Great Britain as allies and colonial powers, and with the Soviet Union and China as the leaders of the communist bloc.

The specific tenets of American policy were placed within the larger framework of a domino theory, periodically adjusted to the enemy involved. In 1940, the Roosevelt administration assumed that should Japan succeed in consolidating its control of Indochina, Tokyo would next attempt to seize Thailand and continue to press further southward in the Philippines, Malaya, and the East Indies.[3] Nevertheless, this assumption did not immediately commit the United States to the area: after the fall of France in June 1940, Roosevelt refused to provide the French governor in Indochina with the aid that the latter had requested to resist Japanese demands. But following the enlargement of Tokyo's "Greatest East Asia Co-Prosperity Sphere," Indochina became "the watershed that separated peace from war in the Pacific."[4] Understood as a test of America's determination to contain Japanese expansion in the Pacific, Indochina now required more attention. The American government, Secretary Cordell Hull argued, could not "sit perfectly quiet and be cheerful and agreeable, but static, whilst most of Asia is 'Manchurianized.'"[5] On the very day when Tokyo struck at Pearl Harbor, the so-called Hull note proposed that Indochina's neutrality be guaranteed by America, Great Britain, China, Japan, the Dutch government in exile, and Thailand—with all six countries but not France to be given equal treatment in trade and commerce with Indochina.[6]

In early 1945, with Japan about to be defeated, President Roosevelt regarded Indochina as a test case of America's determination to end colonialism. The colonial system, believed Roosevelt, "means war. . . . Americans would [not] be dying in the Pacific . . . if it had not been for the short-sighted greed of the French and British and the Dutch. Shall we allow them to do it . . . all over again?[7] In a new variation on the domino theory, Roosevelt contended that "India, Burma . . . Indochina, and Indonesia—they're all interrelated. If one gets freedom, the others will get ideas. That's why Winston is so anxious to keep de Gaulle in his corner. De Gaulle isn't any more interested in seeing a colonial empire disappear than Churchill is."[8]

By the end of World War II, America's policy in Indochina therefore aimed at preventing the French from returning as the effective colonial overlords in the area. As recorded by his son Elliot, the American president "felt that the French would have no right after the war, to simply walk back into Indochina and reclaim [it] . . . for no reason other than that it had been their colony."[9] "The case of Indochina," stated President Roosevelt on another occasion, "is perfectly clear. France has milked it for one hundred years. The people of Indochina are entitled to something better than that."[10] The case was all the more convincing as French policy from 1940 onward had been to preserve nominal control of Indochina at whatever cost, regardless of the effects that French concessions to Japan might have upon U.S. interests in Asia. As first outlined at the interallied level in March 1943, the French were to be replaced by an international trusteeship made up of three commissioners—an American, a Chinese, and a Briton.[11] This trusteeship was later enlarged to include as many as two Indochinese, a Russian, a Frenchman, and a Filipino.[12] With the support of the Soviet Union and China, the United States foresaw complete independence for the Indochinese states—an independence to be achieved, however, after a length of time that was never clearly specified. In line with such a policy, the American war department refused military assistance to the de Gaulle government when, in March 1945, Tokyo broke its modus vivendi with France, swiftly deposed the French administration, disarmed the French garrison, imprisoned French citizens, and created an independent puppet state with Bao Dai as its Emperor.[13] Only after the last organized French units had been destroyed by the Japanese forces did Admiral Leahy receive the president's permission to release American aircraft for support missions in Indochina.[14]

Meanwhile, there had been organized in Indochina a national-front organization—the Vietminh—under the leadership of one Nguyen Ai-Quee, later to be known as Ho Chi Minh.[15] Although largely dominated by the Indochinese communist party, the Vietminh attempted to unite all Indochinese groups against both Japanese militarism and French imperialism. Within a few weeks of Japan's defeat, the Vietminh seized power, and, on September 2, 1945, after the abdication of Bao Dai, a Republic of Vietnam was proclaimed, with Ho Chi Minh as its president. The small official American delegation present at the scene hailed the "liberators of the Vietnamese people" who were urged to break all links with France. At first, American support of Ho's new government was also informally promised. Soon, however, Secretary of State James Byrnes, eager to preserve Paris' support in the growing confrontation with the Soviet Union in Europe, withdrew U.S. support for Ho and denied any American opposition to a French return to Indochina.[16]

Vietnam, however, was already divided. As a result of the Potsdam agreements, Chinese troops had occupied the country north of the 16th parallel and Great Britain south of it, for the purpose of disarming the Japanese and repatriating allied prisoners of war. In the south, the British governor was under strict orders from London to stay aloof from local politics. Nevertheless, he undertook on his own to restore the authority of France by arming the French soldiers. In so doing, and in a move that MacArthur described as "the most ignoble kind of betrayal," he used Japanese troops against the Vietminh in the fighting that accompanied the latter's expulsion from Saigon.[17] In the north, the Chinese opposed French efforts to restore their former rule. But though generally sympathetic to Vietnamese aspirations, the Chinese behaved like conquering armies: they seized what they thought they needed, and they thought they needed everything.

In March 1946, with Japan out of Indochina, the British and Chinese forces prepared to leave Vietnam. At the same time the French and the Vietminh signed a treaty that recognized Vietnam as a "free state with its own government, parliament, army and finances," but as a "part of the Indochinese Federation and the French Union."[18] In theory, the agreement of March 1946 was expected to be a preliminary step toward a larger accord that would grant the Indochinese states full independence. In practice, such an agreement gave the French military entry into the north, thereby providing the means—should they so decide—for undoing the concessions that they had just granted. By avoiding an immediate military confrontation, the Vietminh, too, gained the time it needed to organize its resistance to the French, should this prove necessary. The accord of March 1946 merely meant that the French and the Vietminh were now left alone to settle their differences in a sanguinary war that was officially begun in December 1946.[19] When it ended on July 21, 1954, the war (*la salle guerre*, as it was called in France) had cost the French Union forces 92,000 dead or missing and 72,000 wounded.[20] The Vietminh's casualties ran perhaps three times as high, with countless Vietnamese civilians (estimated by some at 250,000) killed during the fighting.[21]

The American Commitment Takes Shape

As problems with the Soviet Union increased following the end of the Pacific war, America's need to foster unity with the European allies also grew. Following his advisers' recommendations, President Truman urged that every effort be made to assist France to regain its status and its strength.[22] Clearly this included Indochina, whose loss, it was now feared, might be the blow that would bring France to its knees. The loss of Indochina would further weaken the pro-American government in Paris that faced the combined opposition of the Gaullists and the communists, as both could be counted on to channel French resentment into a new wave of anti-Americanism.

In 1949, communist successes in China strengthened the French case for increased American support. In January 1950, the recognition of Ho Chi Minh's government by the two communists giants prompted Secretary of State Acheson to dismiss the nationalist claims of Ho Chi Minh, whom Acheson now described as the "mortal enemy of native independence in Indochina."[23] Consequently, America changed the status of the Vietnamese people, though French-ruled, to that of a "free people" resisting "subversion by armed minorities or by outside pressure."[24] Soon thereafter, on February 7, 1950, in a move that completed America's volte-face, Washington officially recognized Vietnam and each of the two other Associated States of Laos and Cambodia as independent entities within the French Union. Somewhat like Korea, Vietnam had become a theater of the cold war, with Moscow backing up one faction and Washington supporting the other.

In June 1950, the outbreak of the Korean War seemed to confirm the French contention that the conflict in Indochina was "the same war against the same enemy, for the same cause and at the same price of the same sacrifices."[25] To American policymakers, the contention that the free world's determination to resist aggression was being equally tested everywhere appeared plausible. Upon the recommendation of his secretary of state, one of President Truman's first decisions after the attack in Korea was that military aid to the French in Indochina be substantially increased.[26] After Roosevelt and before Eisenhower, the American president was also defining his own domino theory: "We are seeing a pattern in Indochina and Tibet timed to coincide with the attack on Korea, a challenge to the western world. . . . The Chinese communists were Russian satellites. . . . After Korea, it would be Indochina, then Hong Kong, then Malaya."[27]

The theory was hardly disputed at the time, and no effort was made to define more specifically America's interests and objectives in Indochina proper. With circumstances less normal than ever, French and American policy in Indochina became hopelessly confused. The French could no longer make war without American assistance. But with American assistance they could no longer make peace, as such assistance was predicated on the assumption that the French would not quit. "After seven years of conflict," reflected General Henry Navarre, the last French commander-in-chief in Indochina, "we had reached a complete imbroglio, from the plain soldier to the commander-in-chief no one knew why we were fighting."[28] But just as Paris was uncertain whether it was fighting to maintain a colony or to promote the independence of a noncommunist state, so Washington, too, proved unable to define its objective: to help France or to replace it, to "save" Indochina from Soviet communism or from French colonialism? And to those few critics who were already pointing to the danger that American policy in Indochina might eventually escalate into armed intervention,

Secretary of State Dean Acheson simply replied: "I decided . . . that having put our hand to the plow, we would not look back."[29] Unknown to all and never to be declared—thus had begun America's informal entry into a war that was to cost America nearly 58,000 dead and missing.

As allied commander of NATO, General Eisenhower had recommended American assistance in the Indochinese war in order to leave the French with the resources they needed to maintain their role in Europe.[30] Seen from the perspective of NATO, such support also strengthened the alliance between Paris and Washington by reducing France's suspicions of American aims and motives in the area.[31] As president, Eisenhower implemented and escalated the policy of assistance that had been inaugurated by his predecessor. This aid had already reached significant proportions. Estimates in mid-1954 placed the total value of American military supplies sent to Indochina since 1946 at $2 billion, approximately 15% of the total cost of the Marshall Plan. In April 1954, the United States announced that its aid to Indochina for the forthcoming fiscal year would run to $1.1 billion, as compared to the $150 million that had been granted for fiscal year 1950.[32] Altogether, America's contribution accounted for 40% of the total war expenditures between 1951 and 1954, 60% after September 1953, when an additional $385 million grant was received by the French, and 78% by mid-1954, when efforts were being made to liberate the besieged camp of Dien Bien Phu.[33]

Early in 1954, financial assistance alone was no longer sufficient, and American military intervention was seriously discussed. Until that time, the French government, jealous of its prerogatives in the field and still distrustful of United States intentions, had opposed American participation in the war proper. What contributed to a change of mind was Dien Bien Phu, a remote French outpost that had been established on the northwestern boundary of Vietnam in November 1953 as a barrier against any further Vietminh offensives against Laos.[34] With the 15,000 men of the fortress dangerously threatened by General Giap's superior Vietminh forces, the government of Prime Minister Joseph Laniel attempted to secure an American intervention that would save the embattled camp, stabilize the

French position in Laos, and permit a favorable settlement of the negotiations scheduled to open in Geneva that coming spring.

On March 20, a mission headed by General Paul Ely, the French chief of staff, arrived in Washington to elicit American reaction to France's need for additional assistance. In effect, America's commitment to the defense of Indochina had steadily escalated throughout 1953. With increased determination after the Korean War, America warned China that a further deterioration of the situation in Indochina would have "great consequences which might not be confined to Indochina."[35] In 1954, some described Dulles' well-publicized January 12 speech on massive retaliation as one prompted by the need to preempt a mounting communist offensive in that region.[36] From the American side, apparently unsolicited by the French mission, came a more ambitious offer. Partly in line with President Eisenhower's instruction to help France save Dien Bien Phu (under attack since March 13) and partly on his own initiative, Admiral Radford, then chairman of the Joint Chiefs of Staff, offered for consideration by Paris an American air raid against the perimeter of the fortress that would be carried out with 200 planes from the Philippines and the Seventh Fleet.[37] Atomic weapons were reportedly available for the contingency of a large-scale Chinese retaliation.[38] Targets in China were even selected, "reasonably related to the area," later said Dulles, although no "great population centers like Shanghai, Peking or Canton."[39]

But Paris' belated approval of the Radford proposal (April 4) came only after the refusal (on April 3) by a group of leading congressmen to approve any such unilateral military intervention.[40] Instead, the Eisenhower administration was urged to act within an international coalition that would specifically include Great Britain. Cognizant of the congressional request, Eisenhower intervened personally with British Prime Minister Winston Churchill to secure immediate action in Indochina. "I believe," the American president wrote to Churchill, "that the best way to put teeth in this concept [of united action] . . . is through the establishment of a new, ad hoc grouping or coalition composed of nations which had a vital concern in the checking of communist expansion in the Associated States, Australia, New

Zealand, Thailand and the Philippines."[41] But Great Britain remained firmly committed to a negotiated settlement through the Geneva Conference and, in the interim, adamantly opposed any action that might undermine its success.

In effect, Dulles was interested neither in the immediate problem of Dien Bien Phu, nor in preparing for negotiations with the communists. Instead, he wanted to pursue the war to a victorious conclusion. To this effect he was willing to offer American intervention, provided he was given commitments by America's allies, including a pledge that France itself would not "withdraw from the battle until it is won" and assurances of complete independence for the Associated States of Laos, Cambodia, and Vietnam.[42] From within, the position of the Eisenhower administration was singularly complicated by the various pledges it had made at home. On the one hand, Eisenhower's early settlement of the war in Korea, as promised during the 1952 campaign, had gained him the enviable reputation of peacemaker, a reputation he was reluctant to sacrifice on the altar of another unpopular war in Asia. On the other hand, the Eisenhower administration had promised an end to communist gains in Asia and elsewhere, and it feared that a refusal to intervene would expose the Republicans to the same charges that they themselves had previously used against the Democrats.

To improve the case for intervention, the stakes in Vietnam were increased by reviving the old domino theory. In his press conference of April 7, Eisenhower reflected on the effect that the fall of one country would have on the others. If one state fell to communism, Eisenhower said, its neighbors would do likewise, in a chain reaction like a row of falling dominoes, and the fall of Indochina would therefore lead to the fall of Burma, Thailand, Malaya, and Indonesia. India would then be hemmed in by communism, and Australia, New Zealand, the Philippines, Formosa, and Japan would all be dangerously threatened. Eisenhower concluded that upon the outcome of the struggle in Indochina could be said to rest the destiny of mankind.[43]

Yet in May, following the fall of Dien Bien Phu, both Eisenhower and his secretary of state tacitly retreated from this doomsday outlook and flatly stated that retention of Indochina was not essential for the defense of Southeast Asia.[44] Unwilling to condone the "loss" of North Vietnam, the American government at the same time refused to participate officially at the Geneva Conference and to join in its final declaration. Thus the stage was set for later violations by both parties of whatever accords might be concluded at the conference table.

1954: The Geneva Conference

The Geneva Conference convened with the Western allies badly divided. After Dien Bien Phu, France no longer had the will to fight; Great Britain had never wanted to fight; and America would not fight if the others did not also fight. Yet, on the whole, the outcome of the conference was quite favorable to the Western allies—"the best," as Undersecretary of State General Walter Bedell Smith declared upon returning from Geneva, "which we could have possibly obtained under the circumstances."[45] Ho Chi Minh was himself under pressure to bring the war to an end. From without, the communist leader was being pressured by his allies. In the middle of the conference the Soviet Union appeared anxious to help the new French government of Pierre Mendès-France on the eve of a decisive vote on the status of the European Defense Community. China, whose presence in Geneva represented a significant diplomatic victory, was not inclined to enter another war with the West less than a year after the conclusion of the Korean conflict. More generally, both Moscow and Peking wanted to experiment further with the more flexible policy that had followed Stalin's death. But Ho Chi Minh was also pressured by the Western allies. From Washington came the ever-present threat of military intervention, a threat likely to be revived if the conference failed; from Paris, French Premier Mendès-France, who had given himself one month to reach an agreement in Geneva, was using the threat of his own resignation as an effective lever against Vietminh recalcitrance; his departure could only result in a new government (probably headed by Mendès-France's arch adversary, George Bidault) bent on continuing the war, and even escalating it through the use of conscripts.[46] From within, but unknown to France and its allies,

Ho Chi Minh's forces were nearing exhaustion; losses at Dien Bien Phu had been considerable, with casualties reaching an estimated 18,000, including 8,000 deaths; and the lassitude of a war-weary Vietnamese population made guerrilla operations difficult to continue.[47]

Under such circumstances, the communists made substantial concessions to the West. They abandoned several provinces that had always shown allegiance to the Vietminh, and they accepted that elections throughout Vietnam should be held as late as two years after the end of the fighting. But the very principle of national elections made such concessions temporary only, as it was widely assumed at the time that Ho's electoral victory was certain.

With regard to Vietnam proper, the Geneva Conference produced two main accords. The first of these accords, a bilateral ceasefire, marked the end of military hostilities between the French Union forces and the Vietminh. The 17th parallel was recognized as a "provisional military demarcation line," on either side of which the forces of the two parties were to be regrouped. Vietnam was to be neutralized: all foreign troops and bases were banned from the country, north and south, and both zones were forbidden to adhere to any military alliance. An international commission, composed of representatives from Canada, Poland, and India, was set up to supervise and control the implementation of the ceasefire agreement and the organization of the general elections. Finally, the agreement also stipulated that any civilian wishing to move from one zone to the other be allowed to do so, freely, before May 18, 1955. (Roughly 900,000 persons moved southward, roughly 150,000 went northward. More importantly, however, approximately 5,000 to 6,000 elite Vietminh guerrillas stayed in South Vietnam and went underground.)[48]

Elections were further outlined in a second accord, the Final Declaration, which was signed by no one but was endorsed orally by the representatives of France, Great Britain, China, the Soviet Union, Cambodia, Laos, and the Democratic Republic of Vietnam. Paragraphs six and seven of the Declaration were the crucial clauses and deserve full quotation:

> The Conference recognizes that the essential purpose
> of the agreement relating to Vietnam is to settle military

questions with a view to ending hostilities and that the military demarcation line is provisional and should not in any way be interpreted as constituting a political or territorial boundary. The Conference expresses it convictions that the execution of the provisions set out in the present declaration and in the agreement on the cessation of hostilities creates the necessary basis for the achievement in the near future of a political settlement in Vietnam.

The Conference declares that, so far as Vietnam is concerned, the settlement of political problems, effected on the basis of respect for the principles of independence, unity and territorial integrity, shall permit the Vietnamese people to enjoy the fundamental freedoms, guaranteed by democratic institutions established as a result of free general elections by secret ballot. In order to ensure that sufficient progress in the restoration of peace has been made, and that all the necessary conditions obtained for free expression of the national will, general elections shall be held in July 1956, under the supervision of an international commission composed of representatives of the Member States of the International Supervisory Commission, referred to in the agreement on the cessation of hostilities. Consultations will be held on this subject between the competent representative authorities of the two zones from July 20, 1955, onwards.

The documents that sanctioned the Geneva Conference formed a not-so-skillful trompe l'oeil, which, designed to please everyone, ended up frustrating everyone. The ambiguity and contradictoriness of these documents was considerable. Provisions were included to protect the freedom of all Vietnamese in deciding in which zone they wished to live. But at the same time, other provisions specifically stated that the division of Vietnam would not last more than two years. Could it be assumed that the Vietnamese people, whose attachment to their land and villages was well known, would be willing to move from one area to the other (with all the risks that such a move might entail) for only two years of relative freedom? To be sure, if unification were necessary, then separation was already implicit, and the notion that a single Vietnam was being dealt with was a weird diplomatic illusion.[49]

The legal dilemmas that the Geneva documents raised were also considerable. With Vietnam recognized since July 4 as a fully independent and sovereign state, how valid was a French general's sanction of matters affecting the administrative and political life of Vietnam? In fact, the South Vietnamese delegation not only refused to sign any agreement at all, but it reserved its complete freedom of action to guarantee the independence and unity of Vietnam as the authorities in Saigon understood them. Subsequently South Vietnam refused to be held by the promise of elections. In adopting this position, the Saigon government headed by Ngo Dinh Diem held one trump card—the support of the United States. Aware that an election in 1956 would in all likelihood spell Ho Chi Minh's victory, the Eisenhower Administration condoned Diem's refusal to hold such elections until the time, in Diem's words, "when all the conditions of freedom are present," that is to say, until the time when North Vietnam would have somehow ceased to be communist and Diem would have become certain of victory.[50] Eisenhower's position was in turn supported by the Democratic opposition in Congress. "I hope," stated then Senator John F. Kennedy in September 1956, that the United States will "never give its approval to the early nationwide elections called for by the Geneva agreement of 1954."[51] American approval was not given, the elections were not held, and the war was soon to resume.

With the Geneva Conference out of the way, the Eisenhower administration resumed its efforts to form an alliance that would permit united action in South and Southeast Asia on behalf of anticommunist elements. Later, in his *Memoirs,* President Eisenhower credited the Indochina War with having alerted London and Paris to the dangers of international communism in Asia and to the desirability of common action to defeat it.[52] Yet the Southeast Asia Treaty that followed was signed despite the Geneva Conference rather than because of it. Only when London proved willing to heal the breach opened in Geneva between Great Britain and the United States and to abandon its plan for reciprocal guarantees in Asia was Dulles able to conclude, in less than six weeks, the desired defense treaty. SEATO linked the ANZUS pact countries (Australia, New Zealand, and the United States) to two of the CENTO members (Great Britain and Pakistan), two Southeast Asian clients of the United States (Thailand and the Philippines), and France. A protocol approved simultaneously with the treaty also extended the protection of the contracting parties to Cambodia, Laos, and South Vietnam.

SEATO differed from the North Atlantic Treaty in that it applied only to a very specific threat. Obviously, the test for inclusion was not geographical location in Southeast Asia: only the Philippines and Thailand met this criterion. The test instead was an explicit commitment to the containment of further communist expansion in the area, thereby excluding from the treaty India and Indonesia as well as such usual parts of the domino theory as Burma and Malaya. Embodied in the treaty was an "understanding" on the part of the United States that confirmed the specific focus of the treaty in such a way as to assuage Indian fears that Washington was now committed to assist Pakistan in the case of a conflict between these two countries.

Yet even such narrowly defined commitment was left somewhat ambiguous. There was no intention to build a defense force on the continent of Asia that would be sufficient to resist direct attack by communist forces. "We do not intend to dedicate any major elements of the United States military establishment to form an army of defense in this area. We rely primarily upon the deterrent of our mobile striking power," testified Secretary Dulles, who added that to do otherwise would risk an "overextension of American military power."[53] Direct aggression would be met in accordance with due constitutional process, thereby effectively permitting each member state to take whatever action it deemed necessary if an armed attack occurred. Subversion and indirect aggression would require immediate consultation. But there was no commitment to defeat it. "If there is a revolutionary movement in Vietnam or in Thailand," explained Dulles, "we would consult together as to what to do about it. . . . But we have no understanding to put it down; all we have is an undertaking to consult together as to what to do about it."[54]

As a result of the first Indochinese War between 1946 and 1954, the United States thus assumed in Southeast Asia a role that it had first sought to convince France to relinquish and then to maintain. But what prospects were there that the United States would be more successful than France? First of all, whereas the French were colonialists, America was motivated by its traditional anticolonialism. As Eisenhower proudly put it, this tradition was "born in the circumstances of our own national birth in 1775."[55] It was hoped that American policies in Southeast Asia would be pursued in conjunction with, rather than against, nationalism, albeit noncommunist nationalism—the only kind the United States recognized. The solution that would make America successful where others had failed was relatively simple: to find a national leader who could promote from within a total determination to resist communist imperialism. This, at least, was the conclusion reached by Eisenhower and Dulles. Eisenhower wrote,

> I am convinced that the French could not win the war because the internal political situation in Vietnam, weak and confused, badly weakened their military position. I have never talked or corresponded with a person knowledgeable in Indochinese affairs who did not agree that had elections been held as of the time of the fighting, possibly 80 percent of the population would have voted for the Communist Ho Chi Minh as their leader rather than Chief of State Bao Dai. Indeed, the lack of leadership and drive on the part of Bao Dai was a factor in the feeling prevalent among Vietnamese that they had nothing to fight for. As one Frenchman said to me, "What Vietnam needs is another Syngman Rhee, regardless of all the difficulties that the presence of such a personality would entail."[56]

The Eisenhower Administration thought it had found a true national leader in Ngo Dinh Diem, and at first Diem appeared to succeed in fostering much national support despite methods that made a sympathetic observer describe his regime in late 1956 as a "quasi police state characterized by arbitrary arrests and imprisonment, strict censorship of press and the absence of an effective political opposition."[57] But the resurgence of communist-led resistance in the south in the late 1950s already presaged the increasing difficulties that Diem and his American sponsors were to have in maintaining the Republic of

South Vietnam in the years to come. Indeed, by 1961, all the difficulties the presence of such a personality as Diem entailed were enough to bring America into a second Indochinese war, a war that was to continue until April 1975.

The Americanization of the War

The Kennedy and Johnson Administrations inherited, rather than originated, the guidelines of American policy toward Indochina. Both Democratic presidents acted on the same assumptions that had motivated their predecessors. The first of these assumptions was America's perception of a monolithic communist bloc. Despite reports already available on the split between the two communist states, Washington refused to conceive of it as plausible at all until 1962. The Kennedy Administration thought it had found in Southeast Asia the first application of a new Soviet strategy. As outlined by Khrushchev in January 1961, this strategy indicated that, in the coming years, Moscow would rely primarily neither on nuclear nor on conventional but on guerilla war.[58] Perceiving the Soviet Union as the implicit enemy in Indochina, the Kennedy Administration resurrected the domino theory, which three previous administrations had previously shaped to suit their needs. More than four years before he assumed the presidency, Kennedy, who earlier had watched the French colonial policy with great skepticism, had in effect endorsed the domino theory. Vietnam, Kennedy had observed in September 1956, "represents the cornerstone of the Free World in Southeast Asia, the keystone to the arch, the finger in the dike. Burma, Thailand, India, Japan, the Philippines, and obviously Laos and Cambodia are among those whose security would be threatened if the red tide of communism overflowed into Vietnam." In short, Kennedy concluded, Vietnam was "a test of American responsibility and determination in Asia," a test that directly involved America's security in any new outbreak of trouble.[59]

The monolithic image of the communist camp and the endorsement of the domino theory were not the only assumptions governing America's policy in Indochina. Also instrumental were fears of a "China on the march," the rigidity of the East Asian establishment at the State Department, still reminiscent of the McCarthy era, the vulnerability of the Democratic party on Asian policy issues since the "loss of China" charges, the lack of substantial American expertise on Vietnam, and the international setbacks early in the Kennedy Administration. All of these important factors shaped America's growing military intervention in Vietnam.[60]

In 1954, the end of the Indochinese war had not meant the end of American aid to Vietnam. In fact, during the remaining years of the Eisenhower Administration U.S. economic and military aid to the Diem government had substantially exceeded that given to the French during the war. Furthermore, military "advisers" began to be sent regularly, and by mid-1961 the United States military mission in Vietnam numbered approximately 2,000.[61] Yet it was not Vietnam but neighboring Laos that, in 1961, posed the most urgent problem to the new Kennedy Administration.

Less than twenty-four hours before entering the White House, Kennedy was briefed by the outgoing president and his cabinet on the impending crisis in Laos.[62] More than $300 million over five years—one of the highest levels of American aid per capita—had failed to transform "neutral" Laos into a Western military outpost. Instead, the pressure that accompanied the aid steadily antagonized neutralist Premier Souvanna Phouma who, in 1958, entered into a political coalition with his half brother, Prince Souphanouvong, leader of the communist Pathet Lao forces that had settled in the two northeastern provinces of Laos where the Geneva accords had specified that the communists were to regroup. By the late 1950s, Laos had implicitly become divided between the United States-backed faction of General Phoumi Nosavan and the Pathet Lao, which was receiving large quantities of Sino-Soviet military equipment—despite the 1954 agreements to neutralize the former French colony, but in conjunction with America's own arms shipments to the Phoumi faction.[63] The situation had so deteriorated that, in the waning days of his presidency, Eisenhower felt that America should consider intervention.[64]

Following some serious military rattling, the Kennedy Administration was able to settle the problems with diplomatic rather than military tools. Apparently both sides failed to find in the Laotians those martial virtues that might have warranted a continued build-up toward armed confrontation. United States ambassador in India John Kenneth Galbraith was reported to have told Indian Prime Minister Nehru, "Americans are practical men and did not set military value on the Lao, who do not believe in getting killed like the civilized races."[65] Moreover, as in April 1954, no ally could be found to support a multilateral military intervention. Finally, the ill-fated attempt at invading Cuba, in April 1961, proved decisive in preventing a repeat performance in Laos. "That operation," narrated presidential adviser Theodore Sorensen, "had been recommended principally by the same set of advisers who favored intervention in Laos. But now the president was far more skeptical of the experts, their reputations, their recommendations, their promises, premises and facts. . . . " As the president confided to Sorensen, "Thank God the Bay of Pigs happened when it did . . . otherwise we'd be in Laos by now—and that would be a hundred times worse."[66] In July 1962, following long and difficult negotiations, a coalition government was formed under the sponsorship of 13 states, including the United States, the Soviet Union, Communist China, and the two Vietnams. It never worked, however, and a still implicitly divided Laos continued to await the outcome of the Vietnam war, between rounds of light combat between the Pathet Lao and the now American-backed Souvana Phouma.

Meanwhile, in South Vietnam the situation had changed from bad to worse. Internal opposition to the Diem regime had reintroduced substantial terrorism as early as mid-1957.[67] Such activities were spearheaded by the Vietminh who had stayed in the south after the 1954 Geneva Conference. In November 1960, a coup led by Diem's own army failed to dislodge him from power. The following month, antigovernment insurgents in the South formed the National Liberation Front (later to be dubbed Vietcong). Although dominated by the communists, the Vietcong, like the Vietminh many years before, included noncommunist, nationalist elements. By the end of Kennedy's first year in office, it appeared that the communists had extended their control to approximately four-fifths of the countryside, cutting off some of the major cities, including Saigon, from their hinterland.

Kennedy's response to the build-up of the communist forces in the South was a parallel build-up of the Saigon forces. In October 1961, a White House team headed by General Maxwell Taylor was sent to Saigon to see what might be done to stabilize the Diem regime. The Taylor mission recommended sending 8,000 more American troops to end infiltration from the North and to assure Diem of America's readiness to join him in a military showdown with the Vietcong.[68] But to win the civil war from within, the team also recommended that major political reforms be enacted by the Diem government. At first hesitant, Kennedy, whose past performance at the Bay of Pigs and ongoing performance in Laos were making him vulnerable to Republican charges of being soft with communism, ordered the proposed build-up: by the time of Kennedy's death, American ground forces in Vietnam amounted to 16,000 men. The letters exchanged between the American and the Vietnamese presidents, like the letters exchanged between Eisenhower and Diem in October 1954, linked the increased American commitment with Diem's pledge of substantial reforms. But though eagerly receiving this increased military assistance, Diem continued to sidetrack the promised reforms.

In November 1963, the collapse of the Diem regime and his assassination signaled the failure of the Eisenhower–Kennedy policy in Vietnam. It was not the Vietcong but the South Vietnamese military, which the United States had so painstakingly built, that overthrew Diem. Thus disappeared the political alternative to Ho Chi Minh on which the United States had counted for so long a time. But fate did not give the American president the opportunity to recoup his losses by embarking, as he apparently intended to, on bold new policies in Vietnam. For John F. Kennedy was assassinated three weeks later.[69]

The transition from Kennedy to Johnson provided little opportunity for a major change in Vietnam policy. The main advisers remained the same, and their assumptions remained unchanged. A difference of some import, however, was Johnson's marked inexperience in foreign policy—an inexperience that left him considerably dependent on his advisers' recommendations. On two previous occasions in the past, Johnson had played an important role in the evolution of America's policy in Vietnam. First, in April 1954, as the senate minority leader, he had been a part of the congressional group that had refused to sanction the proposed Radford Plan without prior support of the allies. As vice-president, in May 1961, he had visited Southeast Asia and had returned to urge the president to engage promptly in a major effort to help these countries help themselves, not only militarily but politically and economically through much-needed domestic reforms. "In large measure," Vice-President Johnson reported to Kennedy, "the greatest danger Southeast Asia offers to nations like the U.S. is not the momentary threat of Communism itself, rather that danger stems from hunger, ignorance, poverty and disease."[70] Having twice demonstrated his reluctance to use force, it was part of Johnson's tragedy to face his first test over Vietnam during a presidential campaign when the flexible military posture established by the McNamara-sponsored reforms allowed him to do what past presidents had been restrained from doing—to send extensive American ground forces to Indochina.

In August 1964, alleged North Vietnamese attacks against American ships in the Gulf of Tonkin caused a sharp increase in American involvement.[71] In Washington, the incident made it possible for the administration to request, and obtain overwhelmingly, passage of the so-called Tonkin Gulf Resolution, whereby the president was empowered by the senate

> to take all necessary measure to repel any armed attack against the forces of the United States . . . to prevent further aggression . . . and to take all necessary steps, including the use of armed forces to assist any member or protocol state of the Southeast Asia Collective Defense Treaty requesting assistance in defense of its freedom.

In Vietnam, the Gulf of Tonkin incident reflected the determination of the Johnson Administration to intervene in the war on an unprecedented scale, as soon as domestic conditions might permit—namely, as soon as the elections were over. On February 7, 1965, the Vietcong attack against the

American camp of Pleiku provided the needed opportunity for enforcing a decision that had been taken months before the attack occurred: retaliatory air strikes against North Vietnam were ordered and then continued regularly against an ever-increasing list of targets.[72] At the same time, an accelerated build-up of American ground forces was undertaken: their number reached 267,000 by mid-1966. These two developments transformed a civil war, fought in the South with outside aid by North Vietnam in the manner of a guerilla war, into a progressively "Americanized" war, waged with American troops doing the bulk of the fighting against an enemy increasingly directed and manned from Hanoi.

Three years of uninterrupted military and rhetorical escalation followed. American commitment in the area had long since outstripped any reasonable estimation of the importance of the area to America. To muster support for the war among an increasingly skeptical public, the domino theory was once more reformulated so that the war in Vietnam became the test case for halting communist-inspired wars of national liberation that, if defeated in Vietnam, would never again pose a major threat.[73] Critics of the war argued that local conditions would most certainly cause revolutionary uprisings elsewhere, no matter what the outcome of the Vietnam War. Vietnam was also presented by the Johnson Administration as the test of all American commitments throughout the world.[74] But critics asked how America's commitment to defend, say, West Germany—a vigorous, industrial nation with a functioning democracy and with which the United States had a common cultural heritage as well as a common, if troubled, history—could be compared to an ambigous commitment to defend the government of the Republic of South Vietnam—more and more a military dictatorship in a nation whose culture and history were so different from that of the United States as to make even a common political vocabulary impossible.[75]

Militarily the war in Vietnam could not be won without literally destroying South Vietnam, dislocating further the national fabric of America, alienating the NATO allies who were generally critical of United States actions in Southeast Asia, endangering rapprochment with the Soviet Union, and increasing the chances of armed confrontation with China. But, still more important, the political prerequisites for winning the war were not present in America. Having ballooned to include 540,000 men engaged in the war at a cost of $30 billion per year, the war could no longer be fully justified even with the most extreme rhetorical flourishes. Public dissent reached a new peak early in 1968, when General Taylor, by then the United States Ambassador in Saigon, requested an additional troop increase of over 200,000 men. After the presidential primary campaign in New Hampshire, President Johnson decided, on March 31, 1968, to restrict the bombing of North Vietnam in order to clear the way for negotiations to end the war. Disillusioned by the defections of many of those upon whom he had most relied (including Defense Secretary Robert McNamara whose change of heart brought about his replacement by Clark Clifford), embittered by the divisions in his own party, where his leadership was challenged at the polls by Senators Eugene McCarthy and Robert F. Kennedy, and most of all stricken by the political failures of his presidency, which had sacrificed an enlightened policy of domestic reform to the spiraling economic and political costs of the war, Johnson also made the ultimate gesture of political defeat by removing himself from public life. Though peace negotiations were laboriously organized in Paris, the war went on. Difficult to fight in the field, difficult to justify at home, and difficult to end, it had already been lost.

Disengagement

It was a measure of the disenchantment with the Vietnam War that, in 1968, many of its liberal critics were willing to bring Richard M. Nixon to the White House in order to end it.[76] But with 540,000 men in Indochina by that time, the liquidation of the U.S. combat role there was not an easy task.

For one, somehow such liquidation had to be managed in such a way as to provide a "decent interval" between the end of the war and an ever possible (if not likely) collapse of the Thieu government in Saigon. Accordingly, the strategy of the Nixon administration aimed at turning over the role of fighting the war to the South Vietnamese themselves—in other words, "to vietnamize" the war—unless, of course, Hanoi would prove willing to negotiate its end with Washington first. In addition, the U.S. withdrawal had to be phased in such a manner as to preserve the whole fabric of American credibility abroad, especially at a time when new approaches to adversary relationships were being sought and implemented. Thus, a war that had been escalated so often and so much in the name of America's credibility still required to be prolonged and fought in the name of that same credibility.

Disengagement was therefore sought in two overlapping sets of negotiations: with the American public, whose exasperation with the war reached new heights after the Tet offensive in early 1968, and with the North Vietnamese themselves.

Throughout the 1960s, the American public had progressively emerged as the "essential domino." Yet for many years public opposition to the war had developed slowly. Thus, in the elections of 1964, opinion polls commissioned by the National Democratic Party showed that as few as 4 or 5% of the people in many states considered the Vietnam war as an issue of major concern. By that time, too, Vietnam remained an unusual occurrence on television, and only a handful of reporters covered it for the written media.[77] From then on, however, the rise of the critics had been all the more noticeable as President Johnson carefully avoided arousing a war fever in the country, which might have compelled him to escalate the American involvement faster and farther than he wanted. But in 1969, both Washington and Hanoi directed their strategy—the rhetoric and the conduct of the war—to this essential domino.[78] And in this contest for the mind and soul of the American public, Hanoi had accumulated considerable advantages. For following the political shock created by the North Vietnamese Tet offensive, a nationwide desire to withdraw American troops from Vietnam had begun to predominate, regardless of whether or not South Vietnam might endure as a nation.[79] Increasingly, and again to Hanoi's advantage, the democratic shortcomings of the Thieu regime were used as an "alibi for [U.S.] abdication."[80] The North Vietnamese now realized that they did not need to win any battle to win the war. Instead, the way to prevail was to maintain a relentless pressure on the political and psychological American front. This, in turn, would be achieved by keeping American casualties high, thereby enhancing public bitterness against a conflict that would be seen all the more unwinnable as periodic North Vietnamese offensives deep in the South, political sabotage, and assassinations confirmed the prevailing image of an irradicable and implacable adversary. These were relatively modest means needed for the fulfillment of comparatively major goals. Since the dominant U.S. combat strategy was to engage the enemy wherever and whenever it could be found, the Communists could determine themselves where and when hostilities would take place.[81] This made it not only possible for the North Vietnamese to continue to inflict significant U.S. casualties: it made it also relatively cheap in communist lives, as large unit encounters could be avoided up to the spring offensive of 1972. Likewise, and though inevitably more costly, occasional countrywide or nationwide offensives were more political than military as they were meant to deny U.S. claims of progress in achieving the security of local populations by striking deeply and seemingly at will against territories that had been previously reported as safe.[82]

While Hanoi was striving in such a way to topple the U.S. domino precipitously, thereby forcing the United States into an early and premature withdrawal at a time when Saigon was still too weak to take over the responsibility of the fighting, Washington conversely labored to delay its disengagement long enough to permit Vietnamization and pacification to succeed. One of the prices paid for husbanding public support—and thus contain public pressures for quicker withdrawal—was the regular repatriation of U.S. forces. Although such troop withdrawals had at first been made conditional on three criteria (no escalation in enemy activity, progress at the peace conference in Paris, and increasing strength of the South Vietnamese forces), they soon became inexorable.[83] This growing insistence on the withdrawal of U.S. troops left the Nixon administration with little room for maneuver. Had the Paris peace talks shown some progress, public opinion might have rallied and regained some taste for a showdown that might have extracted further concessions from the North Vietnamese (beyond, that is, the return of American prisoners of war). But this avenue was effectively closed by Hanoi's equal determination to prevent a strengthening of America's resolve by demonstrating, through firmness in Paris, that more public support for the war in the United States would only lead to more war in Indochina.

Only Nixon's periodic speeches appeared to slow momentarily this progressive deterioration of public support. For example, his speech of November 3, 1969, revealing Hanoi's refusal to discuss U.S. proposals for complete mutual withdrawal within one year, provoked an outpouring of support for the administration's dual strategy of Vietnamization plus negotiations.[84] On occasion, Nixon tried to soften his opposition at home by incorporating specific demands that had been made by some of the leading proponents of an early withdrawal. In some instances the Nixon administration was blamed for failing to accept proposals that Hanoi had not made, or else for Hanoi's failure to accept the proposals that the administration itself had made at the urging of the critics. But in the end, even though Nixon succeeded in reducing U.S. casualties sharply, opposition to the war grew as no abatement of domestic pressure could last.[85]

Nevertheless, the Nixon administration found it necessary to ignore such pressures in order to force Hanoi into the concessions that might salvage Thieu's regime. But this, too, was not an easy task to achieve, and indeed there could be no North Vietnamese flexibility until October 1972, when Nixon's reelection was all but overwhelmingly assured.[86] In effect, two major concessions had already tumbled into Hanoi's lap; a bombing halt in the north and a withdrawal of U.S. forces in the south. Now, congressional opposition and the 1972 election timetable set the deadline for a final withdrawal and encouraged Hanoi to further intransigence and patience.[87] If a postwar disintegration of the South Vietnamese forces was to be averted, the United States therefore had to maximize quickly the value of its remaining assets to pressure Hanoi for concessions that would permit an acceptable settlement.

The Nixon strategy to escalate the war in order to terminate it had two purposes. On the one hand, striking at communist supply lines, logistics and command centers, and sanctuaries would help gain more time for Vietnamization and pacification to work and take root. On the other hand, such demonstration of U.S. will despite mounting domestic opposition would hopefully lead Hanoi to conclude that its own calculations were wrong and that it could not afford to outwait the United States.[88]

Begun in March 1969, the secret bombing of Cambodia launched the new U.S. campaign. Tastelessly christened "Operation Menu" by the Department of Defense, it was said to respond to a North Vietnamese offensive that had started in late February. Yet as early as January, the then president-elect had indicated his preference for an operation that would "destroy the build-up" in Cambodia, thereby reflecting his intention to expand hostilities without new and specific provocations.[89] This was an instrument of pressure that was all the more convenient as it remained unacknowledged by Hanoi and Washington and unprotested by the Cambodians themselves.[90] Later in the year, the invasion of Laos, too, sent an audible message to Hanoi while remaining sufficiently discreet to avoid an additional inflammation of domestic opinion in the United States.

Initiated, it was said, "not to expand the war in Cambodia but to end the war in Vietnam," the invasion of Cambodia in the spring of 1970 was the most controversial manifestation of the Nixon strategy.[91] Although the expected North Vietnamese divisions never materialized, the incursion severely disrupted their operations and permitted the capture or the destruction of many of its personnel, supplies, and installations.[92] Sir Robert Thompson, the British authority on guerilla warfare, estimated that the resulting destruction of North Vietnamese stockpiles would delay another offensive in the south by two years. His forecast proved to be essentially accurate. Indeed, the military success of the assault—tragically achieved at the ultimate cost of Cambodia's national life—was also reflected in the significantly lower American casualties in the months and years that followed the invasion. It also permitted Nixon to propose, the following October, a standstill cease-fire that reflected his increasing confidence that such actions had sufficiently and convincingly enhanced his own credibility in Hanoi. But with Hanoi's rejection of the new Nixon proposal, time continued to be of the essence. In early 1971 again, the incursion into Laos—launched this time with South Vietnamese troops enjoying U.S. air support—did not achieve military results comparable to those achieved with the invasion of Cambodia; it did succeed, however, in delaying and limiting the offensive that was launched by Hanoi the following year.[93]

The 1971 operation in Laos also revealed that Vietnamization still remained far from reality and confirmed it as the Achilles heel of the Nixon strategy of disengagement. No amount of battle-won concessions from Hanoi could ensure Saigon's survival without the quick and effective transformation of the South Vietnamese army into a competent and motivated force comparable to that of its adversary. To be sure, a measure of improvement could be noticed. Beginning with the Tet offensive, when South Vietnamese forces held up better than anyone anticipated, it is widely agreed that the effectiveness of the government forces improved substantially, "whether judged according to the number of operations with contact, the number of enemy killed or other indices."[94] Yet such progress, and its resulting advantages in the field, stood on tenuous grounds. It remained difficult to assert whether the lower combat effectiveness of the North Vietnamese resulted from a new weakness caused by the costly Tet offensive and the invasion of Cambodia, or whether Hanoi had simply decided to await the completion of the U.S. withdrawal. In any event, such a lull in its actions was likely to be temporary only. And in Laos the South Vietnamese forces showed that they were "simply not yet good enough," thereby, in Nixon's words, "undercutting confidence in the success of Vietnamization and the prospect of ending the war."[95]

In addition, and more importantly, the Saigon regime continued to suffer from a general inability to gain a national legitimacy that would help rally and keep loyalty in the villages. In 1971, the new converts were responding to the security now provided by the South Vietnamese forces: there continued to be little evidence otherwise of a more transcendent loyalty. Instead, villages continued to acknowledge all too readily that a return of the Vietcong in force would bring about a new shift in the allegiance.[96] Such an attitude was no more than the concomitant of survival in a shifting war zone, and it appeared to be shared by the soldiers as well who, "in the end, did not feel that [they] were part of a political community worth the supreme sacrifice [and] saw no reason to die for [the government of South Vietnam]."[97]

Conspicuous corruption among military and civilian leaders further weakened motivation, particularly since President Thieu himself continued to be associated with the very corruptive practices he had pledged to eliminate. Nor did the military at last display the required qualities of leadership that might have helped Vietnamization to succeed. All senior command positions were political appointments. Once appointed, commanders tended to operate independently of the command hierarchy, and the South Vietnamese army remained less a national army than a federation of semiautonomous corps. Under such conditions, much of the South Vietnamese relative success between 1970 and 1973 was attributable to the effective participation of U.S. firepower and did not solve the problems raised by the ineffective deployment of Saigon's army and its incompetent leadership. Between 1973 and 1975, the reduction of this firepower, occasioned by U.S. aid cuts that Kissinger was unable to prevent, together with the disastrous military decisions made by Saigon throughout Hanoi's 1975 offensive, consecrated the failure of Vietnamization and the collapse of the South Vietnamese government on April 30, 1975. Having already lost the war a first time on March 31, 1968, the United States had now lost it a second time—but at last its participation in the conflicts of Indochina was over.

No More Dissent

Long before the Paris Agreements of January 1973, events had shown that the basic premises of U.S. policy in Indochina were generally illusory. First, there had been the illusion that the United States had been fighting in Indochina to help the Vietnamese gain their independence. While Ambassador to the Vichy government of France, Admiral Leahy had correctly predicted the outcome of the war with Japan in the Pacific: "If Japan is the winner the Japanese will take over French Indochina; if the allies win, we will take it."[98] Before 1954, the American illusion was to believe that support of the French would satisfy the Vietnamese claims for independence. After

1954, the illusion was to assume that the Diem government and the plethora of mini-governments that followed were safeguarding Western democracy in Asia. Anticommunist though they may have been, these governments, just like the Bao Dai government under the Japanese and under the French, were external creations that had little support from within the communities over which they ruled. Mostly corrupt, generally inept, and often ignored, these governments made communism the primary issue, because only with that issue did they qualify for the external military support without which they could not survive. Kennedy had hardly settled in the White House than official reports on Diem were describing the South Vietnamese leader with the same words that earlier reports had used to describe Chiang and Syngman Rhee. Diem, concluded a CIA report in March 1961, "is unable to rally the people in the fight against the Communists because of his reliance on virtual one-man rule, his toleration of corruption extending even to his immediate entourage, and his refusal to relax a rigid system of public control."[99]

Second, there was the illusion that should Vietnam (and Indochina) fall, then the rest of Asia would inevitably follow. In 1954, while discussing the then difficult situation in Dien Bien Phu, President Eisenhower had recalled how the Western democracies had "failed to halt Hirohito, Mussolini and Hitler by not acting in unity and in time," thus precipitating many years of stark tragedy and desperate peril. "May it not be," asked Eisenhower in the same tone Truman had used before him and other presidents would use after him, "that our nations have learned something from that lesson."[100] American policymakers apparently followed the ancient warning to remember history lest they be doomed to repeat past mistakes. But it was precisely through the indiscriminate projection of an historical episode that mistakes were multiplied. Fixed in the past, the enemy was elusive in the present, not only in Southeast Asia where the ubiquitous ghost of a local Hitler was seen in Ho Chi Minh, but elsewhere. Whether or not American interests were at stake became a moot point. The Munich syndrome, of which the domino theory was but the Asian expression, made it all one world and one peace, and Soviet communism made it all one enemy against which all peace-loving nations needed to unite.

Such an assessment did not go unchallenged. In June 1964, a CIA memorandum submitted to the president noted that so long as the United States could retain its island bases on Okinawa, Guam, the Philippines, and Japan, it could wield enough power in Asia to deter China and North Vietnam from overt military aggression against Southeast Asia. "With the possible exception of Cambodia," it was accurately predicted, "it is likely that no nation in the area would quickly succumb to Communism as a result of the fall of Laos and South Vietnam. . . . A continuation of the spread of communism in the area would not be inexorable."[101] Although in 1941 Japan did use Indochina as a springboard to take the Philippines, Malaya and Indonesia, the Japanese thrust was made by sea under the cover of air power, both of which Tokyo controlled after Pearl Harbor. But since the end of the war, sea and air power had remained strictly in Western hands. If the domino theory was ever to apply again to a comparable degree, the dominant Asian power would first have to achieve such air and sea superiority. In fact, and as President Kennedy belatedly came to believe,[102] the future of China's predominance in Asia had little to do with what America did in Vietnam—except perhaps for the ironic point that in waging war against Vietnam the United States was actually fighting on China's behalf.

Still other American illusions about Vietnam had prevailed. In 1954, for example, one illusion had been that U.S. support of the French in Indochina might help them accept the European Defense Community in Europe, although France's losses in Asia made it too weak to join the EDC. In 1968, one illusion had been that by waging a war against communism in Vietnam, America would strengthen its commitments throughout the world, although American losses in Vietnam reduced the credibility of those commitments and the destruction suffered by the Vietnamese themselves reduced, in some of the areas threatened by communist expansion, the desirability of having such commitments enforced.

But above all, the illusions that were unveiled during the Vietnam war were domestic illusions: the illusion of a superior efficiency that helped America win its wars by quantifying, planning, destroying, and cajoling; the illusion of a superior morality that had made the American flag the flag of mankind but that was now being torn amidst such revelations as the massacre of civilians in South Vietnamese villages and the tragic destruction of Cambodia; and, finally, the illusion of omnipotence, the illusion that any situation that harms U.S. interests abroad can only exist because of some American foolishness or worse.

There was in all this a curious mixture of three fundamental human features—irony, tragedy, and absurdity: irony in the status of a nation that unveiled its impotence in its hour of greatest strength; tragedy in the behavior of a nation whose indisputable dedication to peace was expressed in policies of brinkmanship and military intervention; and absurdity in the situation of a nation that was transforming its international dreams into a latent domestic nightmare. Entering the 1970s, the enemy had become more elusive than ever as one sought the solutions that would reverse an erosion of national spirit that foreign policy had been instrumental in bringing to surface.

But also entering the 1970s, the meaning of the Vietnam debate for the future was itself very elusive. That the public generally wanted no more Vietnams was not surprising. They had also wanted no more Koreas many years before they had "discovered" Vietnam. To be sure, in another time and at another place another administration might find it more difficult than before to justify another American intervention in the name of self-determination and American security—more difficult but not impossible, and in 1969 it appeared hazardous to predict how much America's disenchantment with its foreign policy would survive the war proper. If it did not, then the debate would probably have been held in vain. If it did, then the real Vietnam debate was only beginning.

Yet, the limits of this debate were also elusive. Given America's power, there was little room for self-retrenchment: America's participation in world affairs had finally been decided by history. But given the nature of power in the nuclear age, few options were available for radical solutions. Perhaps the "new" diplomacy would now be no more than an exercise in futile agitation as it lent itself to few lasting penalties and still fewer lasting rewards.

Any withdrawal by a major power such as the United States would be heavy of consequences, obviously difficult to foresee, probably difficult to control: possibly a measure of self-reliance, but probably much more expansion of adversaries and intimidation of friends.[103] This area of negative repercussions was particularly dangerous, and it would have to be defined with special caution. Assuming that the vast scope of America's imperial commitments had provided the United States for 20 years with a new margin of error, such a margin now appeared to have been exhausted by the Vietnam War. For this war had seemingly shown that a war started at the periphery of the empire could actually come and tear the very fabric of national life: would it be that the Vietnam War actually demonstrated that peace could indeed by divisible although war itself had now become indivisible inasmuch as, from now on, war abroad might also mean war at home?

When withdrawal was mentioned, it was based upon the extension of regional balances (especially in Europe and in Asia) that would be set to contain the expansionist states of the area (especially Russia and China). Western Europe (grouped around Bonn, Paris, London, or any combination of these) and Japan might be delegated a share in America's imperial responsibilities. Conceived as such, however, America's withdrawal would still be minimal: in Europe as well as in Asia, America's surrogates would continue to base their security on the credibility of America's guarantee to come to the rescue should deterrence fail.

Explicitly or not, the criticism of America's foreign policy during the Vietnam War raised the same two questions that in one way or another the United States had attempted to resolve throughout its history. First, what were America's vital interests? Second, assuming a common understanding of these interests, were they actually threatened—how, and by whom? But the Vietnam War added two new questions, both related to the collapse of America's national illusions and, to some extent, to the end of the public's innocence. First, assuming that one knew what these interests were, and how and against whom they needed to be safeguarded, could they be preserved at all? The illusion of omnipotence, which had previously made such a question useless to ask, might ultimately give way to a no less dangerous illusion of impotence. Such a growing feeling of impotence had been apparent when during America's foray into

Cambodia, Nixon's announcement was received with an air of déjà vu, and much of the general public, whether for or against the ensuing demonstrations, assumed the worst. The other question that Vietnam helped raise again was that of America's purpose and the ways in which it could be achieved. Gone was the belief that good intentions purified any action that might be undertaken in their name. The irony—and to many the tragedy—of America's position at the end of the Cold War was that at the height of its power the purpose of the nation had become irrelevant to most of the world.[104]

Increasingly irrelevant because increasingly ill-defined, and it was symbolic of things to come that America's "new" purpose was best outlined by those who endorsed the war most. To George Liska, for example, there was no need for national self-pity. Interpreting the war as a police operation—the first imperial war of the United States fought at the remote frontier of the empire—Liska warned:

> If the United States comes out of the military confrontation in Asia and out of the diplomatic confrontation in Europe with a sharpened sense of how to differentiate its role and distribute the various components of national power in the different areas of the world, it will have ascended to the crucial and perhaps last step toward the plateau of maturity. It will then have . . . become a true empire—a strong and salient power with the sense of a task exceeding its national limits but not its national resources . . . the primary power in the relevant world [whose task would be] to supervise . . . primarily a nuclear peace, even if on the subnuclear level the world order may have to be to a large extent an American order.[105]

Standing on the path toward such imperial maturity, however, were the illusions that had come to be entertained by the critics of the war.[106] Now, the same critics who had uncovered through Vietnam a creeping notion of laissez-nous faire in American diplomacy came close to endorsing a revised principle of laissez-les faire. They complained that "twenty years of intensive cold war 'indoctrination' myths regarding our international role made it difficult to . . . face [foreign policy] issues in a serious way." Unfortunately, such arguments hardly moved the debate further in the direction of the serious and the acceptable, as international relations were now explained as a "struggle to remove the heavy Yankee boot from the necks of oppressed people throughout the world."[107] The rhetorical excess of the Vietnam years would have had the American people stop believing at last that America was born into the world to do mankind service—as President Wilson had once put it—and start believing at once in the "horrifying reality" of a criminal and depraved America. However elusive the enemy might be, it did exist within a hostile and dangerous world that was still characterized by its intrinsic state of war.

What was witnessed during the many years of the Vietnam debate was a resurgence of romanticism among those who, in the name of a new realism, had condemned in earlier years the American romanticism of past eras. America's good conscience in the name of which all evil was expected to be forgiven was being replaced by a bad conscience which labeled everything evil and could find no good in the past and present policies and objectives of the United States. In retrospect, such a damnation of American history would have been nearly amusing if it had not come so close to being a breach of contract between the educators and their pupils—what Morton A. Kaplan has called "a kind of moral rape of the student's mind."[108]

In this sense, deception and self-deception were not the sole privilege of governments engaged in covert operations in Cambodia, Laos, and elsewhere. Scholars, too, and other observers in the media and elsewhere often failed to resist the temptation. Their criticism, when it finally occurred, was but an adjustment to the persistence of a failure that they had been unable to foresee at an earlier and more appropriate time. But while the discovery was late, repentance was total. Frustrated by a war that could not be won, the critic had turned the rhetoric of the apologist inside out and moved from one side to the other of an unmoveable stalemate.[109]

In the end, the Vietnam war was abandoned for the very reason that it did not work. In later years, it would be up to others to "explain" how it could have worked better, or why it was worth the fragmentation of the nation's soul. In the meantime, however, a more immediate and more practical task was at hand. That the Vietnam war had been a bad limited war did not imply that all limited wars should now be avoided. That American power had been used ineffectively there, and possibly elsewhere, did not imply that American power could no longer be relevant in the search for an international order that would remain sensitive to continued U.S. interests. In other words, as two decades of global and undifferentiated cold war were coming to an end, there was a need in the 1970s for a new U.S. foreign policy that would strike a better and more effective balance between power, objectives, and purpose.

NOTES

1. Cordell Hull, *Memoirs*, Vol. 1 (New York: McMillan, 1948), p. 904.
2. See George Kennan's testimony to the Senate Committee on Foreign Relations, February 10, 1966. *Vietnam Hearings* (New York: Vintage Books, 1966), p. 108.
3. Sumner Welles, *Seven Decisions that Shaped History* (New York: Harper & Row, 1951), p. 82.
4. Bernard Fall, *The Two Vietnams* (New York: Praeger, 1963), p. 45.
5. Hull, *Memoirs*, Vol. 1, p. 913.
6. Fall, *Two Vietnams*, p. 46.
7. Elliot Roosevelt, *As He Saw It* (New York: Duell, Sloane and Pearce, 1945), pp. 74, 115.
8. Ibid., p. 72.
9. Ibid., p. 165.
10. Hull, *Memoirs*, Vol. II, p. 1597.
11. Ibid., p. 1597. See also General Joseph W. Stilwell, *The Stilwell Papers* (New York: William Sloane, 1948), p. 246.
12. Fall, *Two Vietnams*, p. 53.
13. Phillipe Devillers, *Histoire du Vietnam de 1940 à 1952* (Paris: Editions du Seuil, 1952), pp. 122–25.
14. Admiral William D. Leahy, *I Was There* (New York: McGraw-Hill, 1950), pp. 338–39.
15. There are several good political biographies of Ho Chi Minh. See, for example, Jean Lacouture, *Ho Chi Minh* (New York: Random House, 1968).
16. Joseph Buttinger, *The Smaller Dragon: A Political History of Vietnam* (New York: Praeger, 1958), p. 231.
17. MacArthur is quoted in George McTurnan Kahin and John W. Lewis, *The United States in Vietnam* (New York: Dell, 1967), p.

24 (revised edition, 1969). This incident is well narrated in Ellen J. Hammer, *The Struggle for Indochina, 1940–1955: Vietnam and the French Experience* (Stanford: Stanford University Press, 1954), pp. 115–19.

18. Buttinger, *Smaller Dragon*, 242.
19. On the agreement of March 1946, see Fall, *Two Vietnams*, pp. 74–77.
20. Richard P. Stebbins, ed., *The United States in World Affairs, 1954* (New York: Harper & Row, 1956), p. 256.
21. Fall, *Two Vietnams*, p. 129.
22. Truman, *Memoirs*, Vol. 1, *Year of Decision* (Garden City, N.Y.: Doubleday, 1955), p. 15.
23. Hammer, *Struggle for Indochina*, pp. 250–51.
24. Buttinger, *Smaller Dragon*, p. 361.
25. In the words of General de Lattre de Tassigny, then commander of the French troops, during an official visit in Washington in September 1950. French Embassy, *Service de Presse et d'Information* (September 20, 1951), p. 2.
26. Dean Acheson, *Present at the Creation* (New York: W. W. Norton, 1969), p. 639.
27. Truman, *Memoirs*, Vol. 2, *Years of Trial and Hope, 1946–1952* (Garden City, N.Y.: Doubleday, 1956), pp. 381, 399.
28. Phillipe Devillers and Jean Lacouture, *La Fin d'une guerre* (Paris: Editions du Seuil, 1960), p. 12.
29. Acheson, *Present at Creation*, p. 674.
30. Dwight Eisenhower, *Mandate for Change, 1953–1956* (Garden City, N.Y.: Doubleday, 1963), p. 336.
31. Truman, *Memoirs*, Vol. 1, p. 15.
32. Stebbins, *United States in World Affairs*, p. 217.
33. Melvin Gurtov, *The First Vietnam Crisis* (New York: Columbia University Press, 1967), p. 32 (paperbound edition, 1968).
34. On Dien Bien Phu see more particularly Bernard Fall, *Hell in a Very Small Place: The Siege of Dien Bien Phu* (Philadephia, Pa.: Lippincott, 1966). See also Jules Roy, *La Bataille de Dien Bien Phu* (Paris: René Julliard, 1963).
35. In a statement made by Secretary Dulles, September 3, 1953. Quoted in Gurtov, *First Vietnam Crisis*, p. 32.
36. Ibid., p. 57.
37. Devillers and Lacouture, *Fin d'une guerre*, p. 70 ff.
38. Gurtov, *First Vietnam Crisis*, p. 95; John Beale, *John Foster Dulles* (New York: Harper & Row, 1959), p. 207; J. R. Tournoux, *Secrets d'Etat* (Paris: Librairie Plon, 1960), pp. 462–63. Reliance upon atomic weapons is denied by Eisenhower in *Mandate for Change*, p. 344 ff.

39. James Shepley, "How Dulles Averted War," *Life* (January 16, 1956), pp. 70 ff.
40. An account of this meeting is found in Chalmers H. Roberts, "The Day We Didn't Go to War," *The Reporter* (September 14, 1954), pp. 31–35.
41. Eisenhower, *Mandate for Change*, p. 347.
42. Speech made at Los Angeles, June 11, 1954. Department of State *Bulletin*, Vol. XXX, pp. 971–73.
43. Sherman Adams, *Firsthand Report* (New York: Harper & Row, 1961), p. 120 ff.
44. "What we are trying to do," said Dulles on May 11, 1954, "is to create a situation in Southeast Asia where the domino theory will not apply ... to save all of Southeast Asia if it can be saved; if not to save the essential parts of it." Stebbins, *United States in World Affairs*, p. 237.
45. Statement made July 23, 1954, ibid., p. 255. Following Dulles' departure, General Smith remained in Geneva as an American "observer."
46. See Pierre Rouanet, *Pierre Mendès-France au Pouvoir, 1954-1955* (Paris: Robert Laffont, 1965), pp. 107 ff.
47. Stebbins, *United States in World Affairs*, p. 236.
48. Ibid., p. 285.
49. Victor Bator, *Vietnam—a Diplomatic Tragedy* (New York: Oceana, 1965), p. 204.
50. Quoted by William Anderson and Wesley R. Fishel, "The Foreign Policy of Ngo Dinh Diem in Vietnam," in Wesley R. Fishel, ed., *Anatomy of a Conflict* (Itasca, Ill.; F. E. Peacock, 1968), p. 206.
51. John F. Kennedy, "America's Stake in Vietnam," an address to the American Friends of Vietnam, September, 1956. Anderson and Fishel, in Fishel, *Anatomy of a Conflict*, p. 146.
52. Eisenhower, *Mandate for Change*, p. 347.
53. State Department, *American Foreign Policy, 1950–1955: Basic Documents*, Vol. 1 (General Foreign Policy Series 117), p. 936.
54. Ibid., p. 937.
55. Eisenhower, *Mandate for Change*, p. 373.
56. Ibid., p. 372.
57. William Henderson, "South Vietnam Finds Itself," *Foreign Affairs* (January 1957), p. 288.
58. Arthur Schlesinger, *A Thousand Days* (Boston, Mass.: Houghton Mifflin, 1965), p. 540.
59. In Kennedy's speech to the American Friends of Vietnam, in Fishel, *Anatomy of a Conflict*, pp. 144–45.
60. See James C. Thompson, "How Could Vietnam Happen? An Autopsy," *Atlantic Monthly* (April 1968).

61. Kahin and Lewis, *United States in Vietnam*, p. 185.
62. On America's problems in Laos, see, for example, Arthur J. Dommen, *Conflict in Laos: the Politics of Neutralization* (New York: Praeger, 1965).
63. Theodore Sorensen, *Kennedy* (New York: Harper & Row, 1965), p. 644.
64. Schlesinger, *A Thousand Days*, p. 163.
65. Ibid., p. 337.
66. Sorensen, *Kennedy*, p. 644.
67. Fall, *Two Vietnams*, pp. 359 ff.
68. Schlesinger, *A Thousand Days*, p. 545.
69. For a plausible account of Kennedy's change of heart on Vietnam, see Kenneth O'Donnell, "LBJ and the Kennedys," *Life* (August 7, 1970), pp. 44–48.
70. "The Pentagon Papers," *New York Times*, July 1, 1971, p. 4.
71. A penetrating study of the Gulf of Tonkin episode is provided by Joseph C. Goulden, *Truth is the First Casualty: The Gulf of Tonkin Affair—Illusion and Reality* (New York: Rand McNally, 1969).
72. See Townsend Hoopes, *The Limits of Intervention* (New York: David McKay, 1969), p. 28. Also, Tom Wicker, *JFK and LBJ: The Influence of Personality on Politics* (Baltimore Md.: Penguin Books, 1969), pp. 184–209. A continuous assumption in Washington had been that a major land war in Indochina could be avoided by simply resorting to large-scale bombing. "North Vietnam is extremely vulnerable to conventional bombing, a weakness which should be exploited diplomatically in convincing Hanoi to lay off South Vietnam." When the bombing was finally ordered, the Johnson administration confidently predicted that Hanoi would yield after two to six months. "The Pentagon Papers," *New York Times*, July 1, 1971, p. 5, and June 14, 1971, p. 31.
73. See Dean Rusk's statement to the Senate Foreign Relations Committee, February 18, 1966. *Vietnam Hearings*, pp. 236–37.
74. Ibid., pp. 247–48.
75. See, for example, David Mozingo, "Containment in Asia Reconsidered," *World Politics* (April, 1967), pp. 361–78.
76. Norman Podhoretz, *Why We Were in Vietnam* (New York: Simon & Schuster, 1982), p. 137.
77. Ibid., p. 71.
78. Leslie Gelb, "The Essential Domino: American Politics and Vietnam," *Foreign Affairs* (April 1972), p. 466.
79. Ralph B. Levering, *The Public and American Foreign Policy, 1918–1978* (New York: Morrow, 1978), p. 130.

80. Henry Kissinger, *White House Years* (Boston Mass.: Little, Brown, 1979), pp. 287–88.
81. Guenter Lewy, *America in Vietnam* (New York: Oxford University Press, 1978), pp. 144–46.
82. Kissinger, *White House Years*, p. 310.
83. Ibid., pp. 283–84.
84. Ibid., p. 307.
85. Ibid., pp. 294–95 and 1482–83. See also Levering, *The Public and American Foreign Policy*, p. 130, and Lewy, *America in Vietnam*, p. 146.
86. Kissinger, *White House Years,* pp. 281–82.
87. Ibid., p. 986.
88. William Shawcross, *Sideshow* (New York: Pocket Books, 1979), p. 90.
89. Kissinger, *White House Years,* p. 241.
90. Ibid., p. 254.
91. Richard M. Nixon, *RN: The Memoirs of Richard Nixon* (New York: Warner Books, 1978), pp. 451–52.
92. Kissinger, *White House Years,* p. 241.
93. Ibid., p. 1009.
94. Lewy, *America in Vietnam,* p. 167.
95. Kissinger, *White House Years,* p. 1009; Nixon, *RN,* p. 499; Podhoretz, *Why We Were in Vietnam,* p. 149.
96. Lewy, *American in Vietnam,* p. 193.
97. Ibid., p. 218.
98. Leahy, *I Was There,* p. 44.
99. "The Pentagon Papers," *New York Times,* July 1, 1971, p. 6.
100. Eisenhower, *Mandate for Change,* p. 347.
101. "The Pentagon Papers," *New York Times,* June 13, 1971, p. 39.
102. According to the columnist Arthur Krock, quoted in Walter LaFeber, *America, Russia and the Cold War* (New York: John Wiley), p. 228.
103. George Liska, *Imperial America: The International Politics of Primacy* (Baltimore, Md.: Johns Hopkins University Press, 1968), p. 110.
104. Robert W. Tucker, *Nation or Empire? The Debate over American Foreign Policy* (Baltimore, Md.: Johns Hopkins University Press, 1968), p. 110.
105. Liska, *Imperial America,* pp. 108–9.
106. See Simon Serfaty, "No More Dissent," *Foreign Policy* (Summer 1973), pp. 144–58.
107. Noam Chomsky, *American Power and the New Mandarins* (New York: Pantheon Books, 1969), p. 4.

108. Morton A. Kaplan, *Dissent and the State in Peace and War. An Essay on the Grounds of Public Morality* (New York: Dunnellen Publishing Company, 1970), p. 32.
109. Daniel Ellsberg, *Papers on the War* (New York: Simon & Schuster, 1972), p. 40.

PART TWO

America
in a Hostile World

CHAPTER SEVEN

Neither Primacy
nor World Order

The Design for Primacy and Order

History does not have any difficulty in locating lost opportunities for peace. And, in the meantime, foreign policy critics find it even less difficult to charge those who have allegedly missed the opportunities that existed in their own time. In so doing, the critics overlook the fact that events have a continuity of their own, which denies the freedom of action that is instead conveniently assumed. In the realm of foreign policy, today's hero often becomes tomorrow's villain—and vice-versa— as observers pass new judgments in light of changed and changing circumstances over which policymakers themselves had limited control.[1]

Consider, for example, the Kennedy administration. In the early 1970s, it became the focus of a semirevisionist literature apparently anxious to expose the shortcomings of the "Kennedy promise" that had been praised by so many earlier. Deploring the "indefinable way in which John F. Kennedy touched people throughout the world," such critics mourned his failure to "understand and use his potential for greatness."[2] They remembered with some melancholy Kennedy's evocation of America's revolutionary heritage as the inspiration for his foreign policy;

yet they observed that "under his administration this nation became the leading defender of the international status-quo . . . [and] the world's most effective counter-revolutionary power."[3] In short, they concluded, Kennedy was a "president in the cold-war tradition of American foreign policy."[4]

Such an indictment is flawed in part because it usually covers a period that starts too late and ends too early. It starts too late to the extent that placing the beginning of the Kennedy foreign policy in January 1961 fails to take into account the legacy of the Eisenhower administration. This legacy was one of unresolved dilemmas and growing crises. It included a damaging credibility gap with the adversaries in the aftermath of the U-2 incident and the aborted summit meeting of May 1960; an escalating conflict in Laos, where an intervention involving U.S. ground forces had been planned; the projected invasion of Cuba; the postponement of a final decision on the difficult question of the antiballistic missile system (ABM); and, not surprisingly, a burning crisis with the Soviets over Berlin and a brewing crisis with the European allies over the delicate issue of nuclear control. Most of these problems matured quickly, from the Bay of Pigs fiasco in April 1961 and the heated summit in Vienna, Austria, in June of that year to the Cuban missile crisis in October 1962 and the Atlantic disarray later that winter. They forced upon the Kennedy administration a wide spectrum of crises that were in a sense inescapable. During these two years, therefore, whose foreign policy was it, Eisenhower's or Kennedy's? Then, as at any other time, could the American president ignore such legacy and simply begin anew? Thus while being exceedingly oblivious to the past, an exaggerated criticism of the Kennedy administration also ends its analysis too early to the extent that the significant policy adjustments that were initiated after the missile crisis (including adjustments pertaining to the search for detente with the Soviet Union, a normalization of the relationship with the People's Republic of China, an accommodation with de Gaulle, openings in the Third World, a withdrawal from Indochina, and arms control talks) are usually ignored or disputed in order to make Lyndon Baines Johnson, too, Kennedy's responsibility, thereby leaving the assassinated president guilty for his successor's subsequent escalation of the war in Vietnam. From Kennedy's politics of expectations to Johnson's politics of crisis to Nixon's politics of confrontation, the progression is deemed to have been neither avoidable nor reversible.[5]

"Statesmen," George Kennan once noted, "inherit from their predecessors predicaments and dilemmas to which they can see no complete solution." Accordingly, Kennan added, "every mistake is in a sense the product of all the mistakes that have gone before it, from which it derives a sort of cosmic forgiveness; and at the same time, every mistake is in a sense the determinant of all the mistakes of the future, from which it derives a cosmic unforgiveableness."[6] Whatever would be said or written of the Vietnam War in later years, by 1969 its main lesson appeared to be that American activism around the world had now outstripped the nation's capabilities—this was, in truth, the product of a number of past mistakes. While the understanding of these mistakes was not, of course, the same for all, critics and apologists, the Nixon administration nevertheless attempted to respond to the resulting demands for change in American foreign policy by devising strategies that would be better suited for these changed and changing circumstances.

"The postwar period in international relations has ended," Richard M. Nixon remarked on more than one occasion.[7] What the American president meant through such an apparently banal observation was no less than the termination of a period in international relations—that of the cold war—which had been marked by an extraordinary dominance of the United States, whose willingness to use its surplus of military and economic power had resulted, especially following the outbreak of the Korean War, in commitments that were occasionally marginal to the nation's interests. Now that the postwar surplus of American power had been exhausted, the Nixon administration hoped to build a new structure of peace within which past obsessions with ideology would be muted, arms would be controlled, and negotiations with adversaries would be launched over a wide range of issues linked in such a way as to permit a more efficient use of America's residual power. In Kissinger's words, "The postwar order of international relations ended with the last decade. . . . Gone was the rigid bipolar confrontation of the Cold War. In its place was a more fluid and complex world—with many centers of power, more subtle dangers, and new hopeful opportunities."[8]

Accordingly, the Nixon–Kissinger New Look was based first of all on a reassessment of the past role of idealism and ideology in foreign policy.[9] "It is part of American folkore," Henry Kissinger had complained in 1966, "that while other nations are concerned with equilibrium, we are concerned with the legal requirements for peace. We have a tendency to offer our altruism as a guarantee of our reliability."[10] Such specifically American philosophy of international relations had made it difficult for past U.S. administrations to articulate U.S. national interests in the world.[11] Adherence to the abstract principle that the United States must resist aggression everywhere had caused an undifferentiated proliferation of American commitments.[12] But without a clear explanation of the interests that prompted these commitments, the American public had withdrawn from the policymakers the support that was required to carry out these commitments in full.

Spurning the ideological basis upon which containment had evolved over the years, the Nixon–Kissinger foreign policy administration attempted to substitute geopolitical for moral imperatives. The failure of extended containment had been its propensity to overstate American stakes everywhere through the double imperative of the domino theory and a Manichean view of international conflict. But every crisis and every change anywhere in the world were manifestly not life-and-death battles for the survival of democracy. "We must outgrow the notion," Kissinger claimed shortly after the American retreat from Vietnam, "that every setback is a Soviet gain or every problem is caused by Soviet actions."[13] Now that the past claims of ideological purity had been somewhat exposed in the course of the Vietnam War, the preservation of America's global primacy under the circumstances of devalued American power demanded that U.S. leaders recast their appeal for domestic support in some new political coin. Ironically, the general approach that the Nixon administration chose to follow implied a change to the sort of power politics that the American people had bitterly opposed throughout most of the history of the Republic.

Such a change did not however, mean the end of containment, but rather its continuation by other means and for different (or differently formulated) purposes. Left alone, Kissinger argued, "obsession with ideology may translate into an unwillingness to confront seemingly marginal challenges, depicting them as unworthy because they appear not to encapsulate the ultimate showdown."[14] Instead of focusing on the pace of domestic reforms in the Soviet Union and instead of holding negotiations captive to an elusive reading of Soviet intentions, the United States would first elaborate its own purposes and interests vis-à-vis the Soviet Union. These would be defined within a general framework of global equilibrium: again in Kissinger's words, "In an era of growing Soviet boldness and radical quests for ascendancy, an American failure to deal with the geopolitical challenge would risk the global equilibrium as surely as a failure to preserve the military balance."[15] But while the containment of Soviet expansion would thus be pursued, the Nixon administration would nevertheless negotiate with its main adversary "on the concrete issues that threaten peace" and because "the nuclear age imposes a degree of cooperation and an absolute limit to conflicts."[16] Thus, the search for peaceful coexistence with the East was now being provided with a respectability that it had sorely lacked in the past when, as Adam Ulam has put it, "next to an all-out war, the prospects of negotiating with the Communists inspired the most fear in the bosoms of American diplomats."[17] This is not to say, of course, that negotiations were not held during the cold war years. But the objectives of these negotiations remained a maximization of satisfaction that made any lasting agreement unlikely: "only amateurs believe in one-sided deals."[18] When taken at face value, such misleading historical analogies as appeasement and Munich ended the search for a negotiated settlement of existing differences even before the search could be initiated. If negotiations necessitated concessions, they would also imply appeasement, thus reducing one's credibility and in the process opening the gate either to further concessions or to war. Accordingly, throughout the 1950s and the 1960s, policy debates in the United States often focused on whether to go to the conference room rather than on what to do once there;[19] in the 1970s, however, the question of whether the United States should be in the conference room at all and whether it should be there now became increasingly less contentious.[20]

This adjustment in the American grand outlook was not so much a matter of choice as it was a matter of necessity. Changes in the realities of the contemporary scene, at home and abroad, dictated such a compromise of otherwise clashing principles.[21] Earlier, the unrestrained and undifferentiated anticommunism of the post-Korea years had conveniently helped to reconcile the country's genuine drive for harmony with its deep-rooted instinct for violence. It had provided the complex web of international relations, which repelled most Americans, with a simplicity that appealed to most of them. In a world that was hostile but not complex, the enemy was said to be everywhere, and its success anywhere was seen as the defeat of democracy, of which the United States was the unchallenged leader. As we have argued, the Vietnam War was the logical outcome of such an obsessive concern with ideology. But with the war painfully coming to an end, the time had come to draw the boundaries of American behavior—not only what could be done but, even more importantly, with and against whom.

Now U.S. relationships with communist ideology would therefore be defined more narrowly in terms of power and influence. Where a communist government was firmly entrenched in power, as it appeared to be the case in the Soviet Union, Eastern Europe, and China, negotiations would be held despite differences in ideologies and social systems. Conversely, where communist parties remained out of power, the United States would continue to oppose adamantly their entry into the government, even if this was achieved democratically—as could be seen during the vocal debate that surrounded the discovery of a so-called Eurocommunist wave allegedly about to sweep Southern Europe by the middle of the decade. Between these two extremes of power and impotence, ideologically hostile governments that still faced substantial opposition from within—as proved to be the case in Chile, for example—would be undermined by U.S. policies that denied such governments the assistance they needed, even while Washington was extending to opposition forces in these countries the assistance they sought.

The search for accommodation between the two super-powers would respond to, and further, permit a rising pattern of political multipolarity. With allies seeing no need to buy the support of their senior partner by adherence to its policies, and with the new nations feeling protected by the rivalry of the dominant powers and thus encouraged to ever bolder displays of self-will, both the United States and the Soviet Union shared a common interest in devising new rules of engagement and restraint.[22] But the failure of these rules would not be borne by the United States alone. As explained by Kissinger, America was now "in a transitional period in which . . . the United States role . . . will be primarily in carrying out the residual moral and other obligations to support by economic aid, on a declining scale, those countries with which we have been associated."[23] Accordingly, the Nixon administration expected to rely on surrogate powers that would act as buffers against communist expansion.

Nixon believed that such an arrangement was now neces-sary because one of many lasting legacies of Vietnam would almost certainly be a marked reluctance on the part of the United States to become involved once again in a similar intervention waged on a similar basis for similar objectives. The war, Nixon complained, had imposed severe strains on the United States, not only militarily and economically, but socially and politically as well.[24] That in Asia and elsewhere—particu-larly in the Persian Gulf, where Iran was an especially appealing candidate since in its case the United States would get the benefits of surrogate relationship without ever having to foot the bill—the promotion of viceroys was often tantamount to the enhancement or the consolidation of authoritarian regimes that shared common interests with the United States, was neither new nor surprising. Unlike the exasperating inability of democracies to deliver on defense issues, dictatorships showed an attractive dependability. Apparently, a single meeting between Nixon and the Shah of Iran in 1972—when Nixon authorized the sale of any arms, short of an atomic weapon, to Iran—had sufficed to make the Shah the guardian of the Gulf.[25]

The Nixon administration now hoped to end the nation's self-defeating sensitivity to the persistent ambiguities of the American posture on the issue of human rights.[26] Surely enough, it was hoped, if the American Right was to accept the legitimacy of ongoing negotiations with communist adversaries, the American Left would accept the legitimacy of such expanded relationships with authoritarian friends. Without both, the goal of a stable and lasting balance of power in the world could not be met. In this context, therefore, the end justified the means.

The construction of a new relationship with the People's Republic of China was an intrinsic feature of such a Grand Design. Even though Kissinger had flirted with the prospect of a renewed dialogue with the PRC before Nixon tapped him as his National Security Adviser, the impetus for such an initiative was probably provided by Nixon himself, who had found it imperative that "American policy . . . come urgently to grips with the reality of China."[27] At first, a local containment of China had been contemplated: "the strengthening of non-communist China," Nixon had written shortly before he was elected president, must be assigned a "priority comparable to that [given] to the strengthening of Western Europe after World War II."[28] Most of all, Japan's dramatic economic upsurge qualified it to play a greater role both diplomatically and militarily in maintaining the balance in Asia.[29] In addition, however, Nixon hoped for a normalization of U.S. relations with the PRC as a part of the emerging multipolar world in which, though vaguely, he appeared to believe more, or earlier, than his subordinate, and within which the possibilities of accommodation with both Moscow and Peking would improve American options toward both.

Although at first oversold by an administration anxious to gain public support for a strategy that left many puzzled and concerned, the "normalization" of U.S. relations with the main communist states did not mean an instantaneous reconciliation of their differences. Instead, normalization followed a more hesitant path, still waging a cold war where and when needed, but without a cold war rhetoric and while pursuing accommodation where and when possible. In short, adversary relationships would no longer respond to ideological differences alone, yet they remained relationships among adversaries. "Coexistence to us," Kissinger warned Moscow in the midst of the 1973 war in the Middle East, "continues to have a very precise meaning: we will oppose the attempt of any one country to achieve a position of predominance either globally or regionally."[30] In other words, a relationship of "detente" with the Soviet Union in one area depended on Soviet restraint in other areas. Conversely, the absence of restraint would set in motion a process of action and reaction that would undermine the whole range of U.S.–Soviet relations.

The Promises of Order

Thus, the Nixon administration viewed international relations first and foremost as adversary relations. This, too, was not a matter of choice: in January 1969, an audit of the Soviet political balance sheet would hardly have found it in credit.[31] In addition to the Soviet invasion of Czechoslovakia in August 1968, there was a troubling Soviet intransigence in helping to contain conflict in trouble spots such as Indochina and the Middle East. More importantly, with its sustained military build-up beginning to show its impact, the Soviet Union was at this point coming near to equality in strategic weapons.

As could have been expected, the advent of approximate equality between American and Soviet strategic forces at the end of the 1960s brought new license to the Soviet Union. Easy dominance in many areas of the world at the periphery of East–West contact was no longer available to the United States. Past confidence that the Soviets would not dare to escalate confrontations in which American interests were unequivocal had been based upon the knowledge of clear U.S. strategic superiority. But how would the Soviet Union now respond to equivalence? There was a danger that stalemate would make a future face-off a test of nuclear nerves in which the prizes went to those who were most willing to risk war, including nuclear war.

Earlier, as the confrontation between the United States and the Soviet Union was unfolding, America's first Secretary of Defense, James Forrestal, had pledged a total protection of the country against the horror of atomic war: "We are dealing with a deadly force," he had said, "and nothing less than 100 per cent security will do."[32] Now, however, a president who had done much in the past to help crystallize the cold war outlook of the preceeding two decades appeared to accept an inescapable measure of insecurity for the nation. "Although every instinct motivates me to provide the American people with complete protection against a major nuclear attack," Nixon acknowledged on March 14, 1969, "it is not now in our power to do so."[33]

Shortly after he left the Pentagon, Robert McNamara had defined the essence of security as "assuming a worst plausible case, and having the ability to cope with it."[34] Prior to, and throughout his stay in office, the worst plausible case had repeatedly determined the security policies of the United States. Already visible at the turn of the 1950s, when, as we have seen, the Truman administration had launched a first massive build-up of U.S. strategic forces, this pattern proved to be especially significant during the latter half of that decade. Thus, after Moscow's dramatic launching of the Sputnik satellites in October and November 1957, intelligence estimates placed Soviet missile production at a new high as they envisaged more than 200 Soviet intercontinental ballistic missiles (ICBM) in place by 1962 at the latest, and perhaps as early as 1960.[35] Given the calculations that were made at the time and according to which 125 to 175 such missiles would be sufficient to preempt all the strategic air bases (SAC) in North America while Soviet medium-range missiles already deployed preempted SAC bases overseas, the Eisenhower administration feared that the U.S. deterrent was now, or was about to become, obsolete.[36] Eisenhower therefore ordered an accelerated development and deployment of delivery vehicles that included liquid-fueled Atlas missiles, submarine-launched Polaris missiles, and, under his successor, deployable solid-fueled Minuteman missiles. The estimate of an ongoing Soviet build-up was maintained by the Kennedy administration. "Since we could not be certain of Soviet intentions," wrote its secretary of defense, "we had to insure against [it] . . . by undertaking a major build up of our own . . . forces."[37] The Soviet leadership, however, did not increase its strategic forces as Washington expected it to: in February 1962, Senator Stuart Symington, Chairman of the Armed Forces Committee, revealed that intelligence estimates of Soviet missile strength had been revised down to 3.5% of their projected size in December 1959.[38] By 1965, the United States held an overwhelming superiority over the Soviet Union in reliable, accurate, and effective launchers and warheads, both greater than it had originally planned and more than it required.[39]

Moscow's relative standstill is puzzling.[40] Possibly, Khrushchev fell into the practice of studied deception after he witnessed Western miscalculations of the Soviet forces. Given the limited life of many of the systems involved, the Soviet leader may have reasoned that his bluffing would safely outlast the first or second generation of ICBMs, and that Moscow could conveniently catch up at a later date. In the meantime, significant savings would be achieved at a time when the Soviet economy was under considerable strain. Finally, Khrushchev may simply have come to believe in the implausibility of an American first strike. This, coupled with the widespread assumption that losses acceptable to the West were markedly lower than those acceptable to the Soviets, might have reduced Moscow's security requirements.

Regardless of Khrushchev's reasoning, America's growing strategic lead could not fail to affect Soviet planning. Ultimately they, too, would come to define their security according to their ability to deter a worst plausible case. Again in the words of McNamara, "Soviet strategic planners undoubtedly reasoned that if our build up were to continue at its accelerated pace, we might conceivably reach in time a credible first-strike capability against the Soviet Union."[41] A number of options were then opened to the Soviet leaders.[42] First, they could continue to bluff and to claim strategic superiority regardless of Western disclaimers. Second, they could seek short-cuts to nuclear parity. Third, they could accept strategic inferiority and seek detente. Fourth, they could join the race until they regained at least strategic parity. All of these options were pursued by the Soviet leaders in the 1960s, often in combination with one another. Moscow undertook its own massive build-up, in part at least, in response to America's own build-up, itself undertaken, in part at least, as a response to a perceived Soviet build-up. The search for security had led to still more insecurity.

But now the Nixon administration was coming to office at a time when the decisive U.S. superiority that had prevailed throughout the entire postwar period was coming to an end.[43] To be sure, American strategic power—consisting of 1,054 ICBMs (including 1,000 Minuteman), 656 Polaris SLBMs, and more than 650 long-range B-52s—was hardly significant. Assuming that each missile carried one nuclear warhead and each plane four bombs, the United States had at its disposal approximately 4,200 nuclear warheads, plus several thousand "tactical" nuclear weapons (some of them five times more powerful than the Hiroshima bomb) located within range of the Soviet Union. These numbers, however, represented self-imposed ceilings that the Soviets would soon match and eventually pass. Already by 1969 it was estimated that the Soviet forces included over 1,200 ICBMs, more than 300 SLBMs, and approximately 150 long-range bombers, plus a considerable number of intermediate-range missiles and planes that could be used against targets in Western Europe. Although the Soviets probably had fewer nuclear warheads (approximately 1,800) than the United States, their destructive potential was roughly identical because the Soviet delivery systems had a heavier payload, their bombs were generally of greater yield, and the American population was more concentrated in urban areas.

Accordingly, at his first press conference, on January 27, 1969, President Nixon recognized the need for new criteria of "sufficiency," a term he then considered more appropriate than either "superiority" or "parity."[44] All in all, sufficiency would downplay the urge to have more for the sake of sheer numbers and even accept inferiority in some areas, as long as the resulting imbalances would be balanced elsewhere. Central to this new approach was the assumption that there existed a point beyond which additional weapons lost either political or military significance as they permitted no further advantage for either side.

This nuclear stalemate did not seem likely, however, to produce the overall stability that was required. With both sides able to ensure the devastation of the aggressor following the absorption of its first strike, it had become even more unlikely that either would attack the other with nuclear weapons except in response to a direct nuclear attack.[45] Equivalence at the strategic level thus appeared to place the burden of escalation upon the victim of a conventional attack. In such a situation clear advantages would accrue to the party with a preponderance of local conventional forces. In the retrenchment certain to follow the Vietnam War, the United States would have that advantage in fewer places: the change seemed to forebode new opportunities for Soviet pressures in the Third World and a weakened ability of the United States to deter Soviet challenges to American allies in Central Europe where the Soviet Union also enjoyed conventional preponderance. Less costly and more flexible forms of pressure had to be found to counter the increasing inadequacy of the military tools required to ensure containment.

Detente was the answer to these dilemmas in strategy and method. It sought to prevent confrontation with its greater risks and operational costs by cultivating a Soviet interest in good relations with the West. By making arms control the main pillar of detente, the Nixon administration recognized a Soviet interest in arms reductions at a time when the Soviet leadership faced the necessity to respond to the increasing appetite of Soviet society for consumer goods. Yet it was imperative that such negotiations should not be held within a vacuum, and that they would add momentum to progress in other areas.[46] In other words, issues would be "linked." As stated by Nixon in his news conference of January 27, 1969, "Simply reducing arms through mutual agreement . . . will not in itself assure peace. . . . We [must] have strategic arms talks in a way and at a time that will promote, if possible, progress on the problem of the Mid-East and on other outstanding problems (such as Vietnam) in which the United States and the Soviet Union, acting together, can serve the cause of peace."[47] In addition, linkage would force restraint, as the Soviet Union would be caught in an inescapable web of related agreements that mixed rewards for responsible behavior and penalties for renewed adventurism.[48]

Even though the central element of the Nixon–Kissinger strategy—the Strategic Arms Limitation Talks (SALT)—was launched in November 1969, a number of obstacles made progress initially slow and uncertain and brought SALT to a near halt by the fall of 1970. One such obstacle was the mutual mistrust that had been and would remain an intrinsic part of the negotiations between two ideologically incompatible adversaries. Another such obstacle was raised out of the difficulties the Nixon administration encountered in formulating a credible negotiating position at a time when the Congress was relentlessly cutting the defense budget. A third obstacle, and from the perspective of the Nixon–Kissinger design perhaps the most arduous one, was a direct Soviet global challenge that the U.S. administration found especially alarming in the Caribbean and the Middle East in the fall of 1970.[49]

In the Caribbean, the placement of Soviet nuclear submarine servicing facilities at the Cuban base of Cienfuegos would have violated security interests deemed essential by every U.S. president since Kennedy. The Soviet action therefore challenged not just America's global posture but also its national interest, however narrowly construed.[50] With construction of the base nearly completed by the time the evidence had been gathered, little time was left for preventive diplomacy, and both superpowers were facing a dangerous collision course. But since the resulting showdown would have occurred in an area where the United States continued to enjoy a preponderance of applicable force that permitted low-risk escalation for the fulfillment of vital security objectives, a Soviet withdrawal was quickly achieved.

In the Middle East, the crisis in Jordan, which occurred simultaneously, was precipitated by a Syrian invasion aimed at reinforcing the Palestinian rebellion against King Hussein. Had the King's forces begun to mutiny, or had they been on the verge of losing to the Syrians, U.S. intervention would probably have followed, and a superpower confrontation might have ensued under circumstances that, as in the Caribbean, were all the less favorable to the Soviets as the United States had more at stake and would therefore risk more than the Soviet Union. Advance knowledge of this, the availability of Israeli forces for entry into Jordan and even Syria, and the superiority of American naval strength in the Mediterranean (where the Sixth Fleet was placed on limited alert) would have attached high costs and risks to an active Soviet support of Syria, especially if accompanied by an air-lift of supplies. In fact, there is strong evidence that the Soviets were unenthusiastic about the Syrian invasion, and after it ran into trouble they counseled the withdrawal that took place on September 25, a mere five days after Syrian tanks had crossed the border with Jordan.[51]

Neither crisis could have started without Soviet encouragement, or at least in the absence of explicit Soviet discouragement. Neither crisis could have been defeated, or at least defused, without U.S. involvement. They both represented an exercise in brinkmanship, which had been, however, conducted with a great sense of control. Nixon and Kissinger were elated by the outcome of each sequence of events. With this initial "testing" of U.S. will within the context of public dissent over the Vietnam war now over, a major rule of detente had been defined and demonstrated. As later described by Kissinger, the rule read that reasonable relations between the superpowers could not survive the constant attempt to pursue unilateral advantages and exploit areas of crisis. "The Soviet leaders," Kissinger postulated, "should be made to understand that they cannot expect to reap the benefits of cooperation in one area while seeking to take advantage of tension or confrontation elsewhere."[52]

Soon afterward, a breakthrough in the SALT negotiations was achieved as the Soviets agreed to a long-standing American proposal on the limitation of offensive strategic weapons in return for an active American role in helping conclude the Berlin negotiations. By perceiving that Moscow was willing to concede on the former in order to secure a recognition of the territorial status quo in Central Europe (as offered in 1969 by Chancellor Willy Brandt in exchange for an improvement of Western access to West Berlin), the Nixon administration was making its linkage policy pay off. There had been no one-sided deal on any one issue alone. In Kissinger's words, "we had kept SALT and Berlin in tandem and substantially achieved our goals. And, of course, the Soviets were reasonably satisfied by Brandt's concessions."[53]

The linkage strategy appeared to work in Indochina as well. From the beginning, both Nixon and Kissinger had believed that adroit diplomacy in Moscow and Peking would eventually compel compromise in Hanoi.[54] In 1969, it had been hoped that Cyrus Vance, who was not serving in the government at the time, might go to Moscow as Nixon's personal envoy to engage in simultaneous discussions with the Soviets on SALT and, secretly, with the North Vietnamese on Indochina.[55] Even though the plan never materialized (as the Soviets were not overly enthusiastic about any arrangement which, as had been the case in 1954, would see Soviet pressure permit a peace that was potentially unfavorable to Hanoi), Nixon and Kissinger did not lose their conviction that some degree of big power leverage was available to the United States to settle the Vietnam War. Accordingly, even as detente took more tangible forms, Moscow was repeatedly warned that Hanoi's intransigence would not only lengthen the war in Indochina indefinitely but also create "a complicated situtation" between the two superpowers.[56]

Overtures to Peking carried somewhat less guarded enticements.[57] Although tentative at first and temporarily hampered by the U.S. actions in Cambodia in 1970 and in Laos the following year, the trend toward a Sino–American rapprochement was unmistakable. The so-called ping-pong demarche of April 1971 led rapidly to Kissinger's secret trip to Peking the following July, and the Shanghai communiqué that recast Sino-American relations was issued in February 1972.

To be sure, at no time in the course of such diplomatic maneuvering did either Moscow or Peking cease to support Hanoi—but it is unlikely that the White House hoped for so much. Instead, Nixon and Kissinger used detente and the Sino–Soviet rivalry to create powerful inducements for better relations with the United States, inducements that effectively demoted and isolated the interests of their client in Hanoi. The true test of this strategy came in May 1972, when despite his scheduled visit to Moscow Nixon mined every port on the Gulf of Tonkin and bombed Haiphong. Not only did the Kremlin confirm its invitation to the American president shortly thereafter, but the Soviet and Chinese responses to the American action remained significantly pro-forma, and mild beyond precedent.[58] As it now became clear that neither the Soviet Union nor the PRC would act to relieve the resulting reduction of communist supplies to North Vietnam, Hanoi embarked on a more sober stock-taking, which included its first major step toward compromise at the Paris Peace talks in August 1972—and which became increasingly evident as Nixon's reelection appeared ever more likely, and even certain.[59]

That the simultaneity of U.S.–PRC and U.S.–Soviet detente eroded the support that both communist states extended to Hanoi should come as no surprise. Moscow faced dangerous tensions on the Sino–Soviet border at the same time as continuing instability in Czechoslovakia endangered the stability of its European frontier. A settlement of the European boundaries would permit the Soviets to give greater attention to the Sino–Soviet tensions—but such a settlement was not possible without U.S. agreement. In addition, SALT, too, offered important incentives for the Soviets, especially in the light of Nixon's threat to deploy an ABM system that would negate many of the Soviet gains in nuclear striking power. In sum, the Soviets could hardly afford new disruptions in U.S.–Soviet relations while watching a rapprochement between Peking and Washington.

But Chinese motives were no less compelling. By the late 1960s, the North Vietnamese war effort bore little resemblance to Mao's celebrated "people's war." From its reliance on heavy artillery to its use of large-unit combat forces, Hanoi's military strength had become all but conventional. As it did, Hanoi's dependence on Moscow increased, and Peking's influence suffered. Now that an eventual communist victory and an American withdrawal had become next to certain, Peking became restive at the contemplation of a unified Vietnam that would be militarily powerful and highly indebted to Moscow. Later, it was now feared, Hanoi might be tempted to unleash well-known territorial ambitions of its own (in Cambodia and elsewhere), thereby causing a further expansion of Soviet influence around Chinese borders. In any case, like any other great power, China would always prefer to have divided and weak neighbors on its doorstep, even if these were technically its allies.[60] Paradoxically, China began to favor a less precipitate U.S. withdrawal from Indochina.[61]

The successful conclusion of the Berlin negotiations, the prospects for further progress in the SALT negotiations, and the Soviet apprehension over Nixon's trip to China in February 1972 provided the necessary ingredients for an unprecedented U.S.–Soviet summit in Moscow in May 1972. Now, the rules of detente were refined further as it was agreed that the "bilateral development of normal relations based on the principles of sovereignty, equality, non-interference in internal affairs and mutual advantage" would take place irrespective of differences in ideology and in the social systems of the two countries.[62] Moreover, the United States and the Soviet Union—which Raymond Aron called the "warring brothers"[63]—agreed that they shared important stakes in preventing the development of situations capable of causing a dangerous exacerbation of their relations. In this context, the United States and the Soviet Union would "always exercise restraint in their mutual relations, and [would] be prepared to negotiate and settle differences by peaceful means. Discussions and negotiations on outstanding issues [would] be conducted in a spirit of reciprocity, mutual accommodation and mutual benefit."

These principles appeared to incorporate almost fully the original design of the Nixon administration for a new structure of peace. Included was the adjustment the two sides would make vis-à-vis each other's ideology, but this adjustment would apply only in their mutual relations. The United States and the Soviet Union would not accept the infiltration of each other's ideology into their respective spheres of influence. Accordingly, both countries agreed that efforts to obtain unilateral advantages at the expense of the other, directly or indirectly, would work against a reduction of tensions. Consequently, the requirements for maintaining and strengthening peaceful relations between the two protagonists were "the recognition of the security interests of the Parties based on the principle of equality and the renunciation of the use of threat of force."[64] Under these terms, the United States and the Soviet Union would avoid provocative policies toward each other's areas of influence.

The SALT I Interim Agreement that was also signed at the Moscow Summit was the result of two and a half years of difficult negotiations. As we have seen, the two superpowers had entered such negotiations because they recognized that unless they were able to agree on the terms of the emerging strategic parity between them, they would be involved in a destabilizing arms race. By 1969, however, the American strategic arsenal appeared to be virtually frozen.[65] To be sure, the Johnson administration had relied on the U.S. lead in MIRV technology (multiple, independently targeted reentry vehicles) for the Minuteman ICBMs and the Poseidon SLBMs to preserve a marginal strategic superiority.[66] In September 1967, following a long and tedious debate that had begun under Eisenhower, Johnson had also opted for the development of a "thin" ABM system, the Sentinel,[67] because a "heavy" system, McNamara explained, would "strongly motivate" the Soviets "so to increase their defensive capability as to cancel out our offensive advantage."[68] Yet these decisions hardly compared with the dramatic pace of the Soviets both for offensive and strategic capabilities.[69]

As a way of gaining some leverage in the upcoming negotiations, Nixon opted in March 1969 for a Safeguard ABM system, whose principal mission would be to protect the U.S. land-based retaliatory forces against a direct Soviet attack. According to President Nixon, Safeguard would provide for "local defense of selected Minuteman missiles sites and an area defense designed to protect [U.S.] bomber bases and . . . command and control authorities."[70] With Safeguard perceived as qualitatively superior to the Soviet Galosh system, the Nixon administration hoped to have found the much-needed bargaining chip that would help to curtail the build-up of Soviet offensive missiles.[71]

The negotiations that started in November 1969 came to an impasse by late 1970 over the U.S. insistence that any agreement to limit the ABM deployment must be tied to an agreement to limit the deployment of offensive strategic weapons. As we have seen, the impasse was broken by linking the SALT talks to the Berlin negotiations. The United States would agree to the Soviet request for an active American role over Berlin only if the Soviets yielded to the American position in SALT. With the arms talks therefore resumed in earnest following the breakthrough of May 20, 1971, new concessions were made by both sides on both defensive and offensive weapons. Initially, the United States had insisted that ABMs, including those systems under construction, be frozen at existing operational levels. Because the Soviet Union had only one such system—protecting Moscow—while the United States had nearly completed two such systems—around two ICBM sites—the Soviets insisted on an equality, which was achieved as the final agreement limited ABM defense to two sites of 100 launchers each, one site to protect an offensive missile field, the other to protect the nation's capital.[72]

With regard to offensive weapons, the announcement of May 20, 1971, had made it clear that the initial settlement would be an interim agreement that would freeze only selected categories of weapons at certain levels. While such limitations were to include ICBMs, there had remained much disagreement as to whether the settlement would also cover U.S. forward-based systems (FBS) and/or SLBMs. The Nixon administration was adamantly opposed to the inclusion of the FBS. Deployed in order to offset over 600 Soviet intermediate- and medium-range missiles pointed at Western Europe, these were outside the purview of the SALT negotiations.[73] Whereas the Soviets were ready to abandon their claim on these systems, they insisted that SLBMs, too, be excluded from the talks. But with the Soviet sea-based forces expanding at a yearly rate of 100 SLBMs while the U.S. sea-based forces were frozen, the United States faced a disadvantage that might increase in the near future. To be sure, the Nixon administration was actively seeking funds in Congress to develop the Trident and MX systems (the focus of much debate in later years). But even under the best possible circumstances these new weapons would not be deployed for at least another five years or longer.[74] Thus the Nixon administration insisted that the SLBMs also be made part of the five-year freeze on ICBMs, a demand that was accepted by the Soviet leadership in return for the American acceptance of the Soviet position on ABM deployment.[75] This series of trade-offs permitted the conclusion of the SALT negotiations during the Moscow Summit and the signing of what came to be known as the SALT I Agreement on May 26, 1972. Under SALT I, the Soviets were allowed to build up their ICBM forces to 1,618 while the United States would remain at their existing level of 1,054. Moreover, the Soviets were allowed 950 SLBMs and 62 submarines, while the United States was confined to 710 SLBMs and 44 submarines. But the agreement was an interim agreement in the sense that important systems that were left out of the accord— bombers, land-mobile ICBMs, forward-based forces of less than intercontinental range, and multiple warheads—were to be the subject of further and more comprehensive negotiations that were expected to be concluded by October 1977.[76] Thus, detente now appeared to be well on its way: from the confrontations of the fall of 1970 to the compromises of the spring of 1972, the strategy of linkage had worked.

The Illusions of Primacy

On the general premise that U.S. military interventions in the 1970s had become more problematic domestically and operationally, detente called for preventive diplomacy in such a way as to preserve American global influence while reducing its dependence on the projection of military force. Yet if this was to succeed, deals at the top, of the SALT variety, had to be combined with skillful preventive action at the local level as well. To do otherwise was to court two faulty assumptions: that the center could control the periphery, a premise repudiated by increasing nationalism everywhere in the Third World; and that Moscow would so value the benisons of detente that it would subordinate and even oppose the interests of its allies if these endangered the Soviet–American relationship.[77] Yet even before the Moscow Summit the Nixon administration showed a marked predilection for global diplomacy at the expense of local factors, as it was first exposed in Southwest Asia.

The separation of East from West Pakistan by 1,000 miles of an historical rival country had been a precarious arrangement since 1947, when Britain jury-rigged it to separate India's Moslem from its Hindu population. In the late 1960s the situation was complicated further by the growth in East Pakistan of the secessionist Awami League, whose electoral victory in December 1970 prompted President Yahya Khan, on March 25, 1971, to send 40,000 troops to impose military administration on an area that was now seeking independence.

The Nixon administration was concerned over the serious possibility of another war between India and Pakistan. With an estimated 10 million Bengalis fleeing into bordering West

Bengal, one of the most separatist Indian states, an Indian military response was indeed likely not only to ensure the independence of East Bengal but also to use the occasion to threaten the western half of Pakistan as well. As a CENTO ally, Pakistan could then invoke uncertain U.S. treaty obligations in the face of an aggression launched by a country allied to a communist state. Yet even if warranted, an American intervention would be domestically explosive at a time when the Vietnam War was still raging, and in the light of Yahya Khan's widely reported brutality. But, conversely, U.S. inaction or insufficient action on behalf of an ally, whose strategic location on the Indian Ocean in the south and bordering Iran on the west was vital, would raise apprehension among other allies in the region as well as in the People's Republic of China, for whom Pakistan was serving as an intermediary with Washington. Since India's military forces were supplied by the Soviet Union, it might also have suggested, in Kissinger's words, that "Soviet arms and diplomatic support were inevitably decisive in a crisis."[78]

American "friendly" advice to the Pakistani president, to move toward autonomy for East Bengal, proved to be ineffective; the Indian invasion was launched on November 22 and spread to the west two weeks later. That more forceful U.S. pressure to force the pace of events in East Bengal would have been ruled out reflected the constraints of the then-emerging "triangular diplomacy" between the United States, the Soviet Union, and the PRC. As Kissinger narrates it, the United States had "every incentive to maintain Pakistan's good will. It was our crucial link to Peking; and Pakistan was one of China's closest allies."[79] Yet, was it necessary to make U.S. policy hostage to the China opening? Chinese interest in a rapprochement with Washington rested upon the Sino–Soviet conflict, not upon Sino–Indian rivalry. Had Pakistan spurned its go-between role, Peking would have found another intermediary. Moreover, even if Sino–Soviet and Sino–Indian considerations overlapped to demand the preservation of West Pakistan, a comparable case could hardly be made for silence and inaction during the repression in East Bengal, whose eventual autonomy Nixon and Kissinger considered as inevitable.[80]

Not surprisingly, the result of such solicitude for China and its ally was only to worsen the dimension of the crisis and to enlarge U.S. involvement. As the predicted Indian advances in West Pakistan began to threaten its disintegration, an American fleet entered the Bay of Bengal, U.S. treaty commitments were brandished ominously, and hints were dropped about the eventual cancellation of the Moscow Summit. Even though damages were ultimately limited (Bengali independence was ensured, but so was the status quo in the West) the crisis belied one of the essential premises of Kissinger's emerging detente diplomacy: the center manifestly did not control the periphery. While Soviet pressure (at U.S. bidding) may have prevented India from pursuing its maximum goal of annexing Kashmir and other parts of West Pakistan, there is no evidence that the Kremlin could have dissuaded Prime Minister Ghandi from the minimum goal of Bengali secession. Even a Soviet threat to cut off supplies would have been moot given preexisting levels of Soviet-supplied arms and the relative penury of Pakistani arms.

Similarly, the 1973 Middle East War displayed the limits of superpower cooperation in defusing and resolving crises. Despite the injunction in the 1972 Moscow "Statement of Principles" against efforts to exploit tension for unilateral advantage and to gain special influence in various parts of the world, it was precisely such advantage and influence that each superpower sought to extract from the October War.[81] Rhetoric aside, both the United States and the Soviet Union viewed the conflict as one in which some degree of superpower confrontation was permissible and even desirable to shape the postwar political situation in the region to their respective advantage.

Although President Sadat's decision was even more autonomous than Ghandi's in 1971, it is likely that the Soviets considered they had little to lose. Even a modest success, which was as much as the Soviet leadership could have hoped, would have reflected upon Soviet arms and diplomatic support. Alternatively, Soviet pressure would prevent a failure from turning into a rout, again displaying the effectiveness of Soviet friendship.

Ever since the Six-Day War in 1967, U.S. prospects in the Middle East had been seen as promising.[82] Israel's overwhelming victory, and its subsequent occupation of a substantial amount of Arab territory, had made the American leadership hopeful that intensive diplomatic efforts might make the Arab states responsive to genuine negotiations on the basis of which the occupied territories would be returned for a measure of peace. Accordingly, the Nixon administration had produced a peace plan—the Rogers Plan—that was based essentially on Resolution 242 of the United Nations Security Council.

One of the main obstacles faced by the Rogers Plan had to do with the internal differences that beset the Nixon foreign policy administration. Thus, according to one account, the reaction of the White House to the proposals prepared by the State Department was "only mildly supportive at best, and on occasion was distinctly negative. Bureaucratic rivalries became personalized in the Rogers–Kissinger quarrel. On the whole, Nixon sided with Kissinger. As a result, United States policy during this period was particularly ineffective and inconsistent."[83] In effect, Kissinger reasoned that the Rogers proposal was based on an inherently fallacious premise, namely, that in the absence of an American initiative the status and prestige of the Soviet Union would increase in the Arab world. To Kissinger, the reverse was true: the longer the stalemate continued, the more obvious it would become that the Soviet Union could not deliver what the Arab states wanted. Time, therefore, was on America's side: sooner or later, the persistence of an intolerable status quo would force a reappraisal of even radical Arab states left impotent by their continued military inferiority.[84]

Following the signing of the Paris Agreements in January 1973, the Nixon administration found it possible to turn more directly to the crisis brewing in the Middle East. The earliest expulsion of Soviet advisers from Egypt, coupled with the opening of secret talks between Egypt and the United States, had appeared to confirm Kissinger's analysis. Increasingly in control of U.S. policies toward the region, Kissinger now favored a step-by-step approach that would seek an interim agreement between Egypt and Israel[85]: President Sadat's complaints that "everyone [had] fallen asleep," and his warning that "the time had come for a shock,"[86] thus remained unheeded until October

6, 1973, when Egyptian and Syrian troops invaded their respective Israeli-held territories.

Subsequent charges that the Soviets had broken the rules of detente by not warning the United States in advance were hardly warranted. Even if Soviet foreknowledge could be proven (the Kremlin knew at least as early as October 3 when it ordered an evacuation of its embassy personnel from Cairo), it would have been asking a great deal of detente to expect the Soviets to warn the United States, and therefore Israel as well, of Egyptian and Syrian plans.[87] Accordingly, detente—as defined in Moscow the previous year—played little role in the crisis. The behind-the-scene diplomacy of both superpowers on behalf of their respective allies changed with the evolution of the military situation, and not as the result of detente leverage. Despite increasing interest by both Nixon and Brezjnev in a settlement imposed by the two superpowers, Kissinger's hurried trip to Moscow on October 20 did little more than ratify the American cease-fire proposal while preserving the separation between immediate military and ultimate political objectives.[88]

Nor did detente appear to figure prominently a few days later, when Sadat requested U.S. and Soviet forces to come to the Suez Canal to implement the U.N. cease-fire resolution and to prevent the destruction of the Egyptian Third Army, by then trapped by the Israeli forces. Fearing the possibility of a Soviet–Israeli confrontation and the renewed Soviet influence, Washington sharply opposed Sadat's proposal and the Soviet threat of a unilateral intervention should the United States not participate. At the risk of a major deterioration in U.S.–Soviet relations, the Nixon administration relied on the threat of military force—including a rarely used maximum (DEFCON III) state of alert—to contain and prevent a Soviet intervention. It is not clear, however, how influential the U.S. alert was in forcing a Soviet retreat on October 25, since on that morning Sadat complicated the Soviet position by retracting his invitation and asking instead for an international force.

Nevertheless, the crisis brought about drastic alterations in the perceptions of Henry Kissinger, who was now all the more in charge of foreign policy as he had become secretary of state under a president who, due to the escalation of the Watergate scandal, was increasingly weak. In contrast to his previous assumption, Kissinger now concluded that an effective management of the Arab–Israeli conflict was urgently needed because the dangerous exchange between Washington and Moscow had shown once again how quickly a local conflict might grow into a major clash between the two superpowers. In addition, the 1973 war exposed the vulnerability of Israel, which suffered significant setbacks during the early stages of the war. Finally, the introduction of a new weapon—the oil weapon—during and after the war revealed a vital weakness of the West in the face of Arab determination to achieve a favorable resolution of the Arab–Israeli conflict.

Kissinger's original intention was apparently to build upon U.S. and Soviet cooperation (as it had emerged, however reluctantly, in the later days of the war) and agree to the convening of a conference in Geneva to seek a comprehensive settlement of the conflict. However, such an approach was soon discarded as Kissinger returned to a step-by-step strategy that was carried out within the framework of a much-publicized "shuttle diplomacy."

The results of Kissinger's new approach were not insignificant. The longstanding dispute between Egypt and the United States was defused at the expense of the Soviet Union (now excluded from the unfolding peace process), and the differences between Israel, Syria, and Egypt were somewhat narrowed with the conclusion of three disengagement agreements between Israel and Egypt in January 1974, Israel and Syria in May 1974, and Israel and Egypt again in September 1975.[89] In the process, however, Kissinger continued to postpone indefinitely the fundamental Palestinian issue.[90] Previously, it had been the responsibility of Jordan's King Hussein to represent the interests of the Palestinians. But with the U.N. recognition of the Palestinian Liberation Organization (PLO) as "the representative of the Palestinian people," and with the Arab League's unanimous endorsement of the PLO as "the sole legitimate representative of the Palestinian people on any liberated territory,"[91] strict limits were placed on any negotiation in the region: Israel staunchly refused to deal with what it considered a terrorist organization that denied Israel's right to exist, and Kissinger sought to reassure the Israelis with a formal pledge that the United States would not negotiate with the PLO as long as it had not recognized Israel's rights.

Ideally, Kissinger needed time to bring the Palestinian issue into his step-by-step approach, but such time was made unavailable by the upcoming presidential elections of 1976: any attempt by President Ford to pressure Israel toward a comprehensive settlement was likely to mobilize the American-Jewish constituencies and harm Ford's uncertain reelection prospects. Consequently, in 1976 the peace process came to a halt, and following Ford's defeat the challenge of a Middle East policy was left in the hands of the incoming Carter administration—but not before Kissinger had mistakenly permitted, and even encouraged, the entry of Syrian military forces into Lebanon, at a price that would have to be paid dearly in subsequent years.

In 1973, the Middle East War brought into focus a new and formidable obstacle to the Kissinger Grand Design from an unexpected direction. Until then, Kissinger had treated the nations of the Third World with a nonchalance which, as we have seen, had been replaced with a measure of panic only in those instances when U.S.–Soviet rivalry appeared to be directly at stake. The earlier nonchalance could be attributed to Kissinger's concern with questions of power and questions of structure.

"The new nations," Kissinger had written in 1968, "weigh little in the physical balance of power." To be sure, their evolution would affect the moral balance of the world. But this was the "world of tomorrow," which had not arrived yet.[92] When its time at last came, past neglect would be explained partly in terms of America's preoccupation with other areas in the world and partly in terms of an absence of local structures "in many of these countries [where] the primary process going on was the formation of a national idientity, a process in which we could not participate directly."[93] Yet even then Kissinger remained ambivalent in his assessment of what U.S. policies could and should be. Certainly, he was now aware of the problem on its own merits: "If you have an enormous gap in a global society in which nations are now closer really to each other in terms of communication than most nation states were in the previous century," he lectured the Senate Foreign Relations Committee prior to his confirmation as secretay of state, "and if this gap continues to grow, revolutionary upheavals in the world that will profoundly affect international stability are inevitable."[94] But all that Kissinger could conclude "at this point" was that "the problem was urgent," and that its resolution would "depend upon our ability to make some contribution."[95]

There were several reasons behind Kissinger's belated efforts at damming the post-1973 flood of Third World pressures.[96] First, the oil crisis in 1973–74 had shown the economic and political vulnerability of the West (including Western Europe and Japan) to the manipulation of vital economic parameters by Third World countries over which traditional coercive methods were no longer as effective or as permissible as they had been in the past. The threat was now said to be elsewhere, and some observers were predicting the imminent escalation of a North–South cold war that would make the East–West cold war pallid in comparison. Second, in a sense, the Nixon–Kissinger Design for continued American primacy in an age of diminished American power required that the new influentials that had been uncovered in the midst of the OPEC challenge be won over. Even if they did not condone U.S. primacy, at the very least they had to be kept away from further Soviet influence. And, third, the growing tug-of-war between the Executive and the Legislative over the directions and methods of U.S. foreign policy evolved increasingly around Third World issues, which many in Congress and throughout the country wanted to see decoupled from East–West preoccupations and the sordid calculations of power politics.

While Kissinger's acknowledgement of a new foreign policy agenda was first, and most comprehensively, stated in his address of September 1, 1975, to the General Assembly of the U.N., the most significant expression of this new look at Third World issues was seen at the time of the secretary's visit to Africa in late April 1976. As outlined in a speech delivered in Lusaka, Zambia, on April 27, American policies were engaging in a dramatic turnaround from the assumptions that the Nixon administration had entertained earlier. With the setbacks in and over Angola during the previous months probably acting as a catalyst for such a reversal, Kissinger was focusing on Southern Africa to demonstrate a new American attitude that would help "put aside slogans and ... seek practical solutions."[97]

Thus, having once again repeated that America could not do everything simultaneously, Kissinger attempted to put aside the lingering memories of earlier policy recommendations that most had interpreted as a tilt toward South Africa—the so-called Tar Baby option—as he now spoke of an "unequivocal commitment . . . [to] self-determination, majority rule, equal rights, and human dignity for all the peoples of southern Africa." More specifically, with respect to Rhodesia, U.S. policy would now be based on the proposals made a few weeks earlier by Great Britain: independence preceded by majority rule, itself achieved no later than two years following the conclusion of negotiations. On the Namibia question, Kissinger condemned as illegal South Africa's continued occupation of its former mandate territory and asked that self-determination and independence be attained under U.N. supervision. And on the matter of South Africa's internal policies of apartheid, Kissinger came closer to endorsing the position of black African states than any American official had previously. "The United States," Kissinger said, "appeals to South Africa to heed the warning signals of the past two years." While he conceded that there was still time for a peaceful reconciliation of South Africa's peoples, he pointedly warned that there was "a limit to that time—a limit of far shorter duration than was generally perceived even a few years ago." In this context, Kissinger finally elaborated on U.S. policies vis-à-vis South Africa, as follows: "The United States will continue to encourage and work for peaceful change. Our policy toward South Africa is based upon the premise that within a reasonable time we shall see a clear evolution toward equality of opportunity and basic human rights for all South Africans. The United States will exercise all its efforts in that direction. We urge the Government of South Africa to make that premise a reality." In the meantime, the three southern African issues were linked as Pretoria was summoned to take immediate steps on Namibia and to promote a rapid negotiated settlement for majority rule in Rhodesia.[98]

From the Middle East to Africa, Kissinger's new and belated focus on Third World issues responded to an ever more pressing dimension of the East–West conflict. From the start of detente, there had been a troubling ambiguity in the premises on which peaceful coexistence between the two superpowers would henceforth rest in the largely uncommitted areas of the developing countries. To be sure, the third "basic principle" agreed upon at the 1972 Moscow Summit had pledged both states to do "everything in their power so that conflicts or situations [would] not arise which would serve to increase international tensions." In addition, the United States and the Soviet Union had agreed that they would "seek to promote conditions in which all countries [would] live in peace and security and not be subject to outside interference in their internal affairs."[99] Yet, especially from the 1973 Arab–Israeli war onward, Soviet behavior and policies in the Third World provided much evidence that Moscow was now ready to use its military power to expand further the boundaries of its permissible political behavior at a time when a growing public predilection for a U.S. disengagement from the world constrained any American reaction.

The Fate of the Design

Paramount among the problems that came to plague Kissinger's New Look were the uncertainties and ambiguities of detente. In theory, the triangle of detente was compelling. With each communist state fearful of the other, both were expected to turn to the United States and make the concessions required to secure a measure of U.S. support against the other. The sole holder of the balance, Washington could accordingly maximize its leverage on its two major adversaries.

Such a scheme, however, was easier to outline theoretically than to apply practically. To start with, both processes of normalization were based on an initial and crucial contradiction. As China might have seen it, American overtures were the result of increasing tensions between the United States and the Soviet Union, tensions that such overtures would now exacerbate further. Certainly, the Chinese understood the U.S. concern over an eventual reconciliation between the two communist giants. But they also assumed that Soviet suspicions of U.S. motives in the Far East might generate additional clashes between the two superpowers. The closer the United States grew to China, the greater would the rift be between the United States and the Soviet Union. In the short term, even Taiwan was secondary to diverting U.S. hostility away from the PRC and toward the Soviet Union.

At first, Kissinger may well have underestimated the importance of the China factor. "The world," he had written in 1968, "has become militarily bipolar. Only two powers—the United States and the Union of Soviet Socialist Republics—possess the full panoply of military might."[100] Significantly enough, Kissinger had also assumed that over the next decade the gap in military strength between the two superpowers and the rest of the world was likely to increase rather than diminish. But in the fall of 1969, sharp Sino–Soviet tensions opened the door to new diplomatic opportunities, which Kissinger continued to evaluate primarily in terms of U.S.–Soviet relations. An American rapprochement with China, Kissinger now reasoned, would be of such concern to the Soviet Union as to facilitate a rapprochement with the West. In 1950, the Soviet leadership had played the card of East–West collision to isolate the PRC and make it dependent on Moscow for the support it needed against the United States. Now the United States would play the card of U.S.–Chinese collusion to isolate the Soviet Union and make it more sensitive to the support it might need from Washington against Peking. In other words, while both the Unites States and the PRC sought normalization to influence Soviet behavior and policies, the United States wanted this to result in a minimization of U.S.–Soviet enmity, while the PRC wanted it to result in a maximization of that enmity. Indeed, by the end of the Ford administration, Kissinger's closest aide on China policy (and the Director of the State Department Policy Planning Staff) would candidly acknowledge that a hedge against Soviet diplomatic and military pressures had been seen in Peking as first among the advantages to be derived by the Chinese from a rapprochement with the United States, while improved prospects for a global equilibrium had been placed at the top of the list of benefits gained by the United States from such a rapprochement.[101]

With regard to normalization between the Soviet Union and the United States, there was also an early and fundamental contradiction. The leadership in Moscow understood detente as the recognition of the status quo in Europe, but without denying the permissibility of change elsewhere (especially in Africa, the Middle East, and even Latin America). Washington, however, wanted detente to permit a stabilization of the status quo at the periphery, but without denying the permissibility of change in Eastern Europe (as the so-called basket three of the Helsinki Agreement was expected to allow a progressive and graduated defiance of Soviet influence in Eastern Europe).

Thus, even while Kissinger was celebrating the indivisibility of detente, the Soviet Union continued to praise civil and national liberation wars as a way of changing the political and social order.[102] Kissinger equated status quo with stability, and he assumed that even under prevailing conditions of declining U.S. power, stability would entail continued American primacy. "We set," Kissinger declared, "the limits of diversity."[103] This, however, implied that the strategic equality gained by the Soviets at high cost still came together with political inequality. It would be up to the United States to draw and guard the boundaries of permissible Soviet behavior. But this was not compatible with Soviet expectations that not a single question of any importance in the international arena could be solved without the Soviet Union, or against its will. For, in the words of an American scholar, nuclear equality allowed for "a more hospitable environment for success of the Soviet global offensive short of war with the United States and particularly short of nuclear disaster."[104]

Reliance on linkages and nets appeared to limit U.S.–Soviet detente to a choice between functional progression (peace by pieces) or global regression (peace in pieces); hence the gloom or exuberance that often accompanied each setback or each accomplishment. Yet such a confining choice ultimately worked to the advantage of the Soviets, who could use to their benefit concern in Washington over the consequences of global regression in the light of the post-Vietnam mood of the nation.

In 1975–76, the U.S.–Soviet clash over Angola showed that U.S. foreign policy was waging a two-front diplomatic war: with the Soviet Union and other adversaries abroad, and with the U.S. Congress and other critics from the left and the right at home. The former was easier to define than the latter."We were prepared to accept any outcome in Angola," Kissinger indicated in late December 1975. "We can live with any of the factions in Angola, and we would never have given assistance to any of the other factions, if other Great Powers had stayed out of it."[105] Yet the immediate effect of U.S. support for the factions it favored was to undermine the Alvar Accord of January 1975 (which had provided for a cease-fire between the three warring Angolan factions) and to spread word in Luanda (and in the Organization of African Unity) that the United States had opted for a military solution. In October, South Africa's intervention in Angola—rumored to have taken place with U.S. support—effectively ended the previously forceful African criticism of the Soviet role (which included approximately $220 million worth of military equipment to "their" faction during the crucial months of the crisis, between August and November), and created sympathy for a Cuban intervention which by the end of the year numbered at least 11,000 troops.

However justified or justifiable, Kissinger's efforts went against a domestic mood that uncovered in every intervention abroad the seeds of a new Vietnam. In December 1975, the Clark amendment therefore brought such U.S. involvement to a halt and left U.S. policy in Angola in shambles. The danger to detente, Kissinger complained bitterly, was that internal disputes in the United States were now depriving the administration of its ability to impose penalties for aggression and incentives for moderation.[106] More often than not, the U.S. threat to link (that is, to join otherwise unrelated issues for bargaining purposes) could be dismissed by Moscow. To be effective, a linkage policy required a steady willingness to take risks in one area in order to reduce risks elsewhere and the continued ability to sacrifice interests in one area to secure interests in another. But such trade-offs, too, became increasingly difficult because of the rising pressures exerted on the administration by the groups they affected most directly: the farmers and wheat deals or the manufacturers and trade talks, as well as Africa and the congressional restraints or SALT and the liberal constituencies—who was linking what against whom?

Nor did the Nixon–Kissinger methods do much to sustain the required domestic support for their policies. Initially,

President Nixon had sought to centralize foreign policy decision-making around the White House by strengthening the National Security Council (NSC). According to Nixon, the NSC apparatus would ensure that policies be the "products of thorough analysis, forward planning, and deliberate decision," thereby permitting to master problems before they master us." "Real options," Nixon continued, were needed, and "not simply what compromise had found bureaucratic acceptance. . . . Presidential leadership is not the same as ratifying bureaucratic consensus."[107] Such an approach suited Kissinger not only from the vantage point of an apparatus that he now headed, but also from a general philosophical perspective, which made him deride "the modern bureaucratic state [which] widens the range of technical choices while limiting the capacity to make them."[108]

With so many foreign policy illusions shattered in the course of a harsh and protracted debate over the Vietnam War, the American public had welcomed at first the opportunity thus offered to slide into the more comfortable and more passive role of spectator. After so many foreign policy setbacks, the public had also generally welcomed Kissinger's acrobatics: the China initiative, the SALT negotiations, and the Middle East shuttle had all required a degree of secrecy and a centralization of authority that had been either overlooked or tolerated by a public increasingly weary of foreign affairs. (By 1974, the 10 leading national priorities all had to do with domestic affairs.)[109] Yet, the Vietnam syndrome was now accompanied by a Watergate complex, which had the nation question the intentions of its leadership at home even as it was debating the purposes of that same leadership abroad. Congressional inquiries of illegal practices at the White House coincided, therefore, almost logically with congressional investigations of illegitimate covert operations abroad. In the realm of the former, what began as a number of investigations over allegations that the Nixon administration was involved in national security wiretapping of American officials and newsmen gave way to a number of investigations over revelations that the Unites States was waging covert political and economic warfare of destabilization against numerous regimes it deemed unfriendly.

Such a pattern of congressional preoccupations was enhanced in the aftermath of the bloody coup in Chile in 1973. Reviewing the circumstances that had surrounded the coup, a widely publicized Senate report did in fact exonerate the U.S. administration from any direct complicity.[110] But, simultaneously, evidence showing that the Nixon administration had actively sought to foment a military coup in Chile in 1970 in order to prevent Salvador Allende's election tarnished Kissinger's image and eroded further a personal credibility already affected by a growing sense of discomfort over the rise of his overall influence in the conduct of foreign policy.

In 1974, the Cyprus crisis appeared to merge these two congressional concerns over human rights and decisionmaking. Congressional involvement became all the more pronounced as the specter of two NATO allies plunged into war with American weapons in an area of vital importance to the United States could hardly be seen as promising. Kissinger, it was argued in Congress, had remained for too long indifferent to repeated warnings that the repressive Greek military junta headed by Colonel Ioannides was encouraging anti-Makarios activities by its troops in Cyprus, thereby making last-minute U.S. efforts to avoid Archbishop Makarios' overthrow futile.[111]

At issue between the Executive and the Congress were provisions of the Foreign Assistance Act, which made a country receiving U.S. military assistance ineligible for additional aid if it used such assistance against another recipient of U.S. aid. In response to the Turkish invasion that followed Makarios' overthrow, members of Congress already under considerable pressure from an increasingly assertive Greek lobby sought the imposition of an arms embargo against Turkey.

During his confirmation hearings, the secretary of state-designate had assured the Senate Foreign Relations Committee that in devising and implementing the nation's foreign policy he would always abide by statutory law. "Once the intent [of the law] is clear," Kissinger had stated at the time, "we will implement not only the letter but the spirit."[112] To be sure, the Turkish invasion of Cyprus had introduced legal grounds for an immediate arms embargo against Turkey. Yet Kissinger now argued that the imposition of such an embargo would place undue constraints on his "efforts both to advance the Cyprus peace negotiations and to safeguard [U.S.] wider security interests in the Eastern Mediterranean" since "instead of influencing conduct in ways we desire, cutting aid is likely to harden positions."[113] Thus Cyprus was transformed into the focus of a major and bitter debate between the Executive and the Legislative Branches over the conduct of U.S. foreign policy. "[Beyond] the general requirement of advice and consent," Kissinger argued on January 24, 1976, "the legislative process—deliberation, debate, and statutory law—is much less well suited to the detailed supervision of the day-to-day conduct of diplomacy. Legal prescriptions, by their nature, lose sight of the sense of nuance and the feeling for the interrelationship of issues on which foreign policy success or failure so often depends."[114]

Yet, despite the efforts of the Nixon administration, the arms embargo against Turkey went into effect on February 5, 1975. One week later, Senator Thomas Eagleton captured the catalytic role played by the Cyprus crisis as he merged it together with all kinds of issues—Vietnam, Pakistan, Chile, and Watergate—spread over a number of years. Thus defending the action of the Congress, Eagleton pleaded against both the Kissinger and Ford appeals for congressional compliance:

> We must realize that there is no turning the clock back to the institutional relationships of the Cold War era. That period was characterized by a clear understanding of common goals, the acceptance of a common enemy, and the total subordination, largely self-imposed, of the Legislative Branch. . . . The most grievous errors of American policy in the past decade can be traced to a decision-making process which has not benefited from institutional balance.
>
> The American people were too often presented with *faits accomplis* in foreign policy because Congress was unaware of the important commitments being undertaken by the Executive Branch. From Vietnam to the Indian–Pakistan dispute, to Chile, to our current Cyprus policy, initiatives were taken in the name of the American people without the advice and consent of their elected representatives in Congress.[115]

Faced with a congressional onslaught that translated the antinational security mood in the United States into an ever-growing number of resolutions all meant to reduce the administration's room for overt or covert action, the Kissinger rhetoric, too, proved to be ultimately self-defeating. Granted that in the midst or in the immediate aftermath of Vietnam it might have seemed incongruous for the United States to enter into a new round of police actions, still this much-prevailing sense of drift was not helped by the emerging subtleties (why shake the hand of the Soviet communist leader in Helsinki but ignore that of the Italian communist leader in Rome?), the emphasis on limits (one nation among many, to be sure, but one nation that had been born into the world to do mankind service), and the heretofore unknown pessimism (unbecoming for a country which was still, by all measurable standards, the strongest, the wealthiest, and the most just).

In addition, the new rhetoric consecrated the breakdown of a domestic consensus that had grown out of a shared commitment to the worldwide containment of communism. References to the national interest opened a Pandora's box of vested and ethnic interests: against an even-handed policy in the Middle East that betrayed the Israelis; against a strengthening of the southern flank of NATO that sacrificed the Greeks; against free trade that took jobs away; against sanctions that harmed the farmers. With the meaning and implications of containment and superiority more readily understandable than those of detente and sufficiency, the Kissingerian practices and discourse that had been applauded earlier were progressively rejected. The secrecy that had framed the trip to Peking, the negotiations with Hanoi, and the SALT talks was exposed as being responsible for the covert actions in Cambodia and Laos, in Chile, and in Angola; the showmanship that had been well received at first was hurt by the deplorable spectacle of Watergate; the emphasis on adversaries, which had resulted in the constructive initiatives of the first Nixon administration, was seen as having damaged more enduring relationships with the allies and as having caused a self-defeating neglect of the Third World.

The dominant element of the congressional offensive in foreign policy went in the direction of human rights and human needs. "The human rights factor," it was deplored in Congress, "is not accorded the high priority it deserves in our country's foreign policy. . . . An increasingly interdependent world means that disregard for human rights in one country can have repercussions in others . . . [and] consideration for human rights in foreign policy is both morally imperative and politically necessary."[116] To Kissinger, such a focus was, to say the least, intellectually awkward and operationally ineffective. In striking a "balance between what is desirable and what is possible," the policymaker had, of course, to avoid excessively pragmatic policies that would be "empty of vision and humanity . . . and [would] provide no criteria for other nations to assess our performance and no standards to which the American people can rally."[117] Yet the reverse was no less true. "When policy becomes excessively moralistic," Kissinger warned, "it may turn quixotic or dangerous."[118] Who was to strike such a balance? The confrontation came to a head in 1975, when the American secretary of state objected to the idea of presenting to Congress reports on the human rights status of countries that were receiving U.S. aid.[119]

Oblivious to Kissinger's bitter complaints that the growing tendency of the Congress to legislate in detail the day-to-day conduct of American foreign policy threatened its coherence,[120] the Congress continued to vote new restrictions that included amendments to the International Development and Food Assistance Act of 1975 and the International Security Assistance and Arms Export Control Act of 1976. The latter especially directed the U.S. president to "formulate and conduct international security assistance programs of the United States in a manner which will promote and advance human rights and avoid identification of the United States, through such programs, with governments which deny to their people internationally recognized human rights and fundamental freedoms."[121] In this regard, the Arms Export Control Act dictated that the secretary of state "shall transmit to the Congress, as part of the presentation materials for security assistance programs proposed for each fiscal year, a full and complete report, prepared with the assistance of the Coordinator for Human Rights and Humanitarian Affairs, with respect to practices regarding the observance of and respect for internationally recognized human rights in each country proposed as recipient of security assistance." Although the secretary of state could still rely on a claim of extraordinary circumstances involving vital U.S. interests to continue such assistance to countries that did not meet specified congressional criteria, the Congress reserved the right to override such a recommendation and "adopt a joint resolution terminating, restricting, or continuing security assistance for such a country."*

Even though Kissinger gave way over a question which, he conceded, had been brought up "with great integrity and concern,"[122] congressional opposition expanded and forced him to further concessions and retreats on a whole range of issues. No, he now argued, "We do not and will not condone repressive practices" against which "we have used, and will use, our influence;"[123] yes, "as our attention can shift from Southern Asia, . . . inevitably our concern with Africa south of the Sahara will increase,"[124] and thus alleviate Senator Javits' complaint that Africa had been left to Europe;[125] yes, the United States was totally dedicated to seeing that the majority becomes the ruling power in Rhodesia;[126] no, the United States was not favorable to the institutionalized separation of races in South Africa;[127] yes, in meeting the growing threat to the world's food supply, and in line with the spirit of American foreign policy, the United States was ready to join with others in providing such assistance[128] as requested by Senator Humphrey's call for a "more comprehensive and humane use of food assistance abroad."[129] But the retreat came too little too late to pacify the critics. As Lawrence Stern wrote, "while Kissinger's contribution was to purge American foreign policy of the Protestant missionary spirit with which Dulles had imbued it, his failure was in not understanding the imperatives of change among and within nations."[130]

---

*The case-by-case human rights approach of the Carter administration was based on Secretary Kissinger's human rights report prepared for the House International Relations Committee during the waning days of the Ford administration. The Kissinger report had recommended that for strategic reasons Iran and five other human rights violators should not suffer the loss of U.S. military support on the grounds of their human rights performance. With the exception of Argentina, the Carter administration generally followed the recommendations of the Kissinger report closely.

Not that the human rights debate centered only on the internal practices of right-wing dictatorships. Writing in the immediate aftermath of Nixon's resignation, William P. Bundy excessively complained that "in his five and a half years of power, Nixon managed to get on strained terms with almost every democratic government in the world while condoning and cultivating dictatorial regimes both in great and lesser powers."[131] These, of course, included left-wing totalitarian regimes, especially the Soviet Union whose domestic policies were tied to trade incentives during the protracted debate that surrounded the congressional consideration of the Jackson–Vanik Amendment, which aimed at barring Most Favorable Nation status to any communist country that restricted the emigration of its citizens. In Kissinger's view, any legislation designed to use linkage to force changes in the domestic system of the Soviet Union was anathema since it would reflect a return to the ideological premises of containment and would undermine the premises of detente.[132] Already in 1972, a similar amendment had held the U.S. pledge of MFN for the Soviets hostage to the abolition of a newly imposed exit tax on emigrants. Indeed, the Soviets had abolished the tax in April 1973. But now the Kremlin remained apparently unconcerned as it probably relied on the Nixon–Kissinger assurances that the amendment would eventually be rejected by the U.S. Congress. That it was nevertheless passed in late 1974 raised serious doubts in Moscow over the reliability of the United States as a partner in detente. Such congressional practices, Kissinger had warned, would lead other countries "to question whether we understand our own national interest and whether we can be a reliable, long-term partner."[133] Now the Soviets charged that the United States was trying to change the rules in the middle of the game, rules that had been formulated during the summit in Moscow. Moreover, the issues involved much more than economic advantages: greater freedom of emigration was indeed a sensitive matter for the Soviet leadership. This was not so much the result of a Soviet concern about an eventual brain drain, or even possible breaches of secrecy over security issues; more significantly, giving Soviet citizens the option to leave would have substantially reduced the power of the Soviet regime to control their behavior at home.[134] Besides, in addition to the Jackson–

Vanik amendment, the Soviets were also facing new difficulties in getting the Conference on the Security and Cooperation in Europe (CSCE) to ratify the territorial division of Europe without further evidence of a Soviet commitment to freer East–West movement of ideas and people. Thus the Soviet leadership apparently decided that it would now, cautiously at first but more boldly later, attempt to take advantage of opportunities that were opening up in a number of areas (from Cyprus to Angola) where the likelihood of a forceful reaction on the part of the United States was remote in the light of existing domestic circumstances. As for SALT, according to a noted American observer of Soviet military affairs, "the balance of decision within the Kremlin by the end of 1975 appears to have tilted toward the view that there was no compelling reason to make substantial changes in the Soviet bargaining position for the sake of an early SALT II accord and new summit."[135] Detente now appeared to be in disarray. Unlike what had been contemplated and applied in earlier years, the Ford Administration was no longer anxious to link Soviet behavior to SALT. "Limitation of strategic arms," Kissinger argued on January 14, 1976, prior to a new trip to Moscow designed to break the SALT impasse, "is . . . a permanent and global problem that cannot be subordinated to the day-to-day changes in Soviet–American relations."[136] Although some progress was made in the course of the ensuing talks, the Soviets were no longer in any hurry, and it would be left to the Carter Administration to achieve a SALT II Treaty.

Thus, the reluctant partners that Kissinger found abroad as the process of detente unfolded combined with the increasingly restive nation he found at home to undermine the intricate architecture that he and President Nixon had sought to erect in earlier years. The very scope of their ambitions in restructuring America's adversary relationships—often against the grain of American history—forced them to overlook the enduring influence of the past over the present. With Nixon mortally wounded by Watergate, Kissinger inherited a domestic base whose erosion was all the more difficult to contain as the many uncertainties of detente were exposed at the periphery of U.S.–Soviet relations, that is, in areas where the American fear of "a new Vietnam" was most pronounced. In the end, Kissinger failed to gain the legitimacy of the peaceful international order he had wished to build. As one observer put it, "his own drama [was] the attempt to re-create a legitimate order in a world of revolutionary players."[137] Yet Kissinger's reading of the period that inspired him most should have enlightened him better."All of Metternich's colleagues," he had written,"were . . . products of essentially the same culture, professing the same ideals, sharing similar tastes. They understood each other . . . they were conscious that the things they shared were much more fundamental than the issues separating them."[138] But now such homogeneity could not be found or constructed either at home or abroad, then or later, as would be shown during the Carter and Reagan administrations. Thus overburdened, the Nixon–Kissinger design for primacy and order was discarded by an even larger part of the American public either because too much was conceded in the East, as the more conservative critics had it, or because too much was neglected in the West and in the South, as the more liberal critics saw it. Yet, with time the memory of Nixon's and Kissinger's real achievements in foreign policy would dominate the memory of their failures. For, indeed, notwithstanding the tragedies in Cambodia, Chile, and Lebanon, and granted that the best can often prove to be not good enough, their policies may well have been the only policies that could be designed, and the best that could be achieved, under the historically difficult circumstances of Vietnam, OPEC, and Watergate.[139]

NOTES

1. One of the more excessive, and perhaps least acceptable, criticisms of Kissinger's policies and methods is likely to remain that of Seymour M. Hersch, *The Price of Power: Kissinger in the Nixon White House* (New York: Summit Books, 1983). According to Hersch, "Coping with Nixon, pleasing him, and trying to find

out what he really wanted were the most important priorities for Kissinger. They would become even more important than his own convictions about American foreign policy." *The Price of Power,* p. 45.

2. Louise FitzSimons, *The Kennedy Doctrine* (New York: Random House, 1972), pp. 14–15.
3. Ibid., p. 3.
4. Ibid., p. 10.
5. See also Henry Fairlie, *The Kennedy Promise. The Politics of Expectation* (New York: Dell Publishing, 1972).
6. George Kennan, *American Diplomacy, 1900–1950* (Chicago: Chicago University Press, 1951), pp. 50 and 78.
7. Richard M. Nixon, "U.S. Foreign Policy for the Seventies: Shaping a Durable Peace," report to the Congress, February 18, 1970.
8. Henry Kissinger, address to Newpaper Editors, Washington, D.C., April 17, 1975.
9. See Simon Serfaty, "The Kissinger Legacy: Old Obsessions and New Looks," *The World Today* (March 1977), pp. 81–89.
10. Henry Kissinger, *American Foreign Policy,* expanded edition (New York: W. W. Norton, 1974), pp. 91–92.
11. Richard Pfeffer, ed., *No More Vietnams? The War and the Future of American Foreign Policy* (New York: Harper & Row, 1968), p. 13.
12. Kissinger, *American Foreign Policy,* p. 92.
13. Henry Kissinger, address to the St. Louis World Affairs Council, May 12, 1975.
14. Henry Kissinger, *Years of Upheaval* (Boston, Mass.: Little, Brown, 1982), p. 242.
15. Ibid.
16. Kissinger, *American Foreign Policy,* pp. 85 and 90.
17. Quoted in Richard J. Barnet, *The Giants: Russia and America* (New York: Simon and Schuster, 1977), p. 17.
18. Henry Kissinger, *White House Years* (Boston, Mass.: Little, Brown, 1979), p. 833.
19. Kissinger, *American Foreign Policy,* p. 87.
20. By the Spring of 1975, 58 out of the 105 treaties and agreements signed between the United States and the Soviet Union since 1933 had been concluded after January 1969. See Alastair Buchan, "The United States and European Security," in *Western Europe: The Trials of Partnership,* ed. David Landes (Lexington, Mass.: Lexington Books, 1976), p. 197.

21. Kissinger, address to newspaper editors, Washington, D.C., April 17, 1975.
22. Kissinger, *American Foreign Policy,* p. 56.
23. Ibid., excerpts from the Senate Foreign Relations Committee hearings, p. 225.
24. Richard M. Nixon,"Asia after Vietnam," *Foreign Affairs* (October 1967), pp. 113–14.
25. Sandy Vogelgesang, *American Dream, Global Nightmare: The Dilemma of U.S. Human Rights Policy* (New York: W. W. Norton, 1980), p. 266.
26. See William P. Bundy, "Dictatorships and American Foreign Policy," *Foreign Affairs* (October 1975), p. 57.
27. Nixon, "Asia after Vietnam," pp. 121–24.
28. Ibid., p. 124.
28. Ibid., p. 120.
30. As stated by Secretary Kissinger on October 8, 1973.
31. Kissinger, *White House Years,* p. 124.
32. Quoted in D. F. Fleming, *The Cold War and its Origins* (Garden City, N.Y.: Doubleday, 1961), p. 487.
33. *New York Times,* March 15, 1969.
34. Robert S. McNamara, *The Essence of Security: Reflections in Office* (New York: Harper & Row, 1968), p. 52.
35. Charles Murphy, "The White House Since Sputnik," *Fortune* (January 1958), pp. 98–101.
36. George H. Quester, *Nuclear Diplomacy* (New York: Dunellen Company, 1970), p. 160.
37. McNamara, *Essence of Security,* p. 58.
38. Stuart Symington, "Where the Missile Gap Went," *The Reporter* (February 15, 1962), pp. 21–23.
39. McNamara, *Essence of Security,* p. 57.
40. Thomas W. Wolfe, *Soviet Power and Europe* (Baltimore, Md.: Johns Hopkins University Press, 1970), pp. 84 ff.
41. McNamara, *Essence of Security,* p. 60.
42. Roman Kolkowicz et al., *The Soviet Union and Arms Control: A Superpower Dilemma* (Baltimore, Md.: Johns Hopkins University Press, 1970), p. 29.
43. Kissinger, *White House Years,* p. 124.
44. "Nixon: The First Year of His Presidency," *Congressional Quarterly,* Washington, D.C., p. 2A.
45. For a summary of Soviet discussions on the undesirability of nuclear war, see Dimitri Simes, "Deterrence in Soviet Policy," *International Security* (Winter 1980–81).

46. Kissinger, briefing of Congressional leaders, Washington, D.C., June 15, 1972, in *American Foreign Policy,* p. 142.
47. "Nixon: The First Year of His Presidency."
48. Kissinger, *White House Years,* p. 128.
49. Ibid., p. 594.
50. The point was made by Kissinger who quoted directly from Kennedy's news conference of November 20, 1962. *White House Years,* p. 646. See also Tad Szulc, *The Illusion of Peace. Foreign Policy in the Nixon Years* (New York: Viking Press, 1978), pp. 364–66.
51. Szulc, *Illusion of Peace,* p. 328. Kissinger, *White House Years,* pp. 627-31.
52. Quoted in John Lewis Gaddis, *Strategies of Containment. A Critical Appraisal of Postwar American National Security Policy* (New York: Oxford University Press, 1982), p. 292.
53. Kissinger, *White House Years,* p. 833.
54. Richard M. Nixon, *RN: The Memoirs of Richard Nixon* (New York: Warner Books, 1978), p. 511.
55. Kissinger, *White House Years,* pp. 266–70.
56. Ibid., p. 268.
57. A. Doak Barnett, *China and the Major Powers* (Washington, D.C.: The Brookings Institution, 1977), pp. 193–97.
58. Kissinger, *White House Years,* pp. 1190–97, and 1201.
59. Ibid., pp. 1315–16.
60. Michel Tatu, "Moscow, Peking and the Conflict in Vietnam," in *The Vietnam Legacy: The War, American Society and the Future of American Foreign Policy,* ed. Anthony Lake (New York: New York University Press, 1976), p. 24.
61. Ibid., p. 26.
62. "Basic Principles of Relations Between the United States of America and the Union of Soviet Socialist Republics," Department of State *Bulletin,* June 26, 1972, pp. 898–99.
63. Raymond Aron, *Peace and War Among Nations* (Garden City, N.Y.: Doubleday, 1966), pp. 441ff.
64. "Basic Principles," passim.
65. Nixon, "U.S. Foreign Policy for the Seventies."
66. Roger P. Labrie, ed. *SALT Handbook. Key Documents and Issues, 1972-1979* (Washington, D.C.: American Enterprise Institute for Public Policy Research, 1979), p. 5.
67. See Jerome B. Wiesner et al., eds., *ABM: An Evaluation of the Decision to Deploy an Antiballistic Missile System* (New York: Signet Broadside, 1969), p. 4.

68. Quoted in "The Annals of America: 1961–68. The Burdens of World Power" (Vol. 18), Encyclopedia Britannica Inc., 1968, p. 532.
69. Kissinger, *White House Years*, p. 198.
70. "U.S. Foreign Policy for the Seventies."
71. Labrie *SALT Handbook*, p. 198.
72. Kissinger, Briefing of Congressional leaders, Washington, D.C., June 15, 1972, in *American Foreign Policy,* p. 149.
73. Labrie, *SALT Handbook*, p. 12.
74. Kissinger, Briefing of Congressional Leaders, in *American Foreign Policy*, p. 150.
75. Kissinger, *White House Years*, pp. 1148–49.
76. Seyom Brown, *The Crises of Power* (New York: Columbia University Press, 1979), p. 27.
77. Peter Fromuth, "Detente: The Overburdened Design", unpublished paper. Johns Hopkins School of Advanced International Studies, Washington, D.C., 1982.
78. Kissinger, *White House Years*, p. 876.
79. Ibid., p. 853.
80. Ibid., pp. 853, 855, and 866.
81. As argued in Kissinger's statement to the Senate Foreign Relations Committee on September 19, 1974. *American Foreign Policy*, 3rd ed. (New York: W. W. Norton, 1977), p. 153.
82. Kissinger, *Years of Upheaval*, p. 468. Both Nixon and Kissinger apparently thought that the two sides needed a new round of battle before diplomacy could effectively begin. Hersh, *Price of Power*, p. 214; also, Roger Morris, *Uncertain Greatness* (New York: Harper & Row, 1977).
83. William B. Quandt, *Decade of Decisions: American Foreign Policy Toward the Arab–Israeli Conflict* (Berkeley, Calif.: University of California Press, 1977), p. 16.
84. Kissinger, *White House Years,* p. 376.
85. Kissinger, *Years of Upheaval*, pp. 210–27.
86. "The Battle Is Now Inevitable," an interview with President Sadat, *Newsweek* (April 9, 1973), p. 45.
87. See Coral Bell, *The Diplomacy of Detente* (New York: St. Martins Press, 1977).
88. Kissinger, *Years of Upheaval*, pp. 545–54.
89. John G. Stoessinger, *Henry Kissinger: The Anguish of Power* (New York: W. W. Norton, 1976), p. 221.
90. Quandt, "Decade of Decisions," p. 286.
91. "The Middle East: U.S. Policy, Israel, Oil and the Arabs," p. 27.

92. Kissinger, *American Foreign Policy*, pp. 80-81.
93. Ibid., excerpts from the Senate Foreign Relations Hearings, p. 233.
94. Ibid., p. 236.
95. Ibid., p. 237.
96. Stanley Hoffmann, *Primacy or World Order. American Foreign Policy since the Cold War* (New York: McGraw-Hill, 1978), p. 71.
97. Henry Kissinger, "United States Policy on Southern Africa," Department of State Bulletin (May 31, 1976), pp. 672–79.
98. Kissinger's address delivered in Lusaka, Zambia, April 27, 1976, Department of State *Bulletin* (May 31, 1976), pp. 672–79.
99. Declaration of Principles signed by Richard Nixon and Leonid Brezhnev, Moscow, May 29, 1972.
100. Kissinger, *American Foreign Policy*, pp. 55–56.
101. Winston Lord, quoted in Brown, *Crises of Power*, pp. 40–41.
102. Kissinger statement to the Senate Foreign Relations Committee, September 19, 1974. Reprinted in *American Foreign Policy*, p. 153.
103. Quoted in Morris, *Uncertain Greatness*, p. 241.
104. Simes, "Deterrence in Soviet Policy," p. 95.
105. Kissinger's News Conference of December 23, 1975.
106. Kissinger, Department of State *Bulletin*, Vol. VXXIV (February 23, 1973), p. 204. See Stanley Hoffmann, *Primacy or World Order*, pp. 64–65.
107. Nixon, *U.S. Foreign Policy for the Seventies*.
108. Kissinger, *American Foreign Policy*, p. 95.
109. See William Watts and Lloyd Free, *America's Hopes and Fears—1976* (Washington, D.C.: Potomac Associates, 1976), and Robert W. Tucker, William Watts, and Lloyd Free, *The United States in the World. New Directions for the Post-Vietnam Era?* (Washington, D.C.: Potomac Associates, 1976).
110. U.S. Congress, Senate, Select Committee to Study Governmental Operations with Respect to Intelligence Activities, *Covert Action in Chile: 1963–1973*, Staff Report, 94th Congress, 1st Session, 1975, p. 2.
111. See Lawrence Stern, *The Wrong Horse: The Politics of Intervention and the Failure of American Diplomacy* (New York: New York Times Book Co., 1977).
112. Quoted in ibid., p. 143.
113. Henry Kissinger, "Toward a New National Partnership: Congress and Foreign Policy," address to the Los Angeles World Affairs Council, January 24, 1976.
114. Ibid.

115. Stern, *Wrong Horse,* pp. 150–51.
116. As quoted by Vogelgesang, *American Dream, Global Nightmare,* p. 127.
117. Henry Kissinger, address to Pacem in Terris III Conference, reproduced in *American Foreign Policy*, pp. 258–59.
118. Ibid.
119. Vogelgesang, *American Dream, Global Nightmare*, pp. 129–30.
120. Kissinger, "Toward a National Partnership."
121. *United States Statutes at Large*, Vo. 89, 94th Congress, 1st Session, 1975 (Washington, D.C.: U.S. Government Printing Office, 1977), p. 860.
122. Henry Kissinger, "The Moral Foundations of Foreign Policy," address to the Upper Midwest Council, Minneapolis, Minnesota, July 15, 1975.
123. Ibid.
124. Kissinger, Senate Foreign Relations Committee Hearings, *American Foreign Policy*, p. 233.
125. Ibid.
125. Kissinger, "U.S. Policy on Southern Africa."
127. Ibid.
128. Kissinger, address to the United Nations General Assembly, in *American Foreign Policy*, pp. 249–50.
129. Kissinger, *Years of Upheaval*, p. 429.
130. Stern, *Wrong Horse*, p. 162.
131. William P. Bundy, "Dictatorships and American Foreign Policy," p. 57.
132. Kissinger, *Years of Upheaval*, pp. 987 ff.
133. Kissinger, "Towards a New National Partnership."
134. Dimitri Simes, "The Death of Detente?" *International Security* (Summer 1980), p. 17.
135. Thomas W. Wolfe, *The SALT Experience* (Cambridge, Mass.: Ballinger Publishing Co.), pp. 205–9.
136. Press conference, Secretary of State Henry A. Kissinger, Department of State *Bulletin* (February 2, 1976), pp. 125–32.
137. Hoffmann, *Primacy or World Order*, p. 38.
138. Henry Kissinger, *A World Restored* (Boston, Mass.: Houghton Mifflin, 1973), p. 320.
139. Norman Podhoretz, "Kissinger Reconsidered," *Commentary* (June 1982), p. 28.

CHAPTER EIGHT

Neither Allies nor Adversaries

Fading Partnership

Throughout the 1970s, changed circumstances in the relationship between the United States and the states of Europe made of the Atlantic Alliance a fading partnership. These changes could not be attributed to any one U.S. administration, or any American policy over any one issue. Instead, they involved a combination of long-term trends that included the steady reappraisal in Europe of the former image of "America as an exceptional country" and the resulting erosion of its earlier claim at leadership; the devaluation of American military power and the related rise of Soviet power; the deterioration of the American economy and its impact, real or perceived, on the economies of the allies; and the progressive displacement of Western Europe's primary interests toward issues of economic security that involved not only the centralized economies of the communist countries but also—and increasingly—the developing countries of the Third World. Accordingly, the earlier toleration of U.S. policies in Europe and elsewhere, however grudgingly granted by the first postwar generation of European leaders, diminished with the ascendancy of a new successor generation, thereby prompting an ever more visible gap between U.S. policies and those of the European allies. In short, from a European standpoint, the durability of the Atlantic partnership was questioned because of the apparent inability of a "declining" America to protect the vital interests of an "ascending" Europe.[1]

But simultaneously, in the United States, too, there could be seen a growing weariness over the unreliability and selectiveness of Europe's support. Once accepted as a responsibility imposed by the devastations of history and the geopolitical circumstances that came out of two world wars, the states of Europe had now emerged as an increasing burden that offered diminishing rewards. Economic rivals in the contested markets of the Third World and elsewhere, they remained militarily dependent on U.S. protection even as they continued to seek diplomatic separation from U.S. policies. In the United States, too, the Atlantic partnership was questioned because of the inability or unwillingness of a "declining" Europe to follow and support adequately the leadership of America.

Extending over a wide range of recurring political, economic, monetary, and military issues, such divergences between the United States and the states of Europe were new not only because of their intensity but also because of the manner in which, late in the 1970s, they tended to pressure the structures of the alliance all at the same time. Earlier, during the Gaullist challenge, there had remained a stable cluster of common Atlantic interests around which the cohesion of the alliance could be achieved all the more readily as American military superiority guaranteed security, American economic affluence provided prosperity, and over-all political commonalities between the allies permitted compatibility. Thus, Atlantic solidarity proved to be most impressive during the Cuban missile crisis.[2] Coming a few years after the 1956 Suez debacle and the 1960 Summit fiasco in Paris, Western Europe's support for Kennedy's demand that Soviet missile installations be dismantled at once was total and immediate, despite the risks assumed during a crisis that was otherwise unfolding so very far from the European continent. Yet the redeployment of what was then a significant portion of Soviet strategic power into the American security area would have transformed the existing balance of power between the two superpowers. This had ominous implications for the security of Western Europe, especially at a time when Moscow was aggressively engaged in a power play over Berlin. The Cuban missile crisis therefore reflected the united determination of the West—surely the most dramatic if not the last—to preserve strategic superiority over the Soviet Union, by force if necessary.

But in significant opposition to the solidarity shown over Cuba in 1962 stood the disunity shown during the war in the Middle East in late 1973, as most of the allies in Europe simply chose the route of dissociation over that of cooperation: statements of neutrality issued by several NATO members; Turkey's acquiescence in the overflight of its territory by the Soviet arms lift to the Arabs; public prohibition by Turkey, but also by Greece and Italy (as well as Spain, not yet a member of NATO), of landing in or overflying their territories for a similar arms lift to Israel; a parallel, although less demonstrative, prohibition by Great Britain and West Germany; Britain's and France's unwillingness to go along with a U.S.-sponsored U.N. cease-fire resolution that would have urged the protagonists to return to the status-quo ante.[3] Europe's skepticism toward American policies was especially evident over the measures taken by the Nixon administration on October 25, 1973, to counter a projected Soviet military move in the area: where European countries had found it superfluous to consider the evidence in 1962, they now ignored the U.S. fear of a unilateral intervention of the Soviet Union in a region of obvious strategic and economic interest to them, one over which Great Britain and France had last been willing to go to war 17 years earlier. Another six years later, in 1979, the Soviet invasion of Afghanistan caused relative indifference among the allies.

To be sure, in the past, too, the Atlantic allies had often disagreed on the nature and the focus of the Soviet threat and the best and most effective ways to meet it. In earlier years, this had remained a persistent irritant of the Atlantic partnership. The present shapes the rereading of the past—who could say that Stalin had ever intended to challenge militarily the status-quo in Europe? And such a rereading of the past, in turn, affects the vision of the future—should we be condemned to repeat tomorrow yesteryear's alleged errors? Should the Soviet threat be measured in terms of Soviet intentions irrespective of

Soviet power? or in terms of Soviet power irrespective of Soviet intentions? or else, in terms of both, irrespective of the unreliable measurements that could be made of either? Entering the 1970s, the Soviet Union was admittedly more of a military power than ever before. Nevertheless, its intentions toward Europe appeared to concern the states of Europe less than in previous years, as these could not imagine that the Soviet leadership might risk a direct military thrust against them unless provoked by the United States.

Throughout the decade, the irony was there for everyone to see: Soviet intentions were more feared in and by Europe when Soviet power was inferior and stalled than when it was peaking and spreading. That the two major East–West crises had been born out of a Soviet misreading of American policies and allied unity threatened, by the end of the 1970s, to transform the irony into a tragedy. In June 1950, with the alliance still in a state of formation, Stalin assumed that the Truman administration, having previously argued the irrelevance of South Korea to American security, would not respond to its overt invasion by the North Korean forces. In October 1962, as the French challenge to U.S. leadership was gaining momentum, Khrushchev expected that the Kennedy administration, reconciled earlier to the presence of a communist regime 90 miles away from U.S. shores, would also permit the introduction of Soviet missiles there. Eventually, in December 1979, Brezhnev, too, reasoned that the Carter administration, having accepted the "unacceptable" of increased Soviet military activities in Cuba—an issue over which two other administrations had gone to the brink—would now sanction the unsactionable in Afghanistan. Actually, neither Stalin nor Khruschchev or Brezhnev truly miscalculated either in Korea, in Cuba, or in Afghanistan. Instead, their actions could be seen as the predictable outcome of earlier American behavior and pronouncements that pointed to accommodation or compromise in the face of a *fait accompli*. In 1949–50, these had included Truman's passivity toward adverse strategic (the explosion of the first Soviet atomic device) and political (Mao's victory on the Chinese mainland) developments, as well as a narrow definition of American security interests in the Far East. In 1961–62, Khrushchev's gambit was preceded by the Bay of Pigs crisis, when Kennedy's hesitations removed any remaining possibility that the Eisenhower-sponsored effort to topple Fidel Castro might succeed after all; and by the Berlin Wall, which the Kennedy administration saw as an action that demanded conciliation rather than more confrontation. In 1978–79, Brezhnev thought that he could depend on a long list of precedents set by an administration that had wanted to welcome the coming of a new equality in international relations while bidding farewell to the past practices of military coercion. In all instances, the *fait accompli* that Moscow sought in effect almost came to be: the early routing of the South Korean army; the near ability to make the Soviet launching pads in Cuba operational; and the brutal attempt to overwhelm Afghan resistance at once with a large number of Soviet troops. In response to the Soviet actions, the unexpected American reactions precipitated, respectively, a war, a dangerous military confrontation, and a lasting diplomatic freeze between the United States and the Soviet Union. Significantly enough, while the cohesion of the Atlantic Alliance was strengthened by the Korean War (which demonstrated the availability of American power), it was eroded in the aftermath of the Cuban missile crisis (which displayed the dangers of a close relationship with American power outside the NATO area) and fragmented during and after the crisis over Afghanistan (which appeared to expose the new impotence of American power).

Beyond considerations of strictly military power, Europe's vision of America was equally shaped by contemplation of the domestic turmoil that afflicted America following Kennedy's assassination in November 1963. A new image of America-as-a-country-like-any-other now replaced the image of an exceptional nation that Europe, as we have seen, had held in earlier years. Absurd killing or sheer political termination of American political leaders who had best captured the imagination (John and Robert Kennedy) or the respect (Richard Nixon) of the European public; bloody riots in the cities and debilitating quarrels in the Courts and in Congress; a dirty war that would neither be won nor be ended; the rise of national ailments (from unprecedented rates of inflation and persistent budget deficits to the uncovering of political corruption at the highest levels of government) that were thought to be reserved for the old and decadent states of Europe—all this and much more helped to build over the years a picture of hesitation, impotence, and unreliability that inevitably affected the perceived ability of the United States to manage the vital interests of its allies.

But it was not only when it looked at the world outside that Europe pondered America's influence and policies. It was also when Europe looked at itself. During the ten years that followed the formation of the European Common Market, U.S. direct investments in the EEC had increased six times in terms of their book value. Coming at a time when misgivings over the U.S. connection were fed throughout Europe by a vocal and public debate over the so-called *défi américain* (the title of a best-seller in France in the mid-1960s),[4] they added significantly to European grievances that earlier had focused primarily on the more traditional issues of physical security. From the standpoint of many in Europe, the U.S. multinational corporations (MNCs) were just too big, too mobile, and too American. They preempted European credit markets to aggrandize their own assets, maneuvered around national credit control policies and national plans, escaped the surveillance of national banking institutions, distorted intra-European trade patterns through intra-corporate transfers, denied much-needed tax receipts to national authorities by transfer pricing, fueled a politically dangerous inflation, fostered price wars at the expense of the smaller and less competitive national companies, and disrupted traditional relationships. In sum, many argued in Europe, the American MNCs were sapping the ability of the various national governments in Europe to conduct independent and effective macroeconomic policies of their own, thereby affecting national production, employment, prices, and income. With an overvalued dollar that had permitted the cheap acquisition of vital European assets in key national industries as well as in banking, U.S. investments threatened to make the displacement of power from Europe to America irreversible. They disarmed the state in the midst of an international environment that was growing increasingly unstable and precarious.

Defense and money are the two most sensitive and vital areas of sovereign power.[5] It is therefore not surprising that, just as in the case of nuclear weapons, the overall question of national control was at stake in the numerous offensives launched by the European allies against the dollar. Started by the French in early 1965, gold conversions were designed to show the unworkability of an international monetary system based on a national reserve currency. As argued repeatedly in Paris, the dollar had now become the vehicle of American expansionism in Europe where the holders of increasingly substantial dollar balances were forced to pay for the policies pursued by Washington around the world. How such a process actually took place was not always made as explicit as the charge itself. First, it was often argued, the United States exported a measure of inflation to Europe. Within the United States, the increase in domestic money supply—which President Johnson resorted to in the two election years of 1966 and 1968—meant that consumers gained additional funds to buy a constant supply of goods. The resulting inflationary pressures affected European states since, in the absence of substitutes for American-made products, higher import prices now had to be paid. Such increases in import prices were tantamount to a decline in living standard for the foreign consumer. To compensate for this decline, workers demanded related increases in real wages from their employers, thereby spurring an induced inflationary effect. Similarly, the increase in the money stock pushed American interest rates downward and caused an outflow of interest-sensitive capital, creating new problems in managing domestic money supplies in such a way as to combat the inflationary pressures engendered by the rise in import prices.

Ironically, coming at a time when a shortage of international liquidity was said to be a major source of monetary instability, huge capital outflows quickly established the Eurodollar market as a powerful force in the international economy and made the 1968 agreement over the creation of Special Drawing Rights (SDR) generally irrelevant. From 1970, the year when the SDR scheme went into effect, through 1973, total world reserves grew by $59 billion, while SDR creation amounted to slightly more than $4 billion.[6] By late 1969, the EEC summit meeting at the Hague sought a European Monetary Union that might reduce Europe's dependence on the U.S. dollar and shield it from the emerging Eurodollar glut the consequences of which were especially feared for the delicate structure of the Common Agricultural Policy. But even the first modest steps that were agreed upon by the Europeans in 1969 could not survive the monetary storms of 1971.[7]

The energy crisis that erupted following the outbreak of the Middle East War of October 1973 further exposed the impotence of Europe in the face of a manipulation of vital economic and monetary parameters by foreign countries or foreign-based multinationals. "It is inadmissible," complained West Germany's Minister of Commerce Hans Friderichs in April 1974, "that we should be kept in the dark about sales, policies, prices, and profits of the international petroleum companies which are operating in our territory and which are behaving like a state within a state."[8] Although Europe's reaction in 1974–76 was initially one of accommodation (France and the rest of Europe to West Germany, but also West Germany to the United States), it soon evolved into one of renewed rebellion during most of the Carter administration when perennial European misgivings over the durability and reliability of U.S. leadership were sharply exacerbated.[9]

In sum, throughout the 1970s, European countries questioned U.S. ability to provide them with the security to which they had become accustomed since the end of World War II, even while they found the U.S. potential for harming their economic and monetary stability significantly increased. Consequently, the United States was now seen by many in Europe as a part of the threat to its economic security at the very time when the United States was losing some of its past relevance insofar as its treatment of the physical threat was concerned. The Atlantic partnership was fading even while the Atlantic Alliance endured.

The Fall of the Dollar Standard

In 1969, the Nixon administration appeared to be especially anxious to reassert the unity of the alliance with Europe. "Atlantic relations," Kissinger had warned prior to the 1968 presidential elections, "for all their seemingly normalcy . . . face a profound crisis."[10] And Nixon had pleaded in the midst of his campaign, "It's time we begin paying Europe more attention. . . . It's time we begin lecturing our European partners less and listening to them more."[11] Apparently, France, as always the most persistent adversary among the allies, was to be the focus of new American initiatives. "Of the leaders in Europe . . . [de Gaulle] is the giant," reported Nixon upon his return from an early tour of European capitals in April 1969.[12] An independent European Europe was promoted by the Nixon administration as a balance between the United States and the Soviet Union; a promise was made to avoid bilateral talks with Moscow, while the European commissions and other institutions of the European community were pointedly ignored.

But following such an auspicious start, Europe was given little attention since Nixon, as we have seen, concentrated primarily on adversary relationships at the expense of alliance relations. To some, to ignore U.S.–European conflict behind a rhetorical pretense of Atlantic cohesion seemed sensible after years of public confrontation, especially at a time when, it was hoped, French obstinacy might be ended following de Gaulle's departure in early 1969. Yet throughout the first term of the Nixon administration, such neglect of alliance relationships facilitated a renewed European challenge to U.S. leadership, and charges and countercharges between the two sides of the Atlantic took on an increasingly bitter tone, particularly in the area of monetary relations.

During much of the Johnson administration, inflationary expenditures associated with the growing Americanization of the Vietnam War had already begun to underscore widespread demands for a fundamental reform of the international monetary system. The European countries complained bitterly that the American economy had remained immune to the discipline of the Bretton Woods system, a discipline that was otherwise applicable to all other debtor nations. But Western European economies were everything but immune to U.S. economic policies, which were conducive to excessive money creation at home and inflationary pressures abroad. Accordingly, the United States was urged to take steps to restrain—that is, to deflate—its domestic economy and, at the same time, reduce its rising outflows of long- and short-term capital, two-thirds of which went to Europe.[13] It is to convey such concerns that in early 1965 the French government chose to convert into gold some 300 million of its dollar holdings, and to step up its monthly gold purchases from the United States.[14] In so doing, de Gaulle's France—as well as Belgium, the Netherlands, and Switzerland, which soon followed the French lead[15]—hoped to force the United States to acknowledge the unworkability of an international monetary system dependent for liquidity upon a nationally created key reserve currency. They were calling into question the credibility of the U.S. dollar and, consequently, the entire Bretton Woods system that it had come to support and sustain.[16]

The Johnson administration was not averse to lessening the international dependence on exploding dollar reserves so long as the privileges associated with the de facto dollar standard system of the past were preserved. Thus, in 1963–65, the problem of world liquidity had been addressed not so much to confront the consequences of an impending end to continued U.S. payments deficits as to uncover new ways of financing these deficits in the future. The resulting U.S. proposal was the creation of a new international unit of account—the Special Drawing Rights (SDR)—which would be managed by the IMF, over which the United States continued to exert a dominant control and within which it enjoyed the largest quota.[17] Like the Kennedy Round in the area of trade and like the MLF in the area of defense, this American initiative in the area of money ran into a number of obstacles raised by the French with the varying support of other European countries. In the end, because the SDR scheme that was approved in 1968 went into effect in 1970 at the moment when the liquidity problem had become one of excess rather than one of shortage, the relevance of the scheme was moot. Yet the very format of the agreement reflected the growing shift in the balance of monetary power in the West: having the SDRs managed by the Group of Ten (that is, the Finance Ministers of the major industrial countries) would provide the European surplus countries with a veto power over their creation, thereby making it possible for them to resist U.S. calls for increased international liquidity based on automatic IMF credit lines.

Nevertheless, the consequences of such a shift were stubbornly postponed by the Johnson administration as Canada, Japan, Italy, and West Germany all were induced to foreswear direct attacks on the dollar. The case of West Germany proved to be especially telling. The largest recipient of unwanted U.S. dollar reserves, Germany was also the largest beneficiary of much-wanted U.S. troops. Thus the threat of reprisals in broad political and security areas did much to "encourage" German cooperation in international monetary relations: in 1967, Bonn officially declined to join the French offensive against the dollar.[18] In addition, this offensive was significantly stalled by unexpected developments in Europe: in France the tumultuous events of May 1968 greatly weakened the French franc (in crisis in the fall) and temporarily diverted Paris' attention away from the sharp dollar crisis of March of that year; and the Soviet invasion of Czechoslovakia in August served as an apt reminder of Europe's security dependence on the United States. Finally, American evasion of the gold–dollar link was reinforced by the creation of the two-tiered market in gold in March 1968. By agreeing not to buy or sell gold in private markets and not to expand further the total official reserves of gold in view of the impending creation of SDRs, the Group of Ten moved yet another step in the direction of the demonetization of gold, a move that was fully supported in Washington.

The dollar, however, had been left stranded by the developments that characterized the later years of the Johnson administration. No longer sure of its gold value, private holders of the dollar refused to accept it in lieu of other, and stronger, currencies unless interest rates were high enough to justify an otherwise overvalued parity. In other words, breaking the link to gold was only a step toward ending fixed exchange rates altogether.[19] Such a step continued, however, to be postponed: with the collapse of the dollar's two historic postwar rivals as international assets—gold, which could no longer provide for additional reserve growth, and the pound sterling, which had effectively merged with the dollar via the Basle Agreement that followed the sterling crisis of November 1967—countries now had virtually no choice but the dollar.[20] In addition, an unexpected payments surplus in 1969 (due in large part to the domestic credit squeeze that led to massive foreign borrowing by U.S. banks) helped ease somewhat the growing resentment and opposition of the European allies to the passive U.S. policy of "benign neglect."

However, this brief reprieve did little to help control the accelerating pace of systemic decline. The increasingly anarchic character of international monetary affairs was mirrored in the increasing flows of "hot" money from one currency to another. The Bretton woods system had been predicated upon the belief that relative exchange rate stability was necessary to maximize the growth of world trade and investment opportunities in a more open world. Thus, the "par value" system had sought to keep currency fluctuations within a tight band of plus or minus one percent. Although nations were permitted to alter their exchange rates in cases of "fundamental disequilibrium," the Bretton Woods system had become increasingly rigid as virtually no major rate adjustments occurred between 1949 and 1967, with the exception of the French franc devaluation in 1958. The United States, the key reserve country and "numeraire" of the system, had felt itself committed and constrained to a policy of exchange rate passivity. Despite the persistence of significant dollar deficits for close to a decade, the United States accordingly equated the stability of the system with an unchanging and unchangeable official dollar rate. Thus throughout the 1960s the most effective and efficient adjustment mechanism—i.e., a devaluation of the dollar—had been denied to the policymakers in Washington. Since most of the new rate adjustments involved devaluations, the overvalued dollar actually appreciated in value even as it weakened in confidence. But now the huge currency exchange transfers and exchange rate crises that characterized the twilight of the Bretton Woods system (1968–71) indicated all too clearly a diminishing international confidence in the entire framework of existing exchange rate priorities.* The Founding Fathers of the

---

*In 1967–69 such currency crises included a 14.3% devaluation of the pound sterling in November 1967; the dollar and the French franc in successive crises in 1968; a subsequent 11.1% devaluation of the franc in August 1969; and a 9.3% revaluation of the German mark two months later.

Bretton Woods system had been well aware that exchange rates might have to be adjusted in response to relative changes in the real economic position of a given country. But, as the Managing Director of the IMF put it in June 1969, "they did not envisage that a country would have to be so much concerned about the public's changing views on the strength of its currency."[21]

At the December 1969 Hague Summit, the EEC countries took steps to counter the increasing instability of exchange rates. France was especially concerned lest waves of currency speculation wreak havoc upon the delicate structure of the Common Agricultural Policy. Post-de Gaulle France appeared ready to move forward into a new dimension of European integration by accepting for immediate discussion the eventual admission of Great Britain into the Common Market, an admission that had been blocked since de Gaulle's celebrated news conference of January 14, 1963. The Werner Report of October 1970 advocated the creation of a European Monetary Union (EMU) that would help reduce Europe's dependence on the dollar and increase Europe's monetary power vis-à-vis the United States. But as the dollar once more erupted in crisis in 1970–71 and as the Bretton Woods system headed for final collapse, the many pressures working against EMU prevented the emergence of a united European response to the American monetary challenge.

The U.S. balance of payments plummeted to a deficit of $9.8 billion in 1970, two-thirds of which was reflected in increased German reserves. Due to prior "understandings" and still sensitive to U.S. ability to link security and monetary issues at a time when Senator Mansfield was redoubling his efforts to have his amendment calling for a withdrawal of U.S. forces in Europe voted in Congress, the German government continued to have little choice but to accumulate unwanted dollars.[22] When U.S. payments deteriorated at an even more rapid pace in early 1971, thereby prompting a serious run on the dollar in the spring, Secretary of the Treasury John Connally escalated the rhetoric of the administration about the shift in economic power toward Europe and Japan and voiced strong complaints about trade discrimination and unequal defense burdens.[23] "No longer does the U.S. economy dominate the free world," Connally noted in late May 1971, a few months after taking office. "No longer can considerations of friendship, or need, or capacity justify the United States carrying so heavy a share of the common burden."[24] During the 20 years that preceded Connally's complaint, the European and Japanese economies had apparently become more productive and more dynamic than the American economy, and the United States was quickly losing its traditional competitive edge in basic manufactures, including steel, cars, and chemicals thereby causing a fall in the U.S. share of world exports from 16.7% to 13.7%, while the EEC share had increased from 15.4% to 28.6%.

With more than $4 billion in hot money leaving the country during the single week of August 8, 1971, the Nixon administration found it imperative to launch a New Economic Policy. An abrupt and unnegotiated departure from the benign neglect of the previous three years, this new policy was designed to promote noninflationary economic growth largely insulated from balance of payments constraints. The convertibility of the dollar into gold or other reserve assets was therefore suspended, and a 10% surcharge was imposed on dutiable imports while a 10% reduction in foreign economic assistance was announced. Thus, without prior consultation with its main allies (including Japan), the United States had unilaterally changed the rules of the Bretton Woods game: the dollar was in fact significantly depreciated to improve at last the U.S. balance of payments, including the trade balance whose resulting surplus, $7 to $8 billion annually, would, it was hoped, cover the maintenance costs (military and economic) of the American protectorate.[25] Such shock treatment was meant to signal Europe and Japan as well that the postwar days of trade restrictions and discriminations against the United States were no longer tolerated: indeed, the lifting of the import surcharge was for a while linked not only to an overall reform of the international monetary system but also to some basic U.S. complaints of Europe—burden-sharing, trade restraints, and nontariff trade barriers.[26] Now the Nixon administration was determined to have both trade liberalization and a major exchange rate realignment by other countries. In effect, America's allies would be compelled to revalue their currencies or continue to accumulate dollars—or else, open the door wide to further protectionist devices to which they would be all the more sensitive as they remained more dependent on international trade than the United States.

Faced with what was seen by many as a declaration of economic war, the European states failed to reach a common position as their currencies (except the French franc, which clung to its old parity) promptly floated upward in an uncoordinated fashion. Meanwhile, the American position remained adamant. The United States would not take any step to defend the old parity, restore convertibility, or end the surcharge until satisfactory revaluations had taken place. Nor would the United States devalue. Events in the latter part of 1971, however, soon helped to show that the dollar's unchanging parity could no longer be linked to systemic stability. As the U.S. payments deficit rose dramatically to nearly $30 billion in 1971, and the United States ran a trade deficit for only the second time in the twentieth century, the pressures toward devaluation became irresistible. In December 1971, following four months of negotiations, the Group of Ten raised the official price of gold from $35 to $38 an ounce, effectively devaluing the dollar by 8.57%. With the simultaneous upward realignment of most other major foreign currencies, the total net weighted devaluation of the dollar amounted to approximately 12%.

Western Europe's response to the continuing fluctuations of exchange rates was to construct an EEC "snake" in a "tunnel" of wider bands (plus or minus 2.25% of parity) created at the Smithsonian. Launched in 1972, Europe's experiment was consistent with its interest in achieving greater autonomy from the hegemony of the dollar. In principle, such a formula would narrow the margins of fluctuations between member currencies, which would themselves move as a group (the snake) vis-à-vis outside currencies (within the bands of the tunnel). Quickly, however, the system ran into trouble: the pound sterling (together with the Irish pound) floated out in June 1972, soon followed by the Italian lira in February 1973 and the French franc in January 1974. By then the tunnel had long been lost as, in the wake of the second devaluation of the dollar in February 1973 (by 11.1% this time), all the major currencies were unpegged to float, either singly or in groups, in the foreign exchange markets.[27]

Certainly, the existence of conflicting Western European interests did much to contribute to the demise of the snake as originally conceived. Inflation-prone France and inflation-conscious Germany could hardly agree on monetary policy. Furthermore, the weaker members of the snake (including Britain, Ireland, and Italy) were unable to withstand the extreme speculative pressures moving them out of the snake and the tunnel. The crisis of February 1973 only served to exacerbate intra-European monetary and financial discord. Europe would be forced to live with this new world of "dirty" floating rates for the indefinite future, despite persistent French calls for a return to a world of fixed exchange rates that would be admittedly better suited for European nations, whose trade-dependent economies remained relatively open and vulnerable to erratic fluctuations of the dollar and other major currencies.

Reluctant Allies

Following the outbreak of the Korean War, the central purpose of the North Atlantic Alliance had been to protect the area covered by the Treaty from Soviet aggression. It would stand to reason that with the growth of Soviet power in the 1970s, such a purpose would have been confirmed and the Alliance thereby strengthened. Yet this was not the case. Whenever defense issues were raised, they were raised within a framework (detente and arms control) that tended to reduce the allies' attention on, and commitment to, these issues.

A few years earlier, then-Professor Henry Kissinger had praised the development of Atlantic relationships as "the most constructive American foreign policy since the end of World War II."[28] But, he had observed, the promises stemming from such a policy were now "flawed by increasingly sharp disputes among allies." As America dealt with these, Kissinger warned, it would have to avoid the "danger of being mired in the prudent, the tactical or the expedient," and in the process, "confuse creativity with a projection of the present into the future."

Now that the future had become the present, the Nixon administration showed no intention of reopening the heated controversies of the previous decade. As Kissinger told Jacques Kosciuto-Morizet, the French Ambassador in Washington, the United States "would break no lances over the issue of national identity;" nor would it "challenge Europe's right to conduct its own policy."[29] Instead, the Nixon administration hoped to control and reverse the ongoing trends toward an escalation of American–European (and American–Japanese) conflicts by addressing them overtly. With the "acrobatics" on Vietnam, the Soviet Union, and China well programmed, attention could now be turned to alliance relationships. "Nineteen seventy three," Kissinger therefore announced dramatically on April 23, "is the year of Europe because the era that was shaped by the decisions of a generation ago is ending."[30] The "new problems and new opportunities" uncovered by a foreign policy administration that was then starting its second term in office were comparable with those it had perceived when dealing with adversary relationships throughout its first term. But Kissinger's call for new approaches—"a fresh act of creation," Kissinger promised, "equal to that undertaken by the postwar generation of leaders of Europe and America"—proved to be futile at best, as in 1973 it often seemed that America and the countries of Europe were negotiating as if they were adversaries, even as they negotiated with adversaries as if they were friends.

Rather than the ultimatum it was made out to be, the Kissinger proposal for a new Atlantic Charter or declaration of common purpose was substantively a meager proposal. In a period of transition, Kissinger argued, the United States and the states of Europe (as well as Canada and "ultimately" Japan, too) required a shared view of the emerging "changes in the international environment." An Atlantic consensus on the prevailing "new realities"—defense, money, trade, and East–West relations—would hopefully lead to the joint formulation of "new approaches" to problems the allies faced in common. It is such a consensus that Kissinger asked the European allies to formulate.

That despite the extensive consultation that preceded it[31] the proposal would have occasioned such bitterness and acrimony in Europe reflected the gap that had grown between the two sides of the Atlantic during the previous years. The true American objectives, many argued in Europe, were to weaken the European position in the forthcoming trade negotiations with the United States, and to divide European states and fragment European institutions in order to absorb them all into a U.S.-dominated supra-Atlantic area.[32] The European countries were especially concerned over the form and substance of the negotiations between the two superpowers. To be sure, European statesmen could and did travel on their own to Moscow, as de Gaulle had done in 1967 and Willy Brandt in 1970. But in 1972, the unprecedented visit by an American president to the Soviet Union revived charges of a nascent condominium between Washington and Moscow. "Europeans," Nixon has previously noted, "are highly sensitive about the United States and the Soviet Union making decisions that affect their future without their consultation."[33] Now Europe's sensitivity was further sharpened in areas of such vital interest as arms control (Europe's general approval of the SALT I agreement notwithstanding) and the Soviet–U.S. Agreement on the Prevention of Nuclear War (because, some feared, this agreement would open Europe to pressures below the threshold of nuclear war). Moreover, coming at a time when Europe was growing politically (from six to nine members with the admission of Britain, Iceland, and Denmark in January 1973) and economically (although sharp inflationary pressures were already felt), Kissinger's reference to Europe's "regional" interests, as compared to the United States "global" responsibilities, were condescending and ill-advised. These, said French Foreign Minister Michel Jobert, reduced Europe's status to that of a "non-person, humiliated all along the lines."[34] Nor, for that matter, did Europe find the American fulfillment of its global responsibilities particularly compelling: the Christmas bombing of Hanoi in 1972 was harshly criticized even by those in Europe who had previously displayed the most tenacious and most consistent transatlantic faith.[35]

Renewed doubts about the hows of American intervention—clearly distinct from earlier postwar concerns over the whethers of such interventions—encouraged a European mood of regional assertiveness. Thus, in 1972 in Paris, European leaders pledged to achieve political union by 1980, by which time, some publicly dared to foresee, there might even be a European government.[36] Looking into the future with such confidence, Europe found Kissinger's perceived threats of linkages offensive and rejected his argument that economic, military, and political issues were tied by reality. Instead, they insisted that the U.S.–European reality of security issues be separated from the U.S.–EEC realities of economic and monetary relations, thereby leading ultimately to the elaboration of two distinct statements of principles that, even if signed simultaneously, would nevertheless have reduced significantly the subordination that was feared in the linkage of both.[37]

Of course, subordination is not what had been intended in the 1973 call for a renewal of the Atlantic partnership. In effect, the Year of Europe proposal was tantamount to a call for the renegotiation of the Atlantic Alliance. To be sure, this was not a small task, and there were enormous problems of form as well as of substance. Who was to speak for Europe? West Germany and Britain both appeared to be willing to defer to France. But as France stalled, with the moral support of London and the benign acquiescence of Bonn, what was the alternative? Surprisingly enough, the three-country *directoire* (the United States, Britain, and France) which de Gaulle had vehemently advocated in 1958, while now acceptable to Washington (but with the addition of West Germany), was no longer approved by either France or Britain, even though the latter had previously suggested that the idea be resuscitated.[38] The bilateral consultations that Europe seemed to favor instead would have created an endless potential for even more misunderstandings and confusion. The European community, which eventually inherited the role of interlocutor, had no true political authority to negotiate any document binding on the nation states that comprise it. In 1947, comparable negotiations between America and Europe had been made easier by the very nature of Marshall's proposal to the Europeans: an offer, free of charge, of American aid to the recovery and security of Europe. Now, changing circumstances everywhere dictated that Europe define and pay a price for the new agreement that was being sought by the United States.

Not that such an agreement would in any case have been easy to conceptualize and achieve, regardless of the participants and the forum used for the preliminary discussions. Divergences were real and likely to be lasting: currency crises, protectionist rivalries, conflicting interests in the Third World, contradictory aspirations and expectations in the East. The very scope and nature of these divergences, properly perceived by the Nixon administration at the time, had prompted Kissinger's call in the first place. The need for such a call had been stressed by Georges Pompidou and endorsed by Willy Brandt, Edward Heath, and Giulio Andreotti prior to April 1973. Questions of rhetoric and phrasing notwithstanding, and going beyond the personal joust that erupted between Kissinger and French Foreign Minister Michel Jobert, what the Year of Europe needed most was time. This should have been but the first year of the years of Europe. But what proved to be most lacking was, precisely, time.

For one, political circumstances within which these difficult negotiations unfolded soon became disastrous. Within a few days of Kissinger's speech, the Watergate scandal took on new proportions with the abrupt resignation of two of Nixon's most powerful and most trusted advisers at the White House. The sight of an American president besieged from within did little to alleviate the concerns of European statesmen over the true motives of the administration: was Nixon in fact not trying to divert the attention of the American public away from domestic issues, and was he not attempting to regain a new national legitimacy on the basis of some spectacular initiative in the realm of foreign policy? Accordingly, they turned Kissinger's call for a new Atlantic consensus into a European–American confrontation out of which they might have hoped to build a new European consensus.

But in Europe this was not a time for Grand Designs either: if Nixon was the captive of Watergate, Pompidou was the captive of his failing health, Willy Brandt that of his rebellious party, and Heath that of a crippling economic crisis. Before too long they would all be gone.

Such collective paralysis of the leadership of the West muffled Kissinger's initiative; the October War in the Middle East and the oil crisis that accompanied it completed the process and denied it the future it deserved. Now the countries that had criticized Kissinger's reference to their regional interests dissociated themselves from U.S. policies on the grounds that their responsibilities were only regional and that NATO itself was no more than a regional alliance that did not extend to the Middle East. Thus the year 1973, which had been expected to revitalize an admittedly troubled Atlantic partnership, ended with even more discord as President Nixon bitterly complained of European allies who "would have frozen to death this winter unless there had been a settlement" of the conflict in the Middle East,[39] and Kissinger warned against an attitude in Europe that appeared "to elevate refusal to consult into a principle defining European identity."[40]

The Threats Elsewhere

Over the years, the most bitter interallied disputes have arisen over clashes of ambivalent and often contradictory interests outside the NATO area proper: over decolonization, the Middle East wars, numerous African questions, Indochina, and, more generally, the role and influence of industrial states in developing countries. Indeed, there has never been a lasting political, economic, or strategic consensus in the West regarding the structure of its ties with the Third World; instead, competition or even sheer rivalry rather than cooperation have been the rule as the imperatives of world responsibilities for the United States, and the necessities of domestic politics and interests for the European states, have prevented the subordination of American or European policies to purely Atlantic concerns.

Standing in the way of Atlantic unity in the Third World there have been, first of all, the different historical experiences that have shaped America's and Europe's respective relations with these countries. There, the latter's legacy of colonialism faced the U.S. legacy of a liberal tradition that had grown out of a unique and unrepeatable national experience—the Puritan migration to an affluent new world.[41] At times this tradition influenced American policies in ways that went against, or at least delayed, the enhancement or preservation of specific American interests and, as Europeans often had it, Western interests too. This is not to say, of course, that American policies toward the Third World were benevolent. In effect, these policies combined, more or less properly and more or less effectively, the traditional objectives of self-preservation (hence the favourable disposition toward the stabilization of regimes overtly hostile to communist ideology) and self-expansion (hence the emphasis on a strategy of economic development that would help make these countries open for U.S. goods and capital) with less traditional aspirations of self-abnegation.

That Europe's vision of the Third World would have been different from that of America is not hard to comprehend. Whatever the cliche may otherwise pretend, the European Empires were neither an accident nor an aberration—let alone the result of an acute fit of absent-mindedness. Instead, European imperialism was a most logical effort to bypass the natural limitations imposed upon the European continent by geographic circumstances. Initially the leading industrial region in the world because it could draw from its own soil most of the resources it needed, Europe had to secure access to such materials when its own resources were depleted. With its markets often unable to keep pace with improvements in technology and productivity, the continent looked elsewhere for outlets that were at first conquered by force and next preserved or regained by more orderly means. Because it sought to satisfy some of the former colonial objectives, the subsequent diplomacy of trade and aid represented the continuation of empires by other means. Europe became a region engaged in processing raw materials imported from other continents and reselling them as finished goods. And even while the states of Europe dissolved past imperial military, economic, and political structures, they devised a web of organizations, treaties, and cooperation agreements that helped maintain privileged ties despite the newly acquired international sovereignty of the former colonies.

In the 1970s, Europe's efforts were pursued anxiously as fears of disintegration in Africa and elsewhere, oil price explosions, turmoil in other commodity markets, and an increased activism of the Soviet Union and its proxies outside established Soviet spheres enhanced the perception in Europe of a threat that was no longer met by a U.S. foreign policy rendered ineffective by the memories of Vietnam and the vagaries of Watergate. As Claude Cheysson put it before he became France's Minister for External Affairs, "We European countries, with our limited geographic space, do not have the opportunities of the Americans and cannot find at home our essential supplies, markets, and bases of our economy. More than others, we must seek to find an order of cooperation and join with the 'South' of this world."[42]

Europe's vulnerability was found in the area of trade. By 1978, EEC exports to all developing countries, including oil-exporting states, had grown to 38.2% of total exports versus 28.5% in 1973. By comparison, the United States took 13.3% of EEC exports that year and state trading countries another 8.9%.[43] Markets in the Third World (and in the East as well) were made especially important in the light of the considerable trade deficits run by the EEC countries with other industrial states: in 1980, the EEC deficit with the United States amounted to an all-time high of $17.4 billion (twice that of the previous year), while its deficit with Japan reached $10 billion. In addition, the more constant growth of demand in the less developed countries (LDC) made these markets a significant countercyclical factor in buoying up the economies of the EEC states in a period of economic crisis: in 1975, the year when the recession in Western Europe reached its worst level for the decade, EEC exports to the United States fell by 17%, but those to the LDCs increased by approximately one fourth, with those to the African–Caribbean–Pacific (ACP) countries alone by about one third.

Throughout the 1970s, the importance of this trade for individual European countries as well became readily apparent. Thus in 1978, 26.2% of the total exports from Great Britain, 23% from France, 21.8% from Italy, and 16.6% from West Germany went to the LDCs—as compared to 20.8%, 18.1%, 14.2%, and 11.5%, respectively, in 1973. Initially, European exports had followed the flag of old empires. For example, the ACP countries, mostly former French and British colonies, bought more than one fourth of French and British exports to the LDCs, while West Germany and Italy exported more to other parts of the Third World—to Latin America, for example, where the task of their European competitors was made more difficult in the face of large populations of German and Italian ancestry. However, following the 1973 oil crisis, such a trade pattern gave way to a strategy of market diversification that entailed the expansion of competition into former preserves of one industrial state or another. That American markets in the Western Hemisphere would generally have been less well protected from European penetration than were African markets from American penetration, and that various political forces at work throughout the decade in Central and South America would often raise additional obstacles to U.S. interests in the region, increased Atlantic discord and rivalries. In this respect, global interdependence tended to create a boomerang effect as new competition in one regional market encouraged exporters to move into other areas as competitors of established foreign interests. Conversely, protectionist agreements of a supposedly voluntary nature between industrial states occasionally led disadvantaged countries to compensate with more aggressive inroads into the export markets of the allied competitors—or else, helped third countries justify their own protectionist devices. For example, in 1981 restrictions on Japan's car exports to the United States gave rise to charges in some European countries that Tokyo used a double standard—complying with American trade complaints while ignoring those of the Europeans. Yet for many years Italy had permitted a mere 2,300 Japanese cars to enter the country, while France allowed Japanese automakers to take only 3% of its market.

U.S. conflict with Europe over trade issues in the Third World reflected broader differences over the organization of postwar economic order. Traditionally, the United States had favored an open, liberal global economy, with free trade and equal access to markets and investment opportunites for all. The assumption underlying such an approach was that superior American technology, marketing, and financial power would give the United States decisive advantages in this kind of system. Repeatedly, the European countries fought this approach: at first, they resisted decolonization; later, they promoted privileged and generally closed economic communities with their former colonies. With the formation of the EEC and eventual British membership (in part delayed over the modalities of Commonwealth participation), this strategy of preserving exclusive ties with former dependencies was converted into larger multilateral agreements linking EEC and Third World countries. Accordingly, while in earlier years French interests

in Africa had been primarily responsible for the two successive
arrangements that were negotiated in Yaoundé with a small
number of African states, negotiations were now launched with
46 countries in Africa, the Caribbean, and the Pacific and
resulted in the first Lomé Convention of February 1975.* A
similar preference for the development of North–South trade
structures, based on interregional agreements and various
forms of discrimination against third parties, including the
United States and Japan, was behind French proposals for the
unproductive Conference in International and Economic Cooperation and characterized related themes of "organized free
trade" or "orderly growth of trade," both viewed with legitimate
suspicion by the proponents of free trade in the United States.

Similarly, Western Europe continued to depend more than
the United States on the import of raw materials. In February
1975, the European Commission had described this "problem" as
"real and serious. . . . The dangers for Europe in its high degree
of dependence on other continents," the Commission had
warned, have been "consistently growing during the past four
decades."[44] With Europe's dependence on outside supplies of
industrial raw materials estimated at 75% of its needs (as
compared to an approximate 15% for the United States and 90%
for Japan), there was no reason to assume that the problem
would become any less real and serious in the years to come. For
countries dependent to such an extent on raw material imports,
an orderly and stable commodity trade was of vital importance.
In sum, in the words of another EEC report, "given both its
sources of supply and its outlets, the Community depends more
than other industrialized countries on the existence of a
propitious climate in relations between developing countries
and developed countries."[45]

---

*By limiting the Lomé benefits to economic exchanges between the ACP
and the EEC states only, the Europeans strengthened their control of these
markets: at the time, EEC trade accounted for approximately 40% of total ACP
trade, as compared to ACP's 7% share of total EEC trade. Following Lomé I,
EEC exports to the ACP states rapidly doubled and gave the EEC a trade
surplus that contrasted with its pre-Lomé trade deficits with the ACP
countries. Furthermore, with a stabilization fund for export prices (STABEX)
not only kept small but also not fully used, the initial cost for such a privileged
relationship proved to be conveniently moderate.

Accordingly, energy was only one special though admittedly all-important case that was dramatically brought to the forefront of Atlantic concerns in the wake of the Year of Europe proposal. Even prior to the quadrupling of oil prices in late 1973, Europe's dependence on energy imports was impressive: in absolute terms, it exceeded American and Japanese imports combined.[46] The most optimistic EEC Commission projections on increased nuclear power, natural gas, and North Sea oil notwithstanding, Western Europe was bound to remain an important energy importer for the foreseeable future.[47] Under these circumstances, security of oil supplies was of paramount importance, and the actions taken by OPEC (Organization of Petroleum Exporting Countries) after a new outbreak of Arab–Israeli hostilities in October 1973 were seen in Europe as posing a clear and present danger to its survival.

At first no European government would follow the U.S. call for consumer solidarity. The psychological impact of OPEC was such as to cause a general *sauve qui peut*, and European nations even refused to share oil supplies with their embargoed partner, the Netherlands. They lacked the resources to engage in a Project Independence similar to that ordered by Nixon on November 7, 1973, to free the United States of the need to import energy by 1980. Neither did they have the capabilities and the influence that might have enabled them to secure their supplies by delivering on that part of the "European–Arab dialogue" that was of paramount concern to most of the OPEC states, namely the Arab conflict with Israel. While they readily agreed with Kissinger that the situation was likely to get worse, they feared a U.S.-sponsored confrontational stance of which their vulnerability might make them the first victims; and they also feared a self-induced submission that would leave them at the mercy of OPEC's manipulation of vital economic (and hence political) parameters. In the meantime, it was only a slight exaggeration to suggest that some European allies saw the energy crisis as an opportunity to make new inroads in the Middle East and line up advantageous bilateral deals with the producers—principally of the arms-for-oil variety.[48]

Only with the end of the Arab embargo did Europe's panic begin to subside, and a measure of Atlantic unity was restored following the overt display of interallied discord that had characterized the previous months. Even as he was calling for a Conference of Consuming Nations, which would elaborate the structures and define the terms of consumer solidarity, Kissinger's warnings had been gaining an unparalleled intensity. "Under no circumstances," the American Secretary of State told a staff meeting on January 8, 1974, "will we give [the Europeans] a free field for bilateral deals. . . . If they will not work multilaterally we will force them by going bilateral ourselves. If we go bilateral, we can preempt them . . . in most areas."[49] The American discourse had now grown all the more bitter and explicit as the issue at stake was far more significant—because more specific and more immediate—than the issues that had surrounded the debates over the Year of Europe proposals one year earlier. As had been the case during the previous ten years over the major questions of nuclear control, trade negotiations, and dollar conversion, West Germany was the key to the isolation of a belligerent France. Unless such diplomatic isolation was achieved following the mandate the Pompidou government claimed it had received from the EEC in early December 1973, no Atlantic (and Western) unity could be restored. Accordingly, once again the United States relied on a strategy of linkage to pressure the Germans, and President Nixon pointedly informed Europe that "security and economic considerations are inevitably linked and energy cannot be separated from either."[50]

In this atmosphere, the degree of unity that was secured at the Washington Conference of February 1974 emerged at the price of further dividing the European countries. Kissinger's emphatic denunciation of OPEC as the economic equivalent of the Sputnik challenge seemed to justify French apprehensions about a confrontation with the oil producers. Yet, despite the possibly perilous implications of Kissinger's call for Western unity, the other EEC countries viewed France's suspicions as excessive and rejected its appeal for an ill-defined European policy that would be distinct from, and autonomous of, U.S. policy. But their prolonged hesitation and obvious reluctance in joining the United States against the oil-producing nations reflected Europe's growing ambivalence toward American policies in the Middle East and, more generally, the Third World altogether. The view in Europe was now that such policies might increasingly be part of the problems faced by the West in the Third World, and subsequent divisions in the West over U.S. policies in the Middle East, Africa, or Central America would further reflect this outlook.

An Ascending Europe?

Over the years, Europe has been called many names as observers have argued over what it is in order to anticipate what it might become: bargained, finlandized, sheltered, liberated or buffered; nationalist, atlanticist or federalist; ascending, status-quo, astray, or decadent.[51] Yet looking into the future said to be crouching in the present has not been easy, and few scenarios have survived the test of time. Thus, there used to be those who envisioned the enduring status-quo model of a passive Europe that would continue to muddle through the problems of the moment while remaining essentially oblivious to the threats of the future.[52] However, could anyone pretend that the European landscape that prevailed at the time of Kissinger's Year of Europe was the same as the one that had prevailed ten years earlier, when Kennedy was unveiling his Grand Design? At any one point in time, a status-quo Europe still remained a Europe of transition as it evolved toward something else, with either more integration or more fragmentation, either more dependence or more autonomy.

Examining the prospects for such an evolution, some feared a Europe which, no longer satisfied with the shelter provided by the United States, would be finlandized through the sheer weight of Soviet power.[53] Yet during the latter part of the 1970s, even as Soviet power was peaking, Moscow's most trusted allies in Europe—the local communist parties—became increasingly unreliable, either because of what these parties said and did (in Italy), or because of what they did not say and could not do (in France). Marginalized in Spain and in Portugal, and in disarray in France (their belated entry into the government notwithstanding), the communist parties of Western Europe were not doing well even in Italy, up to 1976 the showcase of a

Eurocommunist tide that was allegedly about to engulf Southern Europe.

Nor was the evolution of Western European trade with the countries of Eastern Europe and the Soviet Union such as to warrant repeated warnings against a potential structural trade dependence of the West on the East—an issue that became especially vocal during the first years of the Reagan administration. For one, such trade grew during the years of detente (1970–76) but diminished afterwards. Furthermore, growth in trade, when it did take place, was made possible by a Western willingness to finance Eastern trade deficits rather than by an improvement in the export performance of these countries. If anything, what the respective levels of Western and Eastern Europe shares of trade with each other revealed was a dependence of the East on the West, and not the other way around. As could already be seen by the end of the 1970s, the adjustments that the progressive unavailability of Western financing imposed on the countries of Eastern Europe were painful not only for these countries but also for their outside patron.

Earlier, too, there had been those who had thought of a Europe that would some day "belong to nobody."[54] But had this truly ever ceased to be the case? As we have seen, early examples abound of Europe's resistance to and manipulation of American leadership, whether successful or not. To be sure, Suez remained an especially glaring example of European impotence in the face of U.S. opposition. Yet France fought a war in Indochina against U.S. wishes and ended its part in the conflict at the very time when the Eisenhower administration wanted the French to continue to wage it. Designed to bypass an American proposal for the rearmament of West Germany, the Pleven Plan calling for the creation of a European Defense Community was rejected by the French parliament four years later despite strong U.S. pressures on its behalf. Later in the 1960s, the Kennedy Round of trade negotiations failed to dismantle the trade barriers erected by the countries of the European Economic Community to the immediate benefit of French agriculture and German industry, and the efforts of three successive American administrations to build a Western consensus during the Vietnam War proved futile.

Repeatedly, the lingering faith in an Atlantic Europe continued to exaggerate the permanence of the United States' ascendancy and dominance, the persistence of Europe's decline and impotence, and the convergence of American and European interests. In truth, an Atlantic Europe would have consecrated Europe's final submission to its devalued status in the international arena.[55] Less suspect than the other superpower, the United States would have been acknowledged—with varying degrees of enthusiasm or reluctance—as the natural leader of Western Europe. American leadership backed by American power would service European interests. But, as we have argued, a successor generation in Europe ceased progressively to find the American leadership as irresistible as another generation had in earlier years. In short, if there ever was a time for Europe to embrace an Atlantic Grand Design built around the American model—which is itself quite doubtful—that time was long gone as a new democratic administration was preparing its arrival in power.

In the meantime, for over two decades the development of a politically integrated Europe, associated with but distinct from the United States—and interacting with but distrustful of the Soviet Union—had inched ever closer to reality, however discouraging and tentative the process seemed to be at times. From the beginning, the inner logic of the EEC had been to move steadily from the economic union of a very few to the political union of the many: once consolidated, it was hoped, the economic union of the first six member states would be enlarged and lead to further and more ambitious initiatives in other areas. In part, from failure to failure, this happened. Political parties once hostile to European unity now came to support it, from the least nationalist parties of the left (including the communist parties in Italy first and in France next) to the more nationalist parties of the right (including the Conservative party in Great Britain first and, eventually, the Gaullist party in France next). States once opposed to joining the Community sought, and in a number of cases acquired, full membership—as the Six became the Nine, then the Ten—while states once committed to leaving it at the first opportunity (France in 1958, Great Britain in 1973) remained. Everywhere, there could be found a European presence that was assiduously courted from within the European continent (Spain and Portugal) and from without as well (associate members). The EMU that had been sought in 1969 proved to be stillborn, but the EMS that was conceived ten years later endured, however painfully. In 1979, the first direct elections of a European Parliament held considerable potential inasmuch as it might, in due time, lead to a transfer of power at the expense of the European Council. All in all, over the years, sacrifices of national sovereignty were tolerated by the states of Europe in order to preserve or permit gains sought on grounds of sheer necessity.

That such progressive unification of Western Europe would have had a distinct impact on the relationship with the United States should have come as no surprise. In the past, European integration and Atlantic unity had been imagined all too frequently as one and the same thing. The former was expected to foster the latter. Accordingly, conflicts over either were too readily dismissed as a reflection of temporary personal stubbornness (General de Gaulle) or arrogance (Chancellor Helmut Schmidt), and vain regional assertiveness (France) or anxieties (West Germany), that a forceful display of American power could easily control and reverse: hence John Foster Dulles' threat of an agonizing reappraisal in 1953–55, President Kennedy's successful isolation of France in 1962–63, Secretary John Connally's penchant for economic brinkmanship in 1970–72, and Henry Kissinger's pointed linkages in 1973–75. But while such U.S. reactions promptly restored a measure of Atlantic order, they did not deal with the root cause of the growing conflicts between the two sides of the Atlantic—namely, the recovery of Europe.

Of course, even while united in some areas, Western countries remained hopelessly divided and incapable of any sort of internal consistency in others. In part, this was due to the major difficulties inherent in aligning the national policies of the three dominant European powers. Over the years, the great disputes in Europe over Europe had resulted from an effort by one of these states to bypass either one or both of the other two: to form a concert of Europe around an Anglo–French alliance against Germany; to build a supranational federal state of Europe against French and British objections; to establish a united Europe around a French–West German axis without

Great Britain. More often than not, such disputes had been further fed by American policies not averse to the objective of isolating the voice of Atlantic dissent.

As could be seen at the time of the first energy crisis in 1973–74, this pattern was far from over. Yet, even as it was still persisting, there could be heard a new consensus in Europe that found it convenient to charge the United States with the responsibility for a new round of crises at home, on the continent, and worldwide. Following 25 years of steady economic growth, Europe found a facile explanation for the slowdown of the 1970s in past and current U.S. economic policies. After nearly three decades of unprecedented security, it found a ready and exasperating explanation for the uncertainties of the future in the past misuse of U.S. power, the recent deterioration of U.S. will, and the perceived misdirection of an alleged U.S. renewal. Already questioned in an era of economic and military dominance over allies and adversaries alike, the United States' credibility became even more compromised at a time when such dominance was being overtly challenged not only by its adversaries but by its allies as well. For the United States it had now become imperative, therefore, to restore European confidence in U.S. domestic and foreign policies. For the crisis in the Western Alliance that persisted throughout the 1970s was not simply the reflection of a protracted decline of Europe: it was the reflection of the decline of the United States as well, and there would have been much less penchant for European assertiveness if there had been better evidence of U.S. effectiveness.

The true causes of such discord were not political, even though changed political circumstances *à la* Giscard (and later *à la* Mitterrand) or *à la* Carter (and later *à la* Reagan) might (and would) exacerbate tensions. Over the years, each U.S. president had set new standards of unpopularity in Europe; and over the years, too, much damage had been done to the cohesion of the Atlantic Alliance by conservative majorities in Europe, gaullist or otherwise. Nor was the problem in U.S.–European relations merely a structural problem having to do with consultation procedures: in truth, there could probably be no structure that might succeed in achieving a lasting consensus among democratic and sovereign states where there would be none. Meetings in whatever form would permit, of course, helpful *tours d'horizon*.

On occasion, they did even lead to a few substantive results. But all too often the communiques that followed summit encounters during the second half of the 1970s reflected an optimism of the will that had little to do with the realities of the moment. Thus in 1978 the participants to the Bonn Summit would agree on unemployment as their "main concern"; in 1979 in Tokyo "the most urgent task" was said to be "to reduce oil consumption"; in 1980 in Venice the "first priority" was inflation; and in 1981 in Ottawa the "highest priority" was both unemployment and inflation. In the end, while accord remained in theory on whatever the priority had become from year to year, the policy gap between the participants widened, and the problem worsened. In short, consultation did not create a consensus but presupposed it, and joint declarations did not describe an argument but often imagined it. All could then read such declarations as they pleased and claim the victory they sought as they pursued the policies they preferred within an alliance framework that continued to be eroded by these repeated waves of recurring crises.

Beyond Europe

In the 1970s, the signs of mounting dissatisfaction with the United States among the allies—and with the allies in the United States—were not limited to the states of Western Europe only. They also affected the other pillar of the alliance system built during the years of the postwar era—Japan—and there emerged a striking parallel between the ongoing crisis in U.S.–European relations and a brewing crisis in U.S.–Japanese relations.

The adversarial tone of U.S.–Japanese relations during the whole decade had been set during the 1968 presidential election. In his quest for southern votes, candidate Richard M. Nixon had then pledged protection against textile imports beyond cotton articles to include items made of wool and synthetic fibers. Accordingly, shortly after he took office, Nixon sought an agreement with the Japanese to restrict their exports of low-priced synthetic textiles "voluntarily."[56] Unlike such other pending issues as the territorial status of the island of Okinawa, they were not reflective of a true and serious American national interest. Inspired instead by the narrow interests of one particular industry, they threatened the delicate fiber of international trade on which the Japanese economy was wholly dependent. Where the United States viewed Japan's economy as robust, highly competitive, and generally insensitive to the needs of other countries, Japan viewed its economy as fragile and highly vulnerable to the manipulations of other countries that controlled the supply of such vital imports as food and energy or the access to indispensible markets for Japanese exports.[57] Where Americans viewed the recovery of Japan as the result of rare benevolence granted by a generous conqueror, Japanese viewed their recovery as an incidental by-product of American policies designed first and foremost for American purposes.[58] The United States spoke increasingly of a need for Japanese gratitude, the very commodity that Japan now found lacking in the United States.

Under different circumstances, the textile issue of the late 1960s might merely have been a case of low comedy and selective frustrations, with no durable impact on the state of U.S.–Japanese relations. After all, Japanese exports of textiles to the United States were about to decline dramatically in any case, to the benefit of other newly-industrialized countries in Asia. But the bitterness occasioned by negotiations that were to last 30 months served as background to larger doubts that other issues helped arouse on both sides of the Pacific. Thus, even as the textile agreement was being negotiated, the Japanese were struck by a double shock on security and monetary issues. In July 1971, Nixon's dramatic announcement of his forthcoming trip to China was all the more traumatic as there had been no prior consultation with the Japanese government.[59] Not only had the United States reneged on a pledge that had been made an explicit part of the 1951 Peace Treaty with Japan, it was charged, but in so doing it had altered the ever delicate political balance that prevailed within the ruling party in Japan—where pro-Taiwan and pro-Peking factions had been battling each other for years—and given the Chinese government a strong hand in negotiations, which Japan now had no choice but to initiate at the earliest time.[60] To be sure, many of the Japanese fears proved to be excessive: relations with Peking were restored relatively painlessly, and the resulting break with Taiwan was kept relatively smooth. Yet the episode left a sour taste in a country that had over the years given precedence to its security alliance with the United States over a rapprochement with China, and, in the words of a former U.S. ambassador to Japan, from then on things would never be the same.[61]

In addition, this first shock was soon followed by a second shock with Nixon's adoption of a New Economic Policy on August 15, 1971. As the Japanese saw it, the tariff surcharge imposed on most U.S. imports would strike a serious blow on the Japanese exports of steel, automobiles, and sundry goods, as well as textiles. Most Japanese considered this decision as a political ploy designed to place on other economies the blame for America's trade problems.[62] Their trade competitiveness, they argued, was the result of hard work and sharp business acumen.[63] Their own markets, they were prompt to point out, were open to those exporters who knew how to take advantage of existing opportunities. Thus between 1964 and 1970, U.S. exports to Japan had grown at double the rate of U.S. exports to the rest of the world—16% versus 8.5%. After many years of careful management of Japan's shaky balance of payments accounts, the Japanese resented such efforts to deprive them of the fruits of past labor and saw Nixon's move as a threat to their country's prosperity and future growth. From Japan, there could now be heard a clear and explicit warning, which, in its simplest form, read: "Don't take Japan for granted."[64]

Yet the warning apparently remained unheard by an administration which, in Kissinger's words, hardly "possessed a very subtle grasp of Japanese culture and psychology."[65] Two years later, in June 1973, the Nixon administration therefore revealed yet another surprise, this time in the form of a soybean embargo to Japan. "We wanted to show something to the people who thought our economic strength was low," a former Nixon economic adviser would subsequently explain, and "teach Japan a lesson in international relations."[66] The image of a master-to-disciple relationship that was inherent in such a perception did not suit the prevailing mood. In Japan, past feelings of inferiority and subservience of an earlier generation that had known the humility of defeat and occupation were replaced by a growing feeling of industrial superiority, which contrasted sharply with the perceived decline of the United States and Europe. Ironically, this self-image of Japan as an emerging superpower was often imported from the United States, as the like of Herman Kahn and Zbigniew Brzezinski were displaying the Japanese model as a substitute for failing industrial systems elsewhere, in books that often sold better in Japan than in the United States.[67] But it also reflected a growing disenchantment with an American leadership entangled in a conflict in Indochina that it could neither win nor lose: not merely "the questioning of American 'will' or 'good faith' but rather American sophistication, judgment and competence in dealing with a changing global environment in ways beneficial to Japan and the United States alike."[68]

Fundamental to the bilateral relationship between the United States and Japan was the Mutual Security Treaty of 1951, which, like the North Atlantic Treaty of 1949, was now under increasingly severe strain. With the past surplus of American power clearly deplenished, the United States had become resentful of a Japan that had used its "free ride" in the realm of defense to gain economic advantages at the expense of the American economy. Given Japan's recovery, it was argued, its refusal to share the burdens of defense more evenly was no longer tolerable. Yet while on one side of the Pacific American officials and observers alike urged Japan to take responsibility at last for its security—including the defense of its territory and that of its sea lanes now threatened by the build-up of a Soviet submarine fleet in the sea of Akhotsk—the Japanese retort of noncompliance cited the restriction imposed by Article IX of the Japanese constitution (a war-renunciating clause adopted at the urging of the United States), the crippling absence of public support for increased defense spending, and the destabilizing apprehensions that a rearmament of Japan would create in the region.

In effect, the United States and Japan no longer shared a common perception of the threat—assuming that they had ever shared such a perception in full. As Japan progressively came to see it, the threat was elsewhere and everywhere: not only Soviet power, but also American power; not only in the East, but also in the South. As was the case with the states of Europe, in 1973 the Middle East provided a vivid demonstration of the clear and present danger that friendship with the United States could cause to Japan.[69] Dependent on Middle East oil for nearly 60% of all its energy needs (as opposed to 7.5% for the United States), Japan had cautiously steered clear of any direct involvement in the Arab–Israeli conflict. That it would nevertheless have been a target of the Arab oil embargo on the grounds of its close identification with the United States came therefore as an especially significant new shock. Unlike some of the states of Europe, Japan sensed no guilt toward the Israeli people; unlike the United States, it felt no special emotional ties with the state of Israel. Accordingly, upon recovery from the first oil crisis, Japan quickly engineered an autonomous policy for the region, which relied on a measure of identification with the Arab states over the Palestinian problem. Later in the decade, the crisis in and over Iran caused the same tensions between the United States and Japan as it did between the United States and Europe. Calls for concerted action were ignored all the more readily as American policies were increasingly perceived as part of the problem—no longer as the decisive component of the solution—even if U.S. and Japanese objectives remained similar in most instances.

The unexpected and odd detours of history are conveniently ignored by the leaps of historians who can explain the past through the shortcuts of their own intellectual constructs. In the early 1960s, these constructs had often been euphoric when dealing with the future of the partnership of the industrial countries of the West. In the 1970s, however, instead of embarking upon a new lease of life, the U.S. network of alliances appeared to be shrinking into a fading marriage of convenience, repeatedly on the verge of separation and divorce. To be sure, alliances would still endure for many years to come. As the process of disintegration had continued in numerous areas, it had remained stalled in others, including first and foremost the area of defense, where the allies could seemingly do neither with nor without the American deterrent. Yet in the future the question of allied defense forces not subject to American control was bound to rise again. How and when was, of course, impossible to predict. But that it would arise was all the more likely as it was part of a process of normalization in interstate relations that had begun several years earlier and would continue for many years to come.

NOTES

1. See a fuller development of some of these points in Simon Serfaty, *Fading Partnership: America and Europe after 30 Years* (New York: Praeger, 1979), and "Atlantic Fantasies," in *The Atlantic Alliance and its Critics*, ed. Robert W. Tucker and Linda Wrigley (New York: Praeger, 1982), pp. 95–128.
2. See Horst Mendershausen, *Outlook on Western Solidarity: Political Relations in the Atlantic Alliance System*, The Rand Corporation, R-1512-PR, June 1976.
3. Henry Kissinger, *Years of Upheaval* (Boston, Mass.: Little, Brown, 1982), pp. 708–9.
4. Jean-Jacques Servan Schreiber, *The American Challenge* (New York: Avon Books, 1967).
5. Stephen D. Cohen, *International Monetary Reform: 1964–1969. The Political Dimension* (New York: Praeger, 1970), pp. 19–20.
6. David P. Calleo, *The Imperious Economy* (Cambridge, Mass.: Harvard University Press, 1982), p. 234.
7. "What is necessary," Chancellor Helmut Schmidt later argued, "is to shield the Common Market . . . against monetary turbulence which stems from outside Europe." Quoted in the *Washington Post*, April 20, 1978.
8. Quoted in Romano Prodi and Alberto Clo, "Europe," *Daedalus* (Fall 1975), p. 104.
9. See Simon Serfaty, "Une politique étrangère introuvable," *Politique Internationale* (Winter 1979–1980).
10. Henry Kissinger, *American Foreign Policy*, expanded edition (New York: W. W. Norton, 1974), pp. 69–74.
11. Simon Serfaty, "The United States and Europe," *Washington Quarterly* (Winter 1980–1981).
12. Richard M. Nixon, news conference of March 4, 1969.
13. Calleo, *The Imperious Economy*, p. 46. Despite a relative rise in U.S. interest rates—short-term as well as long-term—in 1964–65, these remained well below prevailing levels in Europe, thereby prompting such outflows of U.S. capital.

14. Robert Solomon, *The International Monetary System, 1945–1976* (New York: Harper & Row, 1977), p. 55.
15. Fred C. Bergsten, *The Dilemmas of the Dollar: The Economics and Politics of United States International Monetary Policy* (New York: New York University Press, 1975), pp. 62–95.
16. As early as 1960, a leading American economist, Robert Triffin, had joined the French economist, Jacques Rueff, in predicting systemic collapse unless fundamental reforms were made in the international role of the dollar. See Robert Triffin, *Gold and the Dollar Crisis* (New Haven, Conn.: Yale University Press, 1960).
17. On the European positions regarding the SDRs, see Solomon, *International Monetary System,* pp. 129–31.
18. Calleo, *Imperious Economy.* p. 24.
19. Ibid., p. 57.
20. Bergsten, *Dilemmas of the Dollar,* p. 90.
21. Reprinted in Gerald M. Meier, *Problems of World Monetary Order* (New York: Oxford University Press, 1974), pp. 87–92.
22. Solomon, *International Monetary System,* p. 177.
23. Ibid., p. 181.
24. Henry Kissinger, *White House Years* (Boston, Mass.: Little, Brown, 1980), p. 952.
25. Calleo, *Imperious Economy,* p. 63.
26. Kissinger, *White House Years,* p. 958.
27. Benjamin J. Cohen, *Organizing the World's Money. The Political Economy of International Monetary Relations* (New York: Basic Books, 1977), pp. 147 and 109.
28. Henry Kissinger, *The Troubled Partnership* (New York: McGraw Hill, 1965).
29. Kissinger, *Years of Upheaval,* p. 148.
30. Henry Kissinger, address to the Associated Press Annual Luncheon, New York, April 23, 1973. In *American Foreign Policy,* p. 101.
31. For an account that preceded Kissinger's call, see Kissinger, *Years of Upheaval,* pp. 137–51.
32. Ibid., pp. 173–74.
33. Nixon's news conference of March 4, 1969.
34. Reported in the *New York Times.* November 13, 1973.
35. According to Kissinger, Nixon was "beside himself" over the attitude of the European allies in early 1973. *Years of Upheaval,* p. 137.
36. Robert Schaetzel, *The Unhinged Alliance: America and the European Community* (New York: Harper & Row, 1975), p. 2.

37. "Partnership," complained the then-Chancellor Willy Brandt, "cannot mean subordination." Reported in the *New York Times*, November 14, 1973.

38. Kissinger, *Years of Upheaval*, pp. 137–51.

39. Quoted in the *New York Times*, October 27, 1973.

40. Kissinger, address to the Society of Pilgrims, London, December 12, 1973.

41. Robert A. Packenham, *Liberal America and the Third World. Political Development Ideas in Foreign Aid and Social Science* (Princeton, N.J.: Princeton University Press, 1973), p. 318. Also, Simon Serfaty, *The United States, Europe and the Third World: Allies and Adversaries* (Washington, D.C.: Center for Strategic and International Studies, 1980).

42. At the time, Cheysson was the European commissioner responsible for development. See his "The Policy towards Development: Generalized Preferences and the Lomé Convention," in *North–South: Developing a New Relationship*, ed. Pierre Uri (Paris: Atlantic Institute for International Affairs, 1975), p. 39.

43. Wolfgang Hager and Michael Noelke, *Community–Third World: The Challenge of Interdependence*, 2nd ed. (Brussels: EEC Documentation Bulletin, 1980), pp. 69–102.

44. "The Raw Materials Dossier," Background Paper, Commission of the European Communities, Information, 1976, p. 46.

45. "Development and Raw Materials—Problems of the Moment," *Bulletin* of the European Communities, Supplement, June 1975, p. 12.

46. Jack Hartshorn, "Europe's Energy Imports," in *A Nation Writ Large?* ed. Max Kohnstamm and Wolfgang Hager (New York: MacMillan Press, 1973), p. 106.

47. Henri Simonet, "Energy and the Future of Europe," *Foreign Affairs*, (April 1975), p. 456.

48. Louis Turner, "Politics and the Energy Crisis," *International Affairs* (July 1974), p. 411.

49. Kissinger, *Years of Upheaval*, p. 902.

50. Quoted in ibid., p. 916.

51. See Lincoln P. Bloomfield, *Western Europe 1965–1975: Five Scenarios* (New York: Bendix Corporation, April 1965); David P. Calleo, *Europe's Future: The Grand Alternatives* (New York: W. W. Norton, 1965); Alastair Buchan, *Europe's Futures, Europe's Choices: Models of Western Europe in the 1970s* (New York: Columbia University Press, 1969); Pierre Hassner, *Europe in the Age of Negotiations* (Beverly Hills, Calif., and London: Sage Publications, 1973); Warner R. Schilling et al., *American Arms*

and a Changing Europe: Dilemmas of Deterrence and Disarmament (New York; Columbia University Press, 1973). See also my *Fading Partnership*, pp. 103–4.

52. Bloomfield, *Western Europe*. See Simon Serfaty, "An Ascending Europe," *Harvard International Review* (September–October 1983).

53. Hassner, *Europe in the Age of Negotiations.*

54. Calleo, *Europe's Future.*

55. Buchan, *Europe's Futures.*

56. I. M. Destler, ed., *Managing an Alliance: The Politics of U.S.–Japanese Relations* (Washington, D.C.: Brookings Institution, 1976), p. 36.

57. As argued by Robert D. Hormats, then the Deputy U.S. Trade Representative, in "U.S.–Japan Economic Relations," *Hearings*, House Subcommittee on Asian and Pacific Affairs (September 1980), p. 171.

58. As argued by Selig Harrison, ibid., pp. 248–80.

59. As Henry Kissinger put it, "in the pressure of events the thought [to consult or at least inform the Japanese] occurred to no one." *White House Years*, p. 262.

60. All opposition parties as well as important factions within the majority party had favored the normalization of Japan's relations with Peking (as did 70% of the population led by all major newspapers). Throughout, the government had found it politically expedient to explain its opposition to normalization as a policy dictated by U.S. preferences. See Graham Allison, "American Foreign Policy and Japan," in *Discord in the Pacific: Challenges to the Japanese American Alliance*, ed. Henry Rosovsky (Washington, D.C.: Columbia Books, 1972), p. 13.

61. Quoted in Leon Hollerman, "The Politics of Economic Relations," in *Japan and the United States: Economic and Political Adversaries*, ed. Leon Hollerman (Boulder, Col.: Westview Press, 1980), p. 220.

62. Eleanor M. Hadley, "Explaining U.S. Trade Problems with Particular Reference to Japan," in Hollerman, *Japan and the United States*, p. 57.

63. See Philip H. Tresize, *Trade Problems Between Japan and the United States* (Washington, D.C.: American Enterprise Institute for Public Policy Research, 1975). Between 1967 and 1972, the Japanese current account moved from a modest deficit to a surplus of about $7 billion. During that same period, the global U.S. current account swung from a surplus of over $2 billion to a deficit of about $6 billion. See Fred Bergsten, "What to Do about

the U.S.–Japan Economic Conflict,' *Foreign Affairs* (Summer 1982), p. 1060.

64. Yasuo Takeyama, "Don't Take Japan for Granted," *Foreign Policy* (Winter 1971–1972).
65. Kissinger, *White House Years*, p. 324.
66. Quoted in Hollerman, *Japan and the United States*, p. 270.
67. Herman Kahn, *The Emerging Superstate; Challenge and Response* (Englewood Cliffs, N.J.: Prentice-Hall, 1970); Zbigniew Brzezinski, *The Fragile Blossom; Crisis and Change in Japan* (New York: Harper & Row, 1972).
68. Harrison, in *Hearings*, p. 254.
69. Nathaniel Thayer, "U.S.–Japan Relations," *Hearings* before the International Subcommittee, House of Representatives, March 9, 1982, pp. 236–37.

CHAPTER NINE

Neither Detente
nor Containment

There was in 1977 little improvisation in the foreign policy of the Carter administration. "Every action we've taken," National Security Adviser Zbigniew Brzezinski explained in May of that year, "was part of a plan for the first 90 days . . . [that] was carried out systematically."[1] A determination to do away at once with the methods and policies of the Kissinger years appeared to shape that plan. The former Secretary of State's predilection for the personal and the covert over the collective and the open would give way, it was hoped, to a collegial administration that would reorder America's priorities to the benefit of the right over the strong.[2] As Cyrus Vance later put it, "a nation that saw itself as a 'beacon on the hill' for the rest of mankind could not content itself with power politics alone."[3]

It is not unusual for a new president to want to assert an identity of his own in foreign policy. Yet, programmed by the occasionally overblown rhetoric of years of step-by-step opposition, this time the attempt was made with a thoroughness that had not been seen since the Eisenhower years at least. Thus, three months after the inauguration, a bulky paper was submitted by the National Security Council to President Carter. Presented as a "vehicle for influencing the general strategic thrust of the foreign policy of the Carter administration," this book of goals was surprisingly tangible not only in setting and describing targets but also in assigning a specific timetable for the completion of many of these objectives.[4] Everywhere success was promised promptly: to achieve deep cuts in the nuclear arsenals of the United States and the Soviet Union and to restrict the level of global armaments, unilaterally and through international agreements; to enhance world-wide sensitivity to human rights and ensure the progressive and peaceful transformation of Southern Africa; to form a web of bilateral relations with the new "regional influentials" of the Third World and improve the state of multilateral North–South relations; to revalue American relations with Western Europe, Japan, and the other advanced industrial democracies of the West; to come to a comprehensive settlement in the Middle East, conclude a treaty on the Panama Canal, and normalize U.S.–Chinese relations. Altogether, these objectives were said to define a "new foreign policy" which, Carter promised, was "designed to serve mankind"[5] at a time when the Soviet Union risked to become "historically irrelevant to the great issues of our time."[6]

To be sure, public opinion remained riddled with doubts over the nation's role and purpose in the world. Yet, in January 1977, there could be seen a resurgence of American nationalism, and although still painfully fresh, the scars of Vietnam and Watergate were healing sufficiently quickly to sustain the philosophy of a policy of "constructive global engagement."[7] "There is a new desire to put an end to what is seen as a weakening U.S. role in the world," noted the authors of a national survey in late 1976, "and to resume the position of being 'number one'."[8] Given this emerging consensus for national renewal,[9] it could easily be granted that the United States needed, more than ever before, a creative vision that would end the pervasive sense of drift that had characterized earlier American policies at home and abroad. Yet such an approach reflected a dangerous predilection for the desirable over the feasible. As initially conceived in 1977, the Carter foreign policy might perhaps be accepted at home, for a while at least; it might even be accepted in the minds and spirits of peoples in a number of countries abroad; but it would certainly not be accepted in the world at large, where the most powerful and more reprehensible of America's foes and friends alike would eventually challenge the directions and intentions of the Carter administration.[10] A foreign policy of aroused expectations threatened therefore to be a prelude to a foreign policy of confrontation. In the past, too, such an escalation had hardly been avoidable. As Truman and Kennedy had shown especially well, words could develop a life of their own: used to explain, justify, or describe a policy, they might soon replace the policy itself.

"Man is not born to solve the problems of the world," Goethe once wrote, "but to search for the starting point of the problem and then remain within the limits of what he can comprehend:"[11] not only of what can be comprehended but also of what can be accomplished. Vis-à-vis the principal protagonist—the Soviet Union—as well as in the vital area of the Middle East and over the difficult issue of human rights, such a sense of limits proved to be particularly lacking in 1977, and the Carter administration abandoned the rules of detente without restoring the means of containment.

Of course, the United States and the Soviet Union had already been on a collision course before the arrival of the Carter administration. As we have seen, in 1974-1976 the continued Soviet military build-up, Soviet activism in Africa and elsewhere in the Third World, and a more visible repression of domestic dissent in the Soviet Union had clashed with the expectations generated by the elaborate Kissingerian designs. Furthermore, any new American administration would have been perceived by the Soviet leadership as less predictable and hence less reliable, regardless of policies, objectives, and methods; this could be anticipated all the more readily as it had been seen before and would be seen again.

If, therefore, the Carter administration could not be held solely responsible for the deterioration of America's relationship with the Soviet Union in 1977, it could nevertheless be declared liable for exacerbating it markedly. For one thing, the emphasis on human rights bewildered the Soviet authorities, which interpreted it as an orchestrated attack against them. To be sure, the Carter administration hoped to use the issue of human rights to rebuild a foreign policy consensus that had been found lacking: how could America's sense of purpose be better recovered than with the renewed claim of an historical birthright, which entitled the United States to expose and condemn the corruption and absence of liberties that prevailed elsewhere? Calling human rights "the soul" of its foreign policy, the Carter administration expected that such servicing of traditional American principles would help it to escape the self-defeating rigidity of the past, which had transformed principles into doctrines and had led to the tragedy of Vietnam.[12] The Carter administration therefore assumed that the Soviet leadership would take at face value its reassurances that American frank statements about injustice—only made from time to time, as Secretary of State Cyrus Vance emphasized—did not single out the Soviet Union.

Yet Carter's focus on human rights might have been more acceptable to the Soviets had it not coincided with a change in the U.S. positions on arms control. Earlier, in 1974, the Vladivostok accord that had been signed with the Soviet Union during the first few weeks of the Ford administration had set upper levels for the strategic arsenals available to both superpowers: 2,400 launchers, of which only a subset of 1,320 could be MIRVed. But now, in early 1977, the comprehensive proposals of the Carter administration not only sought to reduce these ceilings, but also and above all appeared to restrict and limit strategic weapons of particular concern to the United States: a 50% reduction (from 308 to 150) in the number of modern Soviet heavy ICBMs and a ceiling of 550 on each country's MIRVed ICBMs. Significantly enough, this latter ceiling reflected the limit the United States had set for its own MIRVed Minuteman force. Thus, Carter's "deep cuts" would leave the U.S. land-based missile force intact, while Soviet heavy and MIRVed ICBMs (already developed and permitted under the SALT I agreement and the Vladivostok accord) were scaled back.[13] In return, the Carter administration would accept limitations on weapons of specific concern to the Soviets (including the Cruise missile and the MX) but neither deployed, nor under construction, nor even authorized yet.

Appealing as some of Carter's ideas and objectives were, asking too much from arms control at a moment when SALT II appeared to be about to be concluded left the whole process of arms negotiations dangling.[14] Instead, it would probably have been preferable simply to go forward with the Vladivostok formula that had been inherited from the previous administration. Excessive in substance, the deep cut proposals were also maladroit in form. With the Carter administration willing to discuss its offer publicly even before it had been presented to and reviewed with the Soviet bureaucracy, the Kremlin was left with the impression that an acceptance of the American offer would be understood as a one-sided concession of Brezhnev to Carter.[15] Eventually, the Carter proposals and assumptions would be reversed and a SALT II agreement ultimately signed. But by then domestic opinion in the United States had been aroused by a legitimate concern over the continued Soviet military build-up, and there could no longer be found the majority needed for the ratification of a treaty now thought by many to be "fatally flawed."

What was at dispute in 1977 were the objectives and priorities of the Carter administration. If a new SALT agreement was needed before the expiration of the 1972 interim agreement, why not postpone the offensive on human rights? For if there was something to be gained out of a test of Soviet willingness to achieve deep cuts in their strategic forces, why not hold the test under the best possible circumstances? As the Soviets felt provoked, they were likely to question what stood behind the new administration's rhetoric and policies. Did such policies reflect a renewed will for showdown, or would the American president backtrack from his rhetoric if confronted with Soviet inflexibility? With the Soviet leadership thereby inclined to do some probing of its own, the seeds were planted of a crisis in U.S.–Soviet relations which was to become in later years more significant and more serious than the short period of debate and disagreement that President Carter had foreseen instead.

In the Middle East, too, the Carter administration insisted on the need for radical changes and immediate results. In 1976, a much-publicized report of the Brookings Institution had recommended a comprehensive settlement that would include a prompt resolution of the Palestinian issue. In opposition to the bilateral format favored by Kissinger during the negotiations of the previous three years, the report called for a general conference, or for several informal multilateral meetings designed to deal with the wide range of issues involved. The

Brookings report also proposed that because the United States enjoyed "a measure of confidence" on both sides and had the means to assist them economically and militarily, it should play a leading role in the negotiations—but together with the Soviet Union "to the degree that Soviet willingness to play a constructive role [would] permit.[16]

Throughout most of its first year in office the Carter administration followed this blueprint. In early March, the president—who had initially planned "to approach this subject with great caution"—called for a "homeland for the Palestinians" without which, he argued in May, "there can [not] be any reasonable hope for a settlement of the Middle Eastern question."[17] The Carter team found the time ripe for new American initiatives that would help shape a comprehensive framework of principles on the basis of which negotiations would be held on the major issues: the nature of peace in the region, Israel's withdrawal from occupied territories and compensating security guarantees, and a solution for the Palestinian problem. And when the march toward a Geneva conference—initially expected to be convened as early as September 1977—was stalled, a U.S.–Soviet Joint Statement on the Middle East was issued on October 1 in order to enlist Soviet leverage over Arab rejectionist states to ease their opposition to indirect PLO representation in Geneva.

Thus, by October 1977 Israeli Prime Minister Menachem Begin and Egyptian President Anwar El-Sadat feared that they were being pushed to the wall, and Geneva was increasingly emerging more as an end in itself rather than as a device to induce the protagonists to move on substantive issues.[18] Led by Carter—with an hypothetical assist from Brezhnev—everyone would go to Geneva anxious to blame the likely failure of the conference on the other side's unwillingness to compromise. Yet a Geneva that failed might be more consequential than a Geneva that did not meet: this was understood by Sadat all too well. Suspicious of Carter's decision to return to the Soviets a role that the Egyptian leader had tried to end as early as 1972, disillusioned with the more radical Arab states whose inflexibility prolonged a statemate that was having a deteriorating impact on the Egyptian economy (and thus, the stability of his regime), and convinced that the Carter administration would not force a showdown with the Israelis without which, Sadat feared, there could be no agreement in Geneva, the Egyptian president chose to enter into direct negotiations with Israel as a self-appointed spokesman for all Arab interests and with the hope of luring other Arab states into the negotiating process.[19] In Jerusalem he was received on November 19 by an Israeli prime minister who had, ironically enough, reached comparable conclusions with regard to Moscow's projected role, Arab hostility, and Carter's reluctance to engage in a confrontation with Israel.

Sadat's initiative cleary surprised the Carter administration which, in early October, was "still reasonably hopeful that before the end of the year we, in fact, will be having a conference in Geneva."[20] By reneging on the U.S. commitment to a comprehensive approach, Carter and his advisers feared that they would antagonize the other Arab States, including Saudi Arabia upon whom the United States had become especially dependent for support not only for its policies in the Middle East but also for its energy requirements. Moreover, the Carter administration also worried over the exclusion of the Soviet Union from the negotiations, which, it was reasoned, would be sabotaged by Moscow on the basis of the influence it exerted most notably on Syria and the PLO. And, finally, there was some resentment at being forced on the sidelines while Begin and Sadat were starting a game of their own.

In short, Sadat's trip to Israel caused much confusion in the U.S. administration about what should be done next. As reviewed by Carter subsequently, "there had been no time for advance consultations or preparation for further discussions. In the euphoria of the moment, it did not seem appropriate to go back to the timeworn argument about how a peace conference could be arranged or who would attend. The unchanged presumption was that all of us would eventually move toward a multinational Geneva type of conference."[21] But that presumption, too, came to be abandoned quickly: after the failure of the first round of negotiations between Begin and Sadat at Ismailia, Egypt, on December 25–26, President Carter now concluded that the only permanent result of Sadat's visit to Israel might be the cancelation of the Geneva peace conference. The administration was thus reduced to "cast about for some action to be taken," and "prevent any surprises in the future," whether from Egypt or from Israel.[22] As a result, the United States shed the unwelcomed role of "spectator" that had been imposed upon it, however momentarily, by Sadat's intiative, and increasingly assumed the role of an active intermediary between Egypt and Israel.[23] The *ménage à trois* between Carter, Begin, and Sadat had now gone full circle. In the spring and summer of 1977, negotiations between the United States and Israel—held with the malign encouragement of Egypt—had seen the former anxious to save the latter in spite of himself. Next, in the fall, negotiations between Sadat and Begin—conducted with the benign neglect of Carter—had seen the Egyptian president allegedly anxious to enlist the help of the Israeli prime minister to save the American president in spite of himself. In 1978, however, it was Carter's turn to be called upon by both Sadat and Begin to save them from each other in spite of themselves.

Whether by default or by design, from then on Carter played a decisive role in the absence of which no agreement between Egypt and Israel would have been possible and no treaty thinkable. Nixon and Kissinger, to be sure, had paved the way after the 1973 war. Yet Carter's mastery of details and his perseverance in difficult and complex negotiations permitted him to pursue the road to peace much farther than his predecessors.[24] Repeatedly, the American president would be called upon to overcome the intransigence of both sides, momentarily left to their own doubts and mutual suspicions, and risk the acrobatics of personal and shuttle diplomacy between Egypt and Israel to bridge the remaining differences and ensure the signing first of the Camp David Accords on September 17, 1978, and next of an Egyptian–Israeli Peace Treaty on March 26, 1979. If nothing else, the arduous Camp David process launched by Carter in 1978 demonstrated the indispensability of an intense American involvement at the highest possible level if any kind of movement toward peace in the region was to be generated. In the early 1980s, such minute involvement of the American president in the negotiation of any sort of limited or comprehensive peace plan in the Middle East would be sorely missed. Yet Carter's involvement caused an enormous drain on his time and energy, which diverted his attention away from unfolding turbulence elsewhere. The price of Carter's triumph was therefore high. Nowhere was this more evident than in and over Iran.

For many years, U.S. support for the Shah had shown little regard for the repressive nature of his regime. Indeed, during the years of the Nixon–Ford administrations, the United States had made itself deliberately oblivious to the radicalization of key elements of the Iranian society whose opposition had been forcefully repressed by the Shah. For, as we have seen, the regime in Tehran had been identified as a key player in the fulfillment of two of the most vital U.S. objectives anywhere: the denial of Soviet expansion in the Gulf and continued access to safe oil supplies. But now, in early 1977, Carter's overt advocacy of human rights, including the "rights to enjoy civil and political liberties such as freedom of thought, religion, assembly, speech, and the press,"[25] led many an Iranian to assume that the support of such principles—which went obviously counter to existing practice—would prompt the Carter administration to use its tremendous influence to promote political reforms in their country.[26]

The first concrete indication that this would not be the case came in early November 1977, when Iran confirmed its purchase of seven extremely sophisticated American AWAC (Airborne, Warning and Control Systems) planes plus sixteen F-16 fighters. This deal fueled renewed charges in the opposition press published outside Iran—which voiced the concerns of both secular and religious opponents, including those of the Ayatollah Khomeini—that the grateful Shah was thereby providing the United States with the most obvious of Iranian payoffs, namely, the acquisition of weapons intended to serve American, not Iranian interests.[27] Even though the official position of the administration remained that these weapons could in any case be obtained from European suppliers,[28] such arguments were not fully unnoticed. Thus, even before the Shah's visit to Washington in mid-November 1977, a memorandum written at the Policy Planning Staff of the State Department cautioned against the unrestrained sale of expensive weaponry to Iran. Excessive and unjustified military spending, it was argued, would lead to rising social and economic tensions and leave Iran with insufficient financial resources to head off mounting political dissatisfaction, including discontent among groups that had traditionally been supportive of the monarchy. Noting that Iranian socio-economic programs were lagging and that even with huge oil revenues Iran was running balance of payments deficits, the Policy Planning Staff recommended "to slow down and stretch out the building up of [the Shah's] military forces to give him more time and more resources to build a cohesive, prosperous (and nonrepressive) domestic base for his defense effort."[29] Such analysis did little, however, to erode the prevailing perception within the administration that the Shah was in full control and that the discontent was merely the product of some religious fanatics and a few communists.* Instead, whatever illusions the Iranian populace might still have entertained with regard to the intentions of the Carter administration, they were erased by the President's state visit to Iran on January 1, 1978, and Carter's effusive support for the Shah exacerbated a rampant anti-Americanism among the many Iranians who had heretofore hoped for a change in U.S. policy toward their country. Perhaps influenced by his own perception of Carter's penchant for civil liberties and probably affected by his knowledge (not shared with others) of an irreversibly failing health, the Shah's reaction to the turmoil that followed Carter's visit was uncharacteristically spasmodic, and throughout 1978 he wavered between temporary liberalization and fierce repression, until he was forced into exile on January 16, 1979.

The debacle in Iran grew out of the absence of clear goals as the Carter administration remained apparently torn between its own self-proclaimed principles and interests, while a related unwillingness to pay the price that would have resulted from any one choice made the administration move from one worst

---

*Similar warnings were issued after the Shah's visit to the United States. Thus, in an interagency report to the Congress on the "military balance in Iran," the Central Intelligence Agency argued that the Iranian military did not have sufficient skills to absorb any more sophisticated military equipment. Such skills would therefore have to be diverted from the already depleted Iranian industry, thereby causing additional and dangerous pressures on Iran's economy. This analysis, too, was apparently rejected. Extraordinarily enough, a few days before the Shah's final departure from Iran, President Carter still assumed that "the shah and the military would prevail."—*Keeping Faith* (New York, 1982), p. 445.

option to the next. In 1977, Carter did not insist upon the political reforms in Iran that might have reversed the revolutionary trends uncovered by some of his own foreign policy analysts. Having instead confirmed the Shah as America's "island of stability in one of the more troubled areas of the world," he did not move to defend him in 1978, even though Carter still had "no question in [his] mind that [the Shah] deserved our unequivocal support."[30] At times inclined to define him as "the problem," the American president did not take steps to replace him as quickly as possible with a regime more to his liking and to that of the Iranian populace. Nor, in the face of Khomeini's return in early 1979, did Carter move swiftly enough to make contact with the Ayatollah—a failure that apparently dismayed the Shah himself.[31] Later, in November 1979, Carter would similarly reject the military option that he should have endorsed immediately following the capture of a number of American hostages in Tehran. But he endorsed the military option in April 1980 when he should have rejected it, either because negotiations were now progressing or because sufficient capabilities were not committed and thus compromised a military operation which, in addition, was bound to entail costs in human lives which the President remained apparently unwilling to face.

In 1978–79, the uncertainties that accompanied and followed the revolution in Iran exacerbated Western differences to a point that made the observer regret the alleged "ennui" of earlier years. For, as asked in a subsequent study of the events that surrounded the unraveling of American policies in Iran, "if the Americans would not act to support the Shah, under what circumstances could they be expected to move? If the Carter administration did not judge Iran to be a vital interest of the United States, what ally could consider itself truly secure?"[32] In short, the states of Europe (and Japan) now feared U.S. inaction (at home in the domain of energy conservation, and abroad in managing OPEC or in containing Soviet or radical advances beyond, or from, South Yemen, Syria, and Ethiopia) no less than they feared the failure of U.S. actions (against Iran, at Camp David, or over Afghanistan). They feared Soviet intentions before or when a then-expected Soviet oil shortage came no less than they feared Soviet influence if and when their own dependency on the Soviet gas pipeline to Western Europe exceeded the self-imposed ceiling of 5% of their overall energy consumption. And, in the meantime, they feared too much power for OPEC and too much weakness in the OPEC states.[33]

Fears, of course, never add up to a policy, and in later years several of these would be forgotten while new ones were uncovered. Yet the European states, their efforts made awkward by the very insufficiency of their capabilities and the scope of their vulnerability, proved to be an easy release for the growing frustrations of the Carter administration. After the Soviet invasion of Afghanistan in December 1979, the American administration appeared to confuse allies and adversaries, subjecting the former to the pressures and language that it was not prepared or able to inflict upon the later. Indeed, as seen in Europe, the American "punishment" of the Soviet Union seemed to harm the allies more than the adversaries. Although a likely irritant to the Soviet government, the U.S. boycott of the 1980 Olympic games in Moscow also forced the European governments into an unwanted choice between U.S. pressures on behalf of the boycott and domestic pressures against it. Similarly, calls for economic sanctions and, more generally, an end to negotiations were perceived in Europe as policies that hurt the allies (considerably more sensitive than the United States to the actual consequences of such policies, should they be enforced) as much as, if not more than, they hurt the offender. Accordingly, by the end of the 1970s, European countries faulted U.S. policies for their general excesses because they threatened the premature death of detente, even while they pointed to their specific insufficiencies because they did not permit a rebirth of containment.

A Quarter before Reagan

The midwifery of the Camp David Accords, as evasive as they were on a number of key issues, and the signing of the Egyptian–Israeli peace treaty, as fragile as it appeared to be at first, were notable successes for the diplomacy of the Carter administration.* There were others, of course, including the passage of the Panama Canal Treaty in April 1978 (after 13 years of negotiations, which had outlasted three previous administrations), the normalization of U.S. relations with the People's Republic of China in December 1978, and the negotiated independence of Zimbabwe in April 1980. Yet these hardly added up into the "new world system" to which Carter and his advisers had aspired. Instead, the persistent lack of an overall structure left the Carter administration with an inconsistent foreign policy that caused misgivings at home and grievances abroad.

At Notre Dame University on May 22, 1977, the American president had found the Vietnam War "the best example of [the] intellectual and moral poverty" of old American policies that were no longer suited for the new international order. Symbolic of the need for change was the decline of the Soviet threat: "We are now free of that inordinate fear of communism which once led us to embrace any dictator who joined us in that fear," proclaimed Carter. To be sure, the Soviet Union remained a key problem for U.S. foreign policy, but it no longer represented the central problem. As written by Brzezinski in 1973, the "implicitly apocalyptic conflict" of the 1950s and the 1960s between

---

*There were two sets of issues that were debated and negotiated at Camp David: one set related to a peace treaty that would be signed between Egypt and Israel, and the other related to the negotiation of at least an interim agreement for the territories of Gaza and the West Bank. Both were clearly linked: once a separate peace had been signed with Egypt, Israel would find it much easier not to yield on the West Bank and Gaza. Yet, in the end Carter's (and Sadat's) willingness to acquiesce to Begin's vague formulas on the West Bank and Gaza permitted the peace treaty between Israel and Egypt without resolving the territorial issues elsewhere (to be tackled "later on if it was absolutely necessary"). In return for a treaty that was to be signed within a specified deadline, it was agreed that a transitional arrangement in the Occupied Territories would provide the needed framework for later "discussions" or "decisions," the participants to which remained all the more uncertain as Israel's settlement activities were not frozen for the duration of the projected negotiations on Gaza and the West Bank—as Carter had expected and requested—but for the duration of the projected negotiations on the Egyptian–Israeli peace treaty—as Begin preferred and pledged.

the United States and the Soviet Union had been replaced by an "explicitly relativistic competition" which took place within an entirely new global context:[34] in the emerging "2½ +y+z Powers world" (the United States, the Soviet Union, and China, plus Western Europe and Japan), the industrial "technocratic societies" and the "new influentials" of the Third World were competing in drawing the boundaries of a new equality that resulted from a general devaluation of military power.[35]

The Vietnam war had been the catalyst for this new attitude toward force. But this was not all, and changes in the costs of military conflicts—and, accordingly, the relevance of military force—had in fact preceeded the war. Repeatedly, colonial, civil, and foreign wars had shown that the subjugation of groups or people that are determined to organize and resist would necessitate costs in suppressive military measures and repressive political actions that might become so high as to make statesmen tolerate instead the costs of failure or secession.[36] Indeed, pushing the argument to the extreme, some even reasoned that the world was moving to an era in which war between major states might virtually disappear.[37] Given this devaluation of military force, a foreign policy geared to the military containment of the Soviet Union was therefore "too narrow,"[38] and power realism, preoccupied as it was with the traditional issues of international relations, had become "deceptive."[39] Instead, a broader vision would present the world "as a unit, beset by certain common problems."[40] And in such a world the Soviet Union, whose sole asset was its military power and whose historical creed was inequality, had become increasingly irrelevant: it was "not even a rival" of the United States.[41]

Such a vision of the new international system was still present in the second major foreign policy address of President Carter, at Charleston, South Carolina, on July 21, 1977, as he evoked "a new world in which we cannot afford to be narrow in our vision, limited in our foresights, or selfish in our purpose."[42] By that time Carter also insisted that the relationship with the Soviet Union, however important, could not be America's sole preoccupation, to the exclusion of other world issues. Yet already the American president was torn between the planetary vision of a "gentler, freer, more bountiful world" in which genuine accomodation could be achieved, and "the nature of the world as it really is"—namely, one in which "the basis for complete mutual trust does not yet exist."

By mid-March 1978, in a speech at Wake Forest University, the emphasis had shifted away from the early penchant for planetary humanism to the old imperative of power realism. Even in a world that had "grown more complex and more interdependent," Carter now uncovered an "ominous inclination on the part of the Soviet Union to use its military power."[43] Slowly and reluctantly entering the "world-wide political and military drama," Carter was about to urge the Soviets to exercise "restraint in troubled areas and in turbulent times." Charging that the Kremlin was not living up to the human rights provision of the Helsinki agreement, the Carter administration warned against the further expansion of a so-called arc of crisis where Soviet marauders would compel the United States to regain its dominant position if a chaotic fragmentation of the world was to be avoided.[44] In this context, the president now indicated that in the absence of Soviet restraint the projection of Soviet or proxy forces into other lands and continents would lead to the erosion of public support in the United States for cooperation with the Soviets.[45] More specifically, Carter added a few months later, unless Moscow showed further restraint in its attitude toward human rights (in compliance with the terms of the Helsinki agreement) and unless it displayed additional moderation in its own involvement in Africa (and that of its allies as well), it would be "much more difficult to conclude a SALT agreement and to have it ratified once it is written."[46]

Coming a few days after Brzezinski's trip to China, Carter's later warnings appeared to demonstrate a new penchant for linkage in a period of growing strain in U.S.–Soviet relations. Such speculation was encouraged by Brzezinski as he referred to the variety of ways in which the Soviets and the Cubans could be convinced that their intrusions abroad carried consequences that might be inimical to them as well.[47] Earlier, Brzezinski had already noticed that the unwarranted intrusion of Russian power into a purely local conflict would inevitably complicate the arms control negotiations.[48] Now Carter's national security adviser was relying on the so-called China card as he pointedly explained that during his talks with the Chinese leaders he had the "opportunity to discuss the issue" of the Soviet–Cuban intervention in internal African affairs, about which the Chinese, too, had been "very critical."[49]

Whether Carter's decision to dispatch Brzezinski to China was the result of a sudden exasperation over Soviet tactics or the result of a long period of careful study and deliberation within the American administration on the best course for normalization,[50] Soviet reaction showed that the crisis was now deepening quickly. Complaining of "certain leaders who hold high posts in Washington [and] are . . . overwhelmed by anti-Soviet emotions," the Kremlin hinted that they, too, could resort to linkage as they warned that alignment with China on an anti-Soviet basis would rule out the possibility of cooperation with the Soviet Union in arms control.[51] Thus, even though Carter would continue to dismiss the crisis as reflective of "temporary disharmonies or disputes about transient circumstances" and even though he would still point to the "very moderate way" in which he had criticized the Soviet handling of human rights as evidence that he had not "embarked on a vendetta against the Soviet Union,"[52] Carterism was beginning to be spelled Kissingerism—but without Kissinger. Although it would take another eighteen months of bitter internal debates before the final tranformation of the Carter foreign policy—as consecrated in the announcement of the Carter doctrine in January 1980—by mid-1978 the Carter administration's foreign policy was already about to become what it was not supposed to be.

In the course of this transformation, the state and evolution of the military balance with the Soviet Union emerged as a crucial part of the resulting foreign policy debate. Following the Soviet rejection of the comprehensive option in early 1977, the Carter administration had sought a new formula, which included elements of the Vladivostok approach, elements of the earlier comprehensive option, plus elements of another U.S. option called the deferral option. With the prior approval this time of the Soviets, the "three-tier" approach would therefore have included a treaty (SALT II) that would be based on the 1974 Vladivostok accord and run through 1985—with the related aggregate ceilings the main focus of the negotiations; a 3-year Protocol attached to the Treaty that would essentially list a number of contentious issues (such as cruise missile constraints, the Backfire, mobile ICBM limitation, and qualitative constraints on ICBMs) about which more time for negotiations was required; and a joint Statement of Principles, which, together with the Protocol, would serve as a basis for follow-on SALT III negotiations.[53]

Underlying such an approach was the effort of the Carter administration to decouple the issue of ICBM vulnerability from the issue of net U.S. deterrent capabilities. As Secretary of Defense Harold Brown argued, "the survival of Minuteman III's through a nuclear attack and subsequent launch is not the same thing as survival of deterrence, it is not the same thing as the survival of the U.S. military force, it is certainly not the same thing as the survival of the United States, with our military capability, or even with our deterrent capability."[54]

The Carter administration did not deny that the U.S. land-based Minuteman force was, or soon might be, at risk. What was questioned instead was the relevance of such vulnerability to America's security. Even a perfect preemptive strike against the U.S. land-based force, Secretary Brown emphasized, would still leave the United States with nonnegligible capabilities that included the alert bombers and at-sea SSBNs with thousands of warheads. Because a Soviet attack that intended to destroy U.S. silos could still kill at least several million Americans, the threat of a U.S. retaliation would be high, and all the more serious in the eyes of the Soviet planners as it might be aimed at Soviet cities and industries. "The alleged irrationality of such a response," Secretary Brown reasoned, "would be no consolation in retrospect and would not necessarily be in advance an absolute guarantee that we would not so respond. In any event, any Soviet planner considering U.S. options would know that, besides massive retaliation, the surviving U.S. forces would also be capable of a broad variety of controlled responses aimed at military and civilian targets and proportioned to the scale and significance of the provocation."[55]

ICBM vulnerability—"the most urgent problem we face," Brzezinski reiterated a few weeks before the signing of SALT II[56]—did not therefore require additional deployment of land-based systems. To be sure, any advantages or new advantages in force characteristics enjoyed by the Soviets had to be offset by other or new U.S. advantages. But the United States would avoid a resort to one-for-one matching of individual indices of capability.[57] Yet in integrating this argument into the SALT II treaty, the Carter administration appeared to abandon the principle of "strategic equivalence" that had been behind the congressional approval of an amendment to the 1972 SALT I interim agreement and carried the name of Senator Henry Jackson. As Jackson would later testify, a long-standing preoccupation with a definition of equality that was not limited to sheer numbers alone made the Senate insist on "a SALT II Treaty that provided for equal numbers of strategic weapons taking account of throw weight. . . . A team of giants and a team of dwarfs might have equal numbers of players, but they would hardly be equal for most purposes."[58] Instead, the essential equivalence sought by the Carter administration implicitly legitimated the slowdown of a number of vital U.S. strategic programs, even while the Soviets were themselves proceeding with theirs as a result of the Carter failure to limit the Soviet "heavy" ICBM force as extensively as it had sought to do in early 1977.

In 1978–79, the issue of essential equivalence gained therefore a vital importance. SALT II "does not provide for equal missile throw weight," complained Senator Jackson during the hearings that were held by the Senate Armed Services Committee. "It permits the Soviet Union to deploy missiles up to 16,000 pounds of throw weight but it restricts the United States to missiles with no more than 8,000 pounds of throw weight and, as a practical matter . . . it limits the Soviets to 16,000 pounds on a missile and the United States to less than 3,000 for the life of the treaty."[59] Now, Jackson asked, given the growth and improvement of Soviet strategic forces and the growth of U.S. strategic forces since 1975 when a balance of American and Soviet forces had been proclaimed, how could such a balance still exist? "During this period," Jackson continued, "when the Soviets were moving ahead, we suffered slowdowns in the Trident program, delays in the M-X, cancellation of the B-1, slowdown in the sea-launched cruise missile program, the deferral almost to the point of cancellation of the enhanced radiation weapon for theater forces and so on. . . . How do the events of the last 4 years fit with . . . notions of balance and equality?"[60]

Yet, in and of themselves, the terms of the SALT II Agreement that was negotiated under Carter and signed in Vienna in June 1979 could be readily endorsed. The numbers of strategic delivery vehicles for both parties—that is, long-range bombers, ICBMs and SLBMs—were to remain under an equal overall ceiling that was lowered to 2,250 from the ceiling of 2,400 agreed upon at Vladivostok. The treaty also imposed additional sublimits of 1,320 for each side on the combined number of MIRVed ICBMs, SLBMs and ALCM (Air-Launched Cruise Missile)–carrying heavy bombers; and a 1,200 maximum number of MIRVed ICBMs and SLBMs. This last ceiling in turn included a maximum of 820 land-based ICBMs. In addition, for the first time SALT II included qualitative controls on technology and modernization: for example, there would be specific limits on the number of warheads that could be placed on all SLBMs, on existing ICBMs, and on the one type of ICBM each side would be permitted until 1985.[61]

By then, however, circumstances were increasingly unfavorable to an agreement whose "flaws" included the contentious domestic and international setting within which it was being debated as much as the specific terms on which it rested.[62] Abroad, Soviet activities in Indochina were compounded by a rising concern over the activism of their military proxy in Africa and were further aggravated, later in the year, by indications of increasing Soviet involvement in Cuba and Afghanistan and renewed revolutionary fervor with Marxist and pro-Cuban overtones in Central America (Nicaragua) and the Caribbean (Grenada). At home, with the election year approaching, foreign policy issues were all the more distorted as an apparently more conservative electorate was forcing tougher positions upon the more moderate candidates.

Yet even pessimistic observers must have been surprised by the pace and the scope of the crises that accompanied Carter's last year and forced the administration to acknowledge that a ratification of SALT II was, "for the time being, an impossible task."[63] The revolution in Iran in 1978–79, followed by the taking of American hostages in November 1979 and the war with Iraq as of 1980, displayed the instability of a region obviously vital to United States interests. In December 1979 the Soviet invasion of Afghanistan demonstrated an impressive availability of Soviet combat troops and showed further the growing external threat to whatever remained of Western influence in the region of the Gulf. In 1980 the crisis in Poland exposed the alarming potential of new challenges to Soviet control of Eastern Europe as well as American impotence in modifying Soviet actions and reconstructing Western consensus for a united policy toward the area. And in the spring of 1980 the exceptionally bitter feuds with the NATO allies seemed to threaten the very survivability of the Atlantic Alliance.

Under different circumstances such a deterioration of the international scene would have favored an incumbent president, especially as his rival exhibited a lack of experience in foreign policy and a language that were sources of concern to many. A more favorable vision of what a second Carter administration would be like might have been outlined accordingly. Undoubtedly, Carter has accumulated much experience during his years at the White House. A man of details, he had studied fully all major foreign policy issues, always with patience and often with competence. As already indicated, in such cases as the Panama Treaty, Camp David, and Zimbabwe, his political courage and his diplomatic perseverance had been the indispensable prerequisites to the successful negotiated outcomes that followed. But in the end Carter seemed unable to organize the many details he had attended to and to integrate the many ideas he had been exposed to into a coherent vision of the world and of America's role and place in it. Dreaming of an international system that would be orderly, just, and friendly, the American president came to perceive too late and with too many false starts an international system that was disorderly, unjust, and hostile. Instead of SALT II, there were now increases in military spending, more interest in a Rapid Deployment Force, a sudden endorsement of the strategic weapons that had been rejected earlier, a search for a new network of air and naval facilities in the Gulf. In short, in 1980 Carter himself launched the foreign policy of the Reagan administration—just as Truman had done for Eisenhower in June 1950, and Johnson for Nixon in March 1968.

Yet, while waiting for Ronald Reagan, speculation at home and abroad had to be tentative as it rested on a discourse that had centered primarily on the past and said little of the future.

Premature at first, the major themes of the Reagan discourse had come progressively to coincide with the existing circumstances of the 1980s. They stated what the Reagan administration would aim at: restoring American leadership and reasserting its influence in areas deemed to be vital to the interests of the West, reversing the military balance with the Soviet Union, and regaining a measure of unity with the allies in Europe and Japan. Not surprisingly, however, the Reagan discourse had been least specific when explaining how to meet these objectives—and such absence of specificity was to be sorely felt in subsequent years.

Shaping Reagan's vision of the past was an image of the Soviet Union as a country whose internal ineptitude coincided with an expansionist impulse motivated by an abhorrent and evil ideology and fueled by the steady accumulation of military power. That such power had not been balanced, that Soviet expansion had been inadequately contained by the United States after the Vietnam War, and that an American strategy of retreat had been devised instead were seen as the sources of the "clear and present danger" faced by the United States and its allies. Deceived by the Soviet Union, America had abandoned the search for strategic superiority in favor of an ill-defined notion of parity and then become unable or unwilling to defend the terms of strategic equivalence, thereby permitting Moscow to achieve a growing military advantage that eased its penetration into the Third World and culminated with the Soviet invasion of Afghanistan. Confronted with such Soviet advances, the Carter administration, Reagan argued, had persisted in seeking further accommodations that brought about a second SALT treaty whose flaws would have endangered the security of the United States.

Thus distorted by the Soviet perception of their growing military advantage, the past decade of the 1970s had seen excessive American concessions to all. Understanding detente as the recognition of the status quo in Europe and the permissibility of change elsewhere (i.e., the end of containment), the Soviet Union had moved quickly toward a position of primacy, encouraged to military adventurism by the vacillations of the Carter administration (i.e., the end of detente). At home, this strategy of military retreat and political retrenchment had confused and misled the American public. Abroad, it had permitted the fragmentation of an alliance system built under several Republican and Democratic administrations, while allowing additional instability in the Third World, which, whether or not it was directed by Moscow, had brought about costly changes and intolerable humiliations.

Finally, the Reagan foreign policy discourse had repeatedly deplored the moral disarmament born out of the traumatic history of the United States over the previous 15 years. Economic, social, and constitutional crises—most of which had been self-inflicted—had tarnished the self-assured and domineering image of U.S. leadership. Obsessed with a masochistic contemplation of its own imperfections, America had lost the international legitimacy to which it had a right by birth. As if such a self-imposed handicap were not enough, the country had shown a new tendency to abandon its traditional friends abroad, either in the name of principles that were difficult to apply evenly everywhere (human rights), or in the name of vague objections often incompatible with the requirements of regional balance (arms sales), or, finally, in the name of the perceived requirements imposed upon the United States by other policy initiatives (Taiwan and the normalization with China, for example). As a result, the credibility and the durability of U.S. commitments had been eroded further. Anxious to be more "liked" than "respected," the United States was now neither one nor the other—and this, too, had precipitated the making of the present danger in an ever more hostile world.

Thus, a decade that had begun with the admonition that America be thought of like an ordinary nation had given birth to a decade that was opening with the admonition that America be once again dreamed of as an exceptional nation. Where Kissinger had at first succeeded in implementing a policy that combined both detente and containment, Carter had ended with a strategy that appeared to permit neither. In the process, Carter had shown that there were limits to decline: his administration had therefore intended to lead the charge for renewal in 1980; but by then it had little credibility left, either abroad among adversaries and allies or at home where the outgoing president was subjected to one of the most humiliating defeats in the history of the American presidential elections.

It was now up to the new Republican administration to show that there were also limits to renewal.

The Limits of Renewal

Coming after an historical parenthesis that delayed it for three years in 1977–79, a resurgence of American power for the 1980s was a much-needed counterweight to the global drift toward a planetary crisis, comparable in its magnitude and superior in its potential to that which had preceeded World War I. Without doubt, such a resurgence opened dangerous perspectives, as foreign policy critics were once again quick to emphasize: pursued with excess, it might accelerate the very conflicts it was meant to prevent. In the area of adversary relationships, military resurgence without arms control and containment without accommodation would risk a Soviet explosion. In the area of alliance relationships, a political assertiveness that ignored the boundaries of permissible differences among the allies might be conducive to the risks of rupture. And, finally, in the regions of the Third World, a refurbished strategy of global containment that went beyond resisting the advance of Soviet power to close the door on radical regimes irrespective of local circumstances might prove to be self-defeating: aimed at denying the "totalitarian temptation," such a strategy might in fact invite it, as it would once again enhance the image of American policies committed to the defense of an often intolerable status quo.

Eventually, history might well show that such excesses were inevitable. In the meantime, however, a review of American foreign policy since the end of World War II did teach that the greatest and most significant charge that could be made against American policymakers was their persistent failure to define what they wanted out of the U.S. relationship with its most serious and most dangerous adversary on the world scene. Repeatedly, prevailing uncertainties as to the objectives of the United States toward the Soviet Union were inappropriately hidden behind formulas whose operational relevance remained, at best, moot. Accordingly, every American administration since 1945, having tasted the "realities" of Soviet power and ideology, had evolved differently from what had been anticipated initially. So it was with President Truman, whose early appreciation of the limits of American power was abandoned after the outbreak of the Korean War. His reversal paved the way for the Eisenhower policies of expanded commitments and global confrontation—until the crises of 1956 forced a reappraisal that Kennedy criticized in his successful 1960 presidential campaign as a decline of American prestige abroad. But prior to his assassination, Kennedy, too, was on his way toward a new moderation following the 1962 Cuban missile crisis—a moderation that Johnson overlooked in the course of the Vietnam War, whose escalation caused a relative neglect of U.S.–Soviet bilateral relations. Nor did the Nixon–Ford administrations succeed much better in maintaining consistency during their eight years at the White House. As we have seen, the promises of detente proved to be short-lived as an increasingly ambitious Soviet Union came to rely on an ascending military power to turn the strategy of linkage inside out and show that Moscow, too, could effectively link issues to its advantage. In the late 1970s, Carter's initial neglect of Soviet military power was transformed into near panic, to which the Reagan administration added a touch of ideological fervor that had not been heard since John Foster Dulles.

With the Soviet Union too ideologically hostile for conciliation but too militarily powerful for termination, there had been an equal unpreparedness in America for the subtleties of detente as well as for the discipline of containment. It should have been made clear, however, that neither could exist without the other. Perhaps so much time had been spent assessing the uniqueness of the Soviet Union—is she, actually or by design, an outwardly expanding power and an inherently ascending, stagnant, or even declining state?[64]—that not enough time was spent on stressing the need for normalcy in U.S.–Soviet relations. In an historical context, normalcy is for the dominant Great Powers to mix the concessions of accommodation whenever and wherever possible with the intransigence of confrontation when and where no compromise is possible or desirable.

Not every Soviet success ever needed to be construed as a threat to the national security of the United States, nor for that matter had every setback for the United States always originated with Soviet actions devised within the framework of an overall Soviet Grand Strategy. In the 1980s, the resurrection of an indifferentiated strategy of global containment against Soviet expansion was illusory, not only because it had hardly truly existed before but also because it would either face the new assertiveness of Soviet military power or confront the new limits of American power. In other words, global containment would lead either to new Cubas (but with the outcome this time very much in doubt) or to new Vietnams—two prospects that were admittedly of limited appeal.

In writing about "the present danger," Norman Podhoretz was pleading in 1980 for a return to the allegedly unlimited practices of the past: "In resisting the advances of Soviet power . . . we are fighting for freedom and against Communism, for democracy and against totalitarianism. . . . Without such clarity, the new nationalism is unlikely to do more than lead to sporadic outbursts of indignant energy."[65] Yet such a "clarity" could hardly be recaptured: to equate a return to containment with a resumption of the cold war served no significant purpose. What had been known as the cold war was a slice of history whose characteristics had not endured in the past and could not be restored in the future. The only clarity there was had to do with the fact of Soviet power, whose containment was an imperative that even its fiercest critics had never been able to escape fully: they had merely sought to delay its price— "elsewhere, later"—while groping for new and elusive motivations—"to make the world safe for diversity." Emptied of their past rhetoric, the great foreign policy debates of the postwar era had therefore been anything but "great." In all instances, they had raised but not answered the same questions that had been raised throughout the history of the Republic: What and where are America's vital interests? Assuming a common understanding of such interests, are they actually threatened, how and by whom? Given such threats, what are the best and most effective ways of meeting them?

By the turn of the decade, Soviet policies in Africa and Central America were meaningful tests of the relevance and limits of a renewed American strategy of containment. In Africa, the fact of growing Soviet penetration was evidenced by the resources and capabilities that the Soviet leadership had deployed for the enhancement or protection of its friends and clients. Thus, in 1960 Soviet support for Patrice Lumumba had been confined to an offer of a few trucks and a dozen transport planes. But between August and November 1975, during the pivotal months of the crisis in Angola, Moscow provided its clients in Luanda with an estimated $220 million worth of arms brought by sea and air, not to mention the Soviet airlift of most of the 11,000 Cuban troops sent during that period.

This was a major and audacious departure from past Soviet behavior, one that, as we have seen, domestic circumstances in the United States had made difficult for the Ford Administration to contain. Decisive, bold, and successful, the Soviet Union had shown that under the right circumstances it stood ready to expand its sphere of influence beyond Eastern Europe and play a potentially decisive role in Africa.[66] Yet circumstances in Angola had been especially propitious, and it was therefore necessary to avoid drawing general conclusions that might not apply to different circumstances. More specifically, in Angola the Soviet intervention did not aim at the overthrow of an established and legitimate government. Furthermore, Moscow's ability to rely on the armed forces of a willing ally avoided the risk of a heavy and direct Soviet involvement that could not be quickly terminated if the war turned out badly. Such advantages could not be easily repeated elsewhere: on two successive occasions in the Shaba province of Zaire, for example, the Soviets remained carefully uninvolved once the Zairian rebels had crossed the border from their staging grounds in Angola; for not only would a Soviet intervention have aimed at the overthrow of an established government in Kinshasa, it would also have faced the prospects of an intervention by an outside power (as proved to be the case in 1978).

In effect, Soviet policies in Africa displayed a degree of improvisation shaped by Moscow's willingness to exploit opportunities but tempered by a sure unwillingness to take risks. In the Horn, for example, early support for a promising Socialist revolution in Somalia was followed by a show of support for another promising revolution in Ethiopia as the Soviet leadership reasoned, somewhat naively as it was seen, that ideological commonalities would enable it to mediate deep-rooted national hostilities over vital territorial issues.[67] Accordingly, the Soviets lost their position in Somalia and strengthened their position in Ethiopia only after they were forced into a commitment to Ethiopia's victory in a war that they had hoped to prevent.[68]

Repeatedly, the Soviets and their allies did show a clear tendency to exacerbate the instability that prevailed in many African countries and on occasion profit from it. Yet they did not usually cause it. With all Soviet and Cuban forces magically withdrawn from the continent, with any kind of Soviet or Soviet-inspired support for liberation movements ended, and, indeed, with the Soviet Union somehow buried in the graveyard of history, most of the conflicts tearing the continent over economic, territorial, racial, and tribal issues would remain. Accordingly, the debate that split American Africanists—between the so-called "globalists" who were said to confine their assessment of African issues to their East–West dimension and the "pragmatists" who were said to focus instead on the indigenous nature of those issues—was a false debate. No African issue of importance to the United States could escape the arena of U.S.–Soviet rivalry, which remained global; nor could any such issue be decoupled from its most fundamental essence, which remained almost always indigenous. There as elsewhere, the pragmatist who dismissed the outlook of a globalist would distort the strategic realities of the question at hand; but the globalist who overlooked the perspective of a pragmatist would distort no less significantly the political realities of that same issue.[69]

Consequently, an African policy for the United States could hardly be limited to a Soviet policy. Yet, beyond the Soviet Union, the obstacles that continued to hamper the development of an effective American policy in Africa remained considerable. For one thing, there was a glaring lack of true American expertise in African affairs. An historical legacy of neglect and a bureaucratic legacy of indifference in part helped explain such insufficiencies: for too long, the United States had delegated its African responsibilities to European states whose own colonial tradition in Africa was real, to be sure, though hardly of the right variety. Whether in the administration of John F. Kennedy or in that of Jimmy Carter, occasional American attempts to acknowledge the vital importance of African issues had suffered from this historical and political inexperience. But now, entering the 1980s, America's neglect of African issues had become all the more pronounced as the American public and its elite showed an increasing exasperation over the intrusion of foreign policy into the nation's pressing domestic priorities. Thus, in 1982 to the question: "What are the two or three biggest foreign policy problems facing the U.S. today," 3% of the public cited the Third World generally, and only 1% referred to America's changing relations with African countries.[70]

While there were many other handicaps to further American influence in Africa—including self-defeating Western rivalries and the liability created throughout Black Africa by the widespread perception of a U.S.-sponsored and U.S.-sustained white regime in South Africa—none was more decisive that the expanding gap between U.S. objectives throughout the continent and the capabilities available in the pursuit of such objectives. By whatever standard of measurement, whether economic, political, or military, American resources committed to Africa did not keep up with American interests in Africa.[71] Indeed, under the Carter and the Reagan administrations alike, America's illusion of omnipotence in Africa was to assume that everything could be achieved with next to nothing. This, of course, would not suffice, and to prevent further Soviet expansion in a region of vital importance to the United States and the West some of these handicaps would have to be overcome independently of the evolution of bilateral relations between the United States and the Soviet Union.

In Central America, too, an obsessive concern with communism might threaten not only to determine the perception of the regional realities but also the policies that derived from these realities. "The national security of all the Americas is at stake in Central America," warned President Reagan in April 1983. "If we cannot defend ourselves there, we cannot defend ourselves elsewhere. Our credibility would collapse, our alliances would crumble, and the safety of our homeland would be in jeopardy."[72]

While listening to such discourse, the echoes of the past were inescapable. In November 1950, the election of President Jacobo Arbenz Guzman had been a cause of concern to the Truman administration, which had progressively leaned toward covert actions that would clean up Guatemala[73] from the pervasive influence on government thinking by "communist-minded individuals."[74] The resulting determination of the Eisenhower administration to deny Moscow its "first beachhead in the Americas"[75] had shaped U.S. policies in the area for many years to come. "If world communism captures any American state, however small," warned John Foster Dulles in June 1954, "a new and perilous front [will be] established which will increase the danger to the entire free world."[76] By that time, a CIA-sponsored army had already invaded Guatemala and was about to "liberate" it by forcing Arbenz's resignation. In 1965, in the belated wake of Kennedy's disastrous attempt to eliminate Fidel Castro in a comparable fashion, President Johnson bitterly complained of a "rocking chair president" who had "let the communists stay in charge of Cuba, when we could have thrown them out with a few American planes."[77] Now, Johnson feared, it was incumbent upon him to stop rebel leaders, "many of them trained in Cuba . . . to increase disorder" and set up "another communist state" in the Western Hemisphere.[78] Accordingly, 22,000 U.S. troops were dispatched to end a rebellion in the Dominican Republic that was said to involve a group of Communists whose number ranged from 3 to 77.[79]

However, the circumstances that had shaped American interventions in the 1950s and the 1960s were quite different from those that surrounded the evolution of U.S. policies in the region in the 1980s. Earlier fears had grown primarily out of a concern with unfolding changes in the political order of the states involved. In Guatemala and in the Dominican Republic, many who should have known better were apparently convinced that a handful of communists could seize power to the benefit of the Soviet Union simply because they were communists.[80] Consequently, there had been no objective evaluation of the political developments that were taking place at the time. John Foster Dulles' boast that Guatemala marked "the biggest success in the last five years against Communism"[81] did not endure the challenge of time: instead, the intervention served as a catalyst for the growth of numerous revolutionary movements throughout the region.[82] Such movements were all the more effective as, from 1954 on, the Eisenhower administration confidently expected that any new problem, "if it became an open sore, could be dealt with . . . like the Guatemalan problem."[83] When Cuba proved otherwise, Johnson escalated the ante in the Dominican Republic, even though there was hardly any evidence that the internal strife then plaguing that small island had much to do with external forces.

But now the fact of a Soviet–Cuban challenge to American security interests in the region was widely acknowledged. Thus, in January 1984, a presidential commission headed by former Secretary of State Henry Kissinger and reflecting a wide range of political opinion asserted: "The use of Nicaragua as a base for Soviet and Cuban efforts to penetrate the rest of the Central American isthmus, with El Salvador the target of first opportunity, gives the conflict there a major strategic dimension. The direct involvement of aggressive external forces makes it a challenge to the system of hemispheric security, and, quite specifically, to the security interests of the United States. This is a challenge to which the United States must respond."[84] Yet in providing the general outline of such a response, the Kissinger commission displayed less clarity than in its presentation of the problem. The use of force was ruled out—except as a vague "ultimate recourse" in Nicaragua and even though the prevailing stalemate in El Salvador "in the long term favor[ed] the guerillas." Aid was promised, of course, but even assuming a questionable congressional willingness to provide the large amounts of assistance required, there remained a nagging linkage between the extension of such aid and "demonstrated progress" in the area of human rights.

As in the case of Africa, then, in the 1980s much of the problem faced by the Reagan administration in Central America grew out of the gap that remained between the interests that were said to be at stake and the capabilities that were committed on behalf of those interests. To be sure, where local governments were not placed at a serious disadvantage by outside intervention, the United States should probably stand aside from internal strife, even if by doing so a radical regime might come to power.[85] But what would be done in cases where there was no Soviet or Cuban restraint?

In January 1980, it is with regard to the region of the Persian Gulf that the Carter administration had outlined a doctrine that heralded America's return to containment. The focus of the Carter doctrine was not coincidental. Over the years, the Gulf had acquired an importance second to no other region. Indeed, an America that would tolerate a creeping Soviet control of the Gulf and accept its oil on Soviet terms—or an America that would wish to escape the responsibilities of its power by learning to live without that oil regardless of the fate of its allies—would have abdicated any pretense at world power and sought refuge in a new isolationism whose future would remain uncertain and fragile. Yet the Carter rhetoric had remained far ahead of the efforts that followed. The geopolitical outline of an expanded American military presence in the Gulf was drawn, but the predilection for naval and air facilities instead of bases was insufficient: even if it were ever to become a force, the projected Rapid Deployment Force would not be rapid enough unless it was effectively based in the area proper. "We have to be subtle and indirect," Brzezinski had argued in late 1980. "The region [needs] to have some sort of subtle and indirect security relationship with the United States."[86] But the effort proved to be so "indirect" and so "subtle" as to go widely unnoticed. In 1981, Reagan, too, had made the terms of the Carter doctrine his own as he pledged that the United States would "not permit that Saudi Arabia become another Iran."[87] But against whom and how would such a commitment be fulfilled?

That the Soviet Union was "the focus of evil in the modern world" and "an evil empire"—as Reagan claimed in early 1983[88]—and that it imposed upon the United States the burden of a decade of military investments whose magnitude danger-ously strained the American economy might well be true. But what was the operational relevance of such a claim? Did the United States thereby announce its intention to wait for the ultimate collapse of a regime deemed so illegitimate as to prevent any serious diplomatic intercourse? "A struggle between right and wrong, good and evil," Reagan continued, emphasizing that such struggle knew no limits and permitted no escape: in launching an omnidirectional challenge to the Soviet regime on the basis of a "unified strategy" that would combine military, economic, political, and informational tools, the Reagan Administration reasoned that the United States "might one day convince the leadership of the Soviet Union to turn their attention inward, to seek the legitimacy that only comes from the consent of the governed, and thus to address the hopes and dreams of their own people."[89]

To be sure, there was much truth in Secretary of State George Shultz's reminder that "the tone reflects the substance and not the other way around."[90] Indeed, as Shultz emphasized on another occasion, "much of the present day reality is unpleasant. To describe conditions as we see them . . . is not to seek confrontation."[91] Yet the danger of such an approach had been seen 30 years earlier. The identification of a brutal and determined enemy would require the adoption of a brutal and determined response. A discourse thus used to explain and justify a policy might gain such a political momentum as to take precedent over the policy itself—which, in Reagan's case, continued to be more moderate than the words that were used to describe it.

Were this rhetoric and these threats to be taken seriously? The assertiveness of the Reagan administration appeared to be at odds with a continued drift toward disengagement to which the American public, weary of allies and wary of adversaries, had grown increasingly responsive. Thus, in 1982, a survey of public opinion on foreign policy issues showed a persistent erosion of the post-World War II consensus that the national interest required active participation by the United States in world affairs. "Only a bare majority of the public," the authors of the survey concluded, "now believes that . . . international activism best insures the future of the country, while over one-third now say the United States should stay out of world affairs."[92] This was the third such survey to be held in eight years. What was especially significant about its findings was that following a postwar consensus that had always acknowledged the priority of foreign-policy and security issues, the trend was now going in the opposite direction: none of the last four American administrations—from Nixon to Reagan—had been able to reverse or at least stall the erosion of public support for an active and forceful role of the United States in the world.

Even as it spoke of global containment abroad, the Reagan administration therefore confronted at home the threat of global retrenchment.

To combat this trend would not be easy. Thus, in the not-so-new world that had come out of two world wars, a cold war, and the liquidation of several empires, the United States faced the task of acting as a leader toward the outside even as its leadership was being forever criticized from within and its power forcefully challenged from without. In the context of American history, these conditions were entirely novel. During most of its past, the United States had lived apart from the foray of interstate relations. When a mixture of choice and necessity led it to do otherwise, it had still assumed its new role under circumstances of such abnormal dominance over foes and friends alike as to keep the cost of such leadership relatively small. Now, however, the country would have to reconcile itself to the mormalcy of coercion and inequality in foreign policy. This, to be sure, was a sad state of affairs. In a world that was fundamentally hostile, foreign policy could only postpone the inevitable: in the end, wars would be waged and casualties suffered; alliances would be reversed, and compromises struck; morality would be preached, and reality faced.

It is to face these dangerous years that Richard M. Nixon and Henry Kissinger had both sought a "philosophical deepening" of the nation.[93] In a sense their predilection for the tragic had well suited the conditions they faced as a new decade was about to open. Whether for lack of time or lack of skills, however, their efforts to normalize American foreign policy proved to be unable to sustain the required domestic support. On the contrary, following the Ford transition, both the Carter and the Reagan administrations were the radical results of a domestic rebellion against the complexities and the burdens of normalcy. The advocate of certain national values that were thought to have been trampled during the disastrous escalation of the American involvement in Indochina, the Carter administration pledged an era of changes without tears. At last, it was promised, the United States could be on the side of change, since all changes would be on the side of the United States or else would entail no cost to American interests. However desirable such reasoning might have been 15 years earlier when American power was such as to make the price of change negligible, this could no longer be the case by the end of a decade of economic, military, and political decline.

In reaction, the Reagan Administration presented itself as the advocate of a certain historical image of the nation that was thought to have been neglected during the Carter years. Dismayed by the shameful humiliation in Iran, it promised an era of renewal and assertiveness without tears. In the 1980s, it was now pledged, adversaries would be contained until they were reformed. However plausible such ambitions might have been 30 years earlier when Soviet power was such as to make the price of their fulfilment manageable, this could no longer be true after more than a decade of Soviet military ascendancy.

Such vain promises could only meet with disappointments that fed the drift toward disengagement even further. In the years to come, they would have to be abandoned, and the United States would have to learn to distance its rhetoric from the myths of the desirable and adjust its policies to the realities of the necessary. After the Vietnam War had conclusively shown the limits of American power, the crisis in Iran had revealed the limits of American decline. With many dangerous years ahead, the limits of American renewal would hopefully be unveiled without any new tragedy.

NOTES

1. *U.S. News and World Report*, May 30, 1977.
2. Zbigniew Brzezinski,"The Deceptive Structure of Peace," *Foreign Policy* (Spring 1974), p. 51.
3. Cyrus Vance, *Hard Choices: Critical Years in American Foreign Policy* (New York: Simon and Schuster, 1983), p. 29.
4. Zbigniew Brzezinski, *Power and Principle: Memoirs of the National Security Adviser, 1977–1981* (New York: Farrar, Straus, Giroux, 1983), pp. 52–57.
5. Speech at the University of Notre Dame, May 22, 1977.
6. As argued earlier by Brzezinski, "Peace and Power: Looking towards the Seventies," *Encounter* (November 1968), p. 90.
7. Brzezinski, *Power and Principle*, p. 53.

8. William Watts and Lloyd Free, "Nationalism, not Isolation," *Foreign Policy* (Fall 1976), pp. 4–5.
9. *New York Times*, September 18, 1976.
10. Stanley Hoffman, "Will the Balance Balance at Home", *Foreign Policy (Summer 1972)*.
11. Quoted in Hans J. Morgenthau, *Scientific Man versus Power Politics* (Chicago: University of Chicago Press, 1948), p. 207.
12. Anthony Lake (then the Director of the Policy Planning Staff at the Department of State), address before the World Affairs Council, Boston, June 13, 1977.
13. See Roger P. Labrie, ed., *SALT Handbook: Key Documents and Issues, 1971–1979* (Washington, D.C.: American Enterprise Institute for Public Policy, 1979).
14. Richard Burt, "Reducing Strategic Arms at SALT: How Difficult, How Important?" in *The Future of Arms Control,* Part I, *Beyond SALT,* ed. Christopher Bertram, Adelphi Paper no. 141 (London: Institute for Strategic Studies, Spring 1978).
15. Brzezinski, *Power and Principle*, p. 163.
16. "Towards Peace in the Middle East," (Washington, D.C.: Brookings Institution, 1975).
17. Jimmy Carter, *Keeping Faith. Memoirs of a President* (New York: Bantam Books, 1982), p. 275; Brzezinski, *Power and Principle*, pp. 83–90.
18. Brzezinski, *Power and Principle*, p. 102.
19. John C. Campbell, "The Middle East: Burdens of Empire," *Foreign Affairs (America and the World, 1978)*, p. 619.
20. Zbigniew Brzezinski, cited in the *Washington Post*, October 3, 1977.
21. Carter, *Keeping Faith,* p. 298.
22. Ibid., pp. 300–6.
23. Ibid., pp. 111 and 121. "The United States is not just an interested bystander, not even just a benevolent mediator," Brzezinski had pointedly emphasized in early October. Reported in the *Washington Post*, October 3, 1977.
24. Brzezinski, *Power and Principle*, p. 273.
25. "Human Rights and U.S. Foreign Policy," Department of State Publication 8959, December 1978, p. 8.
26. As pledged by Carter in his address to the B'nai B'rith Biennial Convention, September 8, 1976.
27. Richard W. Cottam, "Arms Sales and Human Rights: The Case of Iran," in *Human Rights and U.S. Foreign Policy, Principles and*

Applications, ed. Peter G. Brown (Lexington, Mass.: Lexington Books, 1979), p. 295.

28. Quoted by Scott Armstrong, "The Fall of the Shah," *Washington Post*, October 25, 1980.

30. Carter, *Keeping Faith*, p. 440.

31. According to the then-Ambassador to Iran, William H. Sullivan, the Shah "reacted with stunned incredulity" to Washington's decision to cancel a meeting which had been arranged with Khomeini. "How," asked the Shah, "can you expect to have any influence with these people if you won't meet with them?" For Sullivan's views on dealing with the Shah's opposition, see Martin F. Herz ed., *Contacts With the Opposition: A Symposium* (Washington, D.C.: Institute for the Study of Diplomacy of the Georgetown University, 1979), pp. 1–3.

32. Michael Ledeen and William Lewis, *Debacle: The American Failure in Iran* (New York: Alfred A. Knopf, 1981), p. 231.

33. Simon Serfaty, "The United States and Europe," *Washington Quarterly* (Winter 1980–81), pp. 70–86.

34. Zbigniew Brzezinski, "How the Cold War Was Played," *Foreign Affairs* (Summer 1972), pp. 208–9.

35. Zbigniew Brzezinski, "The Balance of Power Delusion," *Foreign Policy* (Summer 1972), p. 54.

36. Stanley Hoffman, *Gulliver's Troubles or the Setting of American Foreign Policy*, 1st ed. (New York: McGraw-Hill, 1968), pp. 23–4.

37. Robert Hunter, "Power and Peace," *Foreign Policy* (Winter 1972–73), p. 38.

38. Zbigniew Brzezinski, "The Search for Focus," *Foreign Affairs* (July 1973), p. 723.

39. Brzezinski, "The Balance of Power Delusion" and "The Deceptive Structure of Peace."

40. Brzezinski, "The Search for Focus," p. 712.

41. Zbigniew Brzezinski, "America in a Hostile World," *Foreign Policy* (Summer 1976), pp. 93–95.

42. Speech at Charleston, South Carolina, July 21, 1977.

43. Speech at Wake Forest University, March 18, 1978.

44. As explained by Brzezinski to Elizabeth Drew, "Brzezinski," *New Yorker*, May 1, 1978.

45. "President Carter: 1978," Congressional Quarterly Inc., Washington, D.C., April 1979, p. 140-A.

46. Ibid., p. 102-A.

47. In an interview on NBC's "Meet the Press," May 28, 1978. Department of State *Bulletin*, July 1978, pp. 26–28.

48. Quoted in the *Economist*, March 18, 1978. This was promptly denied by Secretary Vance who insisted instead that SALT stood on its own merits.
49. Zbigniew Brzezinski, in an interview on NBC's "Meet the Press," May 28, 1978. See also his *Power and Principle*, pp. 196–202.
50. See Adam Ulam, "U.S.–Soviet Relations: Unhappy Coexistence," *Foreign Affairs (America and the World, 1978)*, p. 561.
51. "On the Present Policy of the U.S. Government," *News and Views from the USSR*, Soviet Embassy Information Department, Washington, D.C.
52. "President Carter: 1978," *Congressional Quarterly*, pp. 108–11-A.
53. Thomas W. Wolfe, *The SALT Experience* (Cambridge Mass.: Ballinger Publishing, 1979), p. 225.
54. U.S. Senate, Committee on Armed Services, *Hearings* on the Military Implications of the SALT II Treaty, Part I, 96th Congress, 1st Session, July 23–26, 1979, p. 28.
55. Harold Brown, "Annual Defense Department Report, Fiscal 1979," February 2, 1978, p. 56.
56. Zbigniew Brzezinski, address to the Chicago Council on Foreign Relations, April 4, 1979. U.S. Department of State, *Current Policy*, No. 62 (April 1979) p. 4.
57. Harold Brown, Annual Defense Department Report, p. 56.
58. U.S. Senate, Hearings on the Military Implications of the SALT II Treaty, p. 30.
59. Ibid., pp. 30–32.
60. Ibid.
61. "SALT Agreement, Vienna, June 18, 1979," Selected Documents No. 12 A, Department of State, Bureau of Public Affairs.
62. Brzezinski, *Power and Principle*, pp. 344–53.
63. Carter, *Keeping Faith*, p. 265.
64. See George Liska, *Russia and the Road to Appeasement: Cycles of East–West Conflict in War and Peace* (Baltimore Md.: Johns Hopkins University Press, 1982).
65. Norman Podhoretz, *The Present Danger* (New York: Basic Books, 1980), pp. 100–1.
66. Robert Legvold, "The Soviet Union's Strategic Stake in Africa," in *Africa and the United States: Vital Interests*, ed. Jennifer Seymour Whitaker (New York: New York University Press, 1978, pp. 174–75.
67. Ibid., pp. 179–80.
68. See Larry C. Naper, "The Ogaden War," in *Managing U.S.–Soviet Rivalry: Problems of Crisis Prevention*, ed. Alexander L. George (Boulder, Col.: Westview Press, 1979), pp. 225–54.

69. Simon Serfaty, "The Soviet Union in Africa: Realities and Limits," *South Africa International* (July 1983), pp. 311–19.

70. John E. Reilly, "American Opinion: Not Reaganism," *Foreign Policy* (Spring 1983), p. 93.

71. Chester Crocker, "Africa in the 1980s," *Washington Quarterly* (Fall 1980).

72. *New York Times*, April 28, 1983.

73. Herbert L. Matthews, *A World in Revolution: A Newspaperman's Memoir* (New York: Charles Scribner's Sons, 1971), pp. 262–64.

74. W. Tapley Bennett, "Some Aspects of Communist Penetration in Guatemala," cited in Richard H. Immerman, *The CIA in Guatemala: The Foreign Policy of Intervention* (Austin, Texas: University of Texas Press, 1982), p. 94. Thomas J. Andahl, "Intervention in Guatemala, the Dominican Republic and Nicaragua," unpublished paper (SAIS, December 1983).

75. John Foster Dulles, "International Communism in Guatemala," radio and television address, June 30, 1954, in *Intervention of International Communism in Guatemala* (Washington, D.C.: Department of State Publication No. 2556, Inter-American Series 48, 1954), p. 31.

76. Quoted in Warren I. Cohen, *Dean Rusk, The American Secretaries of State and Their Diplomacy*, vol. XIX (Totowa, N. J.: Cooper Square Publishers, 1980), p. 199. Yet, Johnson himself indicated that Kennedy would also have intervened in the Dominican Republic. See Lyndon B. Johnson, *The Vantage Point: Perspectives of the Presidency, 1963–1969* (New York: Holt, Rinehart and Winston, 1971), p. 197.

77. Johnson, *Vantage Point*, p. 188.

78. Johnson's statement of May 2, 1965. Quoted in Seyom Brown, *The Faces of Power* (New York: Columbia University Press, 1968), p. 351.

79. Theodore Draper, *The Dominican Revolt: A Case Study in American Policy*, a *Commentary Report* (New York: Commentary Magazine, 1968), p. 159.

80. See Johnson, *Vantage Point*, for his explanation of how Communists can gain control of a revolutionary situation with only a few men, p. 200.

81. Immerman, *CIA in Guatemala*, p. 179.

82. Richard Gott, *Guerilla Movements in Latin America* (London: Thomas Nelson, 1970), p. 201.

83. Quoted in Immerman, *CIA in Guatemala*, pp. 196–97.

84. *New York Times*, January 12, 1984.

85. Robert W. Tucker, *The Purposes of American Power. An Essay on National Security* (New York: Praeger, 1981), p. 185.
86. Cited in the *Washington Post*, November 30, 1980.
87. *New York Times*, October 2, 1981.
88. Reagan's speech before the National Association of Evangelicals, Orlando, Florida, March 8, 1983.
89. William P. Clark, address to the Center for Strategic and International Studies, Georgetown University, May 21, 1982.
90. *New York Times*, April 1, 1983.
91. George Shultz, "U.S. Foreign Policy: Realism and Progress," *Current Policy*, No. 420, Department of State, Bureau of Public Affairs, September 30, 1982, p. 2.
92. John H. Reilly, "American Opinion," p. 104.
93. Kissinger, quoted in John Lewis Gaddis, *Strategies of Containment. A Critical Appraisal of Postwar American National Security Policy* (New York: Oxford University Press, 1982), p. 277.

INDEX

A

ABM *see* antiballistic missile system
Acheson, D., 26, 34, 35, 36, 51, 68,
    72, 73, 95, 96, 109, 112, 116,
    119, 125, 126, 127, 130, 135,
    141, 149, 150, 151, 152, 154,
    155, 173, 190, 191, 199, 201,
    230
  on Chinese civil war, 115
  on meeting strength with strength,
    133
  on NATO, 93
  on Soviet role in Korean war,
    118
  on unlimited interventionism, 27
  on U.S. minimal interests, 111
Adams, J. Q., 7
Adams, R. G., 146
Adams, S., 231
Adenauer, K., 78, 149, 180
  on U.S. leadership, 164
Adler, S., 33
Afghanistan, Soviet invasion of, 288,
    289, 337, 345-46, 347
Africa
  Soviet policy toward, 353
  U.S. policy toward, 353-54
Alexander, Czar, 9, 41
Allende, S., 271
alliances
  global network of, 15
  in a nuclear age, 170-71
Allison, G., 325
Alperovitz, G., 71

Andahl, T. J., 364
Anderson, O. E., Jr., 73
Anderson, W., 231
Andreotti, G., 304
Anglo-American Loan Agreement,
    79
Anglo-American relationship, 79
Anglo-French treaty of Dunquerque,
    91
Angola, U.S.-Soviet clash over, 268-
    69
anti-Americanism, European, 159
antiballistic missile system (ABM),
    238
ANZUS, 15
  pact, 207
Arbenz Guzman, J., 355
arms race, U.S.-Soviet, 247-50
Armstrong, S., 362
Aron, R., 32, 254, 281
Aronson, J., 71
Atlantic Alliance, 87, 92, 95, 96,
    157, 167, 168, 169, 190, 303,
    316, 346
  breakup of, 285-92
  and the defence of Europe, 95-
    96
  in disarray over Suez, 144
  dissension within, 178
  and economic concerns, 161
  eroded by Cuban missile crisis,
    289
  troubled, 175-76, 188-90
Atlantic Charter, 25
atom bomb, *see* nuclear weapons

ABOUT THE AUTHOR

Simon Serfaty received his Ph.D. in Political Science from the Johns Hopkins University in Baltimore, Maryland, in June 1967. Following a brief stay with Business International in New York, N.Y., Dr. Serfaty joined the faculty of Political Science at the University of California in Los Angeles, where he was voted Political Science Teacher of the Year in 1971–72. A member of the faculty of the Johns Hopkins' School of Advanced International Studies in Washington, D.C., since 1972, he has served as Director of the School's Center of European Studies in Bologna, Italy (1972–76) and as Director of the School's Center of Foreign Policy Research (1977–80). He is currently Executive Director of the Johns Hopkins Foreign Policy Institute and Research Professor of U.S. Foreign Policy.

A guest lecturer in approximately 35 different countries, Dr. Serfaty is the author of several books and monographs, including *France, de Gaulle and Europe: The Policy of the Fourth and Fifth Republics toward the Continent* (1968); *The Elusive Enemy: American Foreign Policy since World War II* (1972); *Fading Partnership: America and Europe after 30 Years* (1979); *The United States, Western Europe and the Third World: Allies and Adversaries* (1980); and *A Socialist France and Western Security* (coauthored, 1981). He has also edited or coedited several volumes: *The Foreign Policies of the French Left* (1979); *Portugal since the Revolution* (1980); and *The Italian Communist Party: Yesterday, Today, and Tomorrow* (1980). Finally, Dr. Serfaty is the author of numerous articles that have appeared in leading professional journals in the United States and abroad.